THE FINAL ART-DOWN

With Love,
For Jan,
May you
see only the
joy + light
Spirit + life
love + blessings
that walk along
beside you on
your journey.
Sherri

THE FINAL ART-DOWN

A Step-by-Step Elemental Guide to Strenthening Your Artistic Voice

Sherri Phibbs

The Final Art-Down:
A Step-by-Step Elemental Guide to Strengthening Your Artistic Voice

E-Book ISBN: 978-0-9920727-1-1
Paperback ISBN: 978-0-9920727-0-4

Additional copies of this book may be ordered by visiting the
PPG Online Bookstore at:

shop.polishedpublishinggroup.com

Due to the dynamic nature of the Internet, any website addresses mentioned within this book may have been changed or discontinued since publication.

Psycho-educational expressive artist and workshop facilitator, Sherri Phibbs, Proprietor of W.I.S.H. Studio, utilizes over 25 years experience in watercolour painting and the arts; as well as her unusual approach to creative inspiration, to implement programs for those determined to push their creative boundaries.

A certified Peace Ambassador, a trained teacher of shamanic journeying and healing, and a competent horsewoman, Sherri combines these interests with her studies in expressive art and animal assisted therapies, organic eco-psychology, spirituality and traditional culture to create art projects, workshops and balanced living. She approaches learning as a life long journey and is currently studying for certification in Eco-Art Therapy.

First published in Canada in 2013
By W.I.S.H. Studio, Post Office Box 1143, Station Main
Cochrane, Alberta T4C 1B2

www.wishstudio.ca

Acknowledgements:

To Barbara Barry, Julie Teunissen, and Carlann Thomas, for your wisdom, insightful commentary, community and support, I thank you from every part of my being. You are awesomeness incarnate! Without you, this book and project would have imploded many times. To Alex, for sharing his interest in all things calendar related. You rock! To Kirsten, for much and varied horse time which makes my heart sing. You are the bee's knees. To my husband, Doug, whose patience and tolerance of my deadline driven stress makes life fun. You are so loved. To James O'Dea and Sequoyah Trueblood, for your insight and teachings on peace and harmony, I am truly blessed to have been touched by your lives. To Peter Calhoun, for your year-long coaching through my apprenticeship, many thanks. To Straja Linder-King, Dr. Madeliene Rugh, Dr. Michael Cohen, Vickie Tait, and Ryan Eliason, for teaching/sharing your expertise in your fields. May you bring the same light and joy to all your students that you have brought me.

Snow Ghosts
February 14, 2012

Photography
© Sherri Phibbs

Introduction

As we go about life, the events, emotions and actions we experience, feel or initiate can have a profound effect on our centre or soul; the essence or core of us that makes us who we are and provides us with the direction necessary to function in our physical world. Attending to its care makes sense, but it is not necessarily the first thing on your mind when you wake in the morning. Somewhere between grab a coffee, feed the kids and jump in the car because you're late for work, an important part of self-care is lost. It is almost as though we live a great part of our lives on auto-pilot, merely going through the motions day after day.

For some strange reason, bits and pieces of our core seem to break apart as we go about this daily routine of living, doing, aging in this unawake manner. We wither, get stuck or are even whittled away, and our hearts cry as we adapt to an almost mechanized process of being that leaves us with a world a little less brilliant, a self a little less whole, a malaise or dis-ease with our environment. A numbness or fearfulness settles in, which culminates in feeling disconnected from ourselves and our world. In a sense, we have lost ourselves.

This sense of loss brings to mind a safety warning; one used repeatedly by the airline industry today during their routine flight checks. They tell us to "Please ensure your own air mask is in place before you turn to assist someone else." These airline people know how important it is to ensure ***you*** are able to function before you care for others. Self-care is important, no matter the situation. It is something so powerful it can affect our ability to function effectively in the world. So, take a moment to do a check in, or self-inventory. Are you functioning to your best potential—fully empowered, strong in self—or are you the walking unconscious? Are you truly alive, or has your spirit or soul become numbed? Paying attention to what brings you joy and excitement is the first step to bring you to a balanced, fulfilling and alive life. By paying attention to your thoughts, processes, and actions, you have the ability to be truly, vibrantly, enthusiastically alive in every cell, in every facet, and every dimension of your being. So alive that when you tackle the world each day, you have a focus and attentiveness available to you that makes an undeniable statement. You project to the universe, "This is who I am, and I AM the difference in this world."

When we are children we have no trouble connecting to this part of ourselves. We experience joy, delight, and rapture spontaneously with no preparation, forethought, concern, or worry necessary. It just bubbles to the surface when we smell the sunlight baking the grass or see the play of light and shadow through a veil of leaves. When we taste the wind riding a bicycle down a tree-lined street, we are deeply connected, wholly engaged, and fully present to the magic and wonder of the universe and we know, we feel, our place in it. As adults, we need to be reminded not only to take the time to allow joy into our lives, but also just to remember what it feels like so we may appreciate its value, feel its loss, and seek to reawaken ourselves to its inherent opportunities.

Nature-assisted art and movement are an absolutely wonderful method to remind ourselves of who we really are, to remind us of that joyful, in-the-moment, small child at our centre. The process of creativity acts as the catalyst. It changes us, allowing the expression of things that simmer below the surface, feelings of which we may not even be fully aware but that motivate our actions in our day to day life. It acts as an air mask, allowing us to breathe in life and passion. Add connection with our environment, awareness with fully alive senses, and Nature steps in to initiate an internal healing process within us, a soul reclamation. The expression and review of images produced in this way allows us to make conscious choices, to evaluate clearly and objectively. We know that *this* no longer works for me, or *that* is what makes my spirit sing! We release things that no longer sustain us, make choices that bring a healthier, more whole and joyful life, not only for ourselves but for all those we come in contact with. Joy is contagious.

An Accidental Vision Quest

Many years ago, a certain woman of the people, a mother caring for two young children alone, was stirred by Spirit and began to travel The Path. This woman did not know who she was or even that she was on The Path. She had been separated from the source of the people's understanding when she was very young and raised in isolation by a woman of the Lost People, so she did not value or understand dream teachings or the voices of the natural world; in fact, they were considered evil. The sudden eruption of visions and the speaking of the teachers frightened her. She did not recognize the dreams and guidance she received, and believed the very fabric of her mind was unraveling. Was she becoming one of the Lost People? Already at a difficult time in her life, she decided she must ask for help. She prayed and prayed and prayed for guidance. Finally, in desperation, certain that she must be missing what she was asking for, she prayed, "Creator, I know you are providing me with guidance, but I do not understand! Please! You will need to make it clearer for me! Please help me to understand."

That night as she was about to sleep, a voice called her name! And then it said, "Everything will be all right. You will be protected." Horrified, the woman fell to her knees. "I am losing my mind!" she cried. "I'd rather be dead than crazy!" And then she became very still. Over the next few days, she tried to speak to many different people, but no one seemed to be available to talk to her—no one of spirit, or medicine or even those whose task it was to talk to those in need. She was alone.

In great fear, she finally visited a wise man of the Lost People, and the Great Spirit stepped in to help her so the wise man was not alarmed by the message she claimed to have heard. But the woman insisted that something was wrong with her, and the wise man, against his original wishes, provided her with medicine to sleep and remain calm. Using the medicine did indeed produce that effect, but she noticed something else. Life became flat. Mind became flat, and even sleep became flat. Where was joy? Where was sorrow? Where were love and life and dreams? The woman quickly realized what she would be giving up by continuing the journey in this fashion, and she decided to chance the wild ride unaided by the deadening effects of the potions. And so, she struggled on bravely, in a vain attempt to understand the messages entering her recently opened soul.

As the moon cycles passed, the woman became poorer and poorer. What food she had, she was careful with, but she became thinner and thinner from her fasting. Finally, one afternoon, while she was resting quietly alone, she had a vision. "Wolf turns and locks eyes with her. He is close; so close their noses almost touch. Having her complete and very startled attention, he turns and her eyes follow. Down in a snow-covered valley, she sees herself snowshoeing. The snow is deep, and she is working hard to stay on her feet. One foot in front of the other, she labours, not looking from side to side, completely oblivious to anything other than the struggle. Swish, step, swish, step, snowshoes leaving a wide trail on the crisp, white floor of the valley. Looking down from above, she sees herself. Then she sees something else. Something is in the snow behind her, following her, and it is running, bounding toward her. A wolf! She screams a warning, but her other self does not hear! The wolf leaps and knocks her to the ground. Both selves scream! The wolf's mouth closes in, she struggles wildly and he starts to lick her face."

"What does this mean? I am awake and I am dreaming!" The woman was afraid, and in her pain and confusion she shouted, "Go away!" And the Great Spirit never spoke to her aloud again, and did not send dreams. For a time, this part of the story faded into the dark.

The Final Art-Down: AIR

The Final Art-Down: AIR

So, the journey begins here, with the seeds of a thought . . .

. . . and the seed is Potential. Carried on the bright wings of Spirit, like a divine whisper in a dream, it flows along the currents of AIR until, softly laid to rest beside the journeyer, it waits to be gathered.

Yet AIR's gift goes unnoticed, unremarked by this busily struggling artisan, caught up in the details, bent over an easel bathed in the morning light. AIR persists: Lifting hair, and caressing skin in gentle loving play. AIR sweeps in and whispers urgently, "Look! Be aware! Do you see? It's time to form your vision! Take the first steps!"

With the soughing of the wind in the trees, Potential suddenly takes root and becomes Inspiration, right there at the artist's feet. Joined by Willingness, Commitment, Perseverance, Community and Joy, they create a circle, strong in form; and bear this Creative Being forward on a path outlined by the swirling eddies of the wind.

Thank you for this valued gift, the artist breathes. Thank you for this vision. It will be well-used, and like a breeze rippling the surface of a pond, it will move outward from this point to touch others.

On toward the spring . . . the thought and vision take root and grow, with gratitude.

Awareness of AIR

I invite you to remember where you have felt the wind on your face and sensed the expansive space AIR occupies, and allow yourself to be drawn there again. It might be the top of a ridge, a hilltop, an open field, or prairie. Take along a coloured pencil and a journal. When you arrive at this place, address the area respectfully requesting permission to interact. You will know if you received permission by a sense of lightness or rightness that will make itself know in your mind, spirit and body. Honour a negative response by moving on to another area and repeating your request. When you have permission, make yourself comfortable. Use all your senses to track and be aware of everything in your surroundings. Note the feel of the air...breathe in, breathe out...with gratitude.

When you are ready, begin to form a request in your mind for inspiration and assistance on your journey of creative discovery and integrity. Pay particular attention to the thoughts that flow through your mind, and record them in your journal. Also, note your feelings and physical responses as you interact with Nature in this way, tracking and recording this as well. Are you drawn in a certain direction? Do you feel excited, tired, inspired, or something else entirely? Describe and make note of the experience.

As you complete your interaction with AIR, you may wish to express your gratitude. You may do this verbally or with an offering of sage, sweetgrass, organic tobacco, or cornmeal. You may repeat this interaction with AIR again and again, as a way of getting to know the element, to become connected to your natural environment, and to open your mind to the experience of this Divine and self-sustaining world of which we are a part.

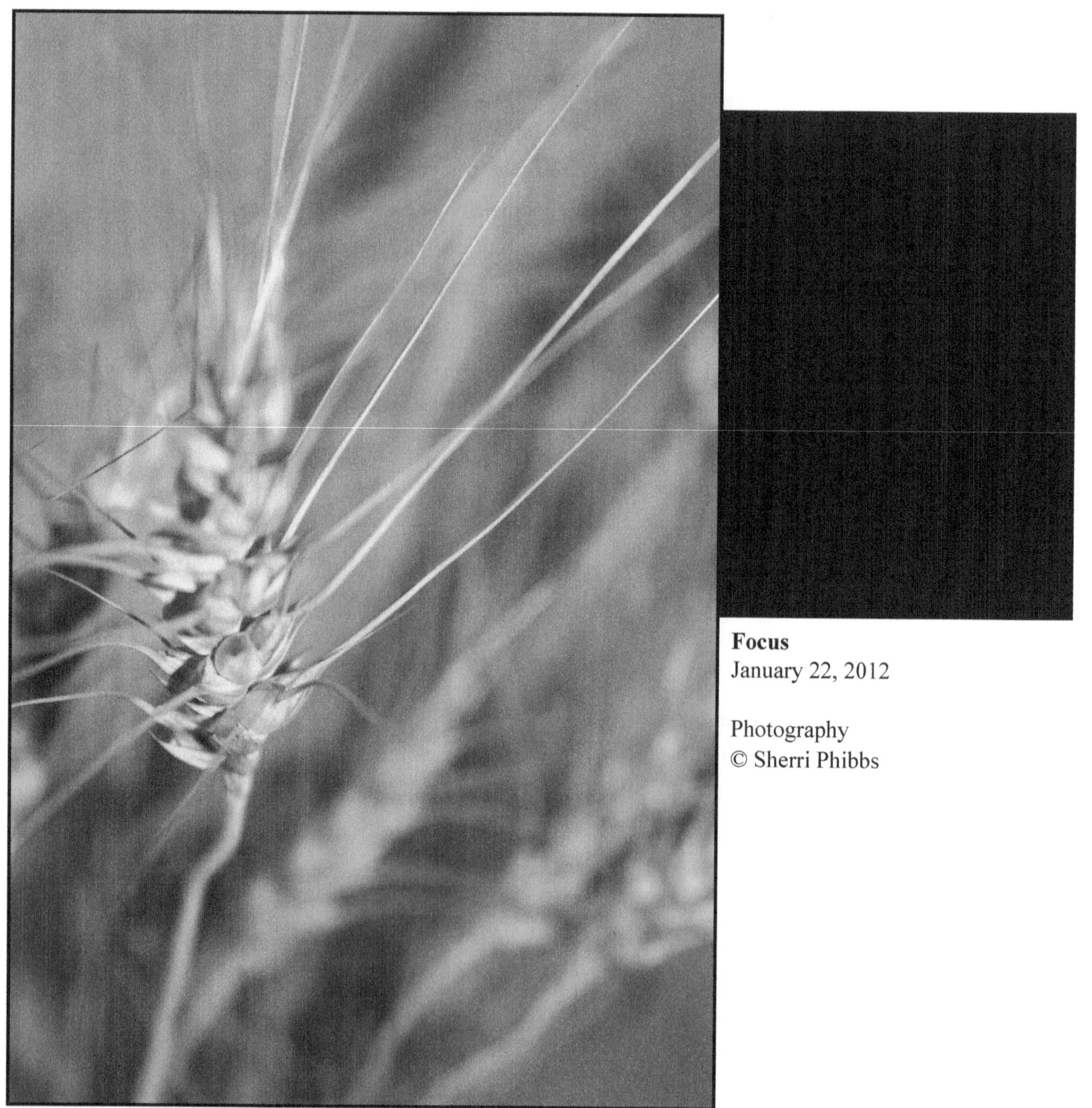

Focus
January 22, 2012

Photography

AIR: The Image

This project came to life in two pieces. The whole, comprised of a written journal of daily life experience matched with a corresponding artistic interpretation, is separated here into its individual parts. So it begins...

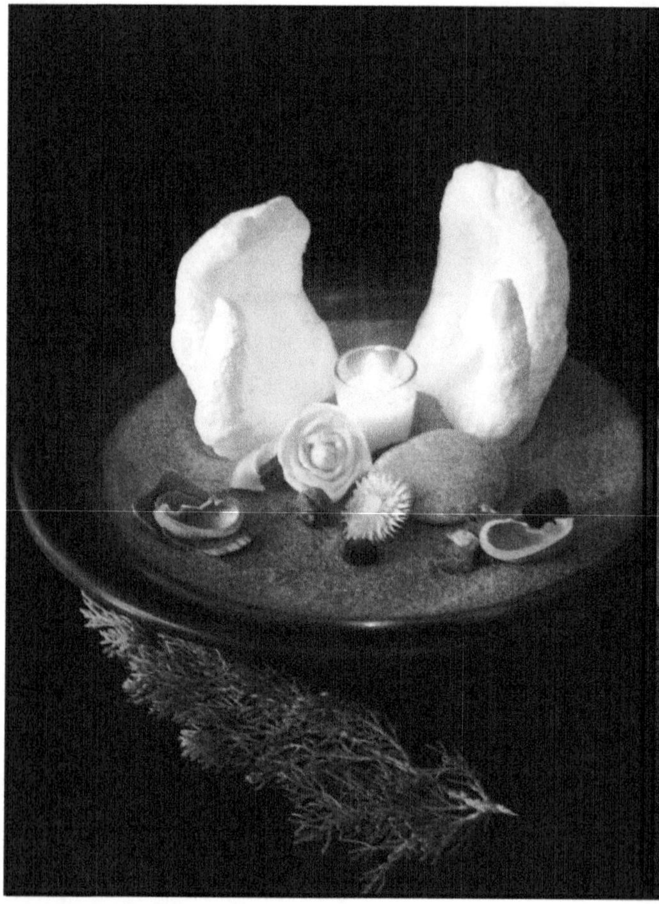

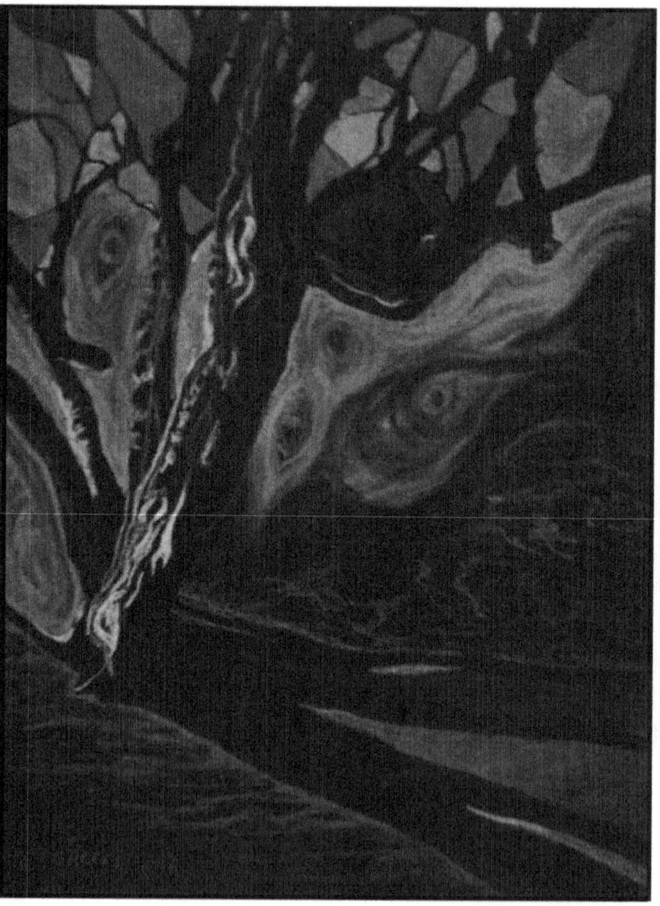

Nurture the Spark
March 6, 2012

Still life photography

Shadow
January 31, 2012

Chalk pastel

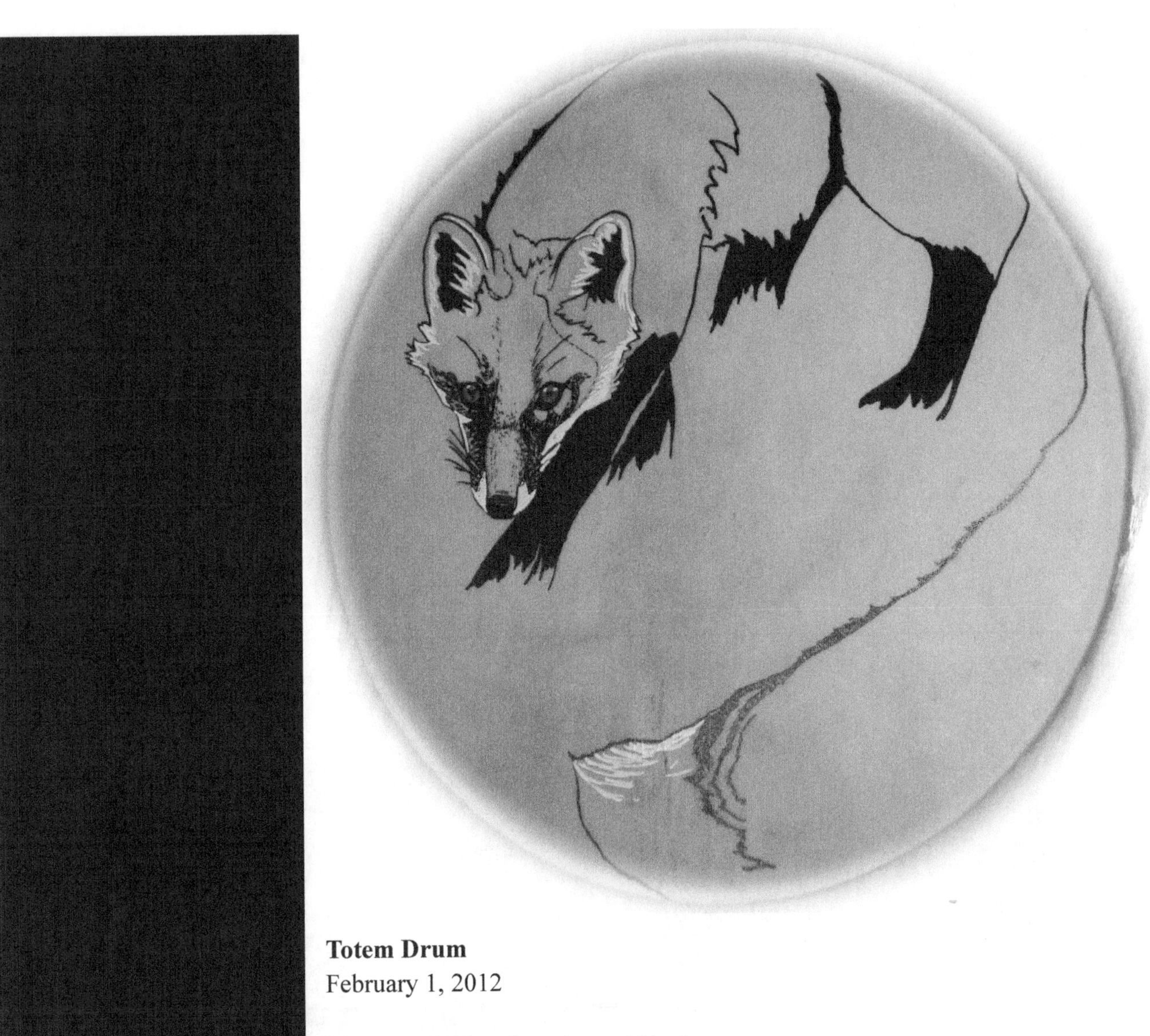

Totem Drum
February 1, 2012

Traditionally hand-made rawhide drum

Battle
February 4, 2012

Chalk pastel

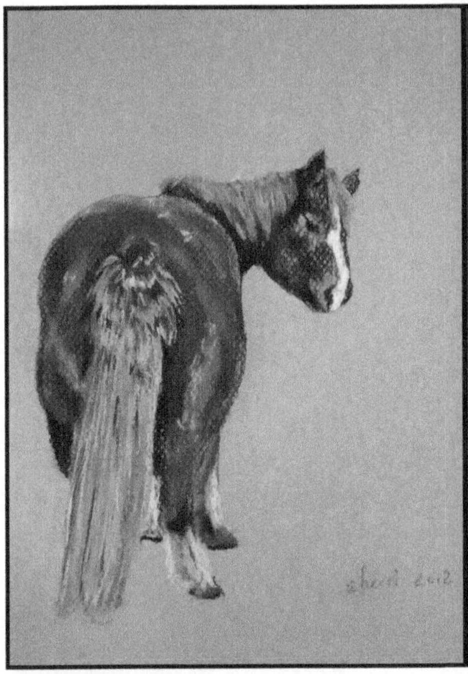

Don't Forget
February 5, 2012

Chalk pastel
© Sherri Phibbs

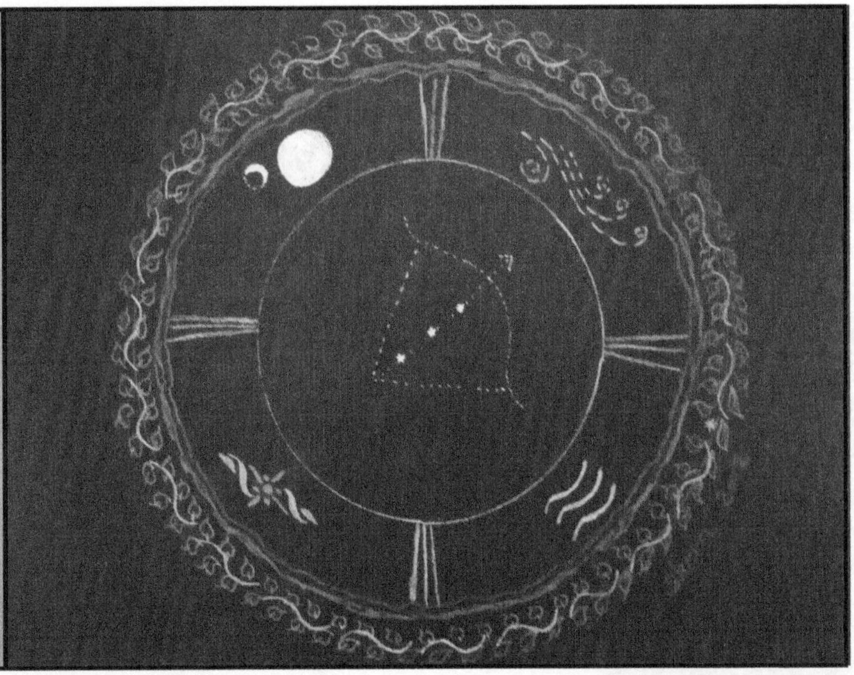

Meditative Mandala
February 6, 2012

Chalk pastel
© Sherri Phibbs

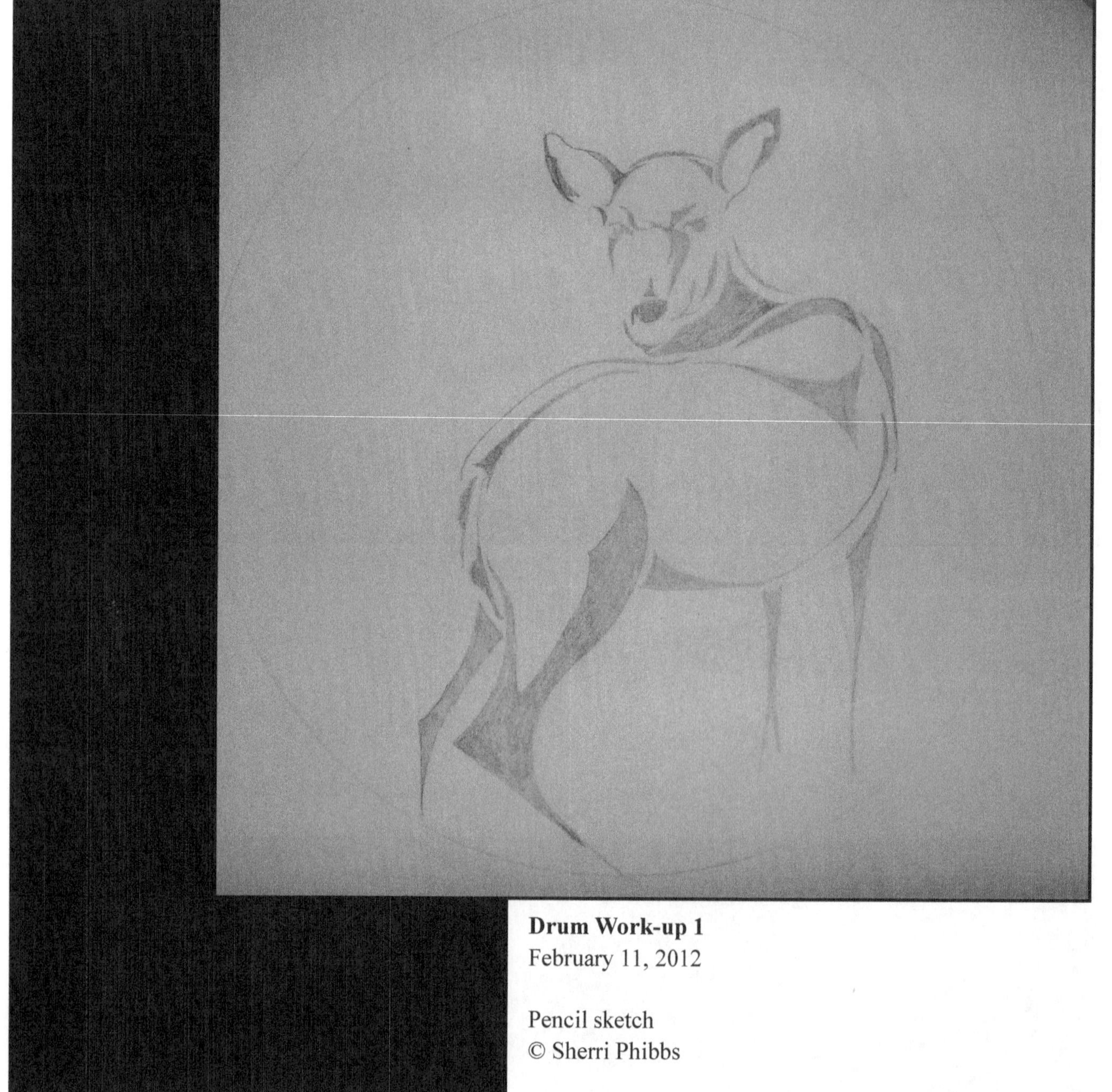

Drum Work-up 1
February 11, 2012

Pencil sketch
© Sherri Phibbs

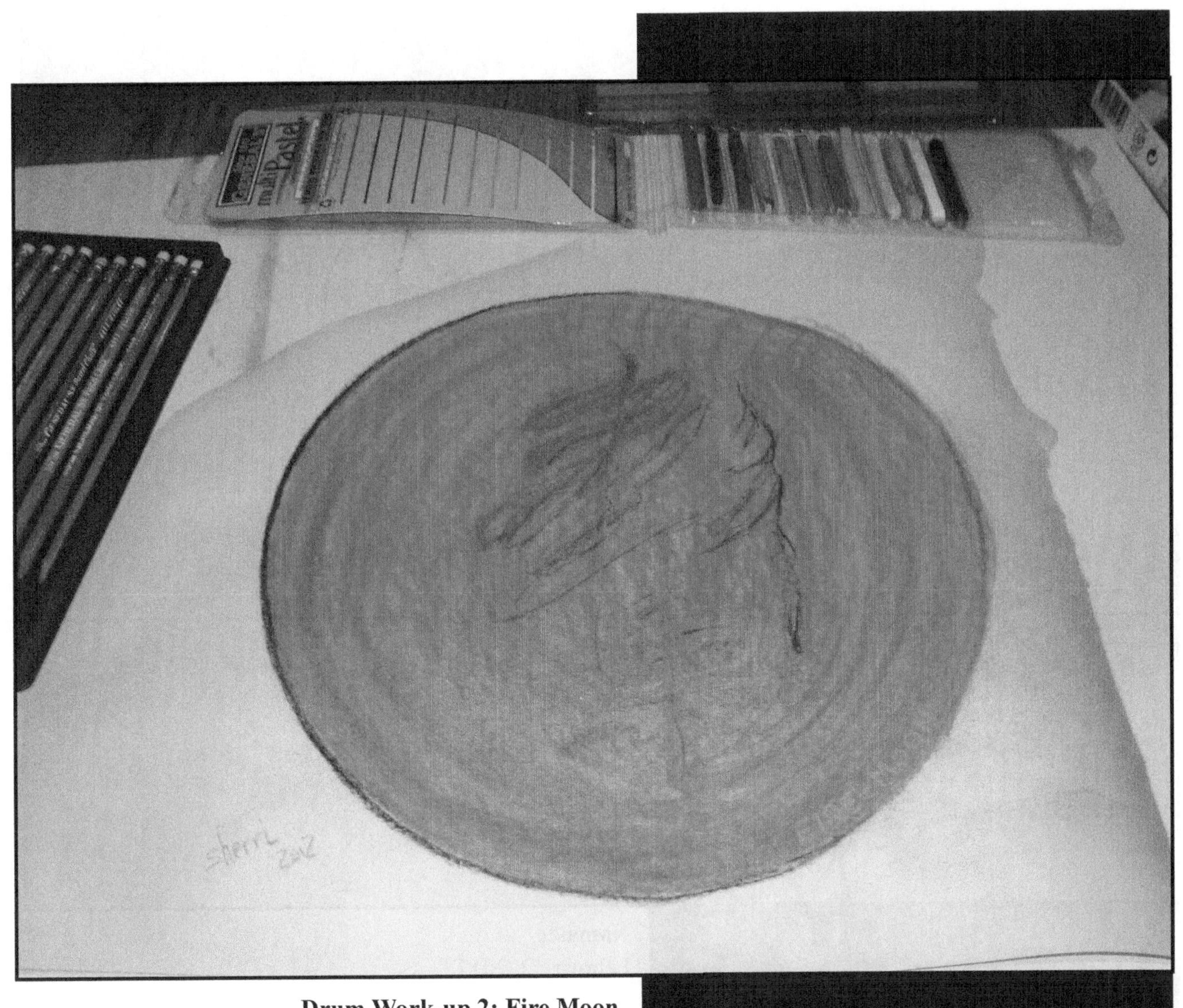

Drum Work-up 2: Fire Moon
February 12, 2012

Chalk pastel

Namaste
February 2, 2012

Wildlife photography

A Gift for You . . .

A Contract for Commitment to Your Own Artistic Voice:

I, ______________________, do joyfully commit to developing my own artistic voice by engaging in a 355 day marathon of personal and creative expression.

Beginning today, and every day until the 355th day from this point, I will engage with the natural world as a source of inspiration, support, and love; I will make a written journal or blog entry; and, I will complete one creative work, daily. I commit to sharing the journal and creative work with others as a way of being held accountable for my initiative.

I agree to forgive myself and get right back up when I fall.

I agree to celebrate my successes, no matter how large or small.

Date: ______________________

Signature: ______________________

Silent Watchers
February 22, 2012

Wildlife photography

From the Inside Out
March 9, 2012

Nature photography

Crystal Clear
February 29, 2012

Nature photography
© Sherri Phibbs

My Journey with AIR

Perched on a large stone embedded in the rock-strewn bank of the Ghost River, I am embraced by the canyon walls on my right, and the tall, angular shapes of the jack pines on my left. The wind stirs my hair as my mind reaches for the sound of the drumbeats cascading over the air currents from the drummers in the water.

Caught up in the rhythm, my own drum remains silent in my hands, and I am feeling the wind. With all my senses, I am engulfed in the sweeping sensation of the air, and I close my eyes, reaching out my arms. Around me, above me, below me, through me, end to end, AIR flows; hollowing me out and leaving me cleansed.

High above the canyon walls, an eagle calls. The drummers hear and are inspired. The drumbeats call to the majestic spirit of this wondrous bird. The eagle sweeps low into the canyon, then soars above the drummers in a free-form sky dance. For long moments, we play together, creatures of the air, sharing sound waves and body, air and soul. Until, at last, as if on cue, the dance ends and we depart.

Sky Dancing
January 4, 2012

Chalk pastel
© Sherri Phibbs

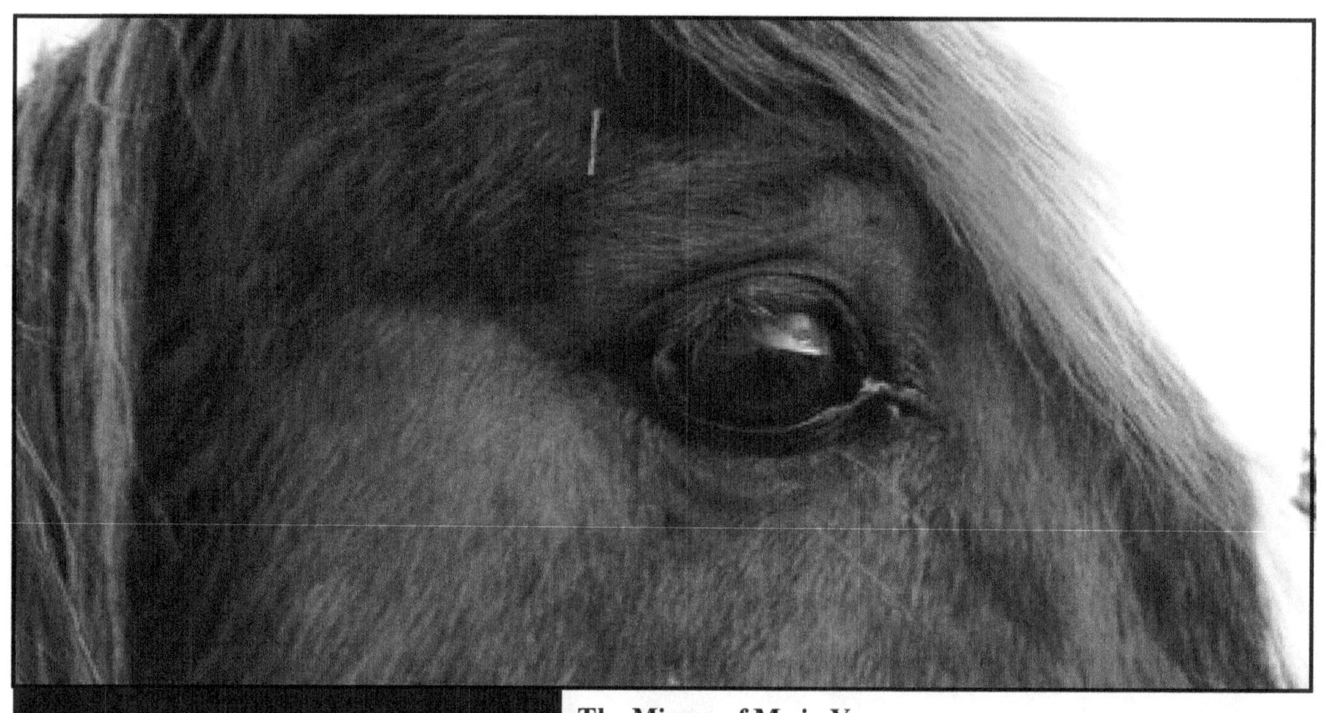

The Mirror of Me in You
March 15, 2012

Pet portraiture

Encircle Rose
January 2, 2012

Watercolour

The One That Got Away
February 28, 2012

Nature photography
© Sherri Phibbs

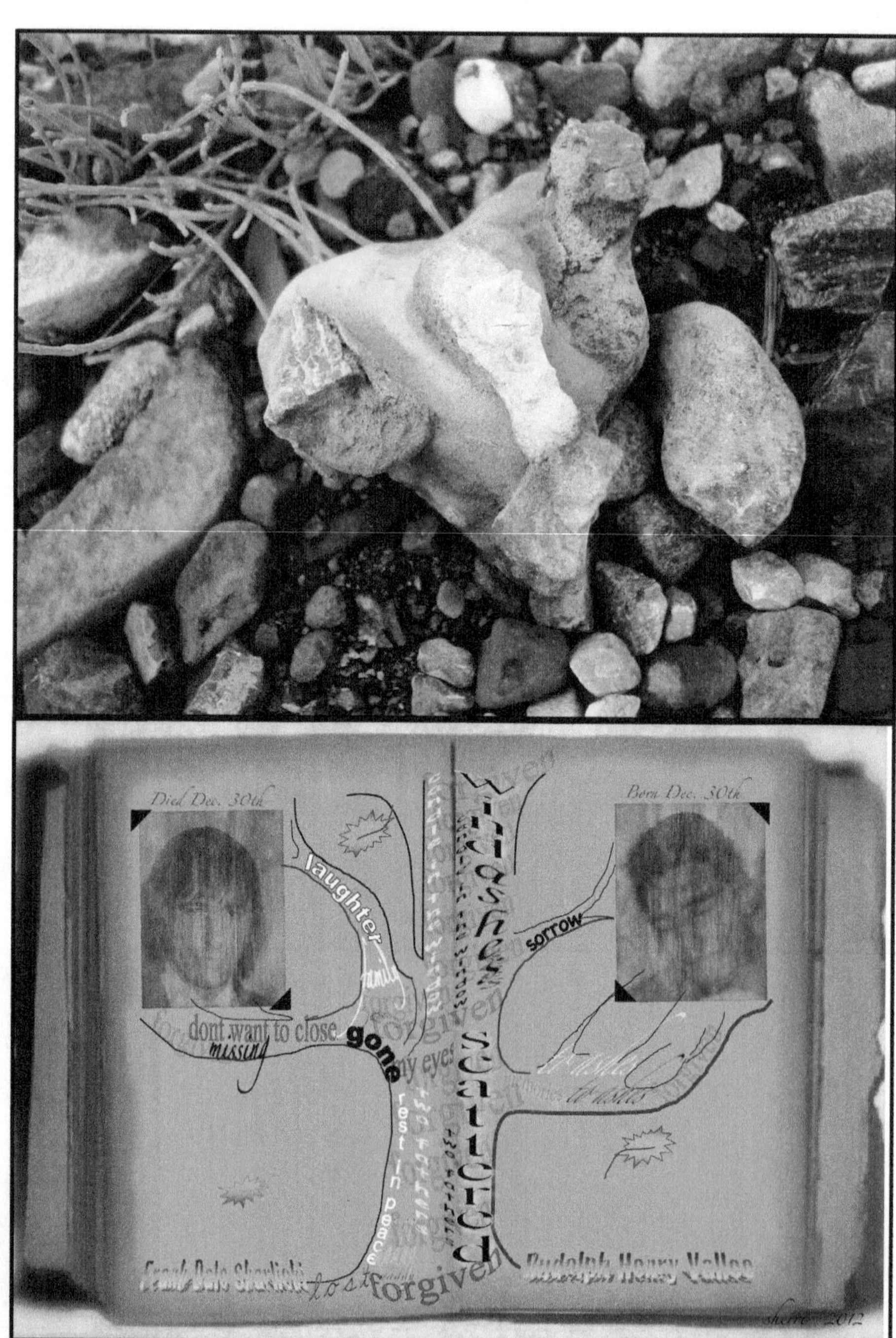

The Tree of Acknowledgement
January 3, 2012

Mixed media collage
© Sherri Phibbs

Happy Ru
March 16, 2012

Pet portraiture

The Inner Circle
December 31, 2011

Still life photography

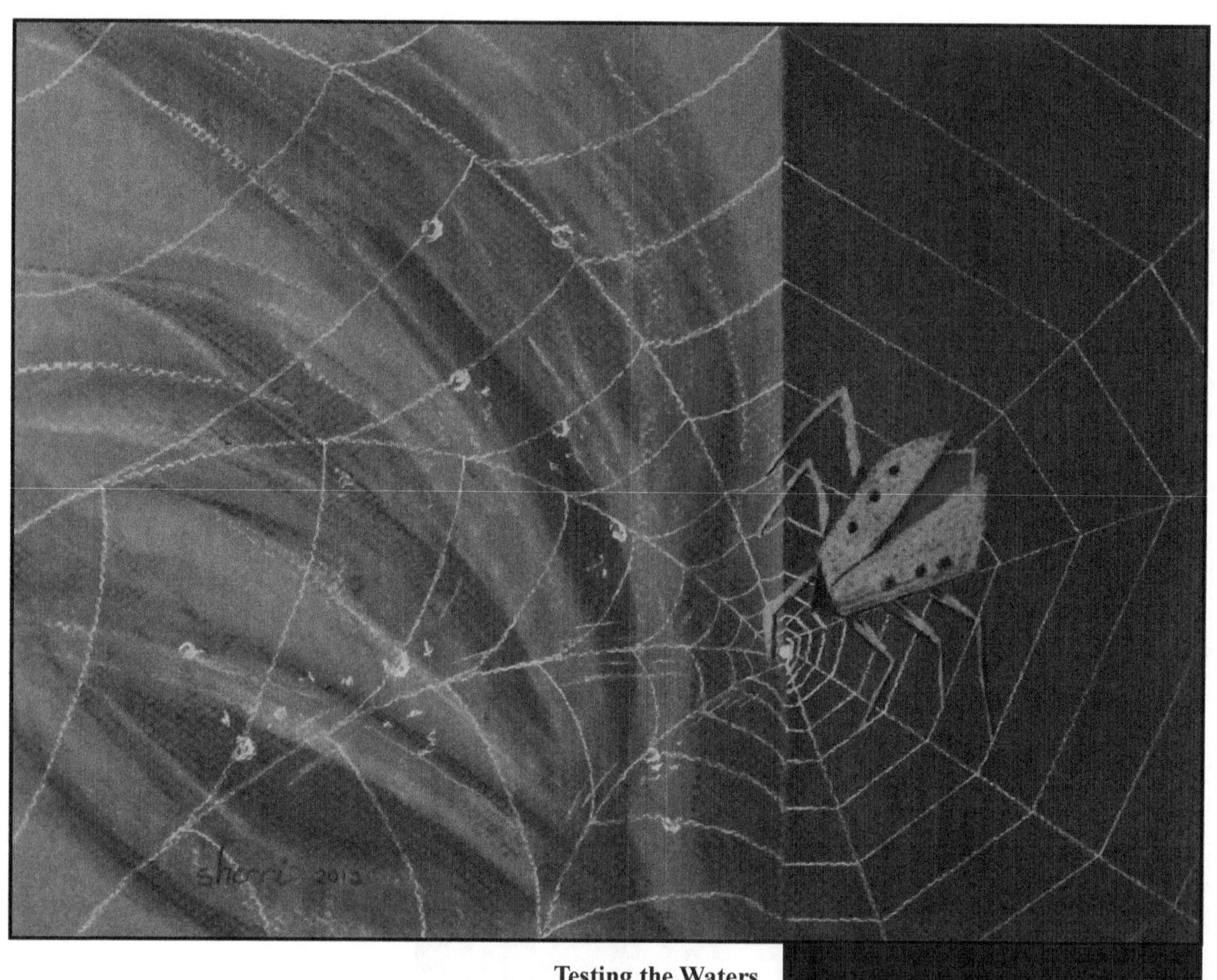

Testing the Waters
January 5, 2013

Chalk pastel

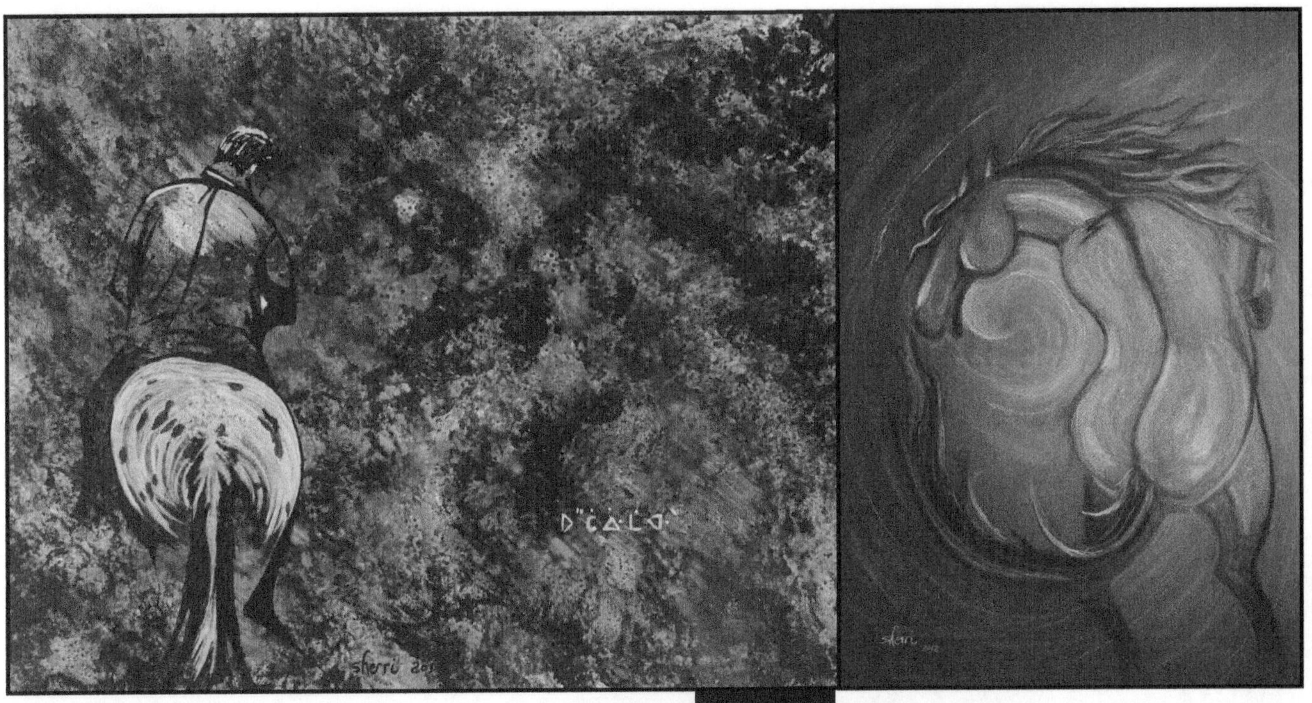

Tracking
January 6, 2012

Acylic
© Sherri Phibbs

Primal Echo
January 7, 2013

Chalk pastel
© Sherri Phibbs

Emergence
January 8, 2012

Watercolour

The Dark Flowers
January 9, 2012

Watercolour
© Sherri Phibbs

Fogged In
January 10, 2012

Chalk pastel
© Sherri Phibbs

Tree Sketch 1
January 11, 2012

Chalk pastel
© Sherri Phibbs

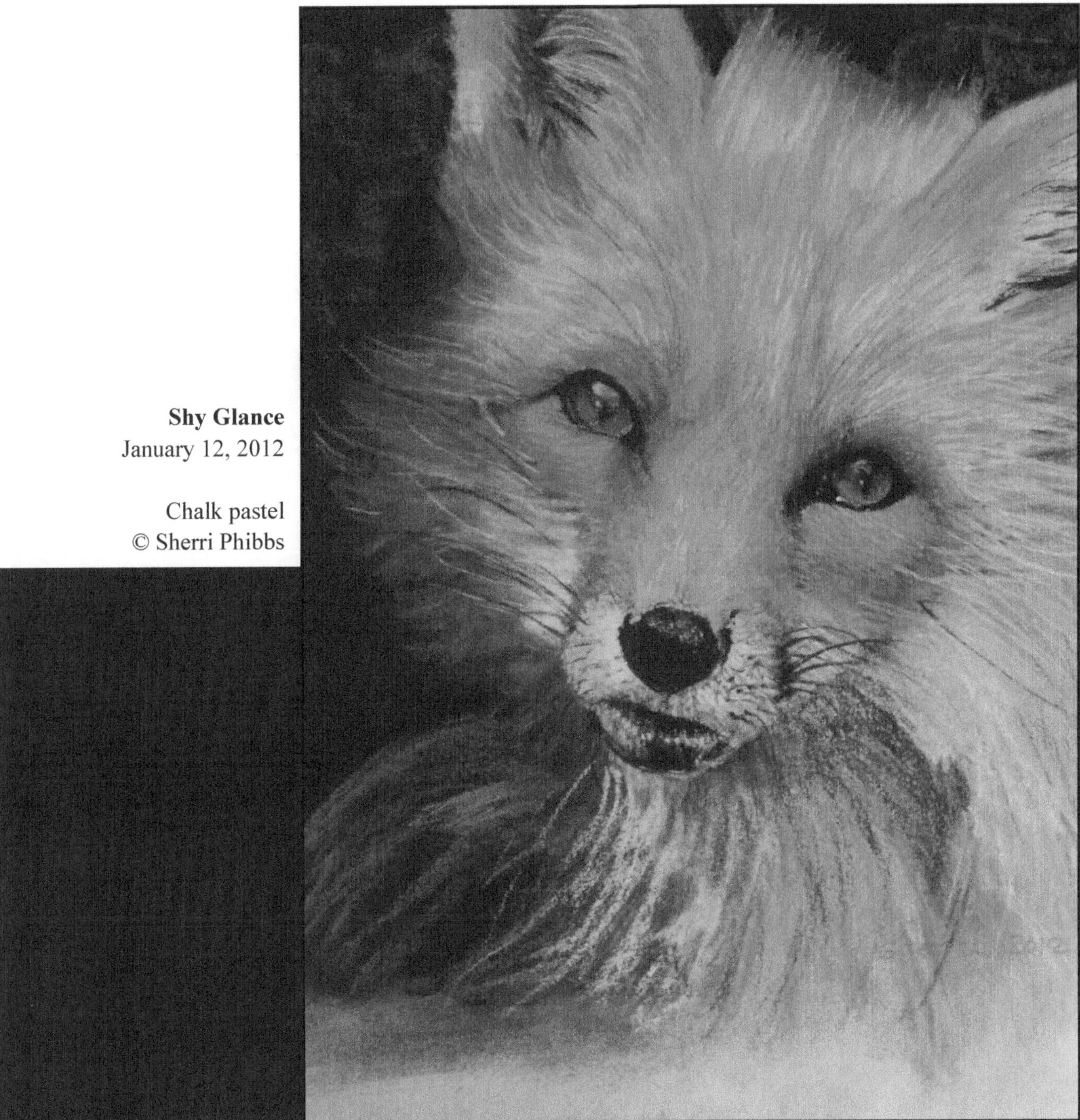

Shy Glance
January 12, 2012

Chalk pastel
© Sherri Phibbs

Sunlight & Shadow
January 13, 2012

Pet portraiture

Iyuptala
January 14, 2012

Digital collage

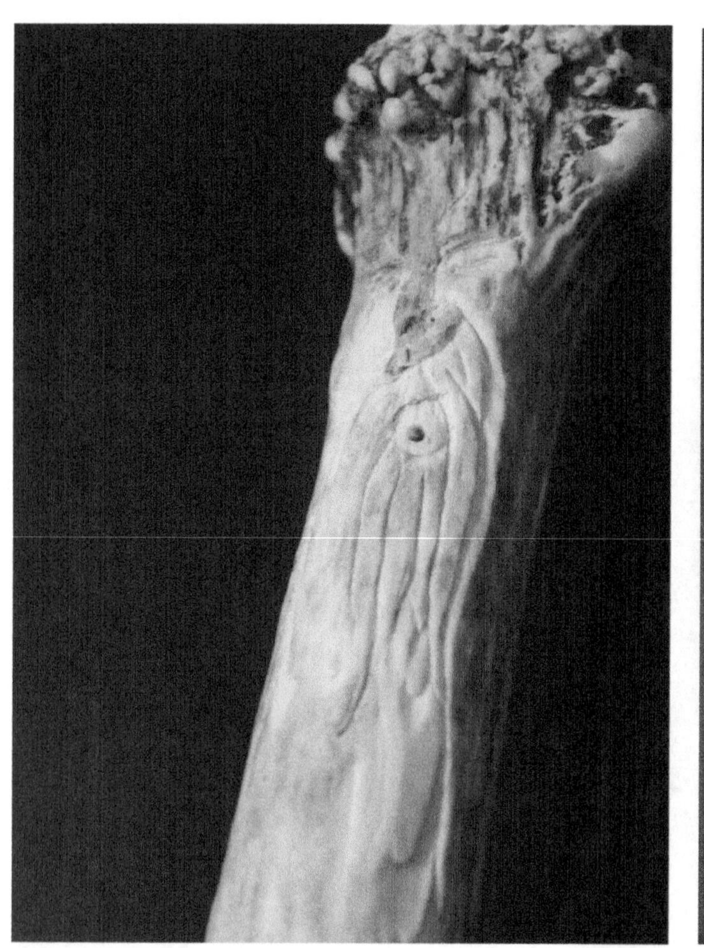

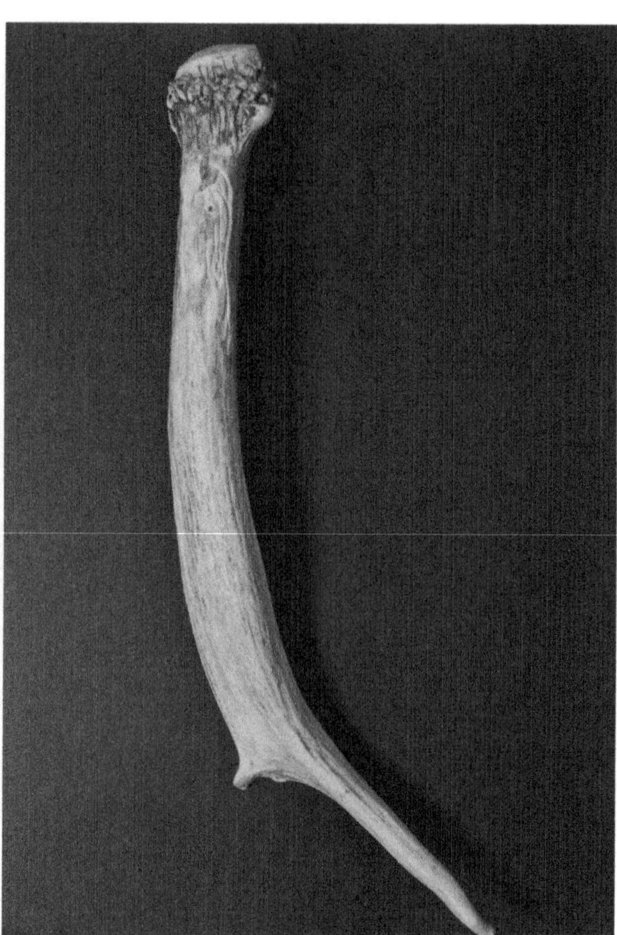

Whistling Elk
January 15, 2012

Antler carving

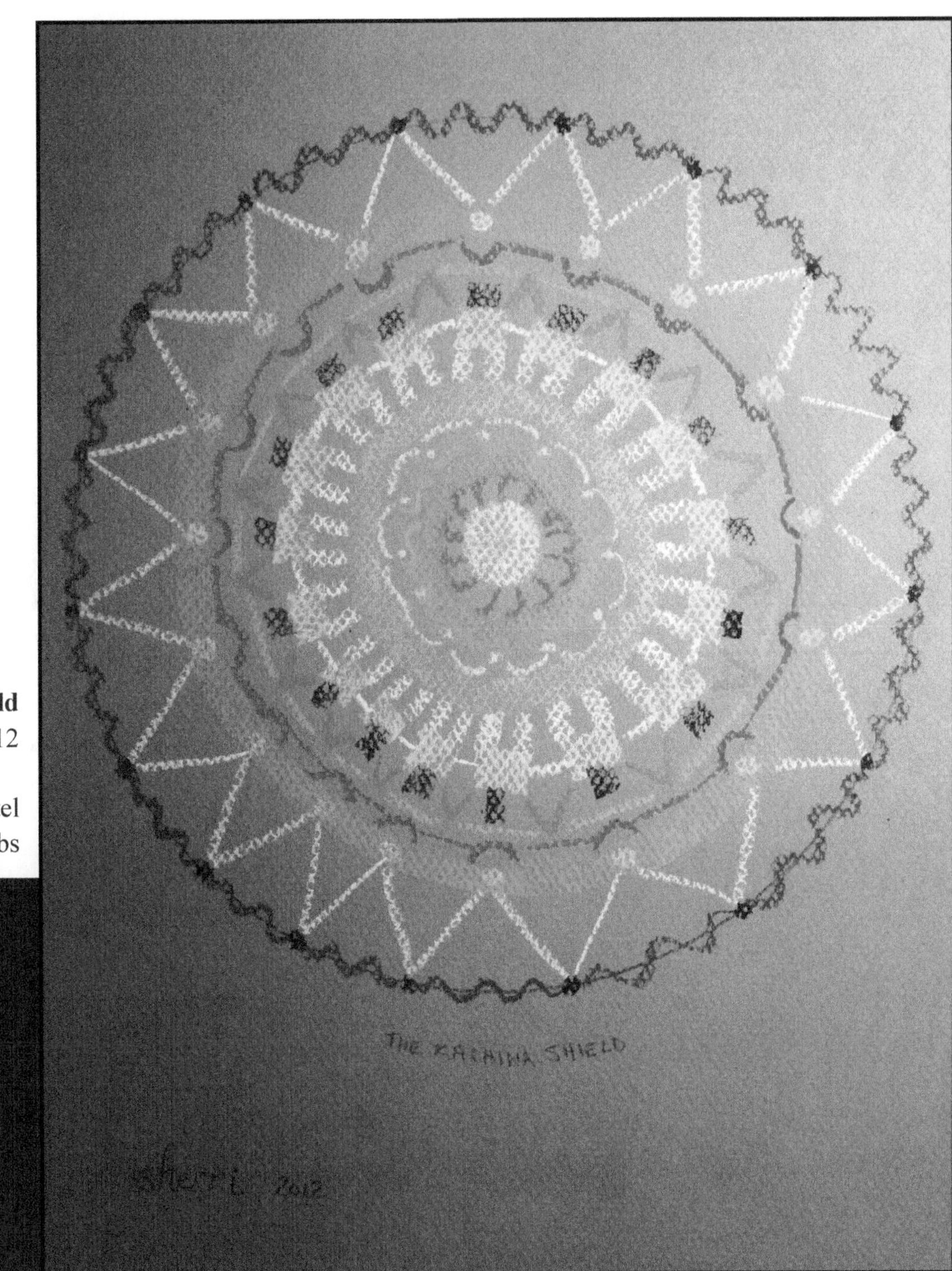

The Kachina Shield
January 16, 2012

Chalk pastel

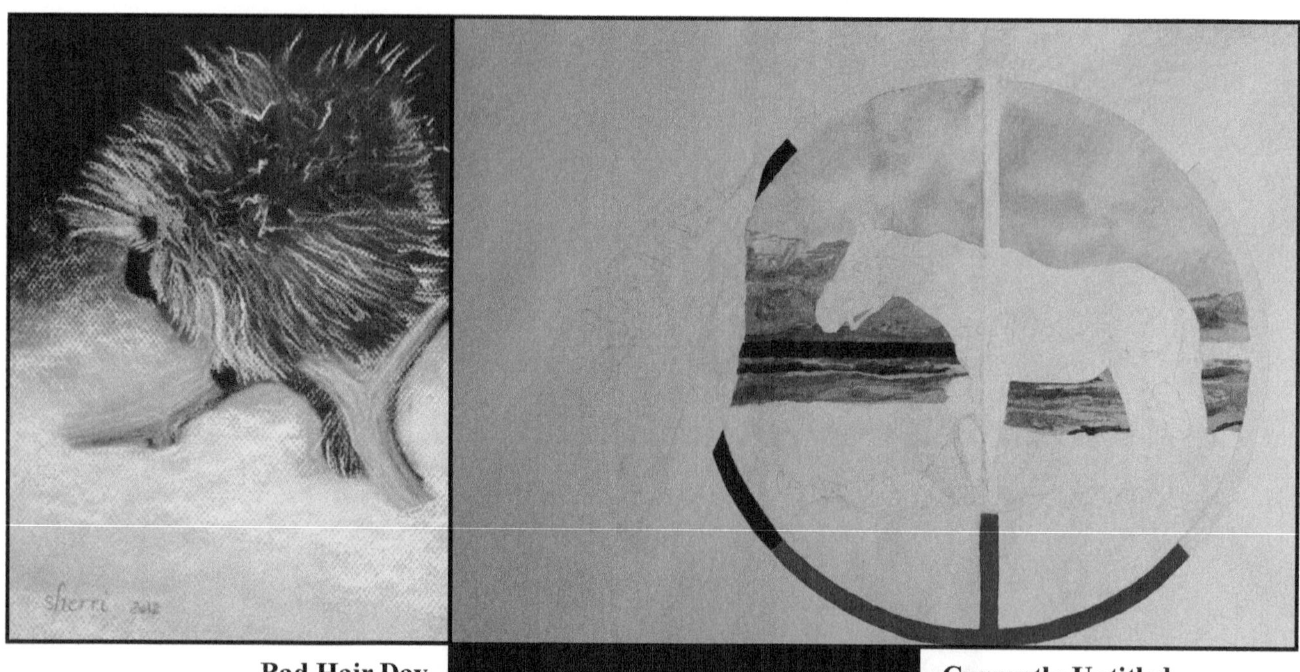

Bad Hair Day
January 17, 2012

Chalk pastel

Currently Untitled
January 19, 2012

Watercolour

Primitive Stallion
January 18, 2012

Acrylics

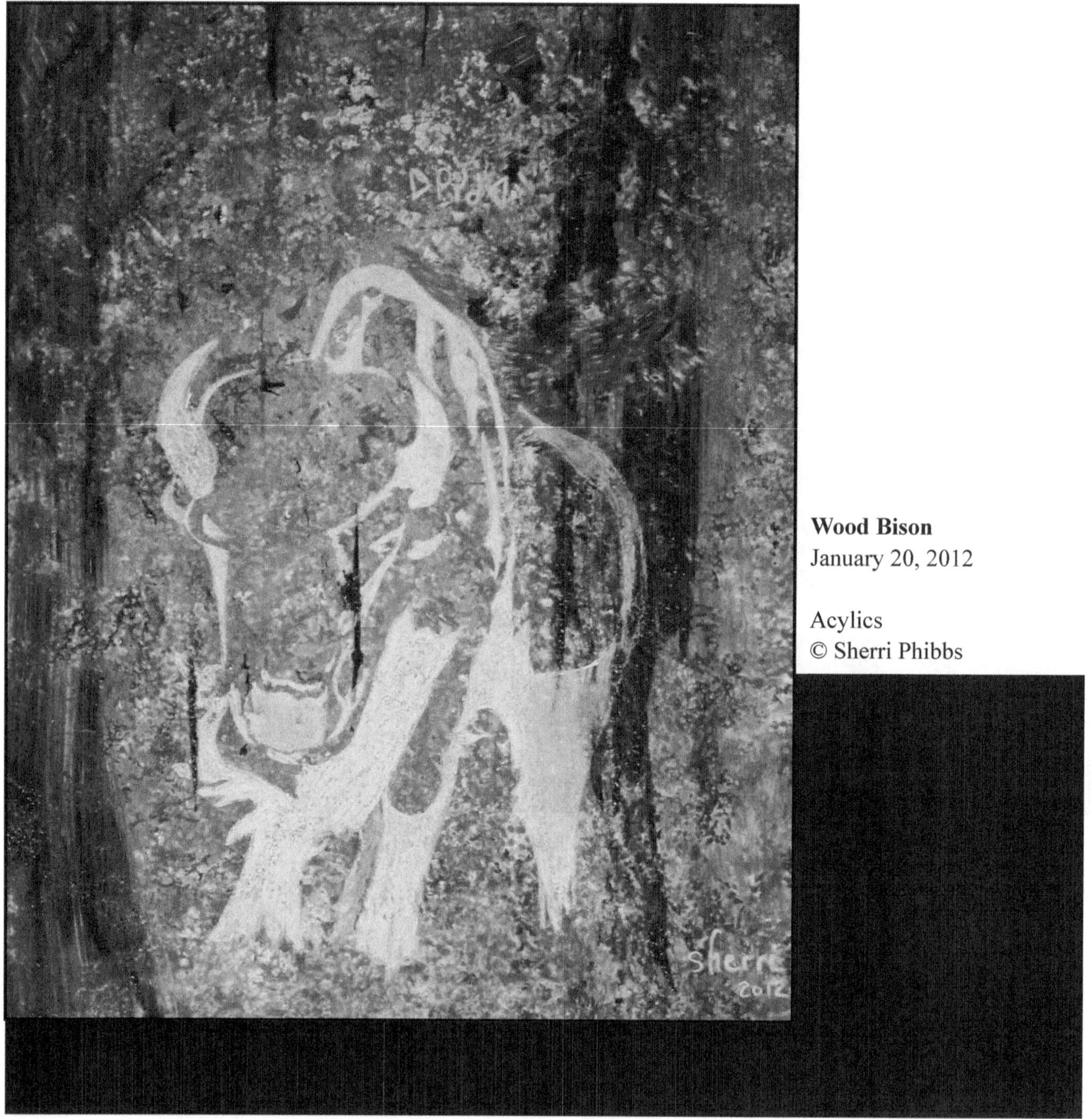

Wood Bison
January 20, 2012

Acylics
© Sherri Phibbs

From Darkness
January 29, 2012

Nature photography

Getting to Know You
March 10, 2012

Watercolour

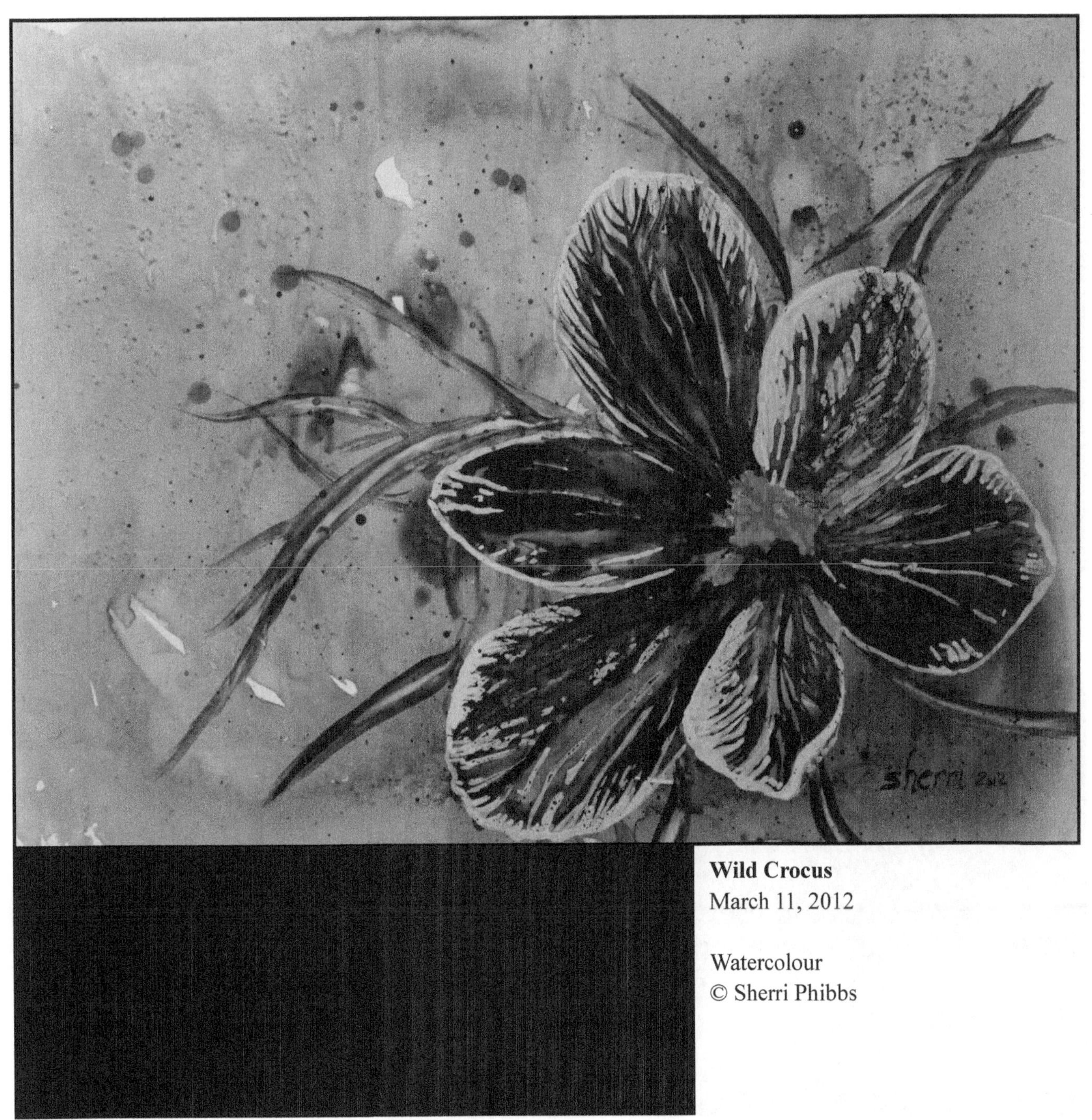

Wild Crocus
March 11, 2012

Watercolour

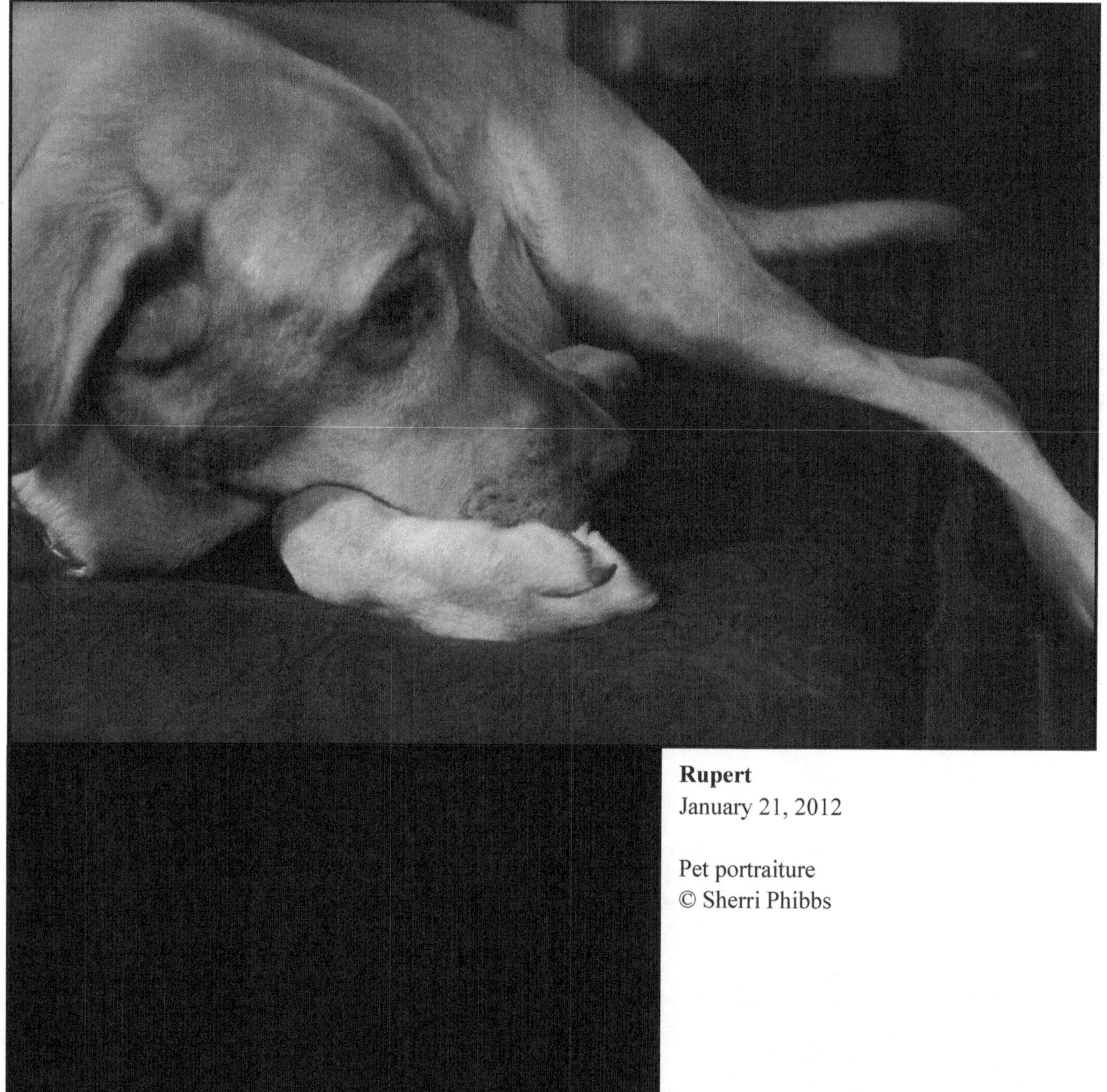

Rupert
January 21, 2012

Pet portraiture

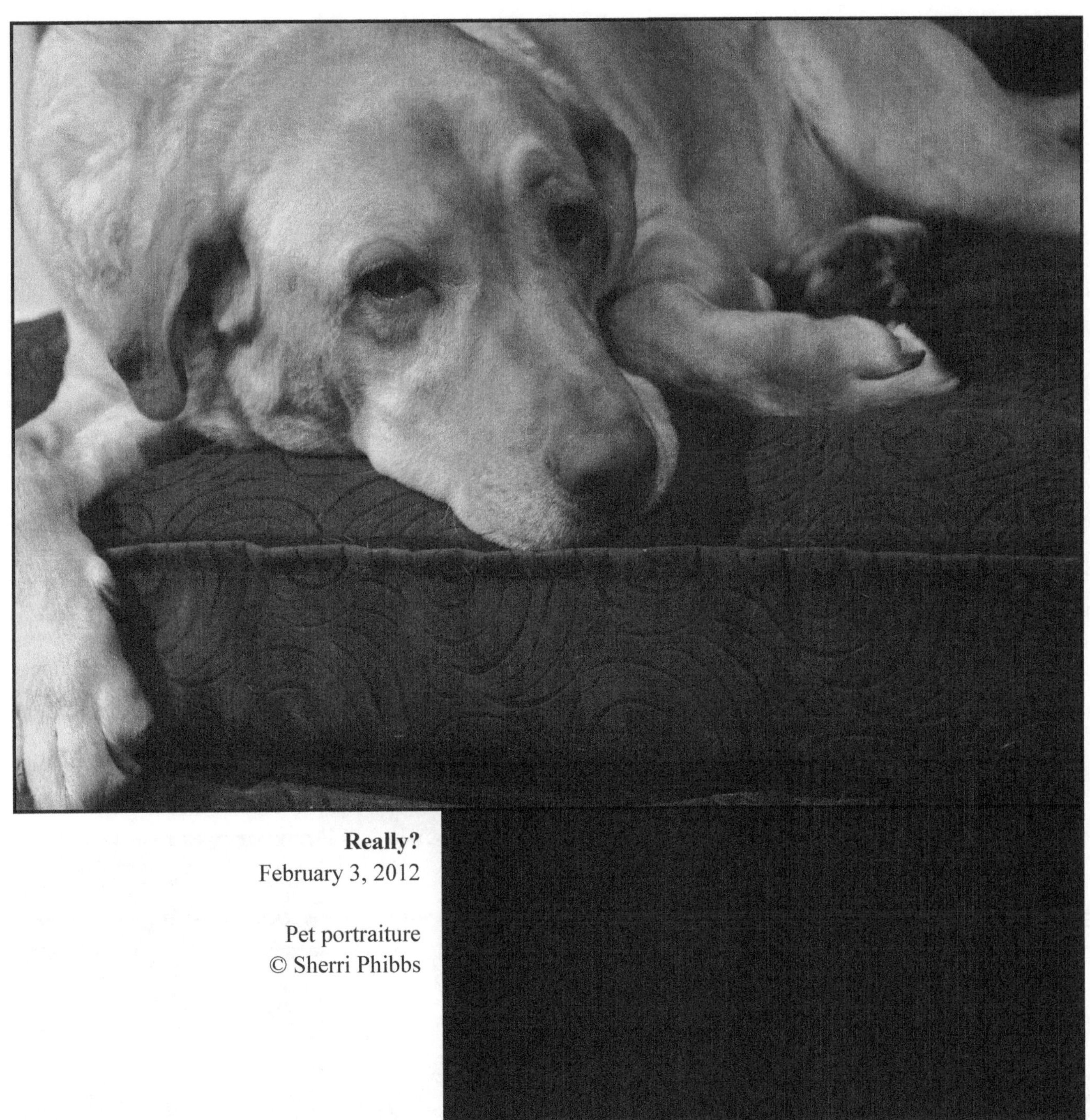

Really?
February 3, 2012

Pet portraiture
© Sherri Phibbs

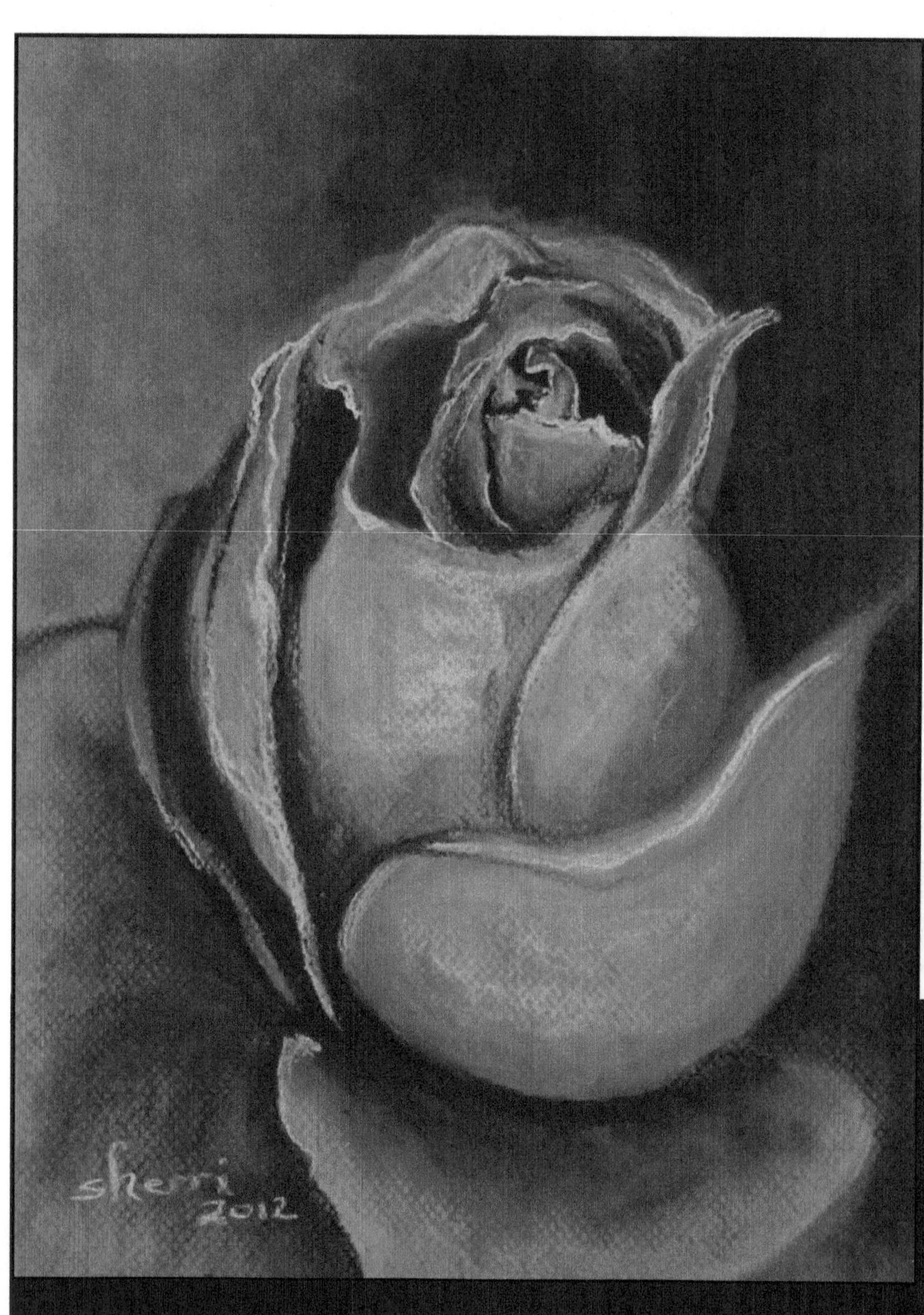

Oh, Seductive Rose
January 23, 2012

Chalk pastel

Suntithenai
January 24, 2012

Digital collage

Stay Bendy
January 26, 2012

Pencil sketch
© Sherri Phibbs

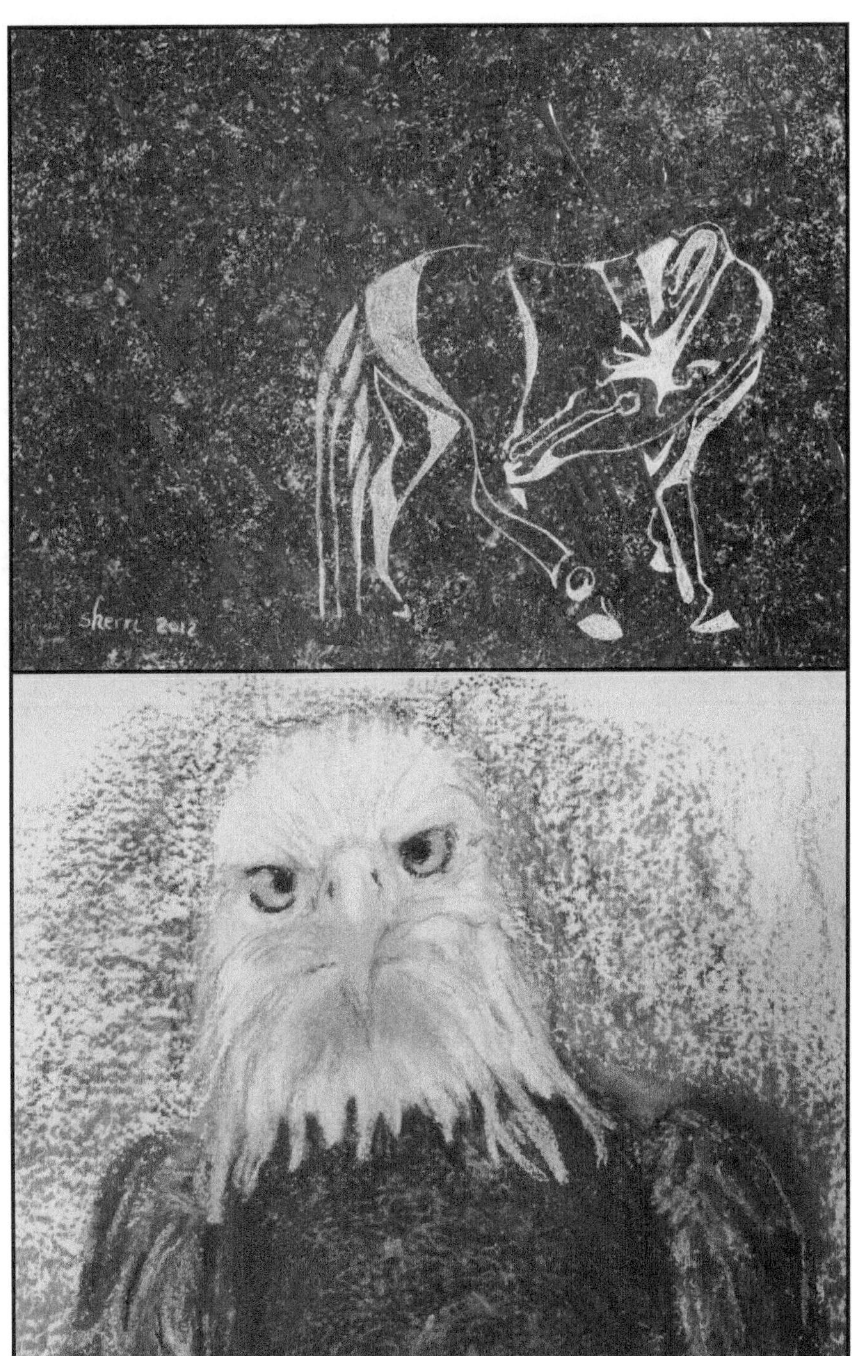

Live Flexible
January 26, 2012

Acylics
© Sherri Phibbs

Eagle sketch
January 27, 2012

Chalk pastel
© Sherri Phibbs

One Is For Sorrow
January 28, 2012

Pencil sketch

Observer
January 30, 2012

Chalk pastel

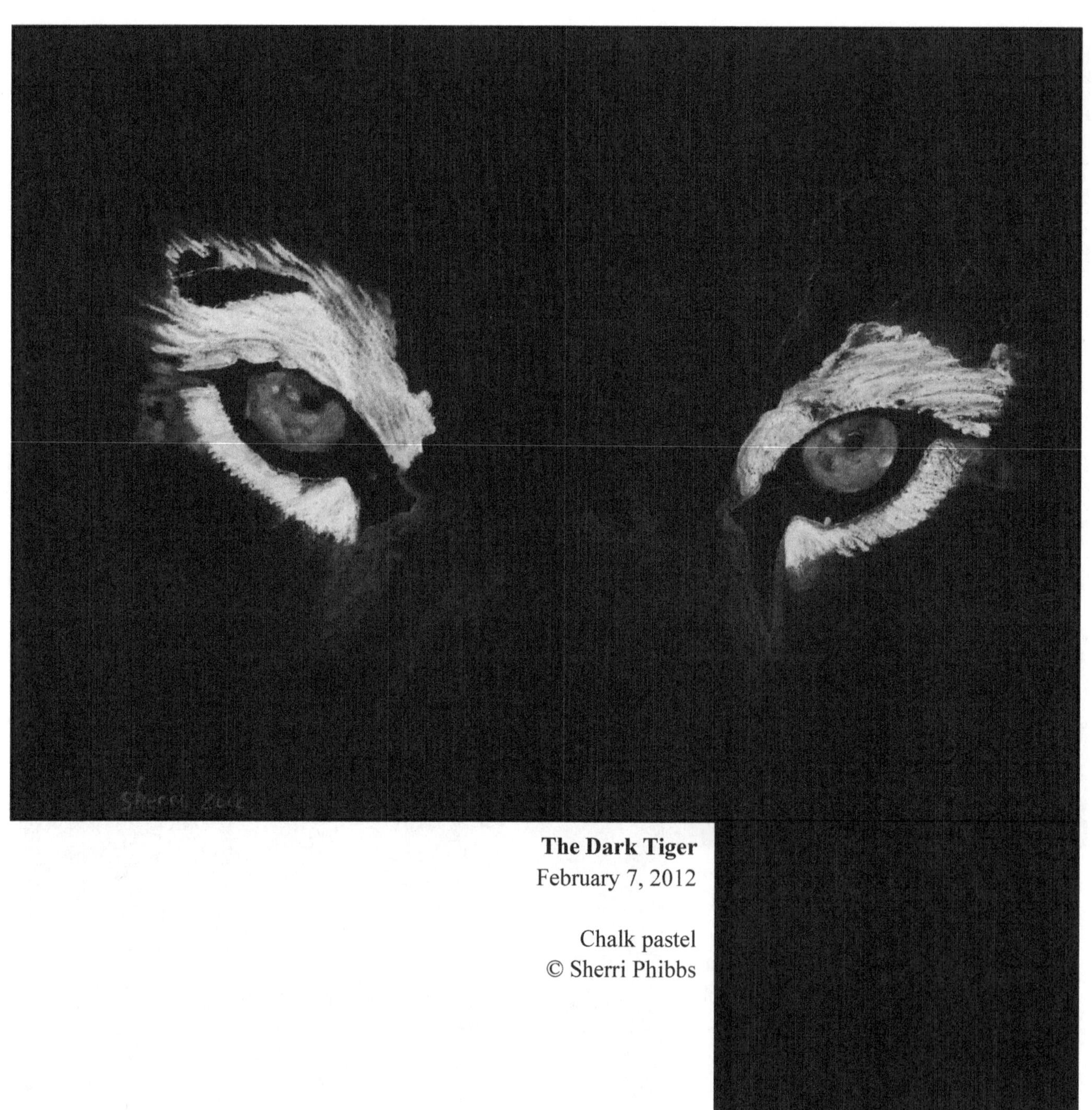

The Dark Tiger
February 7, 2012

Chalk pastel
© Sherri Phibbs

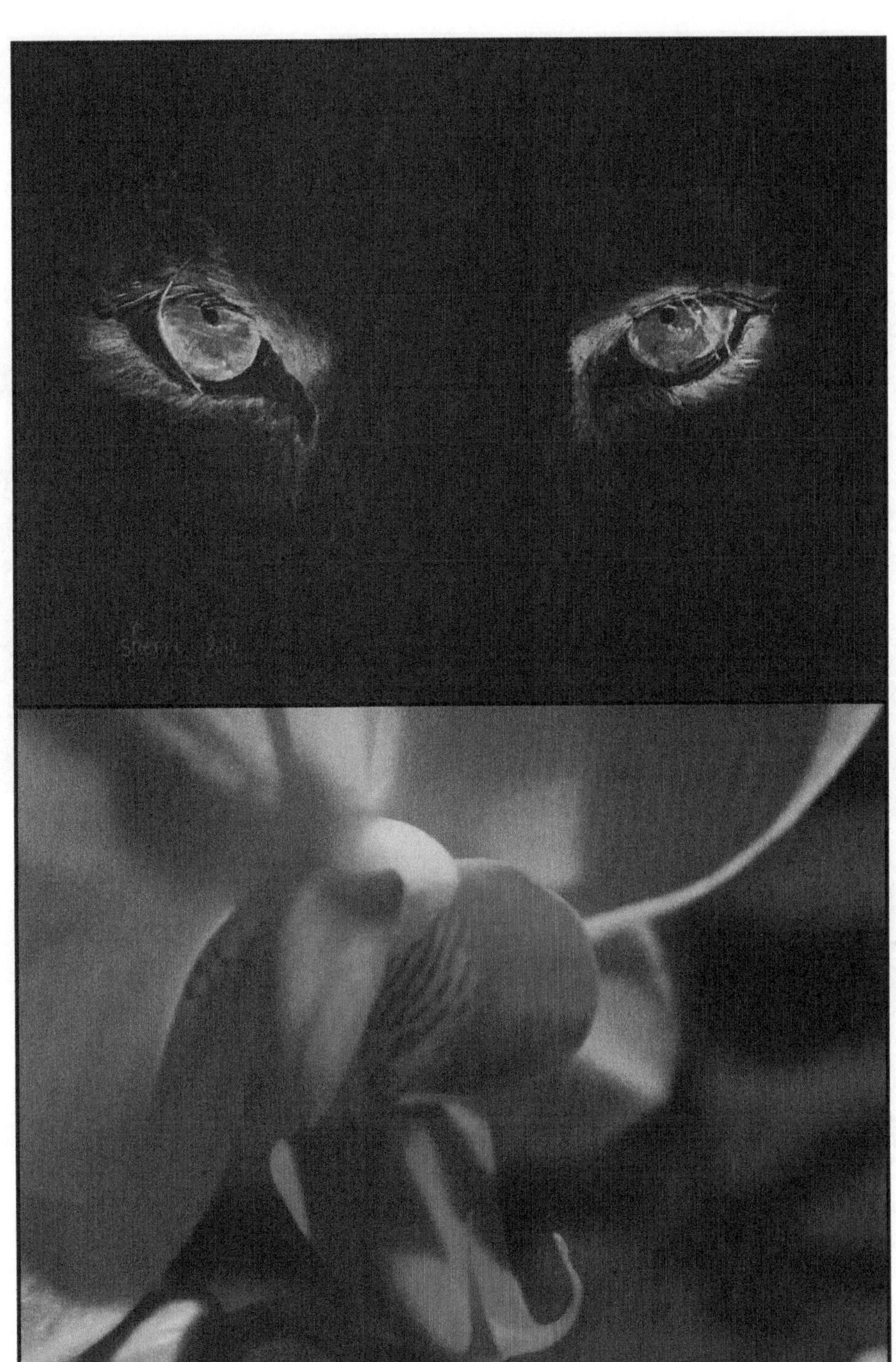

Cougar in the Dark
February 8, 2012

Chalk pastel
© Sherri Phibbs

Beware the Dragon
February 10, 2012

Nature photography
© Sherri Phibbs

Eye Candy
February 9, 2012

Nature photography

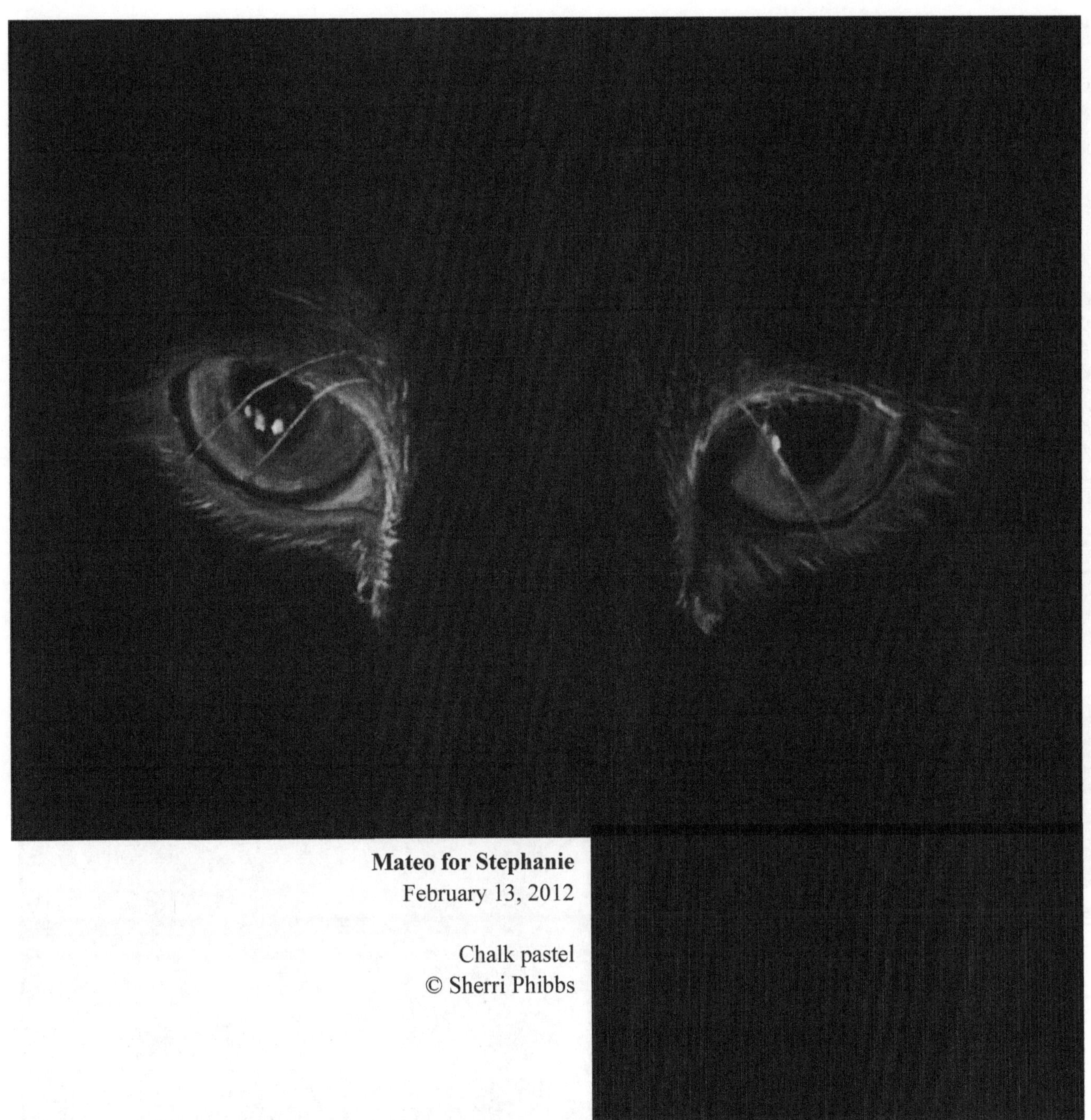

Mateo for Stephanie
February 13, 2012

Chalk pastel

Gravitas
February 15, 2012

Conté

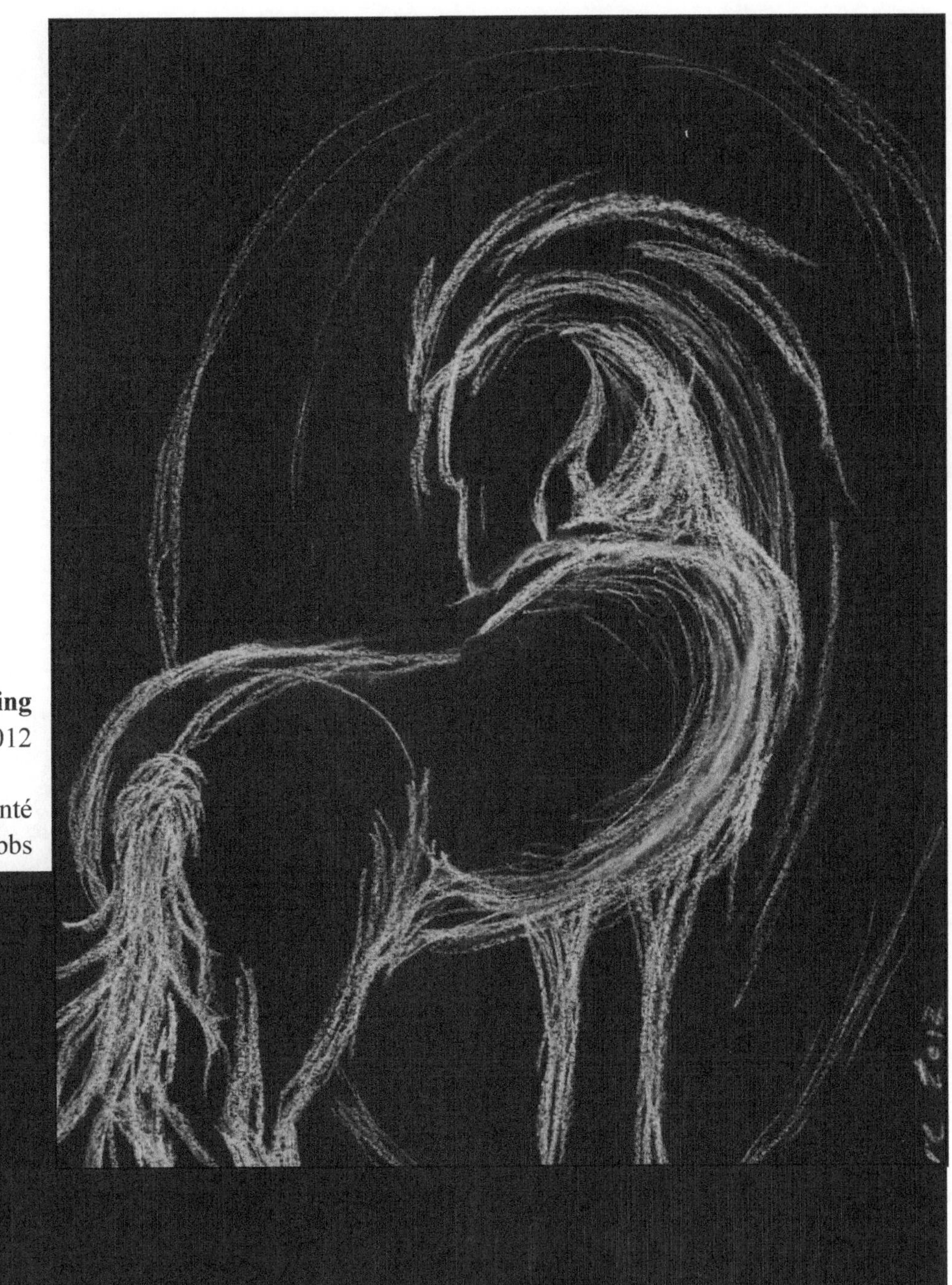

Power Sketching
February 16, 2012

Conté

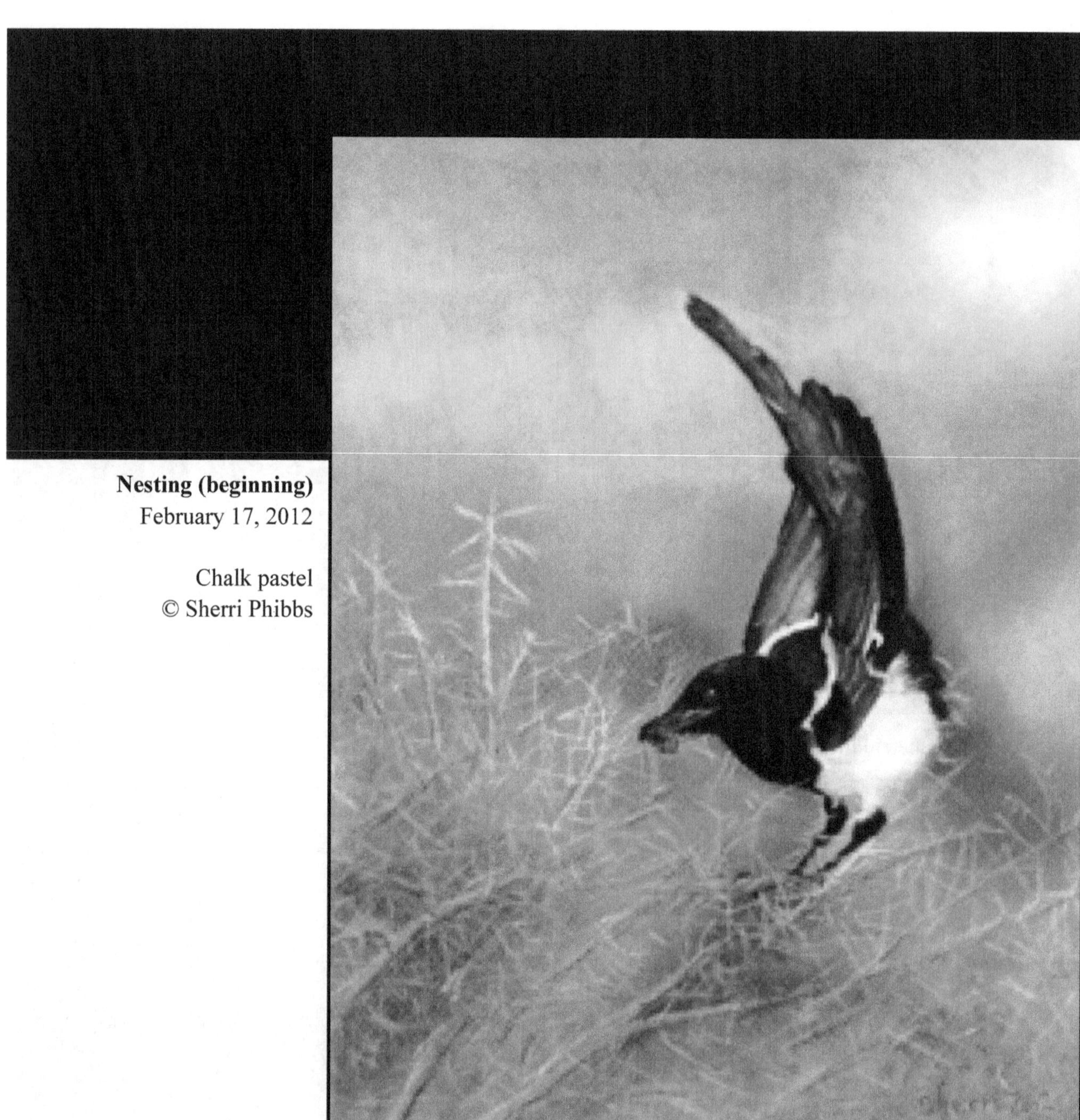

Nesting (beginning)
February 17, 2012

Chalk pastel

A Magpie Moment (complete)
February 18, 2012

Chalk pastel
© Sherri Phibbs

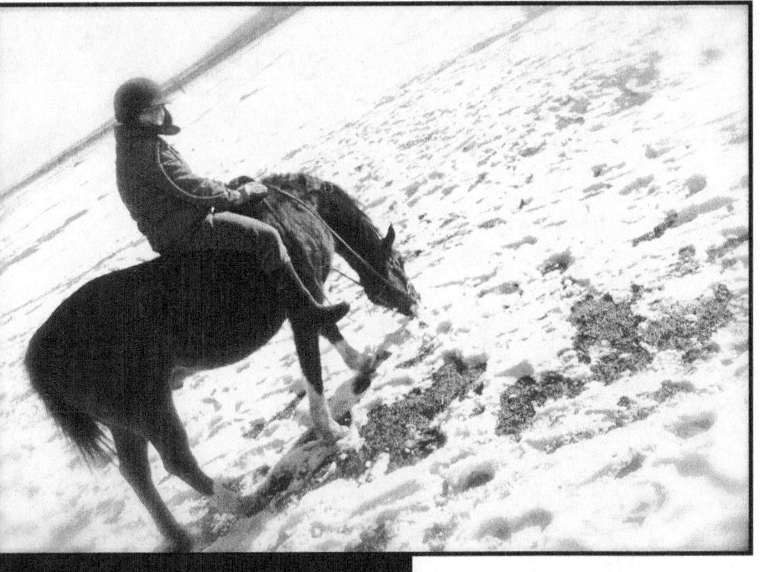

Decidedly Apropos
February 19, 2012

Nature photography
© Sherri Phibbs

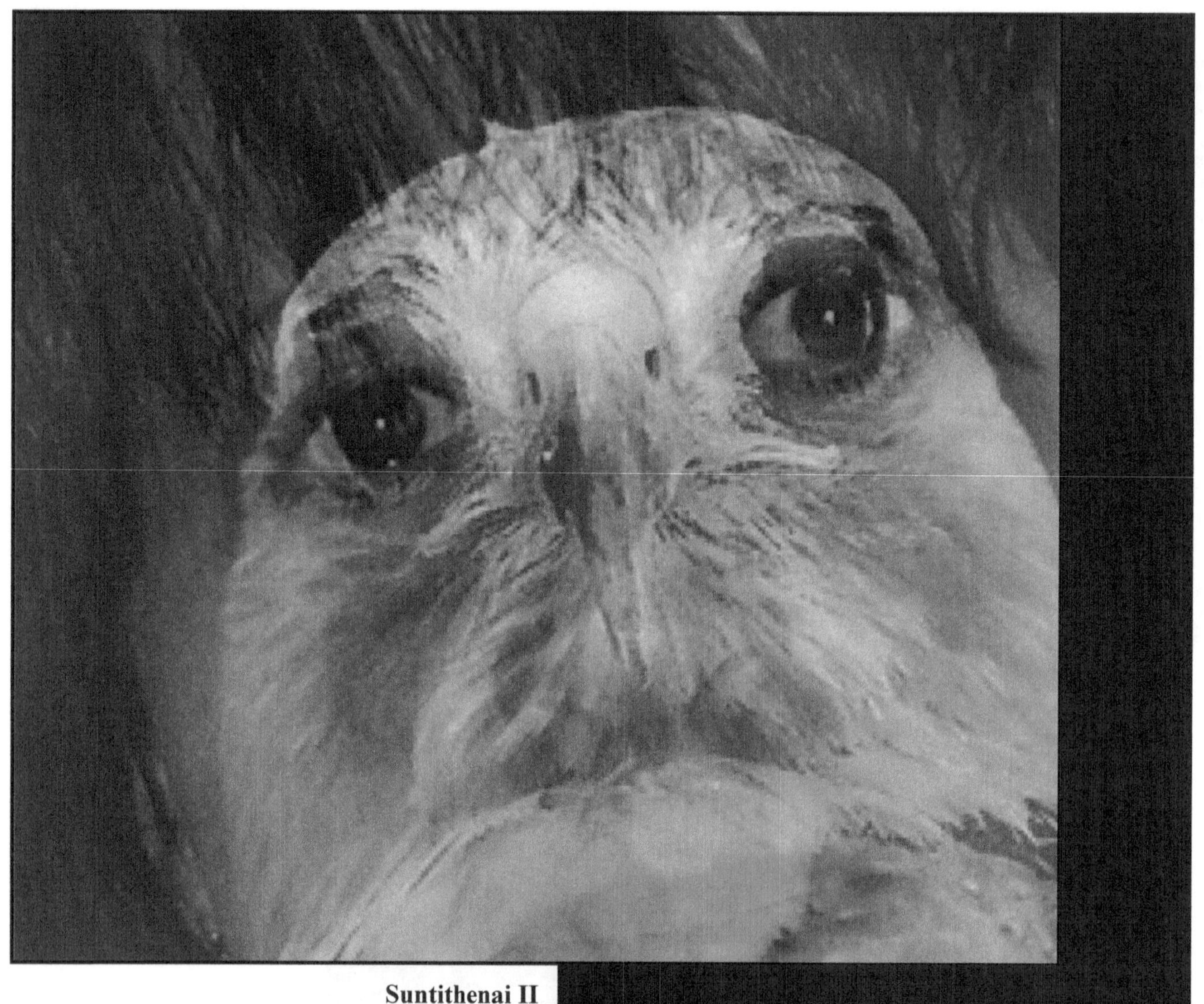

Suntithenai II
February 20, 2012

Digital collage

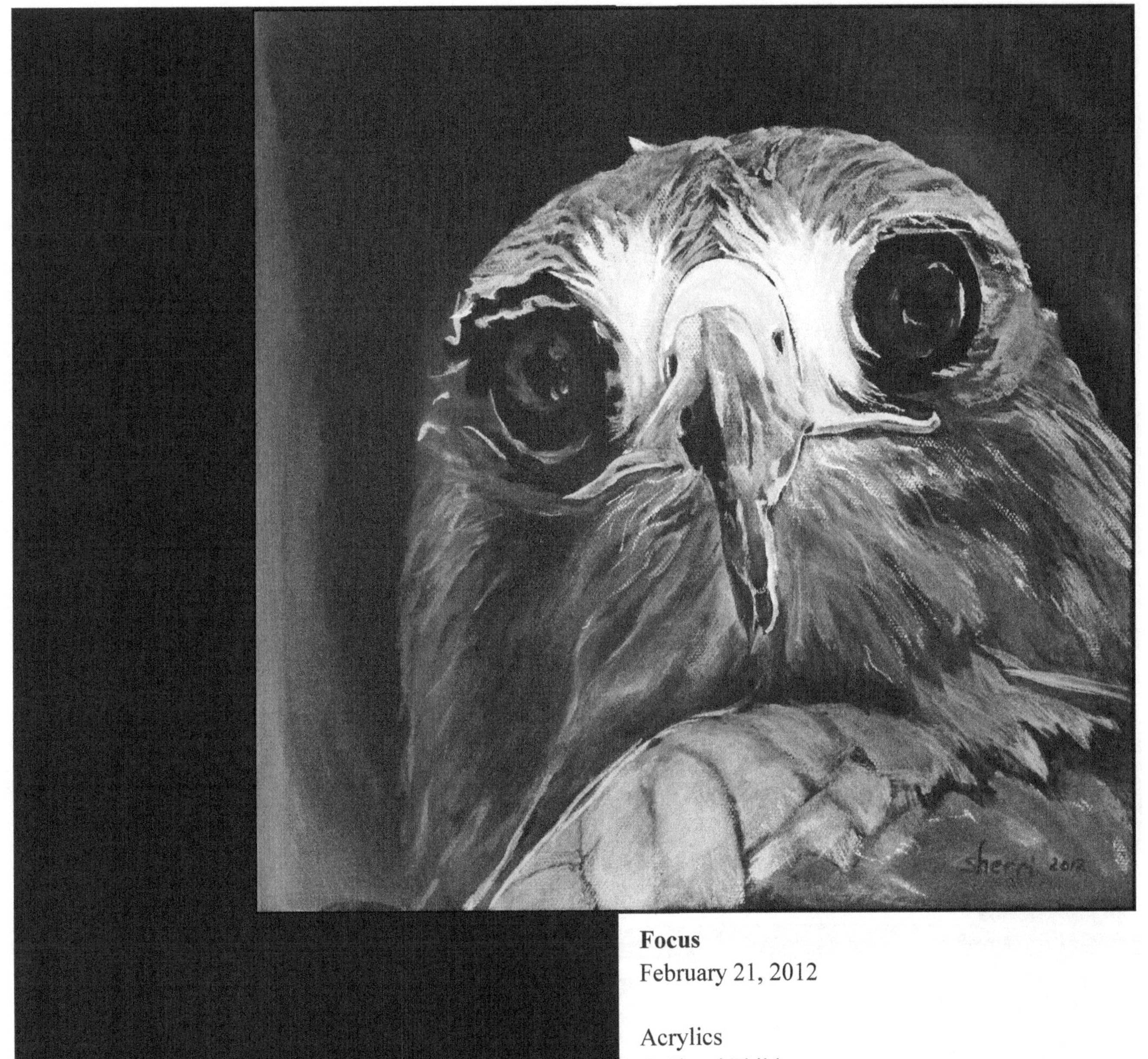

Focus
February 21, 2012

Acrylics

Meditative Mandala
February 23, 2012

Chalk pastel

Shades of the Rock
February 24, 2012

Watercolour
© Sherri Phibbs

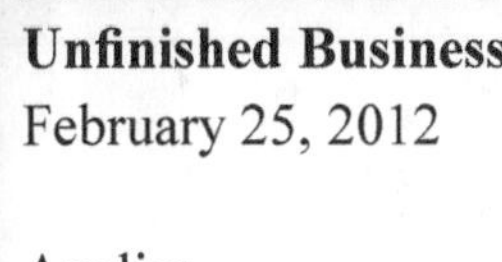

Unfinished Business
February 25, 2012

Acylics
© Sherri Phibbs

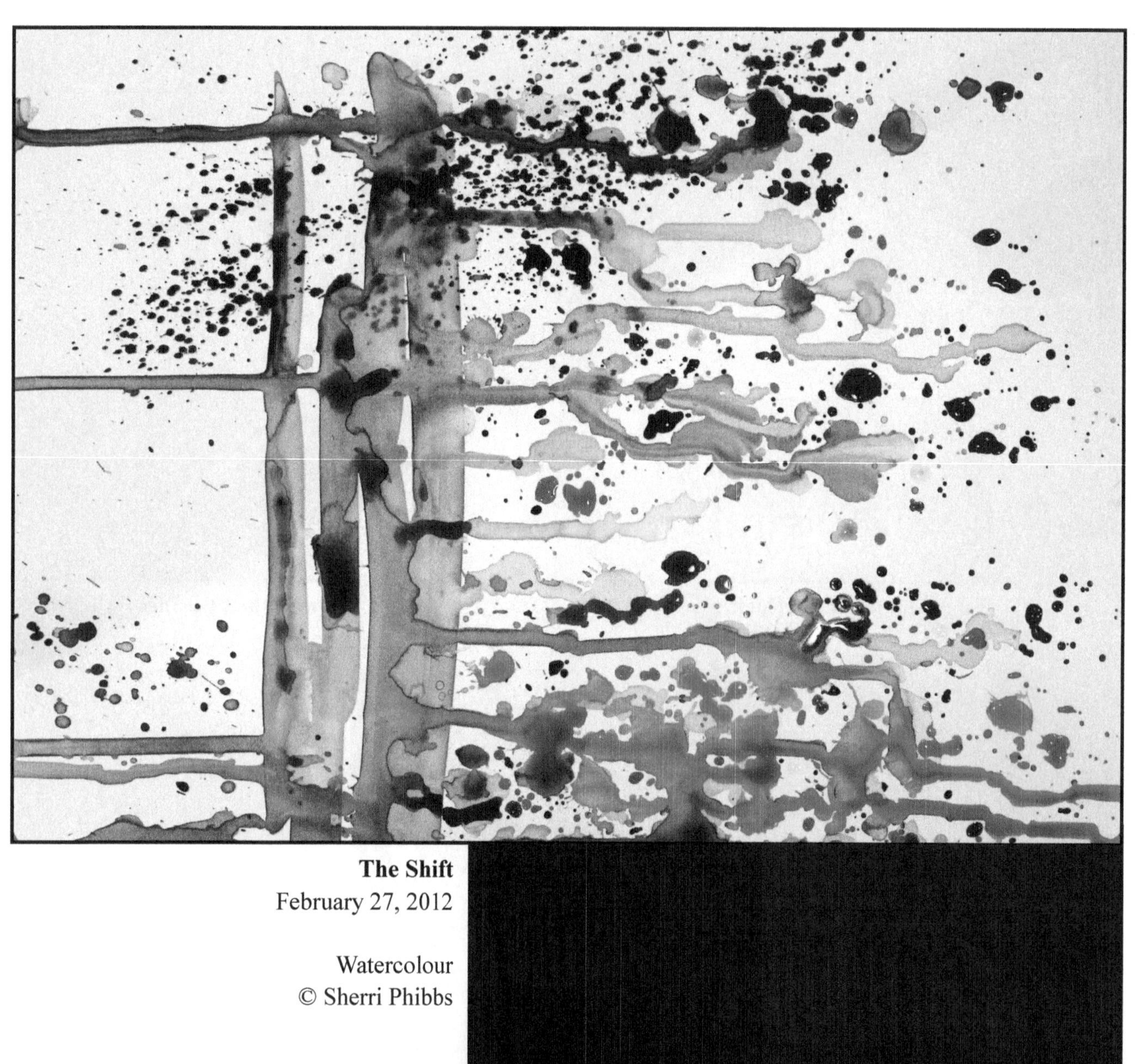

The Shift
February 27, 2012

Watercolour

Trembling Aspen
February 26, 2012

Watercolour
© Sherri Phibbs

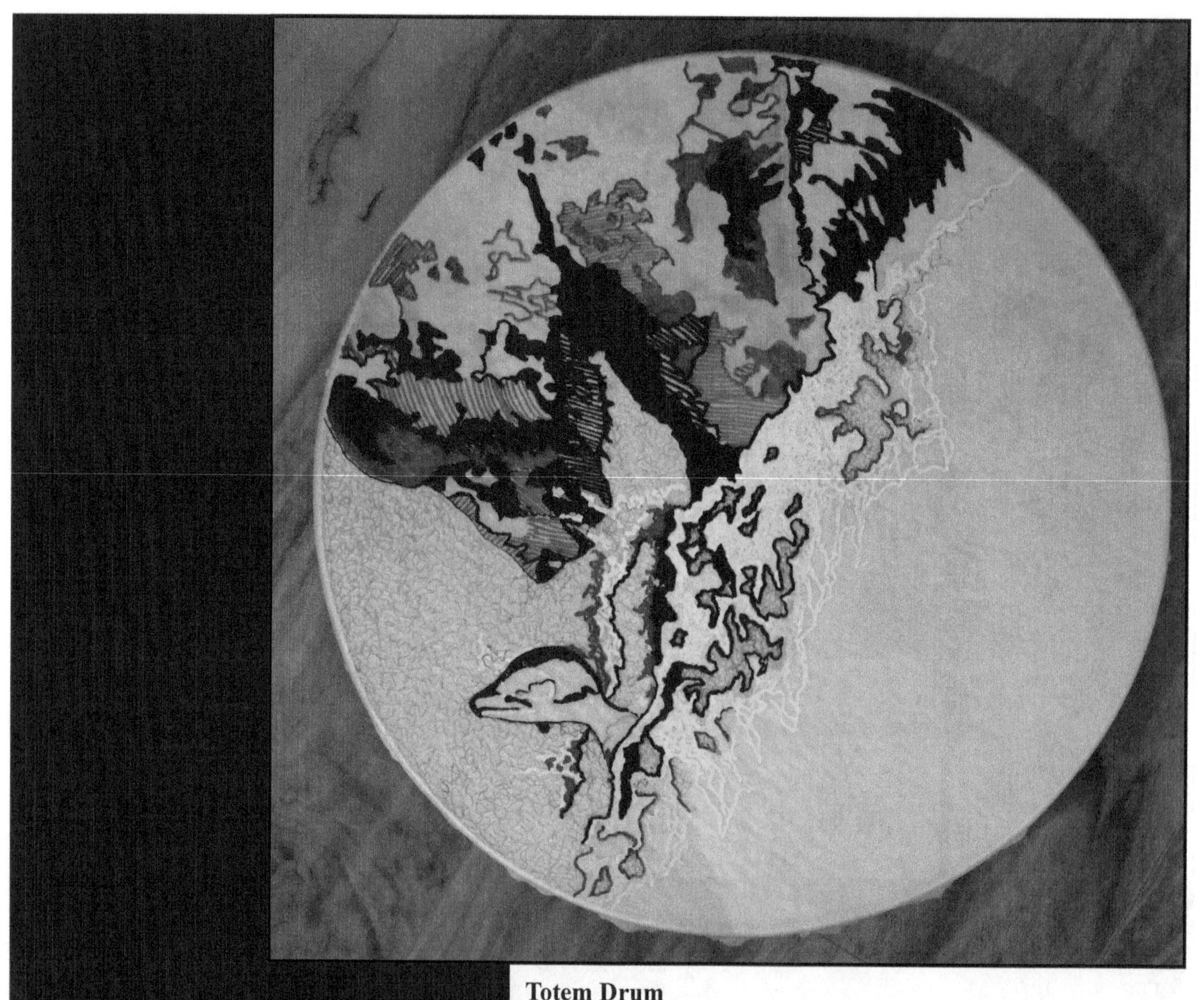

Totem Drum
March 1, 2012

Traditionally hand-made rawhide drum

Weather Sketch
March 2, 2012

Chalk pastel
© Sherri Phibbs

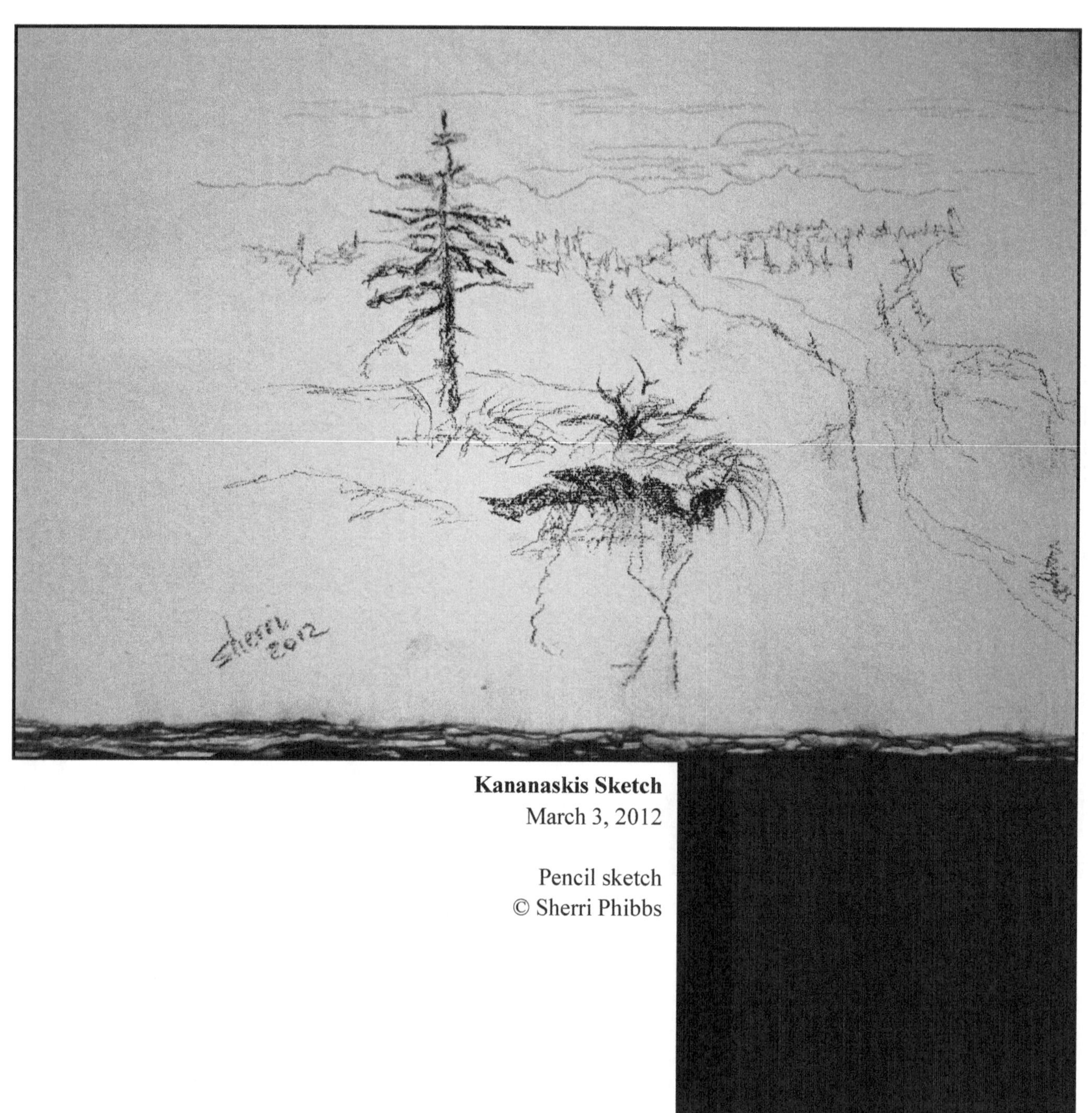

Kananaskis Sketch
March 3, 2012

Pencil sketch

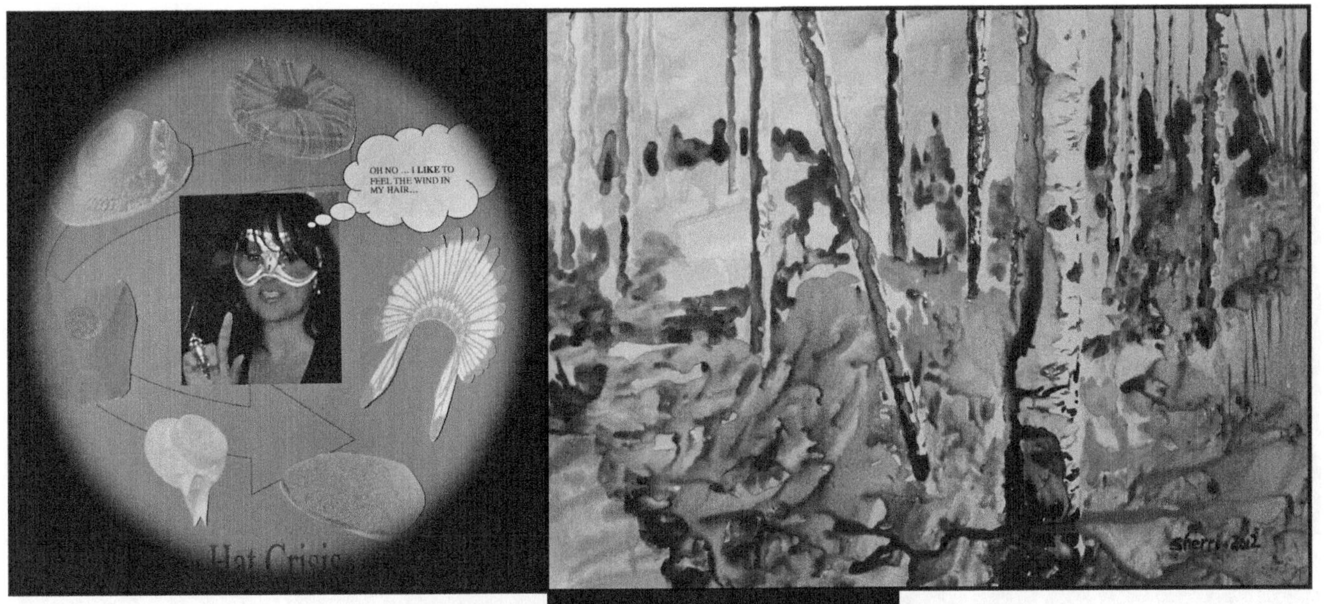

Hat Crisis
March 7, 2012

Collage
© Sherri Phibbs

Changes
March 8, 2012

Watercolour
© Sherri Phibbs

The 10 Minute Orange
March 13, 2012

Chalk pastel

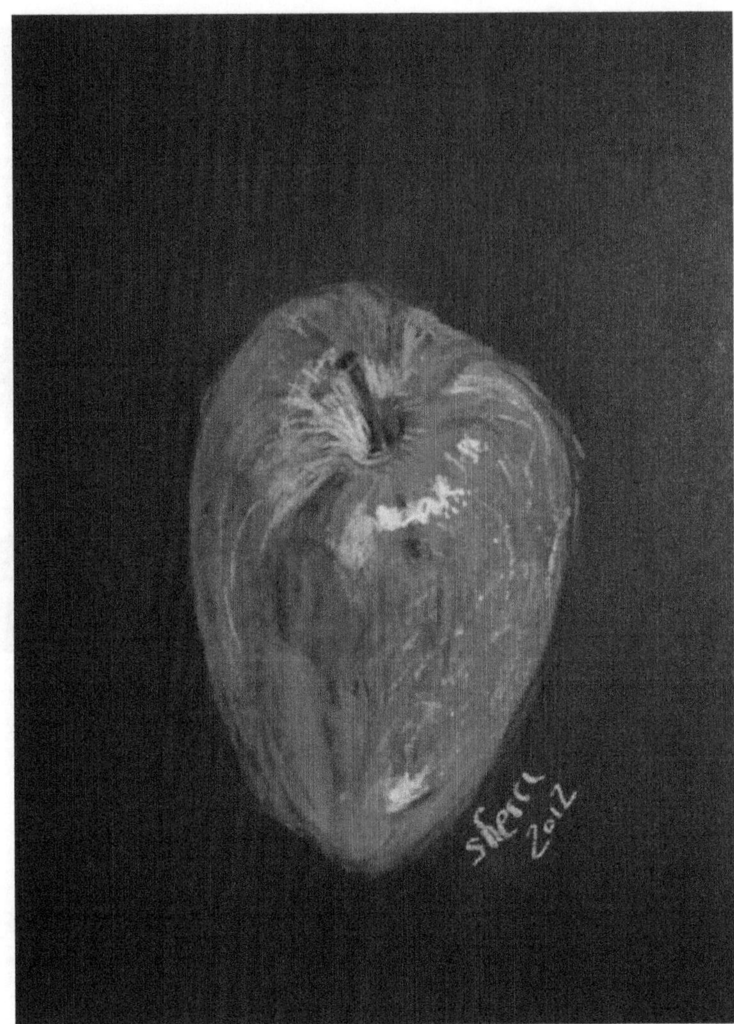

The 5 Minute Apple
March 14, 2012

Chalk pastel

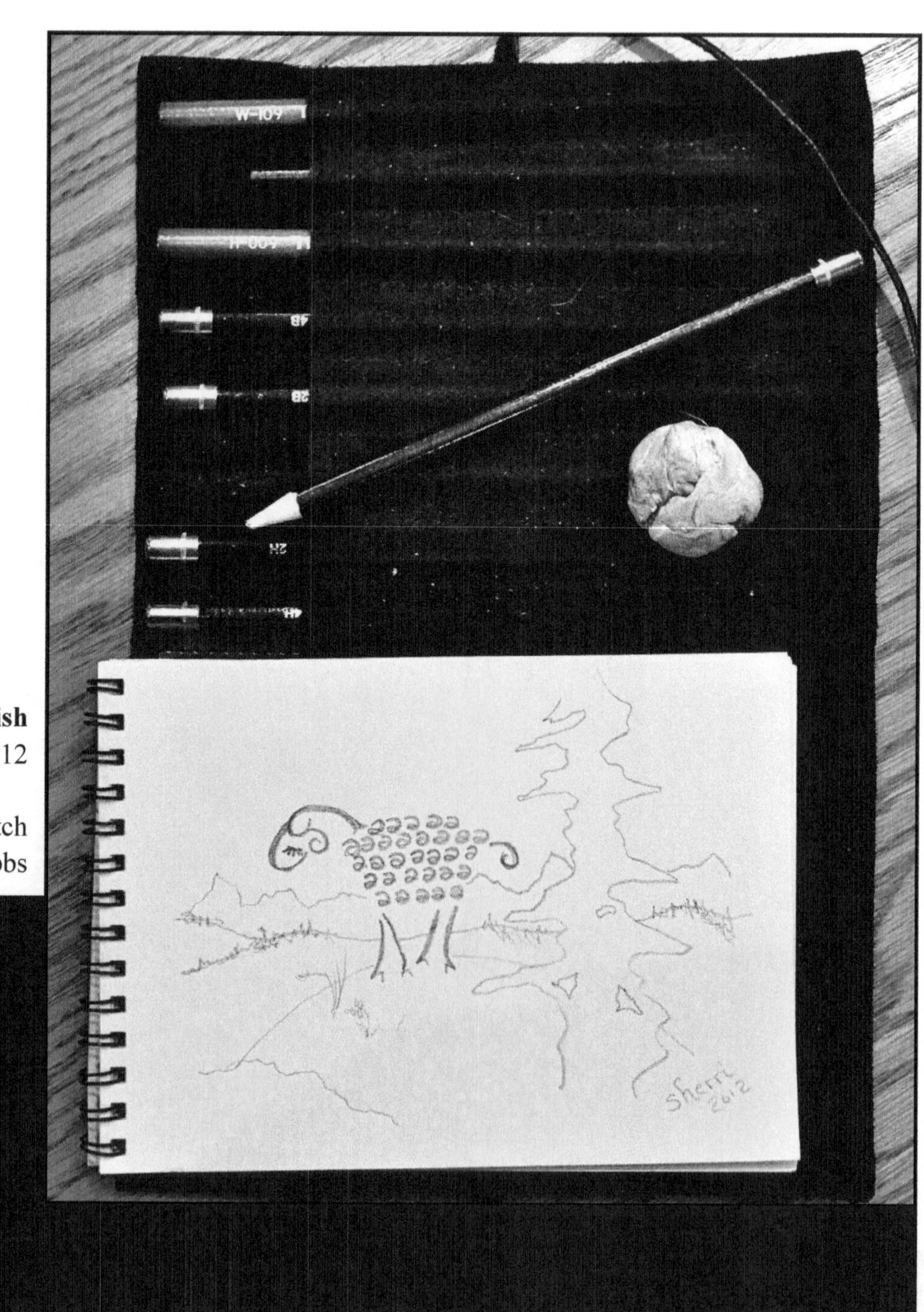

Sheep…ish
March 21, 2012

Pencil sketch

Fierce Display
March 22, 2012

Chalk pastel
© Sherri Phibbs

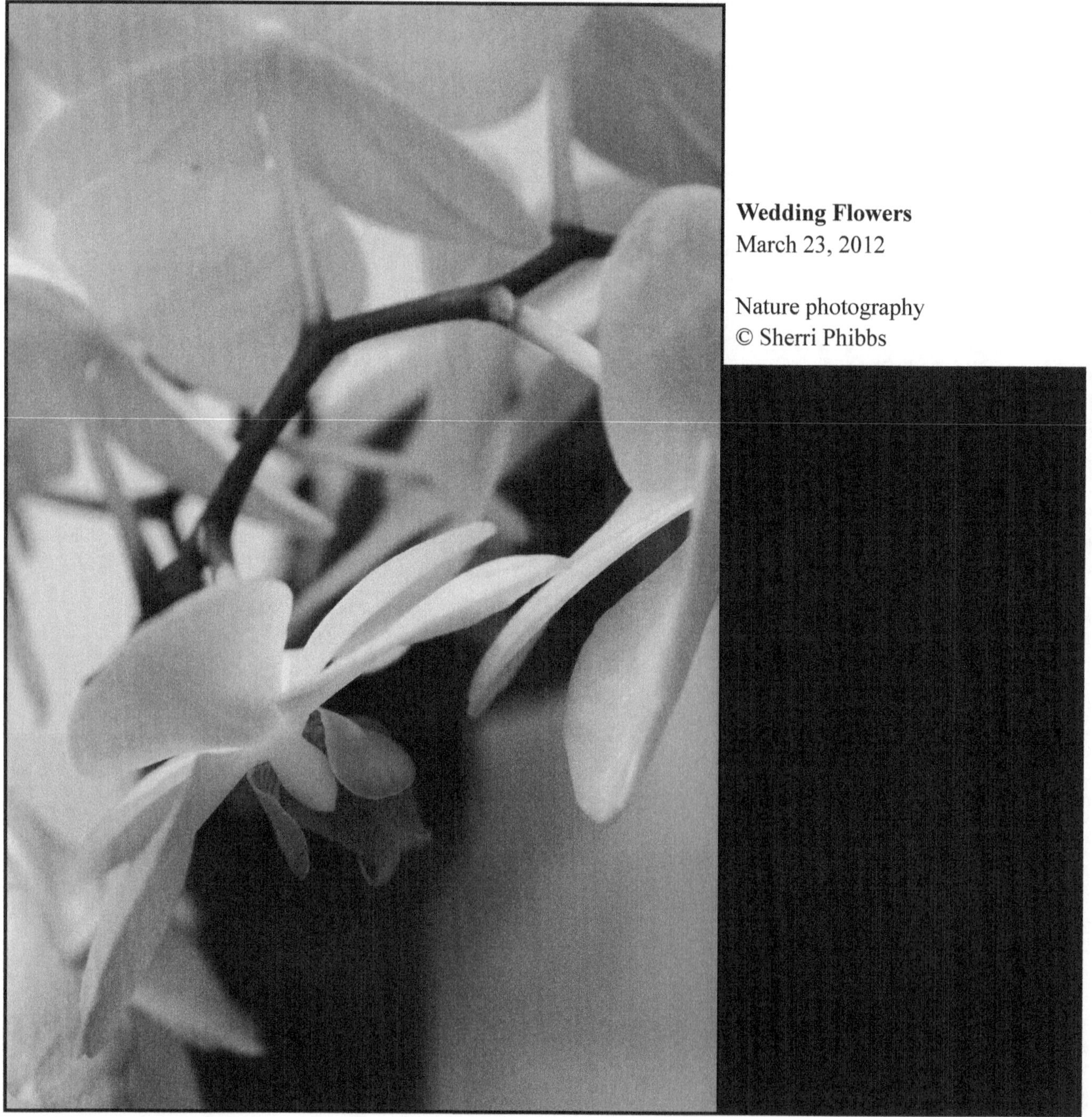

Wedding Flowers
March 23, 2012

Nature photography

Who Am I?
March 24, 2012

Nature photography
© Sherri Phibbs

2012
March 25, 2012

Watercolour
© Sherri Phibbs

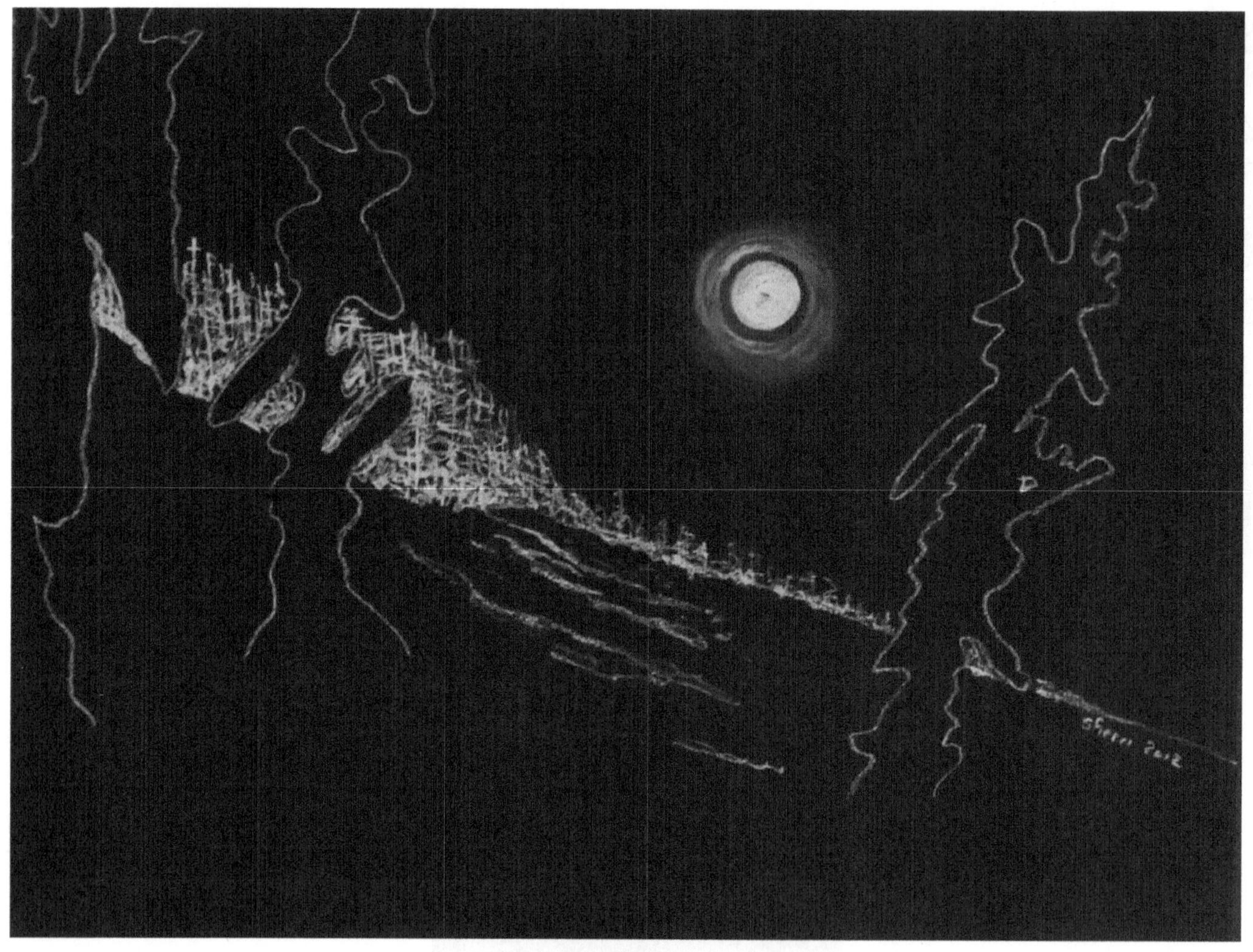

Moonlight Ride
March 17, 2012

Conté

Oxymoron
March 18, 2012

Still life photography

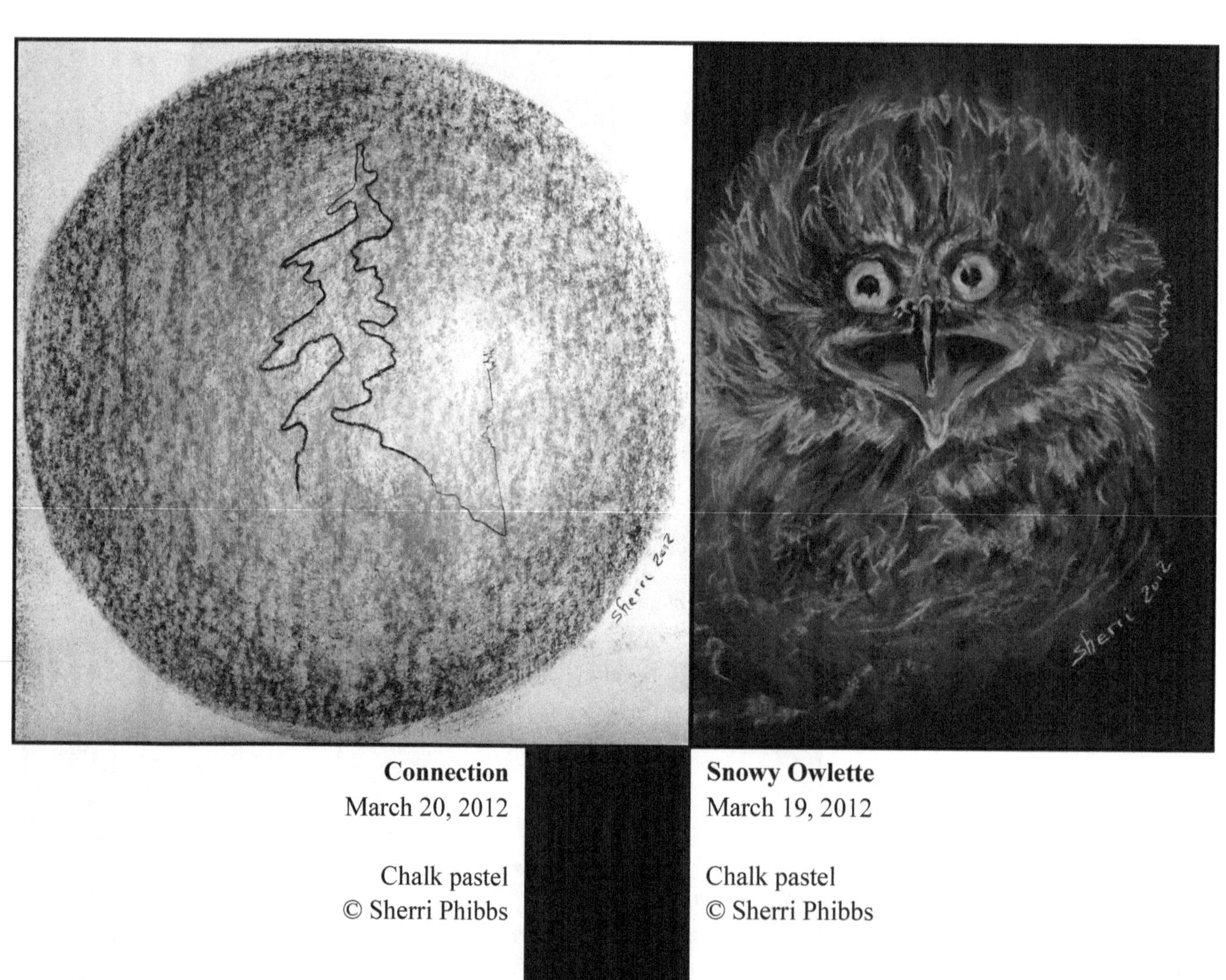

Connection
March 20, 2012

Chalk pastel
© Sherri Phibbs

Snowy Owlette
March 19, 2012

Chalk pastel
© Sherri Phibbs

AIR: The Written Word

Artistic Voice, One Syllable at a Time

January 1, 2012

Starting in 2011, I'd been tossing around the idea of adding a star to further bring to focus the celestial aspect of this drum, but nothing seemed to gel, so I put it aside while waiting for further inspiration. Well, a couple days ago I learned of The Hopi Blue Star Prophecy, which inspired the completion of this piece.

Also of note, the changes in my life this last week have been dramatic. From becoming engaged to the man who has been front and centre in my life for the passed sixteen years, to attending my dad on his deathbed on the birth date of my previously deceased biological father. I understand about emotional roller-coaster rides. Difficult to begin this project...

January 2, 2012

Inspired by imagery seen during a shamanic meditative journey, this rose holds the beat of the drum, the hiss of the rattle, and the protective circle of the human spirit. It is widely known, of course, that a rose is symbolic of love and passion, but it is also a symbol for strength through silence*. In this instance, I draw on the lesser known interpretation. We can only view that which is presented to us, although we are conscious of the possibility of a larger picture and its support system. The whole remains just beyond our awareness; silent, not revealing itself, yet still strongly present.

(*Ted Andrews, 2010, Author, *Animal Speak*, Llewellyn Worldwide)

January 3, 2012

I struggled with this all day, and I am still unsure whether it is appropriate to include this grief drawing as part of the art-down. Yet if this is to be a faithful and literal journal of the year, to ignore this major event would be what I like to call "Wrong."

The release, or clearing, of the spirit I felt during the creation process was invaluable. I moved from anger and spite as I began thinking about the project and prospective designs, to grief, followed by a focused thoughtfulness during development, on to the final addition of the word "forgiven" as giving shape and substance to the support structure of the tree. I realized the issues, gave them voice, and let them go. As a work of fine art —I don't know! But as an illustration of the human spirit during a time of emotional turmoil, this has some merit. So here it is; raw folk art.

January 4, 2012

Today the wind played with the earth. Great waves of earthy dirt sandblasted us as we fed the horses. Clouds of grit and hay and manure, created grand designs on the air currents that swirled skyward, earthward, and everywhere at once. Sending tall grasses bowing and dancing in time to its music, the air teased the river water, tickling up drifts on the surface and sending them outward, cascading in rhythm onto the rocky shore. It was a grand display; breathtaking and clearing, literally.

Studying nature, we learn about ... sky-dancing.

January 5, 2012

I woke up this morning and the internet was down. Hmmm; unusual number of wind warnings, highest temperatures in 90 years, internet goes down ... I hope this isn't foreshadowing! Anyway, I'm struggling with the idea of whether to do the art today, or fudge it and post two or three when the link is back in operation. I'm laughing inside because I know my conscience won't let me do that. Infernal little nag, I love you. You keep me honest, and that gives me a sense of things being right in the world. If I can do it, anyone can. So the question remains: Where do I get my inspiration today?

There was a very real sense of "OMG" when I realized I couldn't get my stuff uploaded. Trying to resolve the issue took up most of my studio time. 1. Reset and test modem. 2. Reset and test router. 3. Buy new router. 4. Run diagnostics again. 5. Feel the stress. 6. Finally call service provider who, by the way, is experiencing higher than normal call volumes. 7. Sit and quietly freak out while waiting the half hour for the call back. 8. Go over steps 1, 2, and 5 with service provider. "But wait," she says at last, "let me check if there are any outages!" Imagine how I felt when she said, "Yes, yes there are." Apparently, 80 houses on my street are experiencing the same thing, and will be out for the next 24 to 48 hours. Wondering why she didn't check that first. Wondering why I didn't check that first?
9. Tomorrow's schedule: return new router and de-stress. This raises another question: Why was I so stressed about being electronically disconnected? It's not like I will never get back online, is it?

Have you ever heard about a web bot? This little jewel of technology was designed to predict, not measure, market trends for stock analysts. It runs out on the web like a spider and gathers intelligence, which it then carries back to its programmers for analysis. Apparently, the beastie is retrieving no data or references to events between December 21, 2012 and May of 2013. Looks like someone turned off the internet? If I stressed over today, what would that scenario—no internet— look like? I give this some thought, and remember.

While looking after a friend's horses today, I experienced a usually aloof, old soul of a horse gently moving into my space to block me from the still strong winds that were chilling my body as I cleaned the paddock. Very slowly, so I wouldn't be startled, he placed his muzzle in the hair on the back of my neck and ruffled it softly with his lips. As I straightened up slowly and looked into his deep eyes, I felt loved and cared for. He followed me as I finished the chores, making certain the other horse moved out of my way when needed. We are connected.

Part of organic eco-psychology revolves around the idea that each and every thing in the universe is connected by web strings. These strings pull or prod us in the direction necessary for our best growth and health. For example, when our body is dehydrated, the webstring attracting us to water is activated and we love the idea: Nameless, Intelligent Attraction Loves.* There are various exercises available to scientifically test webstring activation. The results are repeatable, which is interesting. So I guess if the internet goes down, I'll just go outside and play with some of the webstrings that connect me to the rest of the universe.

* Dr. Michael Cohen, Connecting With Nature, copyright 1989 World Peace University

January 6, 2012

This morning inspiration found me, and I woke with the image completely formed in my mind; so, now to put it on paper. Time crunch!. Oh, the pressure! Maybe, at the end of the age I can put all these meanderings into a book. What would I call it? *Journey to the End of the Earth*?

January 7, 2012

Today the magnitude of the project I've taken on finally sunk in.. Time-wise and commitment-wise, showing up for "Creativity" on a daily basis is not easy. It's easy to watch my favourite TV show, to visit with friends, do chores, but when inspiration is not crystal clear, like it was yesterday, it isn't easy to stick to the program. The key in here for me (and you) is to *do something, daily*, even when [we're feeling] uninspired, tired or cranky. Just show up in the studio and see what happens. Yesterday's piece was one kind of challenge; having the vision clearly in focus but not sure how to get there within the one day time limit. Today's is another thing altogether; it's about feeling as though I have nothing creative to give, and doing it anyway. I've reworked and completed, for the second time, a piece I started in early December: a pastel interpretation of Echo, my daughter's horse. I hope you enjoy the post. And now my tired, cranky self is off to get some sleep. Zzzzzz.

January 8, 2012

I guess sometimes life just isn't pretty. We all know that. The rawness, the intense, powerful and passionate essence surges through our lives like a raging river; crashing into the banks with a force that changes everything. This intensity emerged today, both in meditation and riding. Wind and deer set the perfect stage, and the slightest touch sent my boy leaping forward, catching a nearby horse with a momentum that startled its rider and required a hasty balancing act to keep them centred and together. I felt completely in control, and my horse settled as soon as I asked, but I wondered about the reaction to such a tiny catalyst. Again, once I dismounted, I experienced this same phenomenon. A quick jog from me picked up my horse to trot behind, startled the herd, and sent several other horses off in a panic. As soon as I heard the sound of hoof beats I halted, and so did my horse, but the others kept going for a moment, looking around for the cause of their fear-based flight response that threatened to surge up again at the slightest provocation. If my small, inadvertent motion can cause a reaction so large that the power of fifty stampeding horses makes the ground tremble—a reaction that can unbalance others, or, worse still, cause damage—do I become so frightened of the consequences that I can't move? Or do I trust that my intention for good, my feelings of love for the world and all in it, are enough to smooth out the ripples I generate? Is it enough to bring smiles of delight to others who feel the power of the horses, enough to hone riding skills and help them grow? Overtones of personal responsibility vibrate across my nerve endings. Darn metaphors. The boiled down message from my meditation? Is that we fit together like hand and glove: connected, perfectly. So here's my take on this: Embrace life in all its raw, magnificent, passionate intensity! Trust in the softening power of ripples as you create a wake. Emerge responsibly.

January 9, 2012

Have you ever noticed how the dark makes the light so much brighter? I know, we all hear the cliché in this. "You can't appreciate all the wonderful things unless you are acutely aware of moments when they are not in evidence." But what about balance, what about motion? There are degrees in shading or shadows, just as there are gradations of light. How far into the depths do we need to go in order to appreciate the heights? Can I just dip in my toe? What about the undercurrents? If I jump in, will I be swept away, knocked off balance? Will I drown in it? I experienced a heart chakra clearing today, and while immersed in the sound of the crystal bowl, I felt the twisting and spinning of the Darkness moving. We carry this with us, this Darkness. We built it ourselves, with our own two hands. There's that personal responsibility thing again, darn it. Yet as the meditation continued, I noticed something peculiar: bits and pieces of that Darkness started to break off and spin away, leaving the light showing through behind. To me, that looks like the light is always there; we just paint our darkness in front of it. It makes me go, "Hmmmmm." It's time for a children's story. If you get a chance, read *The Dark*, by Robert Munsch. I'm all for the taped it with tape part. I know, that's confusing … I guess you'll have to read the story.

January 10, 2012

So here we have a day full of light, love, and laughter, and I don't know what to create. It's as though all my creative energy was funneled solely into relationships today. Smiling, joking, and laughing take a lot out of a person, you know, as I'm grinning from ear to ear. So where does that leave me now? Well! Maybe it's time to go to the well? Fill the well? At this point, I'm just going to settle for knowing there is a well. You know the one I'm looking for: that fabled well of creativity—the one that is NOT showing up on my GPS. Go figure. I guess I need to learn how to set waypoints. Ok, then, where did life lead me today? Breathing. Breathe. Breath. This is important stuff, here, this exchange with the world. We breathe it in, we breathe it out. It breathes us in and out. It's kind of crucial, this relationship. It pays to put creative energy into building this one. I'm still scrambling. Okay, when insight is needed, go to nature. It snowed overnight. The wind was cold, and the floor in the yoga room was cold.

The ride was wonderful. I love my horse! Ice bits were stuck all over him, and he glistened in the sunlight. I took my hand out of my mitten to melt what wouldn't brush off his coat. The students were wonderful. The other teachers were wonderful. I'm laughing because I'm starting to see a pattern here: something about being in relationship to (Are we defined by being in relationship to?). My horse and I, we work on communication, and he gets me. I am clear in my presentation (most times), and he gets it. Simple, right? Ok, maybe not so simple. But we move along together, aware of each other, breathing together, connected. On a sub-molecular level, there is no real separation between us, just a melding, meshing bunch of atoms, electrons, protons, etc., all moving together. Connection: not just spiritual or emotional, but physical. We breathe in the world, as the world breathes us out. In the "real" world, what does this mean to me? To you? From a shamanic perspective, it is believed that each person has an animal totem that is with them from birth, as a guide or guardian. Studying this connection becomes a way to learn about how to relate successfully to the world.

January 11, 2012

After last night's work, I'm a little tapped out, so today, I'm taking a breather with just a simple sketch of a hillside in winter. Not good art, but great practice. Just showing up at the easel is an exercise in discipline, especially as not everything is acceptable to me, nor remotely kin to a masterpiece. I make mistakes, recognize what doesn't work, and move on. It's the exploration that allows the learning.

January 12, 2012

I'd like to work on this piece more. There is so much more I'd like to add here, but the clock is ticking. And so, my fox must stand as is; a work in progress, much like the rest of us. Let's see how we develop.

January 13, 2012

Nothing symbolizes the passing of time more truly than lengthening shadows. Even though we have passed the winter solstice, the cold light of the midday sun casts its long shadow across fields of gold grazed to stubble. A bitter wind bites into hands kept too long outside the fleece-lined warmth of leather mittens, and I turn my collar up to stop the chill racing down my spine. Spring may be approaching, but winter's icy fingers still rest firmly on my pulse. Yet I still know the sun's heat. I know fields of gold waving in the warm Chinook winds, blowing off the mountains, and my thoughts turn to; weddings, music, good friends, and family, to summer solstice and vows of love and care. Even the cold winter sunlight brings me warmth. And so time passes.

January 14, 2012

How do you illustrate "being in relationship to"? Is it being in a union or partnership yet remaining an individual within this unity? There is a word for it, *Iyuptala**: a term I had never heard before my introduction to a unique microcosm of horses and people who work to embody the essence of this term. Iyuptala: to be one with. Sounds like a wedding vow to me. "And the two shall become one." Something sacred, maybe: Working together in mutual respect and love to create a whole other entity? Co-creation. Having children. Having a relationship. Being one with. Being in community seems to fit in there, too. Creating something together, something that brings the two entities together. What would our real world look like if we regarded everything we did from a perspective of being one with? I wonder what it would look like if I were "one with" the environment, the elements, the Divine? Wait a minute… I AM! I'm part of a microcosm of the universe, Earth! So are you. Connected and co-creating.

*GaWaNi Ponyboy, 1999, Author, *Horse Follow Closely*, Bow Tie Press

January 15, 2012

What to say about today's work? Ummmm! Okay, this is my very first antler carving, and it will eventually be a door handle for my studio. Go, Dremel, Go! When I first decided to do a sculpture, I was thinking wooden animals, and I'm not really certain how that shifted, other than the face just seemed to jump out of the antler once I really started looking. There was definitely a personality all its own waiting to be revealed. He was winking, blowing, and at the beginning, seemed to be the north wind; but then I realized his sense of humour in the wink. He's definitely whistling. I wonder! Now wouldn't it be advantageous to have a touch of clairvoyance and see a glimpse of the former life of this elk? Must have been a young buck following a herd of does. Wink, wink. Hey, Baby!

January 16, 2012

Rollercoasters have nothing on me today: Physical pain, followed by physio and more physical pain, followed by shock, emotional pain, grief and catharsis. The grieving process is not easy, even when you know the phases and steps. Today's artwork is an art therapy method of processing deep emotions. I'll be using Chalk pastels, which, although fluid and malleable like watercolour, allow control and structure in their dry format. This allows for expression, controllable expression. Art Therapy is all about the process, not the product. I hope you enjoy this one anyway! After the piece is completed, a quick check-in reveals the name, and subsequent research fills in the gaps of the rationale. The Kachina Shield represents the presence of life in all objects that fill the universe.

Everything has an essence or a life force, and humans must interact with these in order to thrive. Eototo, a wuya or main Kachina, represented by a white cylinder with a nest of hair on his head, is considered the personification of nature, the bringer of nature gifts. It appears that this shield also represents a protective circle of nature surrounding the tender flower in the centre.

January 17, 2012

The intriguing thing about porcupines is the way they amble slowly and peacefully about their business, never seeming to be in a hurry to get anywhere in particular. They always stop to smell the flowers. Okay, they stop to eat the flowers, while checking out everything with a sense of wonder and curiosity. And have you seen them dance? Rising up on their hind legs, they sway back and forth, as though listening to some sweet, cosmic music the universe plays for their ears alone. Caught up in just being and experiencing, they roll up in a prickly ball if threatened and only strike out if someone or something with harmful intent comes too close for comfort. There is a lot to learn from our porcupine brother; from protecting sensitive insides from external hurts, to demonstrating how to be strong yet vulnerable. May he bring to you the ability to move at your own speed, take life less seriously, and trust that if you respect others, they will respect you.

January 18, 2012

It's all about the journey. It's about learning how to ride into these new directions and awaken and discover freedom of expression and personal power. As I travel through the Mayan Calendar, the time I spend creating each day is morphing me into something new. What the final image will look like, I don't know, but there is definitely movement. And what symbolizes movement more powerfully than a horse? This black horse speaks to me of protection, birth, and magic. To feel secure in my abilities as I continue on this new and life-altering journey, shall I gift the earth with new trees and flowers? Should I feed the birds, support environmentalism, or is there something else, something deeper and more personal, that I am required to give of myself? Isn't that what art is—a gift of self? And isn't that what this journey seems to be asking of me, more so than anything else: To reach deep inside myself and make my ripples in the air of the world as I fly my magical horse (Art-Down Project) to creative freedom, learning and powerfully expressing who I am as an artist. I am here, and who I am matters! What does your journey require of you?

January 19, 2012

11:00 AM This piece has literally been sitting on my drawing board, as a drawing, for years. Today I intend to work it as close to being finished as I am able.

9:44 PM Wow, what a day! It's a good thing I worked on this drawing earlier because I haven't been able to get back to it until now. This piece terrifies me! I am amazed at how your comments and wisdom have generated such a spark of inspiration that I have picked it up again. I know it will not be completed tonight, but I will post what I have available. I've spent so much time today with wedding plans, and memories of my first wedding, that I am emotionally drained. I met my first husband, the father of my children, when I was seventeen. They are beautiful, and I am glad they are in my life. But I can't help wishing I had known more than I did at that age: that I'd seen the red flags that indicated, especially in hindsight, I was making a mistake. Now I sit here, decades later, hoping that I learned enough during the first round, that I've taken long enough to make the decision this time, yada, yada.… We can't know what the future holds, whether it's the outcome of a marriage or the predictions of a long defunct calendar. We can guess, but until the actual day arrives, we just don't know. It could be merely coincidental that I am hiking down the marriage path I thought I'd never set foot on again at the same time that I am starting a painting I've been sitting on forever—then again, maybe not. Maybe, just maybe, it is symbolic of something going on inside; a reflection of becoming unstuck! Even though I am going forward with some trepidation in both areas, I am also going forward with great joy and excitement. Here's to letting go of the past and getting back up when you've fallen. After all, it's not how many times you fall down, but how many times you get up that really count, and not moving on something because you are afraid of making a mistake counts as a fall in my life. Never try equals never succeed; try, and even if you fall half the time, you've increased your success rate by fifty percent. I'm thinking the odds look pretty good when I try, compared to when I don't. So, here it goes. Moving on with try.

January 20, 2012

Oh no! I've lost the text for this entry! Does anyone have a copy they could send me? It was a thank you to all the "White Buffalo Women" in my life: those wonderful women who change the world with their kind words and wisdom. And yes, you know who you are. In humble gratitude!

January 21, 2012

Since a large portion of the artwork I've done over the years has been picked from photographs I've taken, I thought today's project would be a good time to restock my supply. Near and dear to my heart, the animal companions in my life are always a beautiful way to illustrate the love that surrounds me and walks with me through life. His expression says it all to me: strength, peace and patience. He struggles to convey his thoughts and needs, often resorting to grabbing a toy and squeaking it in order to get my attention, then walking calmly to the door, looking over his shoulder to see if I'm following. He then promptly drops the toy and touches the doorknob. Let me out, please. He has adapted his canine communication skills much more readily to human than I have adapted mine to canine. Last night, I was having difficulty sleeping due to some physical pain, and when it was at its worst, I heard him climbing the stairs and walking to my door. One little whine and I let him in. He trotted over to my side of the bed and laid his head on it looking at me, so I got back into bed. As soon as I was lying down, he cuddled up to the side of the bed and put his head under my hand. The pain didn't subside right away, and the next thing I knew, he went around the other side of the bed and woke up my partner! It was as though he was saying, "Hey, she needs some help over here!" Amazing dog!

January 22, 2012

Today, I experienced the wedding fair as an interesting exercise in determining priorities. What is the vision? Was it the pieces that make it whole? Then, riding my horse, what are the steps to greater understanding and better communication? What do I do first? Can I handle this? Get it right?

When I was working on the photo shoot for the grain, I was startled when I discovered something that really started my thoughts on an unusual path. It reminded me of the organic eco-psychology teachings which cover interactions between humans and nature, an acknowledgement that people are drawn to certain aspects or areas of the environment because they fulfill a need or requirement for the human's well-being. Maybe you've experienced something: going to a certain area, for instance, and then realizing there is something about it that reminds you of someone you've lost and having a good cry? The theory behind this situation is that you were drawn to the spot because you needed to feel that sadness and release to help you feel better. So today, I am drawn to tightly focus on grain. "What does the grain have to teach me?" I respectfully ask. I've focused on what is important to me; everything else is fading into the background, supporting and providing structure, like cast members to the lead actor. This stalk of grain stands upright and clear. Bright and focused, it seems to glow with its own internal light that radiates outward. It has highlights and shadows, spiky spots and smooth seeds full of potential. It is a symbol of inspiration and new life, of promise. If I were to hold this grain between my hands, I could rub away all, leaving only the tiny kernels of that grain. Winnowing, removing the chaff — in a sense, polishing the diamond in the rough and allowing its true beauty to shine. I feel the burn of tears behind my eyes, and know that my life events, not all easy or comfortable, have polished me and made me who I am. Like this grain, I can stand strong, wave in the wind, or if knocked over, start a new life. I was drawn to the grain today because I needed to acknowledge this. What does this grain stalk say to you?

January 23, 2012

Now here's a sight I don't usually see in my artwork: florals full of rich, ripe, earthiness. It's quite a departure from my standard cool coloured fare. What to make of this?!

January 24, 2012

Three hundred and thirty-one days to go, and already I sit here scratching my head wondering how in the world I am EVER going to finish this! And really, why? I'm at my lowest point in the energy cycle at the moment, and I'm questioning everything that isn't a vital priority. What is the value in this practice? Has the exercise, to date, provided any personal growth that might provide incentive going forward? Ultimately, that drive or incentive must come from inside.

I am tired and cranky, and honestly haven't a clue what to do today. Maybe I should draw a porcupine with my nose or a warthog with my eyes? Hmmmm. In ancient Greek there is a word for that, sunthesis, from *suntithenai*, to place together. Is that the talent of a shaman: the ability to place together the individual with their helping totem animal guide, the ability to place together? And how does that appear to the eyes of the shaman? Does the animal-assisted therapist have this ability? Are they able to look at someone and see the animal most able to help? And how would that appear?

It's hard to take oneself too seriously when viewed in this context. Imagine going through life, seeing each person with an animal shadow or overlay. In some instances, it might be rather difficult to maintain composure and not just break out laughing. And really, I am so glad my totem animal is not a warthog. I'm just kidding around of course. I've been way too grumpy and over-sensitive; I neeeed humour.
Is anyone game? I'd love to do this totem juxtaposed with someone else!!! It was interesting to note that the fox drawing and a photo of me fit together in a rather uncanny way. Fun, but really weird. Another weird fact: I'm no longer zz, and I feel energized and focused for the first time today. Go, Fox!

January 25, 2012

Over the last four years of daily horse-time, I've learned a lot about being flexible from my horse, Neo: not just physical flexibility, but mental and spiritual flexibility, as well. The part of horsemanship that deals with listening and relating to our horse can really stretch our understanding of ourselves. Who we are in relation to the horse becomes more about how we are in relation to the horse. Are we soft or light? Are we blending? Do we have an agenda? And how tied in to the exact steps to the outcome are we? Are we able to change our minds? Do we allow input from other sources, like our horse? How much weight do I give to my horse's opinion on our activities together? Is there a limit to love? Many of these lessons come in handy in wedding planning, did you know? Having a vision and goal is wonderful, yet being able to bend in the face of changing timelines, availability, and preferences is an invaluable gift my horse has helped me with. Keeping the relationships front and centre, while managing the details of the vision, is about blending. We are heading in the right direction, so can I bend? Can I be soft? And love, it's just an open-hearted thing that lives in everything, as natural as breathing. Isn't it wonderful?

January 26, 2012

Thank you for your wonderful comments and advice! Go, line drawings! Bringing all that flexibility into living colour (or our day-to-day stuff) makes all the difference in the world. Celebrating life.

January 27, 2012

No matter what, show up at the page*. Regardless of scheduling, time commitments elsewhere, whatever, just carve out the space and show up. Discipline. This piece is a quick sketch, using pastels and handmade paper. The paper itself is highly textured, so the pastels do not adhere to it well. It's an experiment, an exploration—a mistake?

Here are a few interesting insights that eagles have brought into my life:

1. Creativity is a must, and the number three is very significant.
2. A willingness to dive into the ups and downs of life and assimilate the changes this brings about.
3. Being willing to passionately follow your calling, even if it means a little personal trauma.
4. Finding your true emotional self and reveling in it, rediscovering your inner child with pure creative passion that borders on the spiritual or healing.

To me, this sounds like Grandmother Medicine, a call to great healing, wisdom, and creativity. So, the paper and pastel choice becomes not a mistake but a learning experience gained in passionately following my craft. Diving in, fingers tinted and nose smudged, I feel the pastels, delighting in the texture, smell and malleability. All senses become engaged, shoulders roll in long movements, I stand, breathe, and sway. Engaged in a dance, I create.

*Julia Cameron, 1992, Author, *The Artist's Way*, New York: G.P. Putnam's Sons

January 28, 2012

There is a thread running through the fabric of my life, and when plucked it releases bird feathers. Hawks, pheasants, eagles, magpies, ravens, and crows have all made their way into the circle of my attention. Magpie was the first to appear, and has always been dear to my heart.

Although considered a nuisance by many, this inquisitive and mischievous bird has always sparked my imagination. Its bright eyes always seem to see me, not just observe but really see. I've found this an admirable trait to incorporate for my own growth. How many times have we walked through a crowd of people without really seeing anyone? The faces register and are gone, superfluous information quickly tossed aside by our busy brains as we go about our busy business. Yet, people are fine with this. If someone suddenly stops and sees them, they become uncomfortable, as though an invisible thread in the fabric of their lives has started vibrating. Twang! I see you! You there, inside that body, I see you. Hello! It's kinda creepy if the contact isn't broken quickly.

It's almost an invasion of sorts. Yet, as the bird contemplates me, probing and questing, I feel a sense of amusement and perhaps a bit of wonder. What do you SEE when you look at me, little one? Does my smile convey the joy you give me? Do you feel it? What does Nature see when it looks at me? What does Nature see when it looks at you?

January 29, 2012

Wow! What a wonderful day. Surrounded by family and friends, I treasure times like these. I even feel tears welling up. My cup definitely runneth over today. How to illustrate this surge of emotion? I have come through darkness and into the light, and perceive my life with clarity. I feel the tension ease from my shoulders, my back. I breathe easy and free. Hmmm, should I question why today is different from any other day? Or, should I quietly accept the shift and carry on from here, head down and enjoy the ride? I'm not able to do that, apparently. What is it about me that has changed that would affect my perceptions so keenly? Nothing has really changed, yet it has, completely. I've become softer. The consistent, daily check-ins for this project is shifting things for me. The small successes of regular creative endeavours are boosting my confidence; the small steps back with self-doubt are teaching me about my way of being in the world. "Seeing" myself with honest attentiveness rather than a casual glance, I am able to make adjustments. I am much more able to stay "in the moment" than I was less than a month ago. This is a skill I've been working to develop for some time, and this practice seems to be giving the learning process a bit of a lift. You have my gratitude for your support as I started this journey in the valley of the shadow of death. I'm almost at the one-month mark now, and I find the oddest things remind me of Dad. I have a wish for you. May you be happy, may you be whole, and may you be at peace.

January 30, 2012

Hmmm, I think I was channeling Dali while making this one! It's quite a departure from the norm for me, but striking none-the-less. I'm going to let my commentary stop at this point, and toss the ball to you. Any thoughts?

January 31, 2012

Yesterday's work was so fascinating to do. I absolutely love it. I have to try it again! There was definitely a time overrun on this one, but I hope the enjoyment was worth it. I know the enjoyment of making it was. Looking at the shadow side, it's like carving the light out of the darkness. Everything is black, and each stroke of the pastel brings the image up and out of the shadows. Much like our lives, when we focus on and are attentively aware of where the light hits, everything becomes brighter. These are heavy thoughts for a tired brain. I really have to get these done earlier! Off to sleep I go.

February 1, 2012

Start of Month Two! I have a drum offering for you. There is a story behind this one; I hope you enjoy it. A teacher once had a drum that was a depiction of his totem animal. It was painted on the underside of the drum head so that when the light shone through the circle of the drum, the animal glowed. I admired that drum, and the technique used to adorn it, for a long time. Secretly, I wished to have a drum of my own, complete with my totem animal "behind the scenes". Many months passed by, many drums were made, and still I felt that pull in my heart. Then one day, I made a drum that spoke to me, attracted me with the pull of the organic eco-psychology webstrings!* "What is this?" I wondered. Upon examination, an interesting phenomenon was discovered. On the back side of the drum head, only visible with the light shining through the drum, was the image of a running fox ingrained directly in the rawhide itself! My totem drum had found me. To honour this, carefully, so carefully, an image was created on the front so as not to obscure the secret gift behind, yet still bring to light that which is hidden.

*Dr . Michael Cohen, Connecting With Nature, copyright 1989 World Peace University

February 2, 2012

Here we are, back to being flexible! Our local deer liked the feast laid out at the bird feeder in the back yard. I was watching, through the window, how absorbed they were and I decided to grab my camera. I was lucky to get this shot, as it was taken by very quietly and slowly stepping out onto the deck and holding my breath while I took the picture. The series of shots that followed were of deer bounding away in all directions, tails raised in flags. Luckily, I managed to get focused on this little lady. I think she was quite perturbed that I interrupted her feeding frenzy, not to mention alarmed by the sight of some human appearing ten feet from her pointing in her direction. I'm sure she will get over it at some point and venture back for more sunflower seeds and corn.

February 3, 2012

The best part of this picture is all the shapes: light and dark, with the contrast of a variety of textures. Suddenly, I want to get in there and touch everything. Even a monochromatic subject can be interesting and full of life. Tone on tone, there appears the nuances of beauty. Sometimes my life feels like that. Monotone and repetitive, yet when I REALLY stop and take a look, the grace and wonder surrounding me become apparent. I realize that beauty walks with me, always. And when I acknowledge it, there is joy.

February 4, 2012

Apparently I'm not done with the stained glass trees. The air around them seems to be more active, as though a frenzy of the wind is battering the stalwart trunks. These pieces have something about them I just love. Perhaps it's the freeness of expression, or maybe the contrast between the fluidity of the elements and the geometric shapes of the stained glass tree. The tree of life under siege? Certain religious overtones, maybe? The depths of the unconscious subtly exposed. I love art!

February 5, 2012

What a wonderful ride today! Neo has lost a bit of weight since the picture I used as reference for this sketch, but still there is a sense of him here. While drawing him, I felt a closeness, as though I could hear and feel his breath, his sounds, catch his scent. Even quick sketches can evoke a deep emotional and physiological response. That webstring connection that draws us to what we need at a given moment, (e.g., drawn to water when thirsty) is very active between Neo and I. If I pay attention to another horse, I often feel his eyes on the back of my neck, and when I turn this is what I see. Usually accompanied by his nicker, as though to say "Hey, darlin', save the last dance for me*."

PS: I couldn't leave this alone. I admit it, I had to tweak it and re-post.

* Michael Buble, 2006 song lyrics, *Save the Last Dance for Me*, from the album *It's Time*, Reprise Records, 143 Records

February 6, 2012

It's been an interesting day. My herd-bound horse went out with me alone for awhile, although he did keep checking in every so often. I was getting definite "Are you sure?" vibes all the way across the field. Later, I checked tasks off my list as I worked my way through everything that needed doing. I feel as though I'm walking through the hours asleep. I nod and smile, but inside I am tired, so I am aiming for an early night and long sleep. The little skiff of snow that fell last night must be making me think about hibernating. Or more simply, maybe I am just tired, which is definitely making me think about hibernating! ;-)

So, for inspiration today, where do I turn my sleepy head? I pull a rune stone ... it is the Rune of Opening: darkness has been dispelled, and clarity is available in my life. Well, then! Where does that lead me artistically? I hear music "I can see clearly now the rain is gone. I can see all obstacles in my way." Followed by "it's gonna be a bright, bright, sunshiny day!*" Hmmm, let's see. I hear music when I see words, and I smell horses when I focus on drawing one. A teacher of mine once mentioned something about this. Synesthesia; it's something to inspire any artist. Let's see where this goes. If I listen to birdsongs while I work on a meditative drawing, what kind of mandala will I produce? Note of interest: the centre of the mandala wanted to stay void. I had to force something to fill the space. The three stars were all that came to mind, filling them in later with the dots to delineate a constellation. I'm not sure if this is astronomically accurate, but the feeling was right. It's art therapy in basic form.

*Johnny Nash, song lyrics 1972, *I Can See Clearly Now*, from the album *I Can See Clearly Now*, Epic Records

February 7, 2012

Today I've been mulling over the vision for this art-down project; steps through the calendar to a specific point in time. Some call it The Shift, others The End of Time, and still others a Catastrophic Event of some kind. Noises in deep unpopulated forests have been reported, and some debunked, worldwide. Some people are watching, listening, while others prepare with underground condos in abandoned missile silos. Still others continue on, apparently unaffected by the upcoming "deadline". For me, it tickles my mind like an unsolved riddle or puzzle, tweaking my interest and attention. What does it mean? What is the purpose? I must admit to a certain amount of excitement. That being said, I also must admit that the large solar flare activity of a week or so ago, gave me a massive headache that lasted for days on end. The excitement definitely rules the day however. Just to make note here, as the days pass by and the year progresses, I continue with my journey, day by day, moment by moment, planning, creating, and living with a gratitude and appreciation for everything. Yet, the mystery remains, peering out of the dark, whispering of adventure, challenges and change.

February 8, 2012

Yesterday's foray into a meditative journey prior to working has certainly sparked my imagination. I love the sense of a feline visitor quietly contemplating my world. It's as though a silent guardian stands watch, lending strength and energy to my daily tasks. If a cougar backed me up in my decisions, life path changes, or assisted with assertiveness, how would I appear? Would I be able to leap and catch opportunities as they arise? Would I be able to effectively protect and provide for myself, my family? Would I understand this expression of power can be tempered with gentleness, and so adopt that into my life? Many years ago, as a single parent, I was gifted with a glass cougar sculpture of a mother protecting her cub. I've often wondered about a possible similarity. Okay, that just makes me laugh. Grrrowl...

February 9, 2012

Lollipops and pinwheels, these beautiful orchids remind me of trips to the candy store as a young child. Mesmerized by the bright colours of the offerings on the shelves, I'd stand until the last possible moment, finally making a choice based more on the beauty of the display than the taste of the candy. Of course, as I became more of a candy connoisseur, I'd head straight for those that offered both beauty and taste. These orchids definitely do that. No, I'm not going to eat them. I meant they are superbly elegant, exquisitely tasteful, a sensual delight on many levels. My mouth may be watering. It's the cherry and raspberry drops on shortbread cookies. ;-)

February 10, 2012

Yesterday, I was so tired at the end of the day I thought I'd tackle something easy like photography. Ha! Three hours later, after much angst, I was looking at a mass of pictures which didn't feel right, look right, or present the way I had envisioned. The piece posted yesterday was the best, but something about a couple of others continued to pull at me, so I revisited them this evening with an eye to photoshopping some oomph into a lacklustre display. What I found instead was a fresh eye and change in perception had allowed me to see differently. Looking through the lens of today's life experience, I find the aggressive stance and bold statement of this single bloom has become a valid expression of intensity and passion. Stand in personal power, and voila! You're blooming! The title of this piece is a reminder for me. Accept the challenges life presents with grace. Be aware of and feel the emotions as all emotions are valid, then ... let it go. Confronting hurt with hurt only escalates a situation, giving it a life of its own. I will not slay the dragon, but instead befriend it. ;-)

February 11, 2012

This is sooo not done. I've been working it for hours, and the flow is just not there yet. So, best to leave it and come back another time. Forcing it at this point will only result in frustration; this I know from past experience. It is possible to fix it right into the trash. Some of the lines, I love. There is value here.

February 12, 2012

This had a life of its own. With the drums sounding in the background, flutes shrilling and flowing, and no particular direction in mind, I chose colour on instinct only. Red first, deep and sacred like red ochre in burials, I remember thinking, then trees as waves, dancing with the sound. And shadow—the line needed shadow. As the piece progressed, I felt the images of Japan and earthquake, tsunami and fire. I wondered at the show I'd watched today, an episode filmed in Japan earlier. Were the actors still alive? The buildings still whole? I sent out love with each stroke of the colour. The red formed to the side of the trees, winged out above, charcoal was added in streaks around the trees, the Fire Moon. Sometimes, taking a break from the structure involved in "creating" allows the emotion to take centre stage rather than the rendering skill. Emotion and flow can make or break a piece for me. By shifting to the heart centre and letting the mind rest, it is easier to feel that flow of movement, feeling, and passion. It's like taking a mini-vacation while still showing up at the easel. Refreshing.

February 13, 2012

As a request, here is Mataeo. I'll gift you with the original, Stephanie. I know you loved him. Hugs!

February 14, 2012

A rosy tinted piece for Valentine's Day. Got the love. Of course, everything that came up today was about relationship: tea and brownies at yoga; loves songs playing in the horse tie-up area; a lesson with a new student about, you guessed it, relationship; chocolate for children; flowers for fiancé; delicious home-cooked meal (Yes, I did!); and a movie that had me laughing, honestly and with my whole being. Where to find time for artwork? I saw something posted the other day that really hit home for me; it was about the art of living. Today was about that: the art of living, relationship between me and everything else. And you know what? It fills me with a joy that is so huge I feel it is too big to contain within the small frame of my body. It makes me vulnerable, shy and open. And it makes me feel whole; a whole that exceeds the mere physical. The picture above has that expanded feel. The rosy tones speaking of warmth and comfort within a field of divine white light that just goes on forever. Nature has a way of saying it all, expressing it all, without words. Now that's an art!!

February 15, 2012

Tired, uninspired, and cranky? What do I do now? Here I am, looking blankly at a barren wasteland of paper, and what is it doing in return? Is there any sense of inspiration? Any whisper of an image? Excitement? Nope, not a darn thing! I'm totally blank. Now what? Well, honestly, it's not like it's never happened before. Usually, I just take a break and chill with a good book, which, by the way, I actually have on hand waiting for me. However, I made this deal with myself: I will show up at the easel DAILY for the duration of the Art-Down. Unfortunately, inspiration did not make the same deal. All right, I'm going to go grab a single white conté pencil and a grey paper. What shows up, shows up. (Hello? Muse? I could use a little help over here.)

February 16, 2012

Fifteen unfilled minutes: grab materials, now sketch! Quick lines, motions, and feelings. Spirals of energy and power hold the space for the creature at its heart. Regal, proud, and in control, yet gracious and yielding in the curve of the neck, the spine. He stands at the threshold, looking back, checking in. Where do I go from here?

February 17, 2012

It's spring time. Mid-February, and the weather is so beautiful, I can almost imagine that summer is just around the corner. I'm starting to think of planting tomatoes and sunflowers, gardens and long walks surrounded by the warmth of the sun. The beginning of things, emergence, genesis, creation. It's way past midnight, though, and as much as I'd like to keep going with this, my eyes are starting to close all on their own. If I continue, I may sleep right here. It's extremely uncomfortable and absolutely not my idea of restful, so I'll take my tired self off to the Land of Nod. (Sorry, it's a reference to a children's story my mom used to read to me; something about sailing off in a wooden shoe*.) Yawn... I may be dreaming already. ;-)

*Eugene Field, poem, Wynken, Blynken and Nod, 1890, G. Schirmir under the title *Dutch Lullaby*

February 18, 2012

Today, I gave someone advice on how much stress relief can be gained from art, drumming and horses, and I had to step back for a moment to quickly re-evaluate. Prior to the art-down, I would definitely have placed my interaction with all three right up there as the best ways I've come across to relieve stress, with meditation running right along side as a companion to all three. However, I have discovered that even when engaged in something that brings me so much joy and play, I can place such high expectations upon myself that even the best parts of my life become sources of stress. I've learned that stress is not always a bad thing: it can motivate us to achieve great things; it can provide us with a heightened ability for personal safety; it can foster an awareness of the nuances of relationship; and, it can inspire us to resourcefulness and innovation. What I've also learned is that prolonged stress with no relief can burn us out. I know we've all read the books, but for some reason, I had to go the personal experience route for it to really sink in!

February 19, 2012

Some days, art just happens. Effortlessly and with grace, something shows up on the camera that is eye-catching, relevant, and engaging. For me, this photo is a statement on softness and peace: softness and peace in the hands connecting these two species, horse and human; softness and peace in the face of a whole world off balance. It's decidedly apropos.

February 20, 2012

Excerpt from January 24th blog: "In ancient Greek there is a word for that, sunthesis, from suntithenai, to place together. Is that the talent of a shaman, the ability to place together the individual with their helping totem animal guide, the ability to place together? And how does that appear to the eyes of the shaman? Are they able to look at someone and see the animal most able to help? And how would that appear?" Perhaps there is an overlay, a blending that is apparent to the trained eye? Luckily, I've had the opportunity to give this a second try. Thank you, Julie!

While working on this piece, it was amazing to sense a wise knowing and acceptance reflected in the eyes; as though the overlay of these two beings exponentially increased and emphasized this wondrous shared quality. As though quietly affirming, "I am who I am. This is me."

February 21, 2012

This is definitely a bit of a stretch for me, completely out of my comfort zone. An ambitious project for just a few hours, I'm certain I could continue working for hours yet. However, as I've already exceeded my time allotment, I'd best let it be. It's funny about artwork, it is never really done; we just stop in interesting and unique places.

February 22, 2012

A lesson about art with "Life Lesson" written all over it came to mind today. Turn off your inner critic and be gentle with yourself. The deer above are a reminder for me to step back and just be aware of where I am and what is transpiring in the moment. In the past, I remember learning the steps. For the future, I dream of grace and flow, but, the Now, that is where I am. So I practice the dance, mindfully and with awareness. One, two, three ... one, two, three ....

February 23, 2012

Mandala meditation, worked without predetermined plan to the sounds of a northern lakeside: loons, waves lapping at the shore, birdsong, the sound of the water on the sides of the canoe, and fishing reels. I see in this the opening of a flower, or a spider in a web, a sunrise over water or palm trees. *The spider—a cross-cultural symbol of creative power and the magic and energy of creation—is also a symbol of the strength to assert that creative energy. Stunning.

*Tede Andrews, 2010, Author, *Animal Speak*, Llewellyn Worldwide

February 24, 2012

A mountain, a house, trees, a cross, the many shades of humanity—is it a statement on religion, time, change? What does it say to you? What do you see? I present this for comment.

February 25, 2012

Day 56, a day about blending. Not the camouflage kind: I'm talking about the kind you do when horseback riding. Moving along at someone else's pace or direction until you can, with a subtle shift, return to your own set course, only to be nudged outside the lines again and again. Yet, by the end of the day, you realize that despite the convoluted journey, you have arrived where you set out to go, surprised and enriched by the new experiences and understanding garnered along this seemingly arbitrary and meandering path. There is much wisdom to be found on the side roads of my life, and I am grateful.

February 26, 2012

Day 57. Dear Diary, this morning I had the most extraordinary adventure! A young boy I've been working with for the last three years rode a horse independently for the first time. Turning, stopping, choosing direction, he communicated clearly and without stress, guiding Neo smoothly through the field. He has found success against the challenge of autism, maintaining focus and calm. What a delight!

February 27, 2012

"Taking your life from ambition to meaning."

The above is a link to information that may (or may not) be of interest. A change in perspective is always challenging, and every so often I like to shake things up and examine my belief structures. Why do I believe what I do? Is it because this is what I was taught as a child? Does it still have value today? Is it relevant? True?

February 28, 2012

An important point in both shamanic traditions and organic eco-psychology practice is the communication with all aspects of the environment. This communication includes the gaining of an object's permission prior to moving, taking, or using it in an exercise. This permission is determined by honest self-evaluation of personal physical, mental, and emotional perceptions. In the case of this unusual stone, a very strong sense of "leave me here" was communicated despite the fact that we really wanted to take it home for part of our collection. So, honouring the perceived desire, the object was left in peace with only this photograph and our memories of "the one that got away" to mark its impact on our lives. It was an interesting experience to leave it there.

February 29, 2012

Checking in at a favourite place. This beautiful mountain stream is road side in Kananaskis Country. It's sort of a touchstone for me. Whenever I feel the need for an influx of nature spirits, this is where I go. The sound of the water on the stone stream bed, the smell of the wet rocks and mosses, the crisp crunch of snow underfoot ... these things touch my spirit and feed my soul.

Pictures like these as reference, where only a glance takes me back to those soothing moments, inspire the art of living in a healing and balancing way. Nature sustains and heals me, while photography takes note. Now that's an artistic partnership worth exploring!

March 1, 2012

Start of month three! And I have a drum offering for you. There is a story behind this one, too! I hope you enjoy it. A young lady once visited a shaman to determine the nature of her power animal and was shocked to discover she had a bear. She sat with this awhile and did some research. How could she possibly be like a bear? Months went by, and still she puzzled and read up on more bear traits and species. Which one fit? Now, on the last day of this leap year February, she finally announced that it was definitely a grizzly bear. The characteristics just seemed to fit the best, and it felt right to her. Many months prior to visiting the shaman, this same young lady had made a couple of drums, carefully choosing rawhide and wood, then cutting and mindfully placing the pieces together in a traditional two day process. After completion, the drums stayed in her room, moved from surface to surface, occasionally played in drum circles. But mainly they were just there, sort of on the periphery of her busy life. It just so happened that on this same leap-day in February, someone offered to paint a drum for her. Thinking this a good idea, she quickly went to her room to determine which drum to have painted, and as she picked them up, she was shocked to see the outline of a bear in the hide on one of the drums! When compared to the artist's picture, it was noted that the head, nose, and legs of the bear were the exact shape of the outline in the hide of the drum. Freaky or what?

;-)

March 2, 2012

Here is a fun sketch, possibly a preliminary for a future watercolour. With the unseasonably warm weather this winter, I find myself missing the snow!

March 3, 2012

After a very long and exhausting day, I wasn't certain I had the energy to complete any creative project at all. I've discovered depths of stubbornness I didn't know I possessed! Pulling a rune stone, I received an interesting message ... "The life force is available to you. Let your divine nature be fulfilled and maintain your focus." Picking up my conté pencil, I quickly sketched the hills I'd driven by today. Taking artistic liberty, I added cliffs and a distant river. In this perspective, I am standing on the edge of the cliff, looking down the valley at the sun setting over the distant mountains. Divine nature spread out before me; I am blessed.

March 4, 2012

After another very long and exhausting day, I again wasn't certain I had the energy to complete a creative project. So, going to the runes stones for inspiration or encouragement again tonight, I pull a rune stone. The same stone I pulled yesterday: "The life force is available to you. Let your divine nature be fulfilled and maintain your focus." The energy of the universe is floating around me tonight! A little buck was helping himself to the bird feeder, yet again. Looking right in my dining room window, he seemed to be saying, "Thank you." so I sent out a quiet, "You are welcome". Note to self: Need more bird seed.

March 5, 2012

There is a detectable pattern showing up in my life which has no discernible relation to learning "groundhog day-esque" life lessons that I can determine. It is a minor, seemingly innocuous little cycle that is really starting to pique my interest. I'll share it with you and hope to get your take on the matter. For the last year or so, I've organized a gratitude drum circle ending on the spring equinox. The first year it was set up on Tuesdays, and there was a snowstorm every session. This year, I scheduled it for Mondays, and ... snowstorms!! Today's heavy snowfall warning reduced our numbers to three, and the previous one was cancelled for the same reason. Now, I happen to love snow! In fact, I've been wishing for snow for the better part of three weeks. I needed moist, pristine white expanses to ride and walk through, crisp clean air ... you get the idea. However, I was not anticipating heavy snowfall and weather warnings only on the days of the drum circles! Some shamanic practitioners who are skilled in communication with the elements may suggest that I am unconsciously calling the storms as a way to avoid hosting these circles. Maybe we will try again next Monday just to see what happens!

March 6, 2012

Today's segment of the journey had me realizing how much of myself I have let go of in the passed sixteen years or so. I look in the mirror, and I see an older version of the calm, confident, focused woman I was prior to the car accident, prior to the divorce and subsequent years as a single mother. It is as though I had been looking at a shadow portion of who I was, and suddenly something clicked and I am back. I still feel the twinges of post-traumatic stress in the flinching when cars approach quickly, in the feelings that surface unexpectedly at odd moments, the hesitation in relationship, but something has shifted and I have hope. Is it fragile, oh yes. Is it permanent? I don't know, but I feel whole, balanced and at peace for this moment, and I am grateful. I feel Love. The steps to this point have taken me on unexpected and often convoluted pathways. A complete exploration of my values, beliefs, fundamental and personal, through the spiritual practice of the United Church (from teaching Sunday school to leading Basics of Faith programs, and planning services with the Worship Committee and activism with the Social Justice group), to studies of ancient shamanic traditions based on Buddhist theology and North American native traditions, through the lens of the sciences of eco-psychology, art and animal assisted therapies, and the many physical therapies to heal the injuries to my body. It has been a "Spirit Journey", and today my soul is harmonized. I am enjoying life with … Great Thanks, Great Peace, and Great Love*.

*Quoted from the teachings of Sequoyah Trueblood

March 7, 2012

Wow, what a learning day about communication and humour! Directness and humour versus just being plain rude. It was a day about not taking myself or anyone else too seriously, at all, and then maybe regretting it, just a little bit. Sometimes, humour is lost in the translation; you know, somewhere between my mouth and your ear? What's REALLY funny about this? I have never in my life before, ever, made jokes about my small smidgeon of native blood. (Apparently, having one set of great-grandparents who happened to travel with Louis Riel is very important, big deal-type stuff to me). Over the years, I have hidden it, misdirected questions, outright lied about it, and finally owned it and celebrated it; but I have never, ever, made fun of it. It's way too serious a business dealing with the stereotyping, bigotry or myriad other related things that can cause emotional trauma in the recipient. So where did this sudden rash of self-directed humour come from? And what on earth does it mean? I grew up not knowing anything about native culture; the way of life or belief structures. For crying out loud! Where in the world is this coming from ... and what the heck! When my daughter was in film school, a number of students assisted on the film *Two Indians Talking*, which was featured in the 2010 Edmonton and Calgary Film Festivals. This humour is telling. Hmmm, I watched the film. Do you think humour is contagious? Should I be alarmed?

March 8, 2012

Excerpt from "I Am a Peace Ambassador" by James O'Dea: "I am moving from demanding rights to assuming our responsibility to create environments which promote rights and emphasize individual and collective responsibility for an ecologically sustainable, socially just, democratically vibrant, and healthy world." This struck me as pertinent today. I am all about personal responsibility: be the solution. Or as Gandhi so eloquently stated, "You must be the change you wish to see in the world.". One piece of artwork at a time. Great Thanks, Great Peace, Great Love.

March 9, 2012

I went for a beautiful horseback ride under the stars, the northern lights dancing on the horizon. So many stars are visible away from the light pollution of the city; it is magical to be a part of such magnificence! The full moon wasn't yet visible when we headed back in, but that didn't matter. We made an awesome picture: Twenty-two riders and horses silhouetted against the far off glow of the city lights. Now, if I'd only had my camera... Here is a piece taken during a recent hike in Kananaskis with my fiance, Doug. We'd noticed the strange bark peeling patterns and decided to get a bit closer for a look. The snow was deep and crusted until you put your weight on it. But we toughed it out, and I got a couple of nice shots. We noticed that a herd of elk had gone by, and then we saw the cat tracks: big, no claws. As it looked as though they had been made the night before, we followed just to the edge of the meadow where they disappeared into much denser growth. That was enough for us, so we headed back. It was a good day.
Excerpt from "I Am a Peace Ambassador" by James O'Dea "I am moving from being locked into anger and outrage

at war and violence, or being defined as a protest movement, to creating a culture of peace from the ground up, and from the inside out." And an excerpt from a shamanic conversation I had with an apparently dead tree stump, circa April 2010: "It may appear that I am gone from this world, but the truth is, my roots still run deep under the ground. You see that tree over there? And that one, there? We are connected. I am not gone from the world, just changed. From the inside out." And, so am I.

March 10, 2012

Practice strokes with a new brush. Yes, I could do perfectly neat equidistant strokes in sets of five, but I'd rather explore all over the page with movement and rhythm. Wouldn't you? Snap, crackle and pop, says the house in agreement, as it settles down for the night. Click, click, time for sleep, goes the big black exercise bike. And hold the good memories of the day close to your heart. (Do you remember the first time your teenager said they respect you? I think I'm going to cry!)

Excerpt from "I Am a Peace Ambassador" by James O'Dea: " I am moving from making those who disagree with us as the enemy to recognizing the inherent flaw in creating hostility or enmity as a peace strategy. In this way, my work attempts to dissolve polarizing approaches and behaviours." Thank you, thank you, thank you.

*James O'Dea, author, I Am A Peace Ambassador, www.peaceambassadortraining.com

March 11, 2012

Here we are, almost mid-March and for the second time, I've received a notice from the supposedly inaccessible Facebook account of my recently deceased father. It's a bit disconcerting. The first message arrived on Valentine's Day with an "I love you" candy heart. Today, it was a picture of flowers. It's strange, but kind of nice. Interesting note: No one has the passwords, and no one else is getting messages. I could lock out that account, but somehow I don't think I will—unless it starts to get weirder. Then I'll pass them along to everyone else and see what happens! Anyway, here is the art for today. Helen, here is a cardboard crocus just for you. There is definitely room for improvement in my florals, but I am happy with the colours. Just as the crocus pushes through the last vestiges of snow with strength of purpose, there is a delicate cast to this piece, while still maintaining that show of strength. I hope you enjoy.

March 12, 2012

There are times in our lives where we question our purpose, our reason for being. Why am I here? Am I meant to accomplish something? I've often wondered about where I fit in. Like the pieces of the audio file attached, each sound, each beat, has a function within the whole, sending out a vibration or ripple that has an affect on those who encounter it. The point I often have trouble remembering is that the recipient's reaction does not validate or negate the truth in the expression. We all have critics; often we are our own worst. In and of itself, the critic has its place; after all, this is what drives us to improve, to push ourselves into giving our best effort, surpassing our previous personal best. That's part of what this art-down is about: a place to check in and track progress or commitment. However, it is only helpful if it doesn't freeze me in my tracks. So I ask myself, why is drumming important? Well, it illustrates the building of peace between disparate beings. Each person with their own beat, voice, rhythm, is working together in community to create harmony and produce beauty in the world, even if only for a few minutes. What wonder, this creation.

March 13, 2012

Today, my creative energy is being consumed by a flu bug of some kind, so I'll draw on some last minute energy to complete an entry here before I head back to sleep. Funny that my mind should turn to oranges...

March 14, 2012

I'm still not feeling one hundred percent, but immensely better! My horse even allowed me to get on him today; a far cry from the skittish dance sideways he presented me with yesterday. I guess he knew I was sick and had no business being in the driver's seat! I am going to keep the art light today, though, and still turn in early for an awesome night's rest. So today I was going to do "The 5 Minute Banana", but someone opted for fruit salad for lunch and ate my last remaining model: the trials and tribulations of being an artist. But that's okay. Being ever adaptable, I foraged, hunted, and gathered, and found one lone, wrinkly apple that hadn't been offered to the horses. Aha! A five minute model! And so art goes on. With Great Thanks, Great Peace, Great Love.

March 15, 2012

Excerpt from The Earth Charter*: "1. Respect Earth and life in all its diversity.

a. Recognize that all beings are interdependent and every form of life has value regardless of its worth to human beings. Let ours be a time remembered for the awakening of a new reverence for life, the firm resolve to achieve sustainability, the quickening of the struggle for justice and peace, and the joyful celebration of life."

With Great Thanks, Great Peace, Great Love

*The Earth Charter, Earth Charter Commission at the UNESCO headquarters, Paris, March 2000.

March 16, 2012

Today was a day of wedding planning, where the great consumerist machine of the modern wedding rolls along, sweeping the unwary onto paths of great expense. "How do I love thee" becomes "How MUCH … do I love thee?" Serious sticker shock! And yet it is so easy to get caught up in all the glamour, glitz, and details. So easy to lose sight of what's important. When all is peeled aside, what is left is the promises we make together. There is the heart of what really counts: the held hands, the quick meeting of the eyes, the silent laughter and quiet teasing, the moments that build on this commitment, strengthening and deepening the bond. How do I illustrate this kind of day? My first impulse was to ignore the significance of the day and continue on with the 10 minute fruit. I even have grapes in hand. Yet, the more I write and reflect here, I wonder if I do a disservice to this project by trying not to incorporate the more personal and emotional happenings of my days. Art illustrates life, after all. Perhaps I can learn to illustrate avoidance? That's it ... colour me compartmentalized. Art stays art; life stays life. Hmmm. My next impulse was to submit a portrait I've taken of Doug, something that reflects the essence of who he is. Then I realize, no, this isn't something he'd be comfortable with. So, I've decided to showcase his talent instead. Today's artwork is Doug's. I see and honour the artist in you.

March 17, 2012

Ever notice how love jumps out at you when you look for it everywhere? In the smallest things is the most precious spark. The wag of a dog's tail, a nicker from a horse, the smile of a friend, hugs from children, the quiet sharing of a home-cooked meal; all string together in moments that glow like moonlight on the snow. Alive and dancing with joy, the jewel drops of the moon celebrate the love of humanity as we stand witness to the beauty they spread out before us. It brings to mind lyrics of that wonderful Michael Buble song, "Can I just have one more moondance with you, my love?" So, humming softly as I soft shoe (barefoot) down the hall, I remember love, anticipate love, and hold it gently in my heart to share the dance with those whose lives touch mine. Many blessings.

March 18, 2012

An interesting day. A tough day. Threads of pain have been pulled into the joyful fabric of life. The pattern is inextricably interwoven, teasing the eye away from what's real and important as though with a charlatan's sleight of hand. "Focus here, on the knees, on the bones and muscles; all else is irrelevant, it whispers." Yet, even with pain replaying this constant magician's trick, soft focus and soft eyes allow for the entrance of other images: images of care, love between species; images of co-operation and harmony. And the sense of hope inspired by this vision allows for the birth of creativity and of the image above: an image which attracts with contrast, where light and dark struggle for control of the eye. There is a feeling of strength and fragility, a projection of truth and falsity. One of the orchids is a man-made copy appearing as an orchid in truth on the surface but false at the core; the other is natural, flowing with the energy of life. What does your eye perceive? Where do you focus? Do you accept your first glance or do you pursue it further? I invite you to look closer.

March 19, 2012

What an unusual and amazing day! Despite the cancellation of the drum circle this evening, everything about this day shaped up to be remarkable. Spending healthy relationship building, bonding time with my soon to be twenty year old son was exceptionally fun. I watched him bravely feeding then grooming my horse, patiently listening and learning about brushes, combs, and tack, then exercising him by leading him at a walk across the field over various obstacles, and around barrels, bridges and weave poles. All the while, he was struggling with his early childhood memories of being on a horse that bucked. I'm glad I had a chance to help him with this today, and I'm proud of him for how he handled it. He has a wonderful way with animals and horses in particular. We spent the remainder of the afternoon working together to clean out the storage room, in an effort to ready it for setting up his recording equipment. This meant reorganizing all my studio supplies from two tables down to one and a complete shuffle of all items stored in the area. It was a daunting task, but handled with his humour and sense of fun, it was quite enjoyable and the time passed quickly. I was impressed by his initiative and the demonstration of his organizational abilities. He is a fine young man, developing good management skills. So, with my studio space redesigned, but currently not quite reorganized (tomorrow's project), I am left with a bit of upheaval that also seems to be making an impression on me. I don't work well in clutter, so I feel almost compelled to dig in again and clean up before I can settle into art making... Maybe it wasn't so badly cluttered.

March 20, 2012

Well, the disorganization has been dealt with, the electrical has been run, and the recording studio of a young entrepreneur has moved in next door to my art space. Hmmm! I'm not quite sure how this will work out, but I'm sure it will be a fascinating experience in blending and co-operation. I'm confident all will work out for our highest good. Confident: there's a word and a half. I'm moving forward with full trust. Okay, it's time for another meditative mandala! Breathe….

March 21, 2012

The third segment of the Peace Ambassador Certification program was this evening, and it has left me deeply moved. This is the section on working toward inner peace—a difficult state to achieve and maintain consistently. We were speaking of mindfulness practices, listening with your whole being, acknowledging the wounds in others, and taking care of not only yourself in an unsettled situation but also taking care of the "enemy". I've definitely been working on this in my lifetime. I'd love to go into this more, but I am mentally exhausted, so sheepishly, I head for bed. Zzzzzzzzzz….

March 22, 2012

Two hundred and seventy-three days to go. WHAT WAS I THINKING! I started to do a quick inventory of the things on my plate during this time and decided that it looked like complaining, which doesn't reflect how I'm feeling about this at all. Despite the occasional freak out (see above), this is such an incredible learning process for me: building both art and life skills; enjoying the interaction, fun and wisdom of the comments section; and, learning about who I have become. It's a wonderful way to check in, check direction, and check growth.

Sorry for the pun, but it's just checkin' all the boxes for me at the moment. Now if I could just figure out what to do today! Ah ha! Inspiration is looking me in the face, and it has the shape of a screaming hawk. Maybe he's trying to tell me something? Oh, wait! I get it! It's...celebrating life.

March 23, 2012

The thing about art is the emotion it evokes in the viewer, yet Day 83 finds that emotions are stretched thin in the artist! There is a ton of homework waiting to be completed and uploaded. Where can I find time to be creative! How can I possibly spend time in meditation, seeking inspiration, yada, yada ... There is so much to be done! I am reminded to just become aware of the flow and rhythm of life, and step into the stream. Feel the value of being. Who I am, where I am, the way I am … is all part of the whole that plays itself if I just listen and move with the beat. Taking the time to just clear my mind and allow the universe in, rather than being busy, busy, trying to make the universe do calms me. I feel clear and at peace. So here I am, and I am feeling the rhythm of the orchids, softening the background to convey the delicacy of petals, interpreting the pattern through the eye of the lens. And always, always, celebrating life.

March 24, 2012

I started today off with a meditative labyrinth drum walk under the broad expanse of blue sky, which extended west down the valley and right to the roots of the Rockies. Sunlight glittered on the dusting of snow, laid out like untouched diamonds on the ground before us. We were the first human feet to walk there since the snow fell. Breathing in the crisp morning air, we moved through the field to the small dip in the land where the labyrinth was nestled, its stone outline a bas relief against the hollow of its winding pathway. There is a moment of setting intention for the journey to find our own centre, and through this point to connect with the harmony and balance inherent in our natural world, to allow these qualities to fill us as well. As we sound our drums, beginning with the rhythm of our own heartbeats, one by one we enter the labyrinth. Experiencing the path with all of our 53* senses, we track our movements, sounds, thoughts and impulses. Later, after making note of changes in thoughts, body and actions, I was surprised to notice an interesting fact laid out in nature right before my eyes. We had walked on separate paths heading to the labyrinth, our trails plainly visible in the fresh snow. Yet I stood on the point where our paths converged.

Looking behind me into the labyrinth, I realized that when we set our intention for harmony and balance, we walked in each other's footprints…one path ... both into the centre of the labyrinth and out again. One path lay behind me in harmony and peace. It was a touchstone moment illustrated with stark clarity and beauty by the footprints on the pathway, something to remember as our paths diverge and we go on about our day. The footprints on the pathway said it all.

* Dr. Michael Cohen, Connecting With Nature, copyright 1989 World Peace University

March 25, 2012

I am smiling inside and out. The vibrations of joy that have woven vine-like tendrils through the tapestry of my day have reached my heart, and I am singing along in harmony.

And on that note, ends the first element of The Final Art-Down. AIR. Many blessings on your journey.

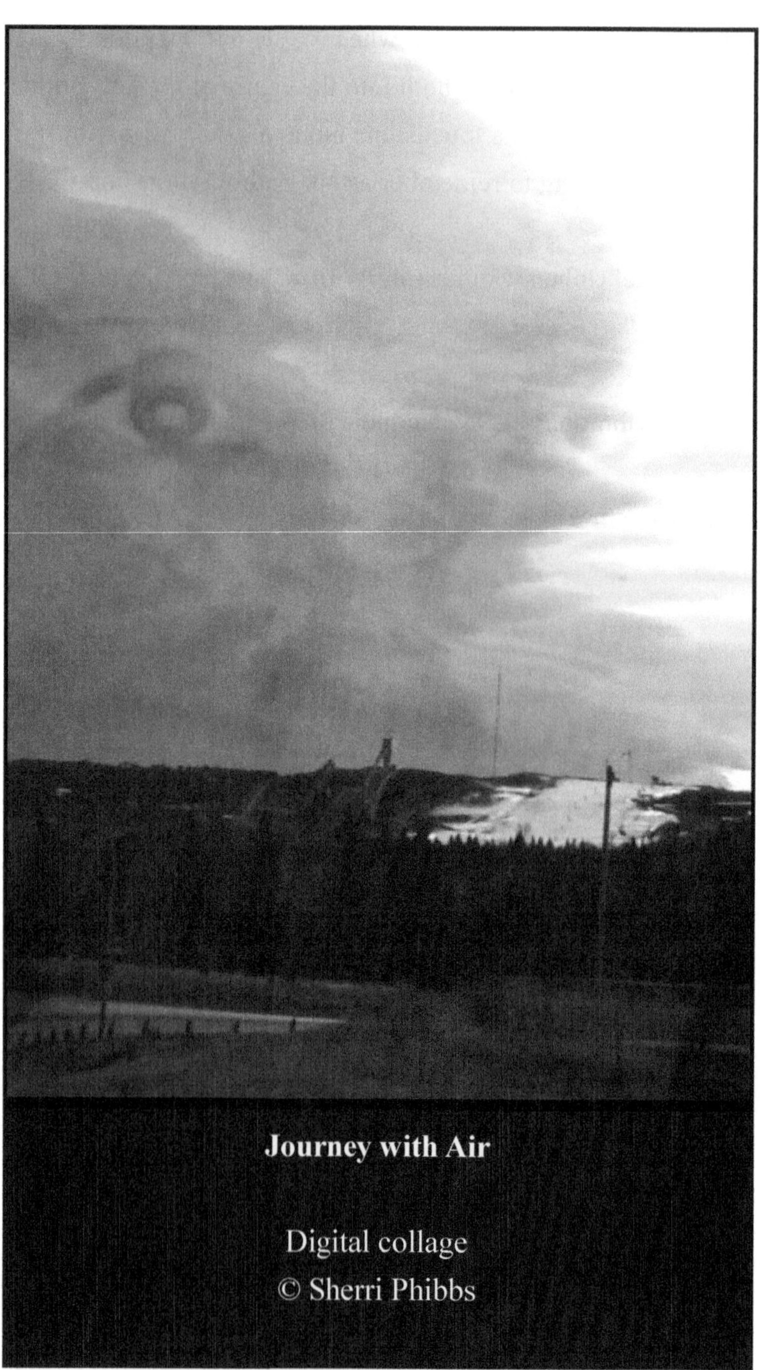

Journey with Air

Digital collage
© Sherri Phibbs

The Final Art-Down: FIRE

The Final Art-Down: FIRE

The journey continues, BUT WAIT . . .

. . . With coffee and keys in hand, one foot out the door, the artisan's mind travels over grocery lists, technical difficulties, home, family and pet care, wedding plans and more. How can this art-down journey possibly continue with everything that needs to be done? Questions of commitment, ability, and sanity float through the ether, touching down on fragile ego like sparks burning holes through dry grass and threatening to take the whole project up in a conflagration of smoke and flames. Is this journey even viable, or worthy of continuation?

Events that interfere with artistic creativity seem to spring to life with the barest breath, leaving only a burnt out, empty hull devoid of inspiration, thought, and excitement. Ashes.

Disheartened and stagnant, the artist sighs, when suddenly FIRE enters, stage left, shifting a spark slightly, focusing the heat a bit more brightly ... flames spark in the soul. Thus is passion born: set alight by FIRE and fanned by community support, the heart is bursting and the artist takes off running.

Running, for band-aids and burn cream . . .

Refocus
March 27, 2012

Nature photography

Awareness of FIRE

Picture in your mind a place in nature where you can feel the heat of the sun and /or sense a connection to the element of FIRE. You may choose a hot, rocky, hillside facing into the afternoon sun; you could light and sit next to a candle or campfire; or you could visit the desert or badlands. Allow yourself to travel, to be drawn to that place you visualized, that place that represents FIRE for you. Take along a coloured pencil and a journal. When you arrive at your FIRE place, address the area respectfully, requesting permission to interact. You will know if you received permission as a lightness, or rightness, will make itself know in your mind, spirit and body. Honour a negative response by moving on to another area and repeating your request. When you have permission, make yourself comfortable. Use all your senses to track and be aware of everything in your surroundings. Note how you feel ... breathe in, breathe out ... with gratitude.

When you are ready, begin to form a request in your mind for inspiration and assistance on your journey of creative discovery and integrity. Pay particular attention to the thoughts that flow through your mind, and record them in your journal. It may be random thoughts, it could be poetry or song lyrics; anything at all is valid. There is no wrong way to be aware of what flows across your mind. Also, note your feelings and physical responses as you interact with Nature in this way, tracking and recording this as well. Are you drawn to a certain spot or location within your FIRE area? What do you see there, taste there, smell there? Are you happy, cranky, inspired, or something else? Does something in particular jump to your attention? Describe and make note of your experience in the FIRE zone.

As you complete your interaction with FIRE, you may wish to express your gratitude. You may do this verbally with deep sincerity or with an energetic offering of burnt sage, sweetgrass, organic tobacco, or even by sprinkling organic cornmeal in the area. You may repeat this interaction with FIRE again and again as a way of getting to know the element, becoming connected to your natural environment, and opening your heart to the experience of love for this Divine and self-sustaining world of which we are a part.

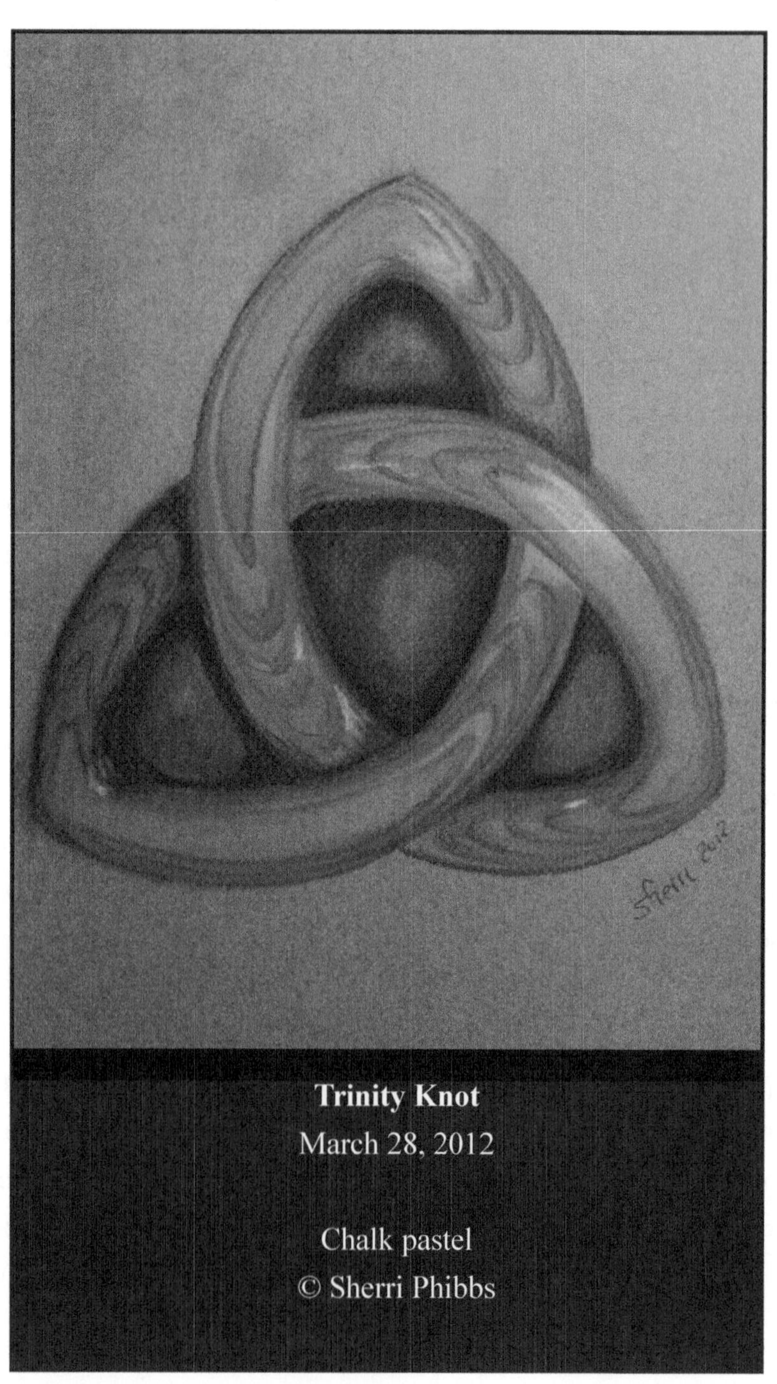

Trinity Knot
March 28, 2012

Chalk pastel

FIRE: The Image

This project came to life in pieces, two pieces. The whole, comprised of a written journal of daily life experience matched with a corresponding artistic interpretation, is separated here into its individual parts. And so it continues...

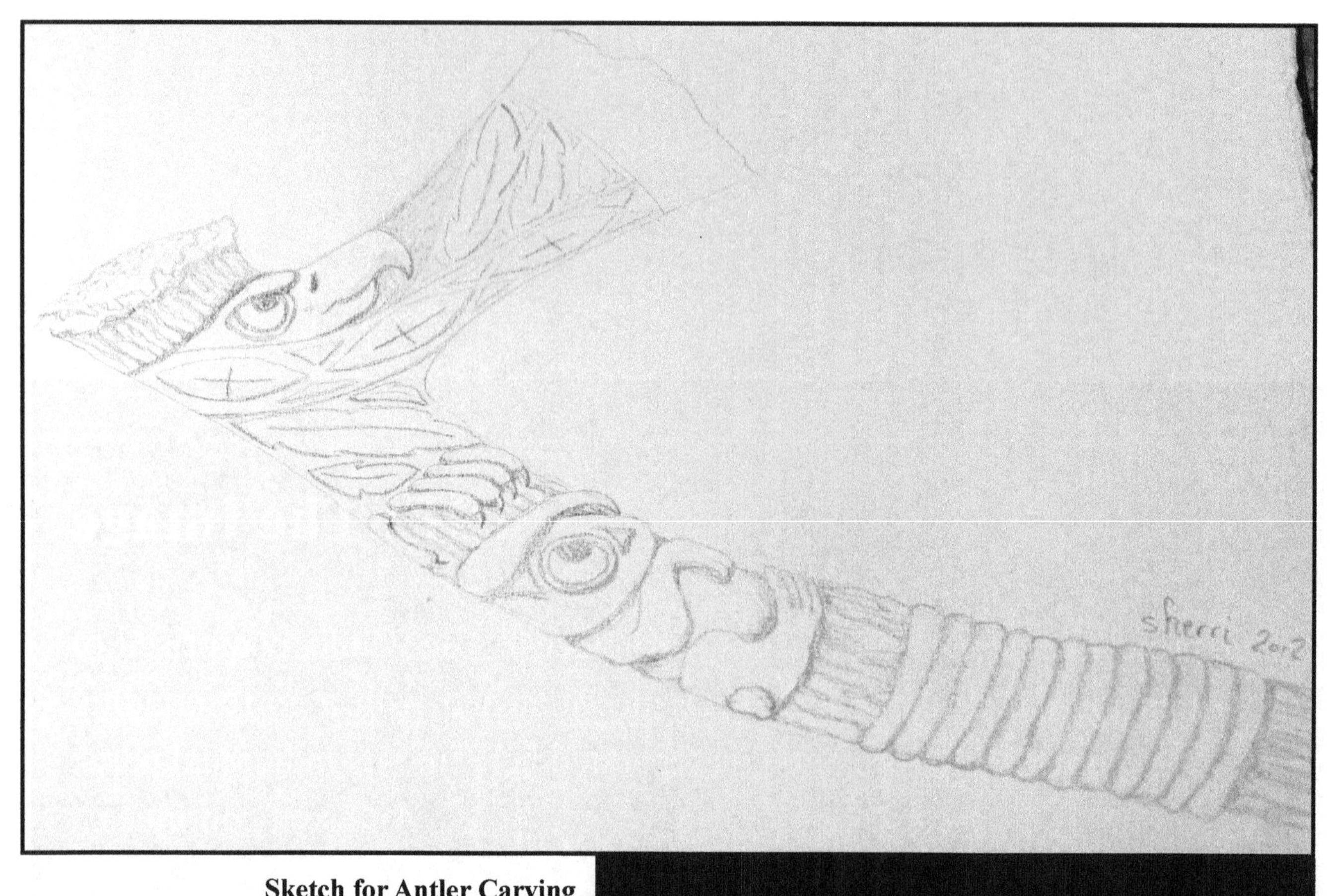

Sketch for Antler Carving
March 26, 2012

Pencil sketch

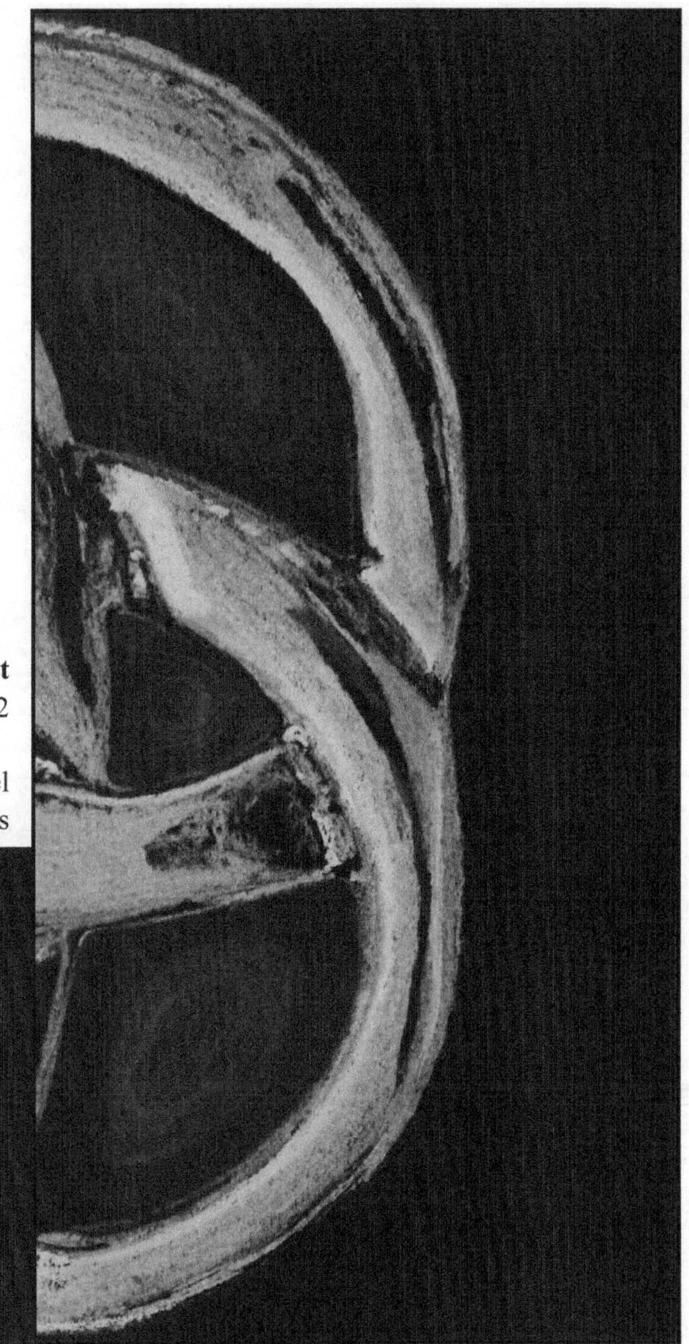

Eternity Knot
March 29, 2012

Chalk pastel

Eternity Knot
March 30, 2012

Chalk pastel

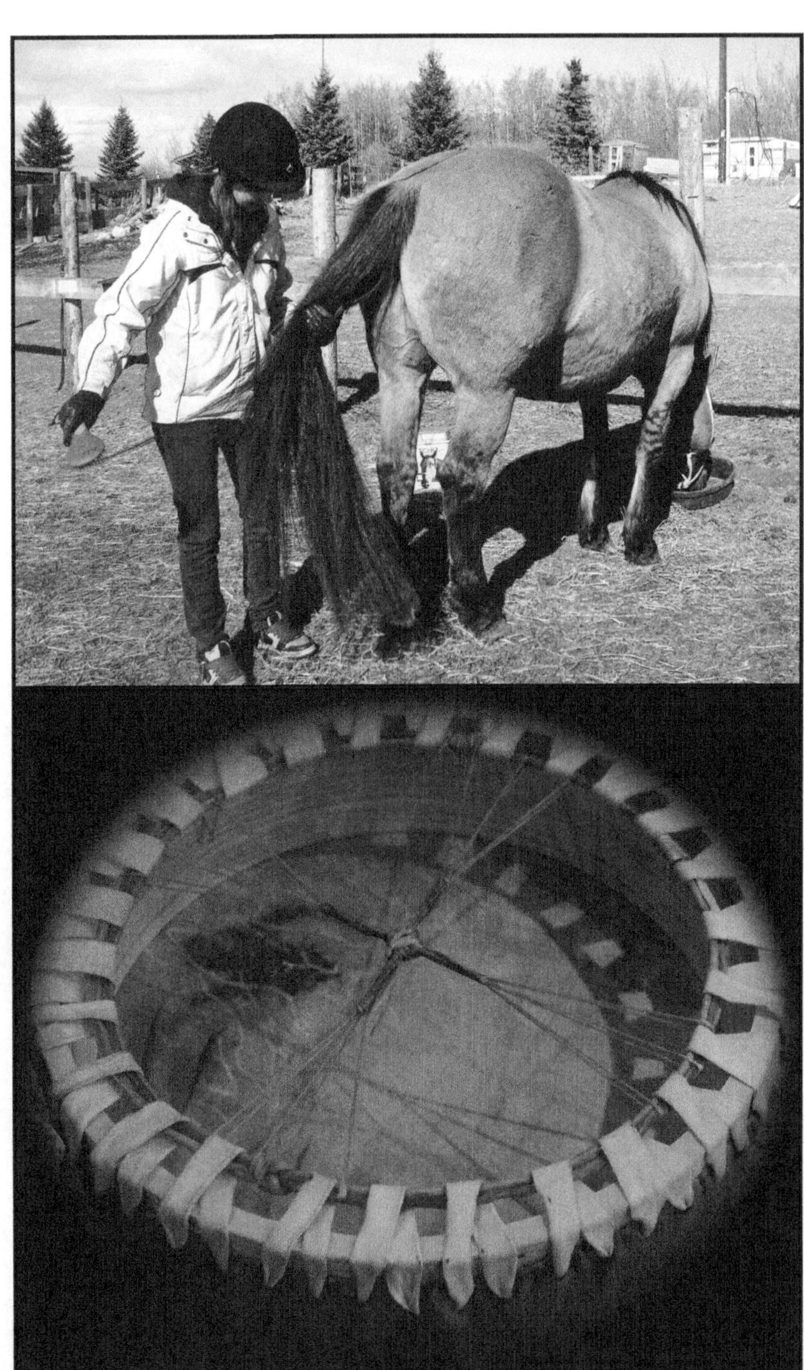

Nothing Says I Care Like…
March 31, 2012

Pet portraiture
© Sherri Phibbs

Naked Glory
April 1, 2012

Traditionally hand-made rawhide drum
© Sherri Phibbs

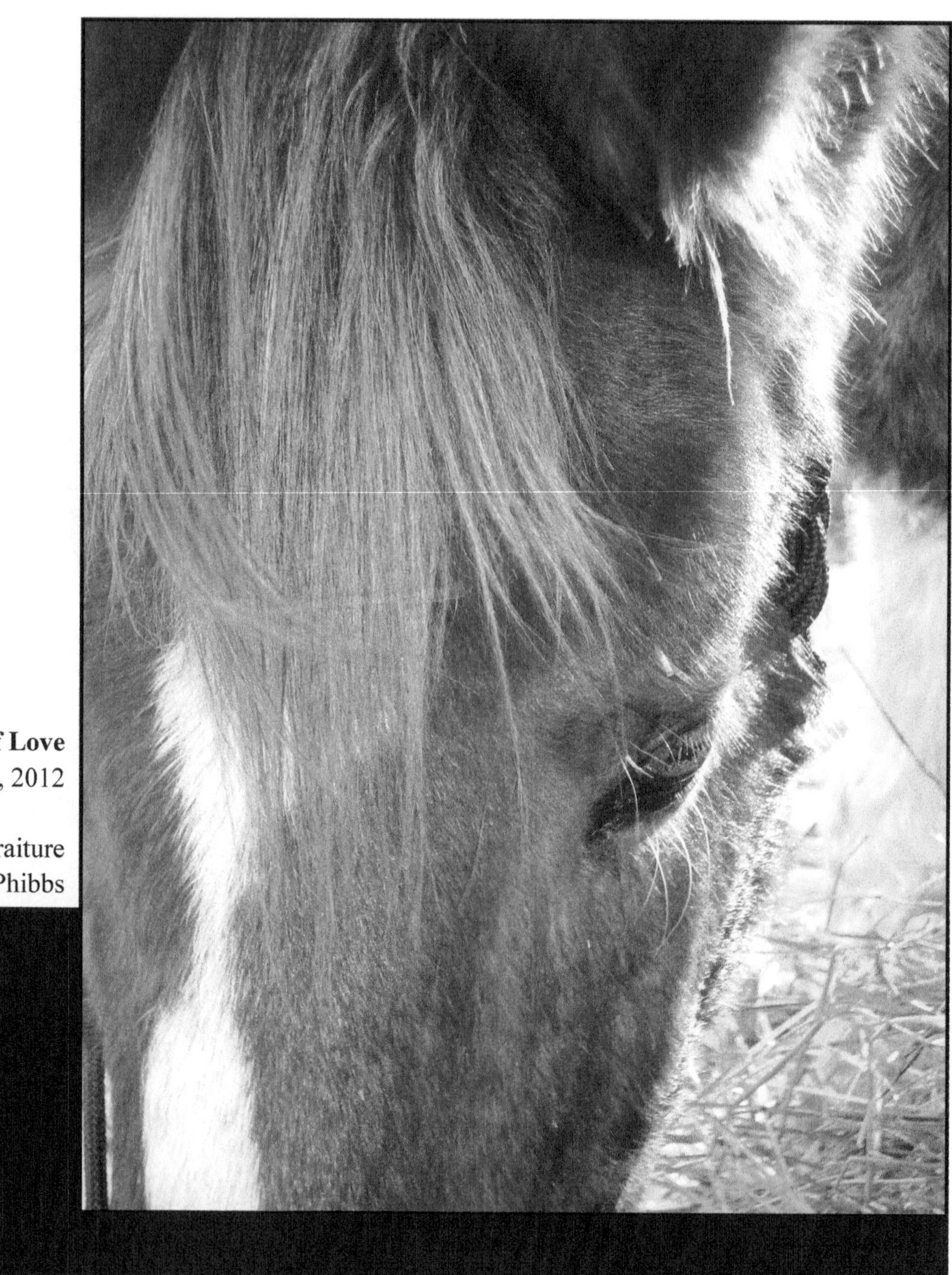

Light of Love
April 2, 2012

Pet portraiture

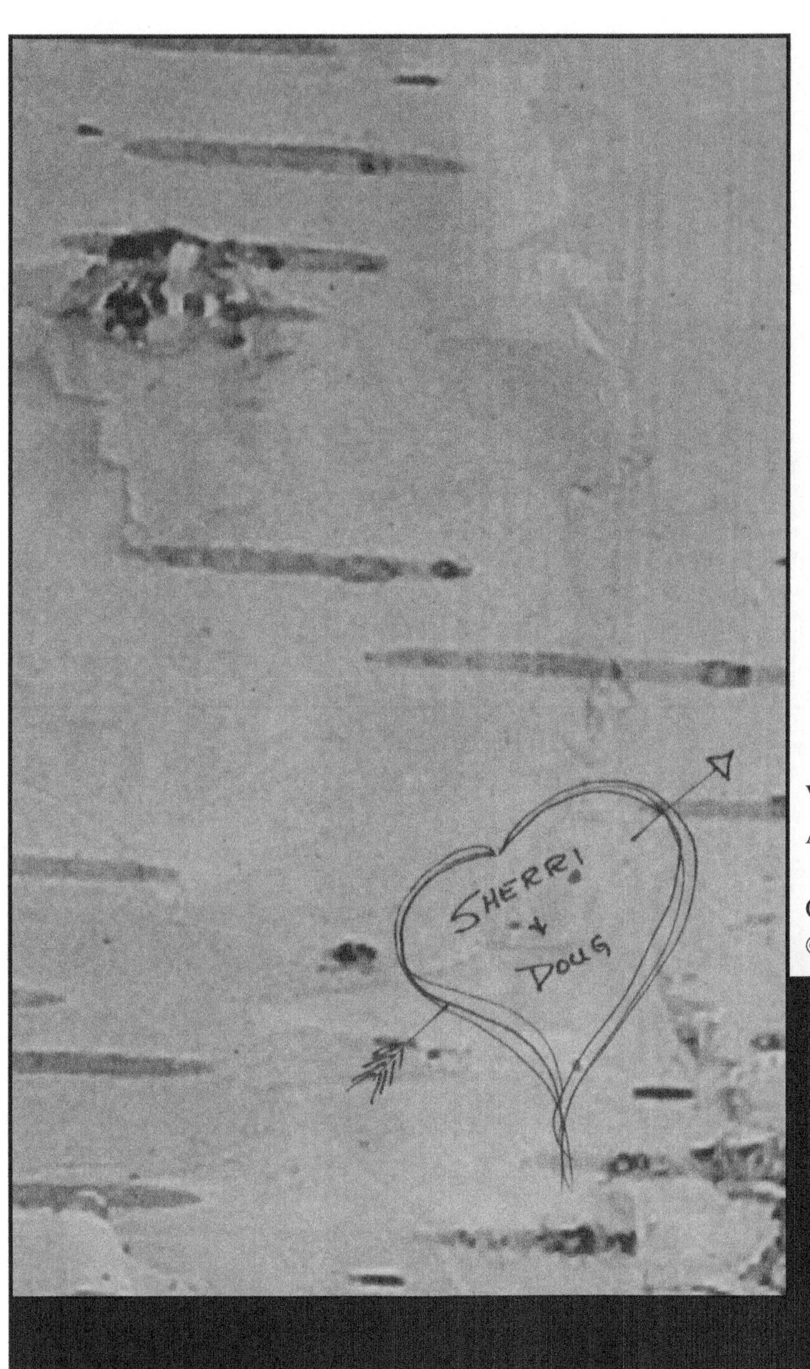

Wedding Program
April 3, 2012

Crafting
© Sherri Phibbs

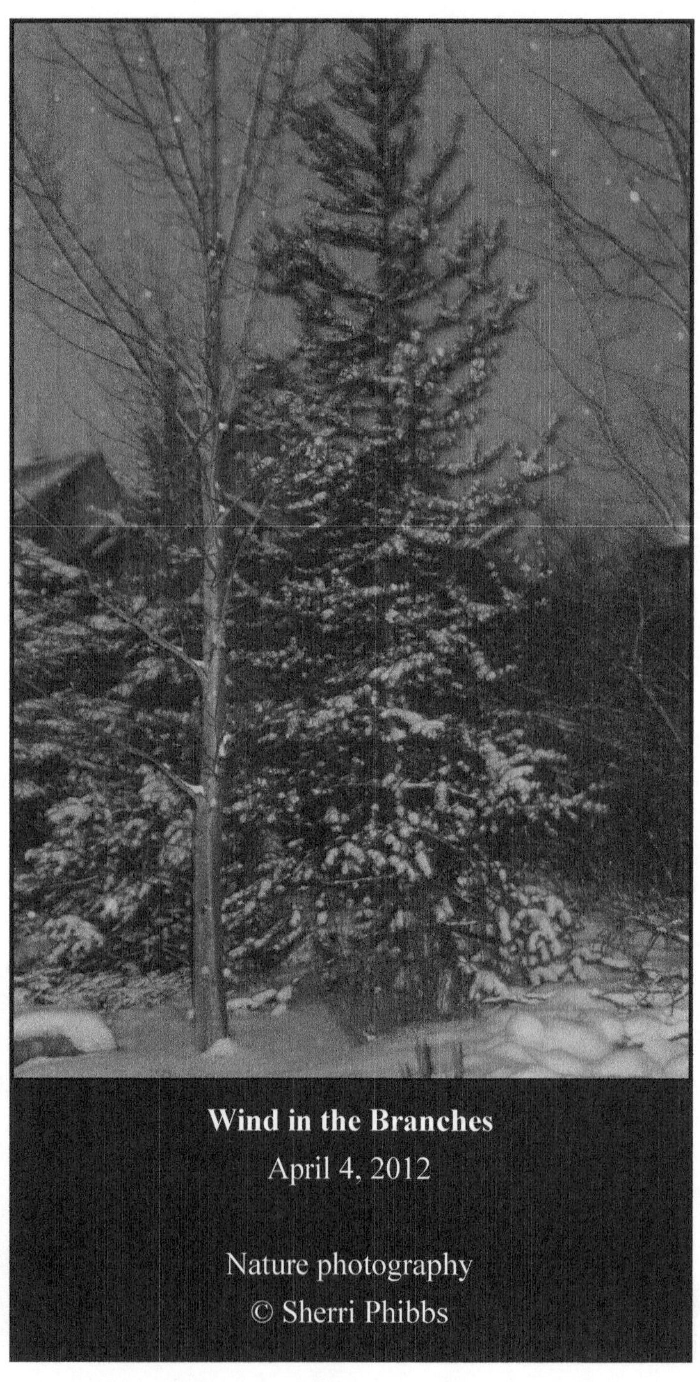

Wind in the Branches
April 4, 2012

Nature photography
© Sherri Phibbs

A Gift For You…

Build Your Vision Collage!

Another tool that showed its extreme value during this project was a Vision Collage. Take a trip with your camera through your neighbourhood, city, or countryside. Anything that catches your attention, represents your dreams and insights, or inspires you to action, gets recorded through photography. Fill in your photo expedition with pictures ripped from wherever (legally, of course) and then assemble all the images with glue on a large, irregularly shaped piece of newsprint or pin them on a cork board, or …. You get the idea; there is no wrong way to display your vision collage. Be creative.

It is interesting to notice that even when our conscious mind is working on other things, our subconscious—or the universe or Spirit—continues to align with our vision. You can come back years after creating a collage, and with a quick look be surprised to find the things represented there have manifested in your life. Powerful stuff!

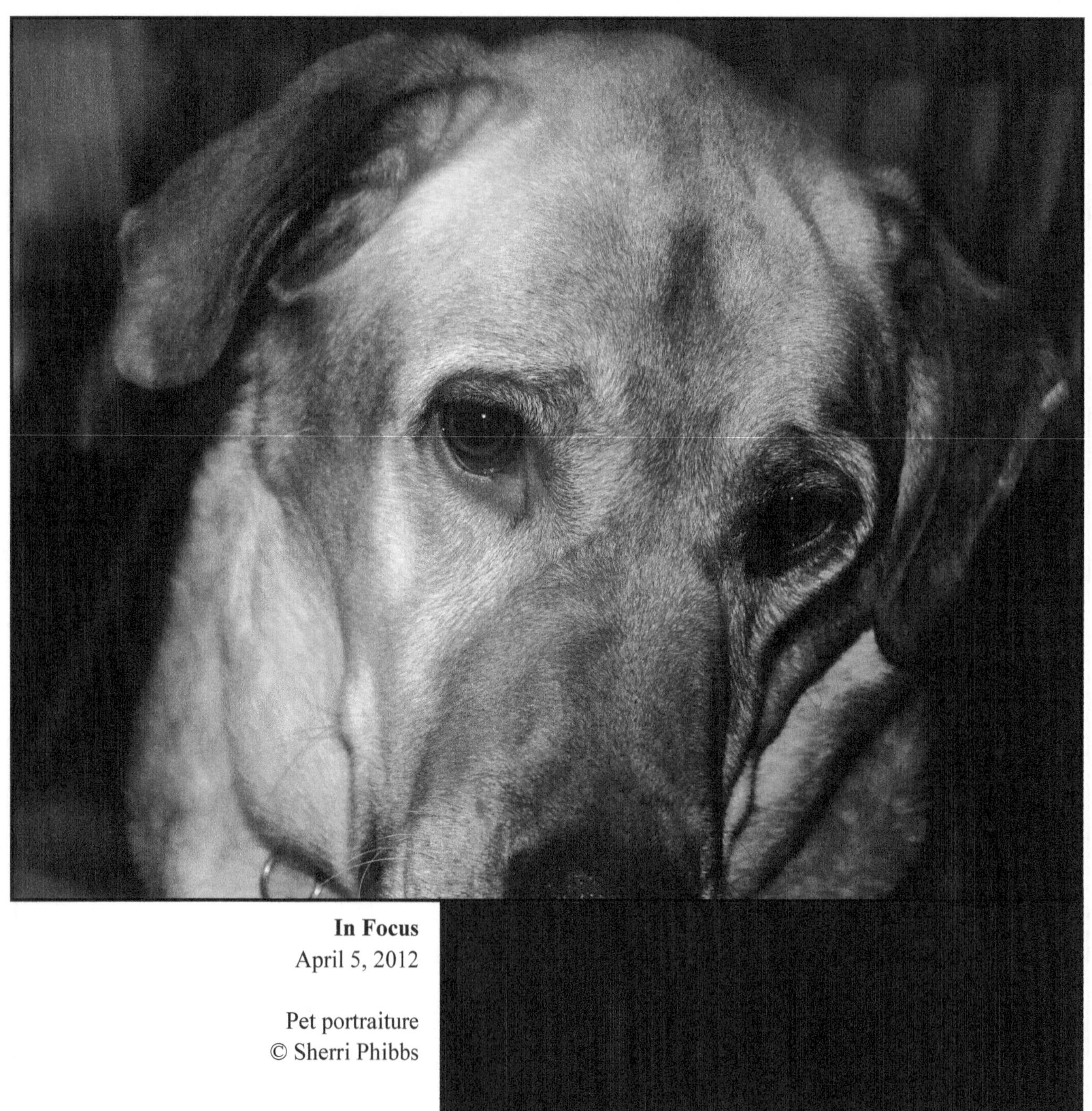

In Focus
April 5, 2012

Pet portraiture

Yum
April 6, 2012

Pet portraiture
© Sherri Phibbs

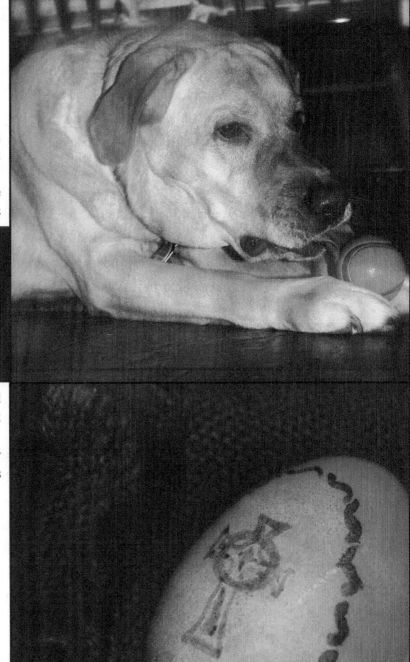

Playing With My Food
April 7, 2012

Still life photography
© Sherri Phibbs

My Journey with FIRE

Many years and countless tests later, a certain woman of the People is shocked to discover she is indeed on The Path. Confronted at every turn by Teachers, Mirrors and the TRUTH in both, she cannot ignore Spirit stirring her soul any more. No longer frozen with fear, more bewildered and mystified, life becomes a series of surprising adventures. Short stories, prose and poetry, Spirit and Creation, all strung together by light, laughter, pain, grief, terror, passion and excitement. Forgiveness and LOVE.

One story began when the woman made a painting of her soul. Free-flowing and strong, with lost and found edges of brilliant colour, it inspired words—calm, peaceful, stirring, relaxing. Yet, when the woman looked at the watercolour image, she saw something else. She did not speak of what she saw out loud; instead, holding it close to her heart, troubled, she allowed her mind to play with the image. At the end of the sun's daily journey, she shared the painting with her husband.

"What do you see when you look at this painting?" She asked.
"I see a fire coming over the mountain! Not a place of rest, that's for sure." He replied.
"Me, too! SOUL ON FIRE!" And she laughed. This man really sees ME.

A few short moon cycles later, and the woman gave in to a very strong and determined nudge from Spirit to take a short journey, a journey that led to a local market. Drawn, she reluctantly followed the pull on her mind, tentatively allowing her inner knowing to emerge. Then she saw it. The woman was amazed, shocked. She breathed slowly in and out, no longer questioning the reason for being in that place at that time. There on the shelf, directly in her line of sight, was a book, cover facing outward: "SOUL ON FIRE", written by a shaman and teacher, Peter Calhoun. With this discovery, a new awareness sets in and the woman of the People steps into the first chapter of another story: an epic poem of traditions, of apprenticeship and learning.

Beginning in TRUTH: the Path of the Wounded Healer.

Fire on The Prairie
April 19, 2012

Watercolour
© Sherri Phibbs

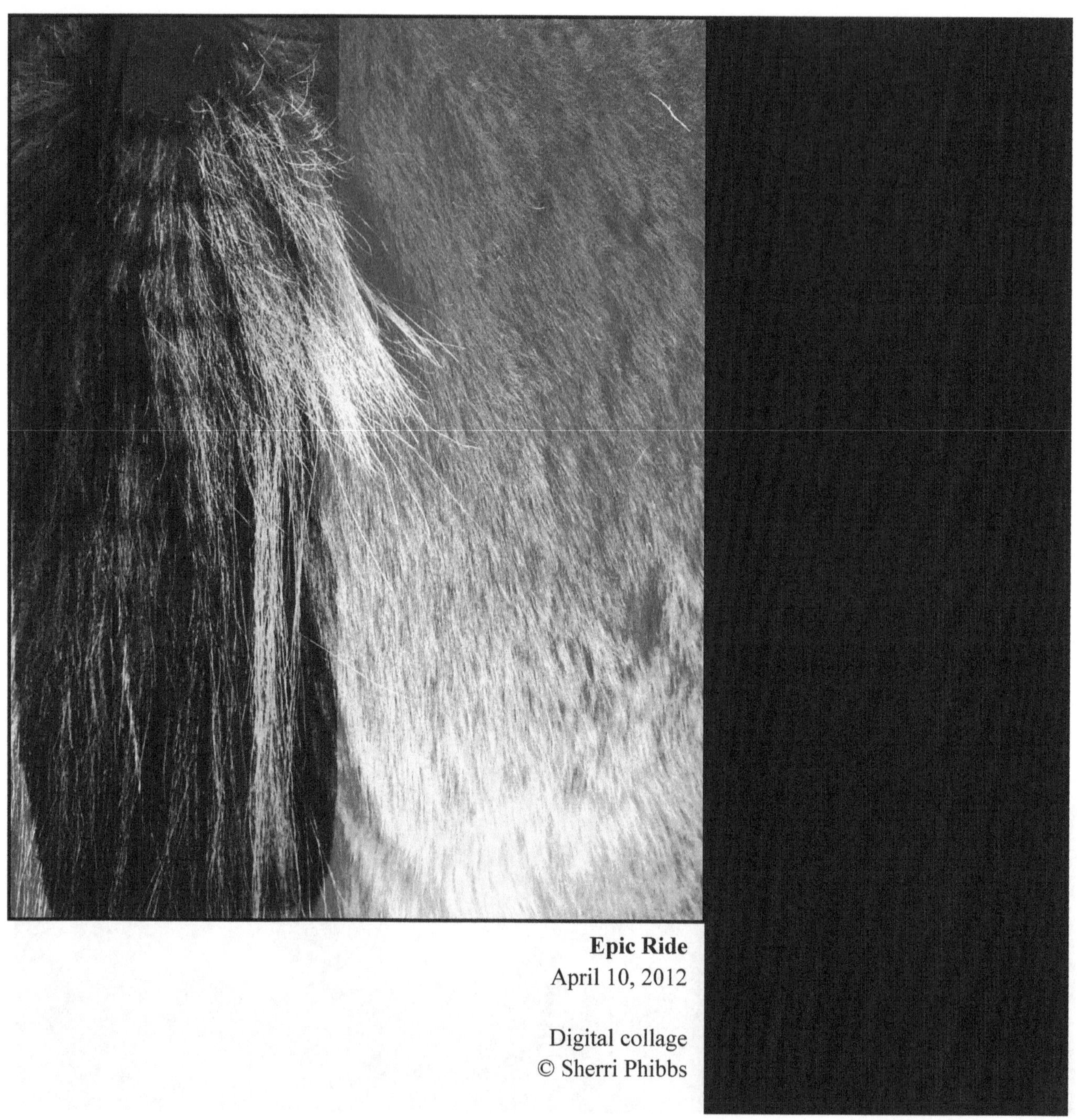

Epic Ride
April 10, 2012

Digital collage

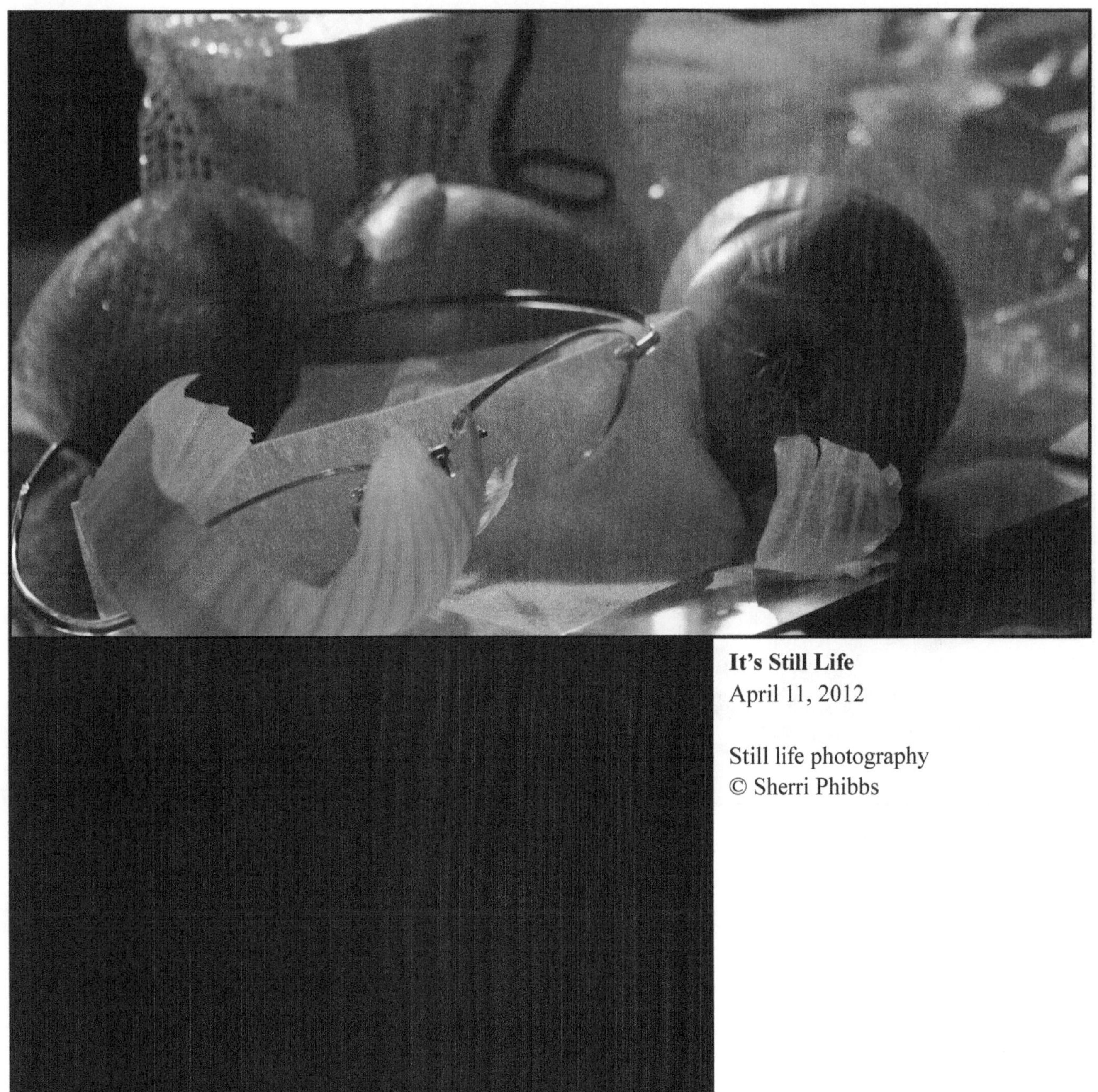

It's Still Life
April 11, 2012

Still life photography

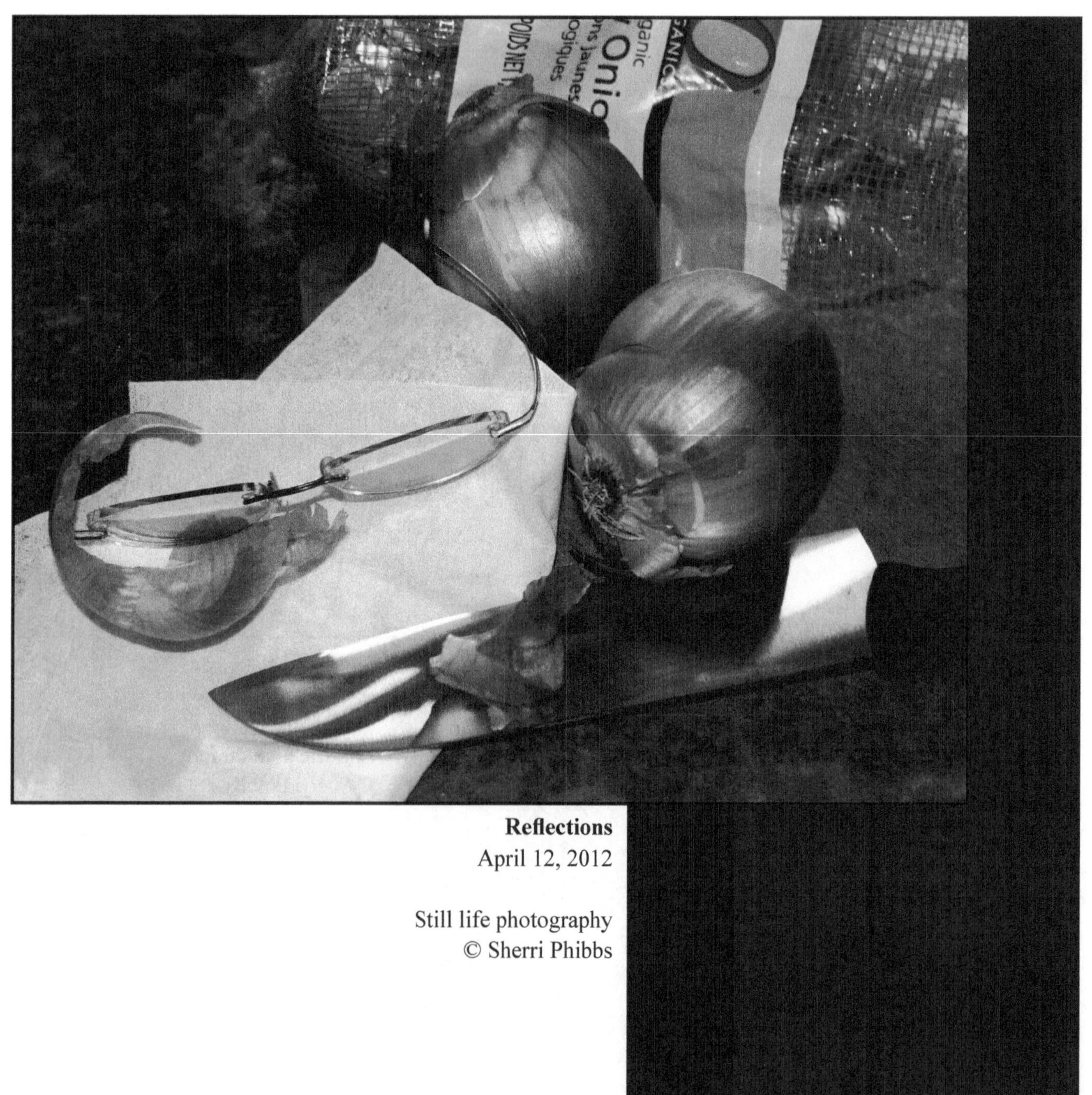

Reflections
April 12, 2012

Still life photography
© Sherri Phibbs

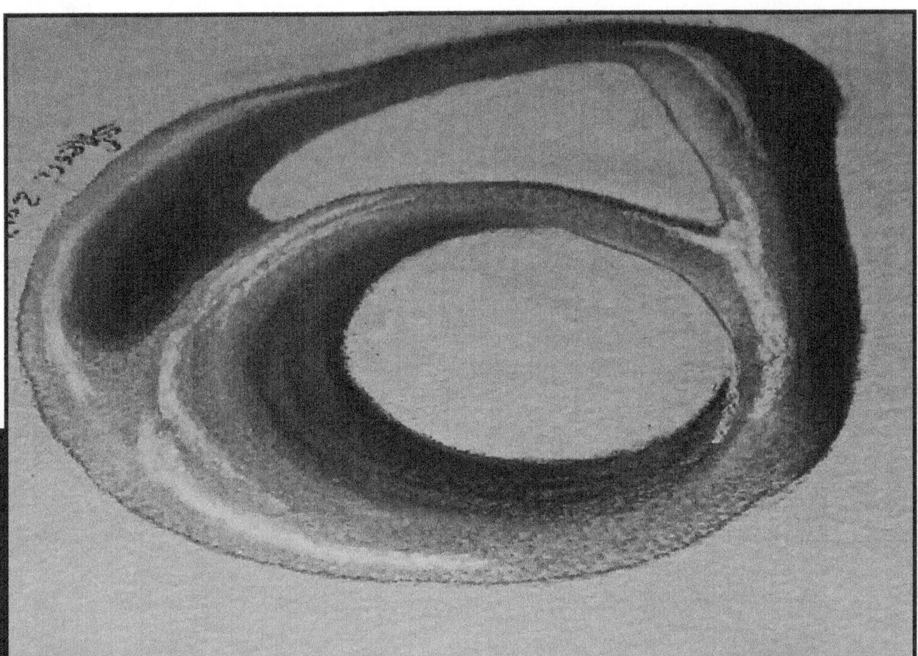

Movement in Jade
April 13, 2012

Chalk pastel
© Sherri Phibbs

Rhythm in Blues
April 14, 2012

Chalk pastel
© Sherri Phibbs

DRUM MAKERS GATHERING

May 12 & 13th 2012

REGISTER NOW

Learn a time-tested traditional method of creating a rawhide hand drum and drumstick.

BUILD IT ... PLAY IT
ENGAGE YOUR SENSES

2-day teaching circle
$220.00 Includes:

- TRADITIONAL CEREMONY
- MUSIC & MOVEMENT
- IMAGE QUEST
- TRADITIONAL & MODERN DECORATING TECHNIQUES

WISH STUDIO

sbohn@telusplanet.net
403-478-4349

Drum Makers Gathering
April 15, 2012

Graphic design *Please see website for up-to-date contact info

Tracking (Framed & Sold)
April 16, 2012

Acrylics
© Sherri Phibbs

A Dark Path (beginning)
April 17, 2012

Watercolour
© Sherri Phibbs

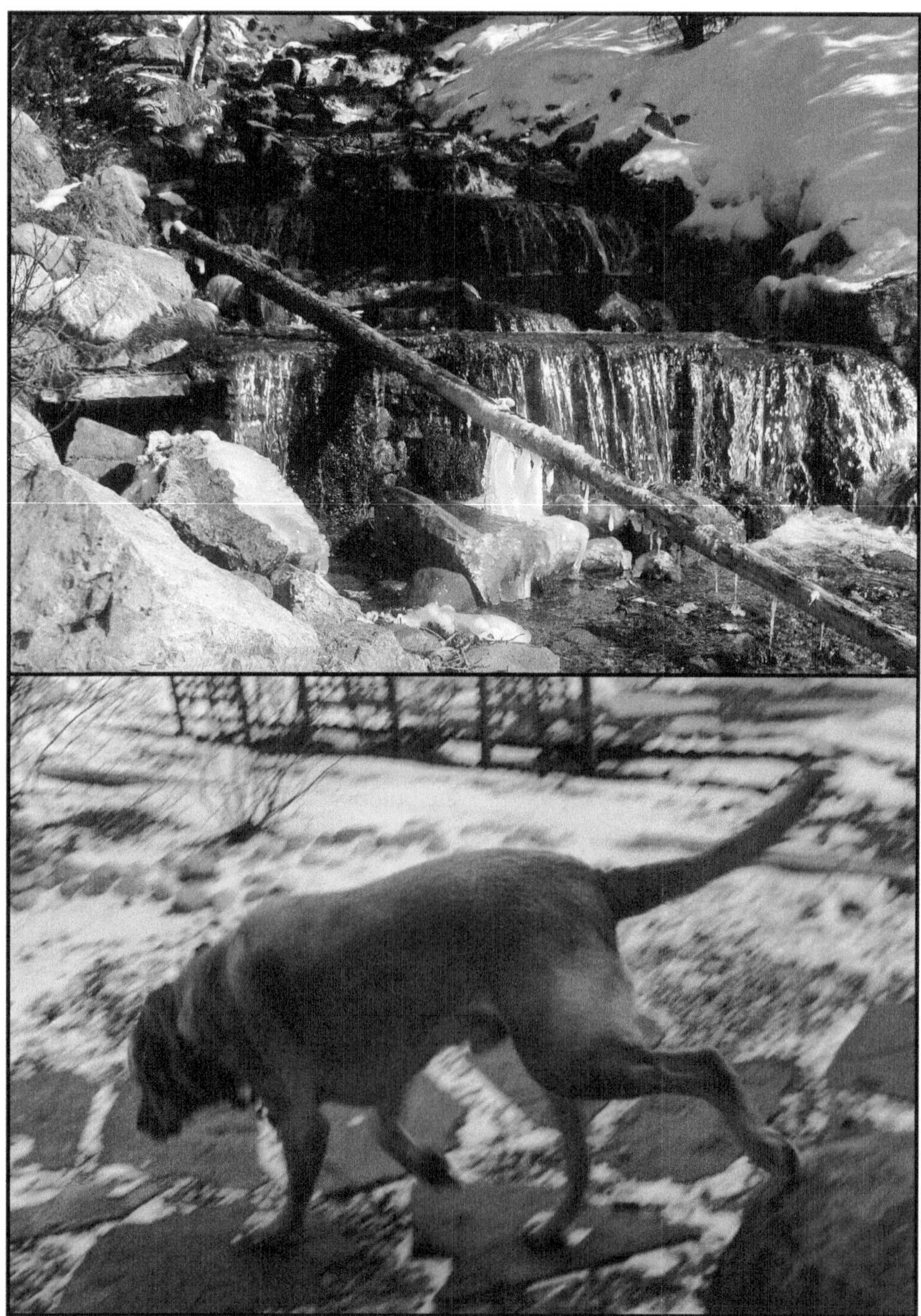

Crystal Clear II
April 20, 2012

Nature photography

Pushing Off
April 18, 2012

Pet portraiture

Egg Wars
April 8, 2012

Still life photography
© Sherri Phibbs

West Coast Sketch
April 9, 2012

Pencil sketch
© Sherri Phibbs

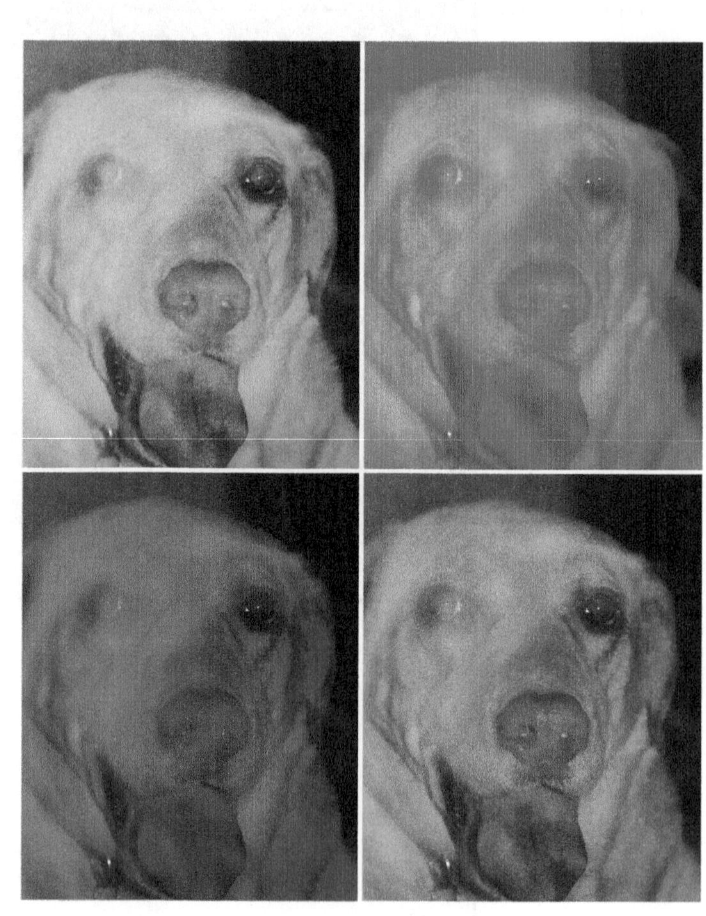

Dogs of War(hol)
April 21, 2012

Digital collage
© Sherri Phibbs

IDK
April 22, 2012

Charcoal sketch
© Sherri Phibbs

Still Motion
April 23, 2012

Pet portraiture
© Sherri Phibbs

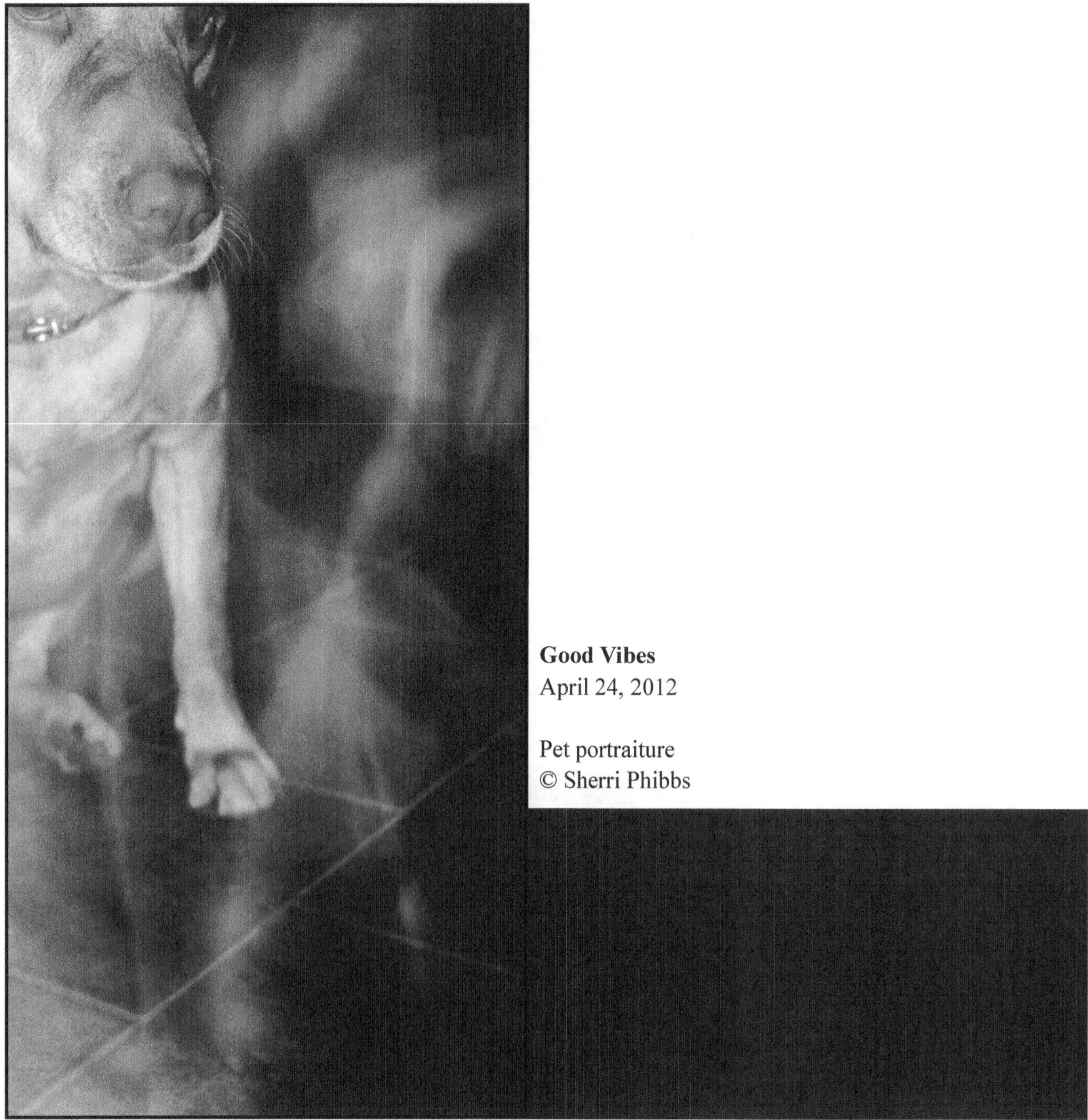

Good Vibes
April 24, 2012

Pet portraiture

Winter Wood
April 25, 2012

Watercolour

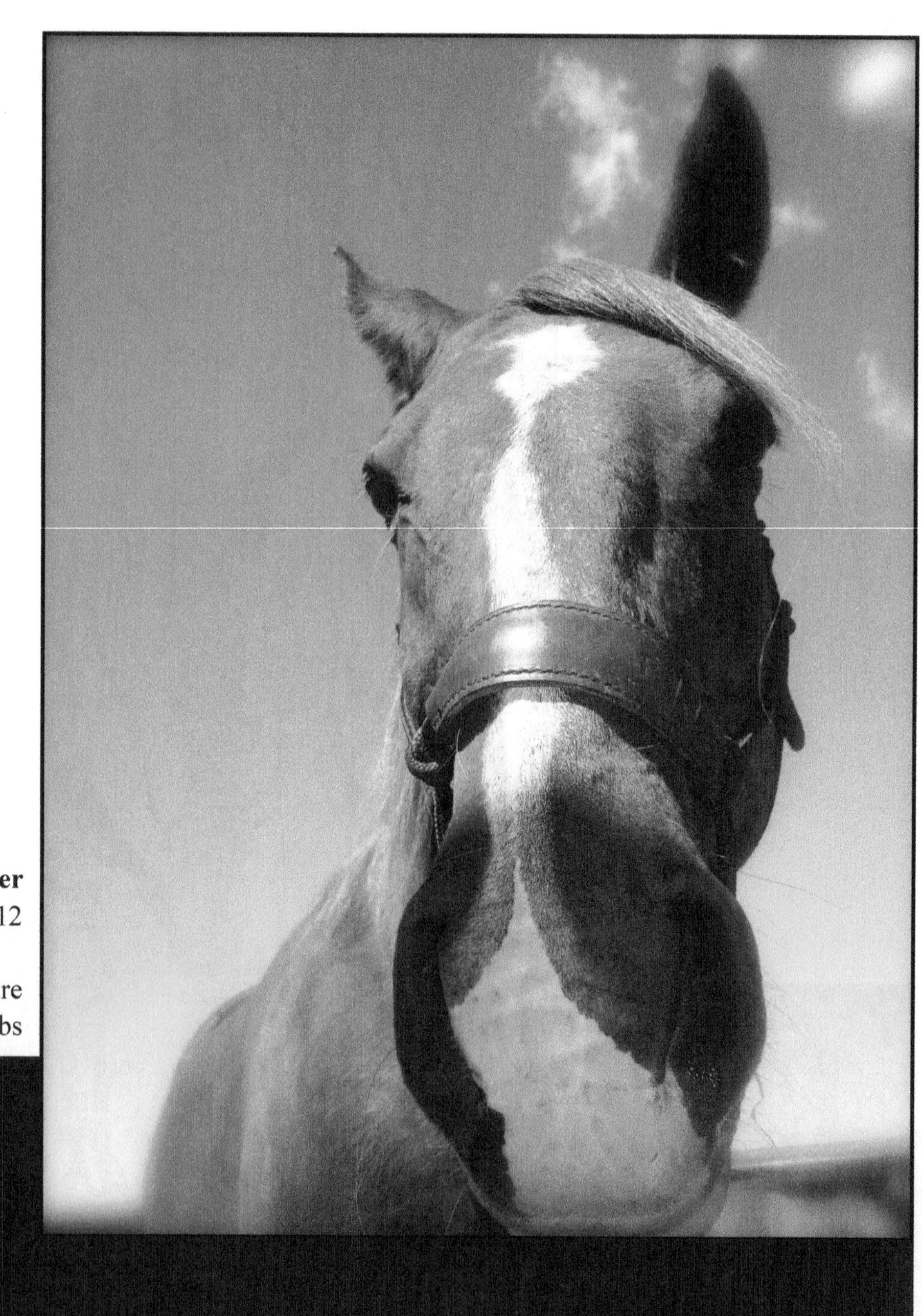

Wisdom Keeper
April 26, 2012

Pet portraiture

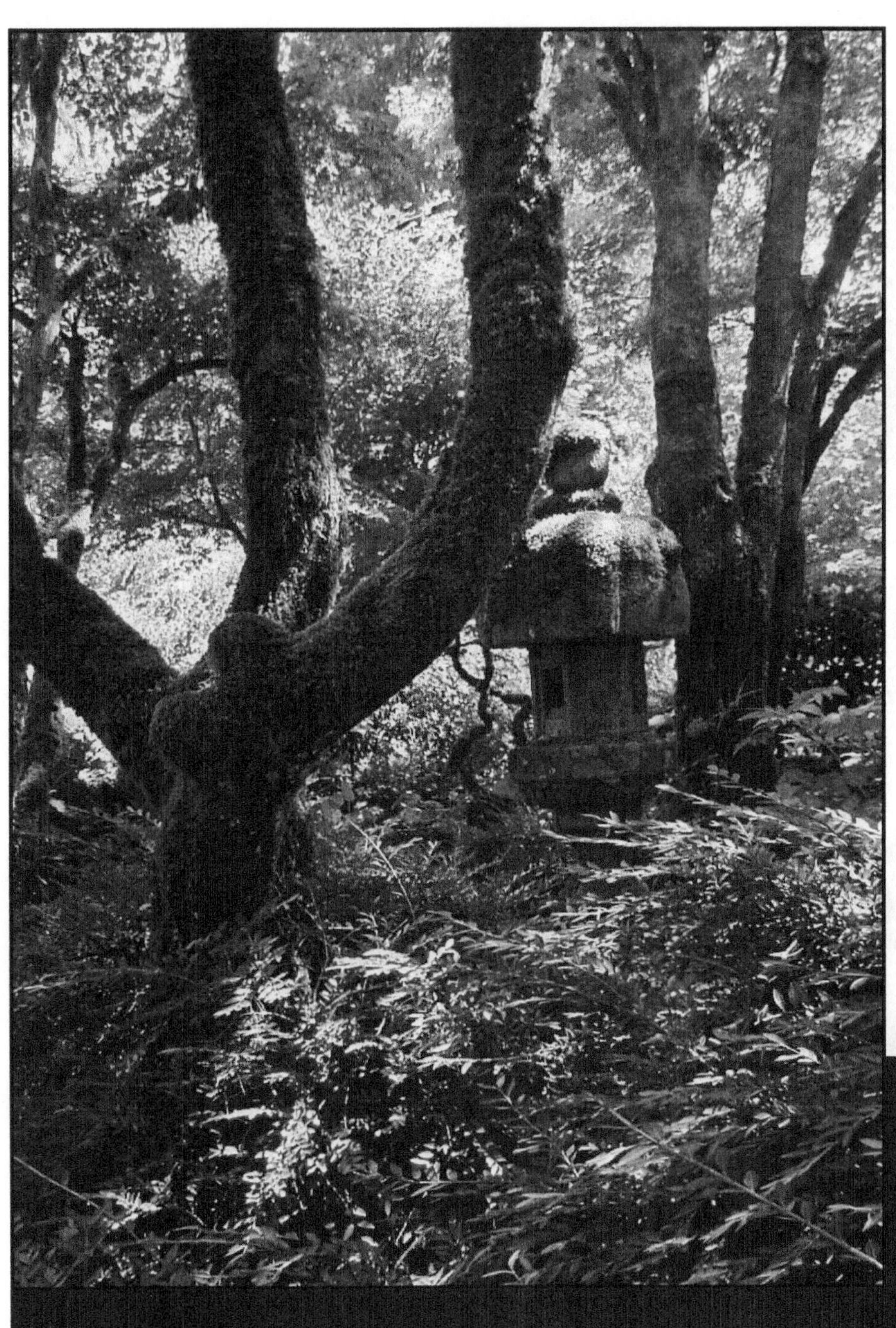

Prepare for Tomorrow
April 27, 2012

Nature photography
© Sherri Phibbs

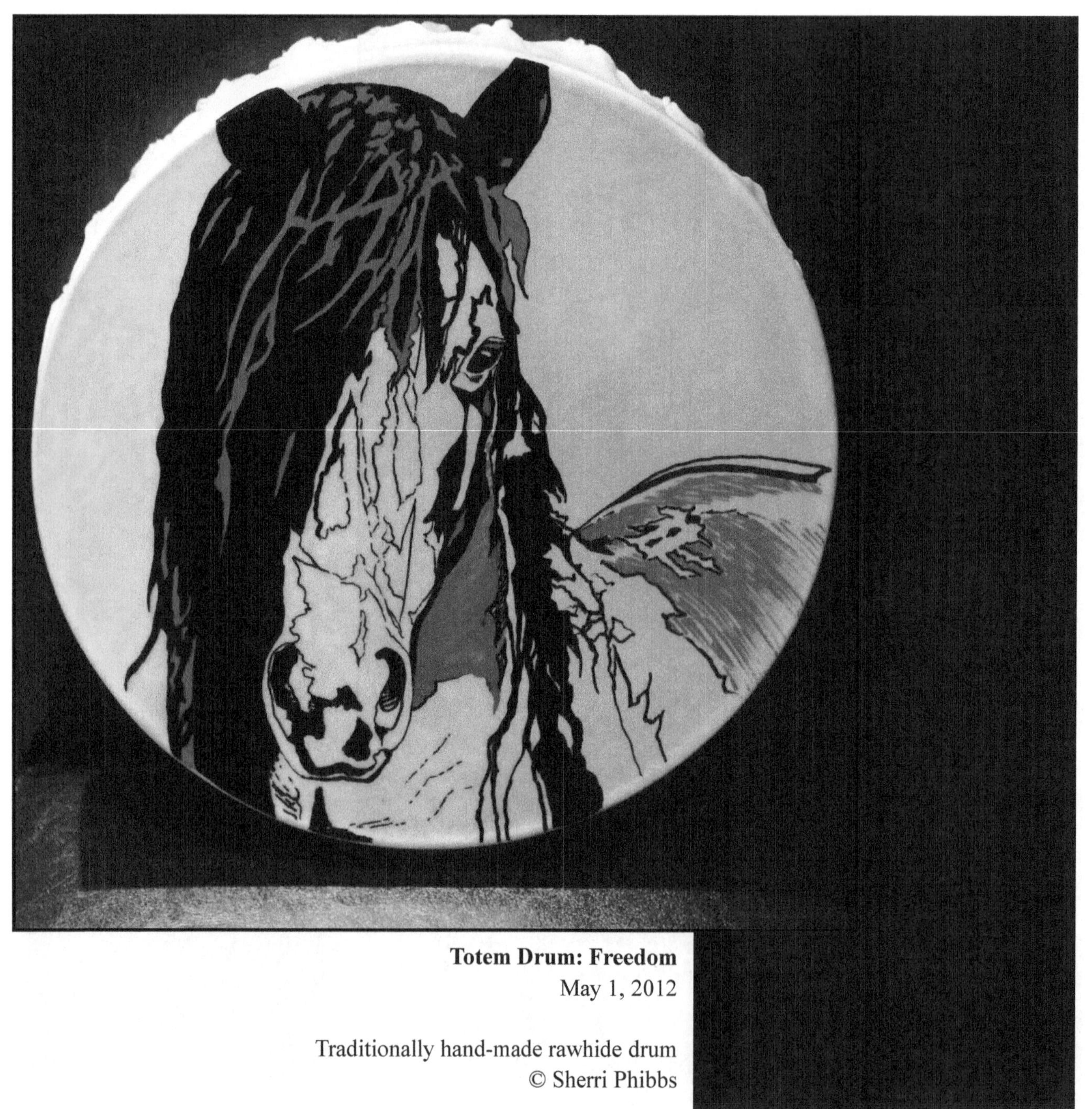

Totem Drum: Freedom
May 1, 2012

Traditionally hand-made rawhide drum

Called Away
May 2, 2012

Still life photography
© Sherri Phibbs

Coquette
April 28, 2012

Nature photography

Quick Sketch
April 29, 2012

Chalk pastel
© Sherri Phibbs

Follow Thru
April 30, 2012

Chalk pastel
© Sherri Phibbs

At Rest
May 3, 2012

Photography

Blue Sunlight
May 4, 2012

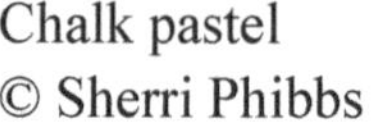

Chalk pastel

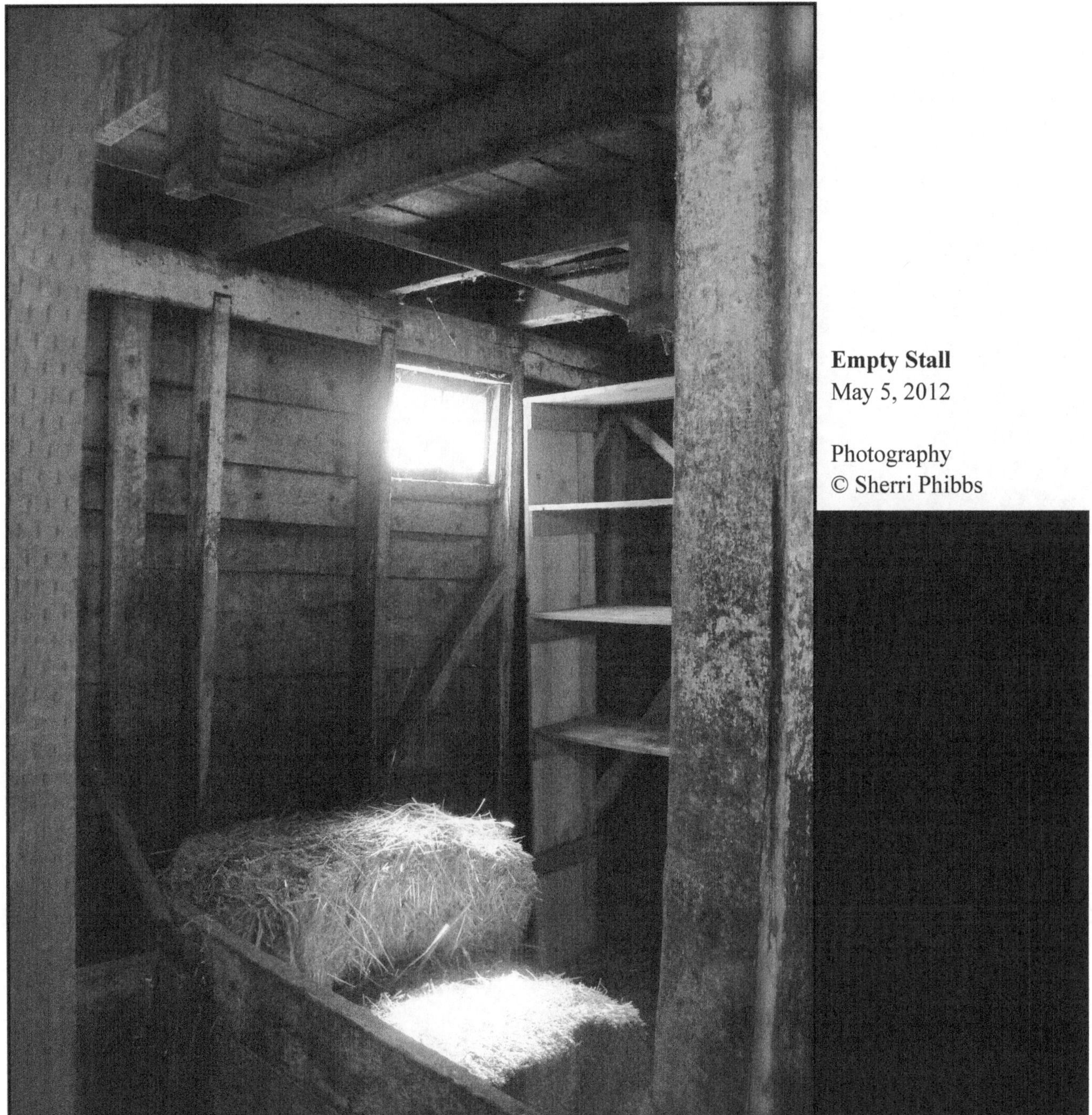

Empty Stall
May 5, 2012

Photography
© Sherri Phibbs

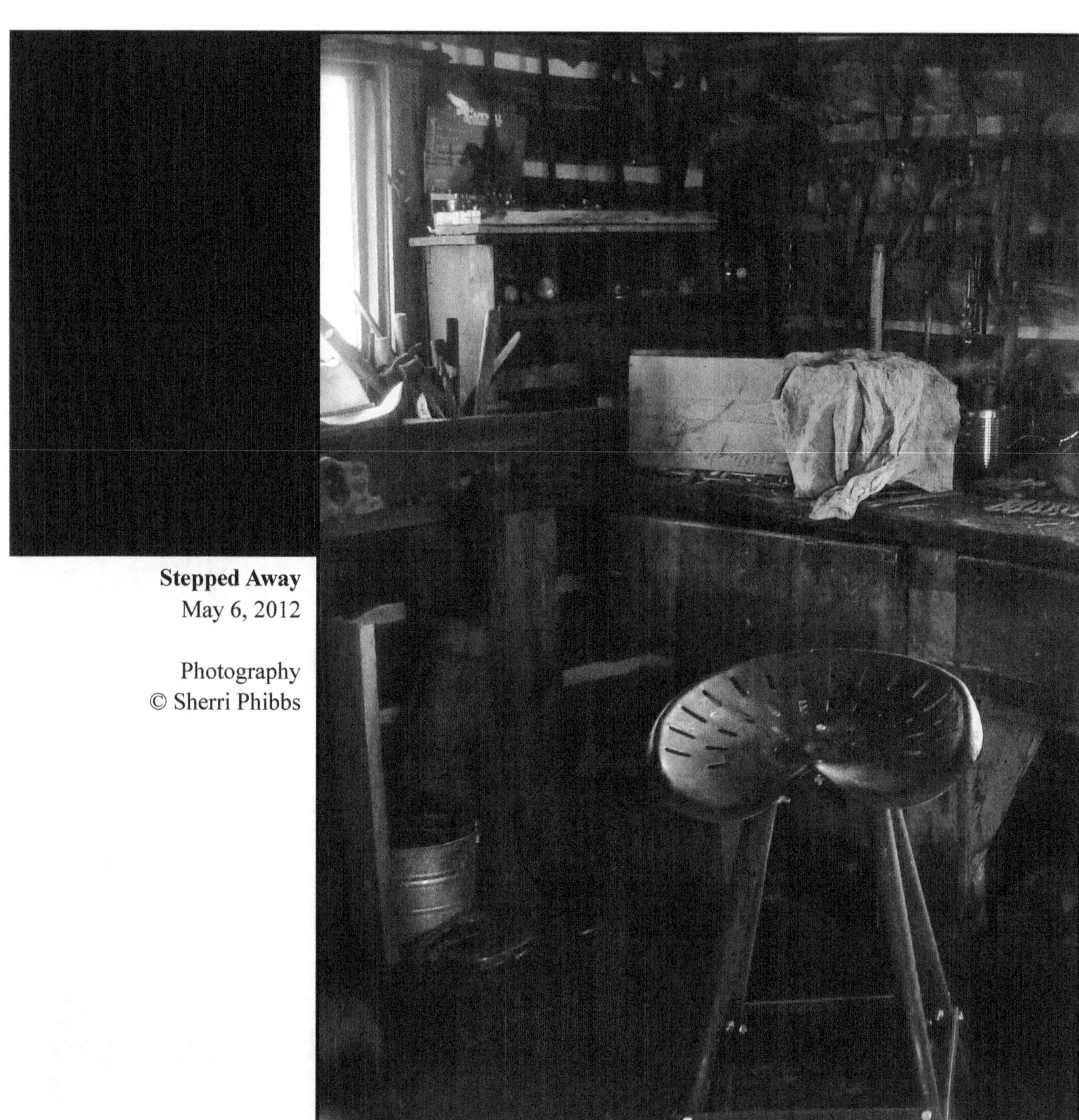

Stepped Away
May 6, 2012

Photography

Off Road
May 7, 2012

Watercolour

Moose Tuft
May 8, 2012

Photographic collage
© Sherri Phibbs

Feminine Beauty
May 9, 2012

Conté
© Sherri Phibbs

A Light unto My Path
May 10, 2012

Still life photography
© Sherri Phibbs

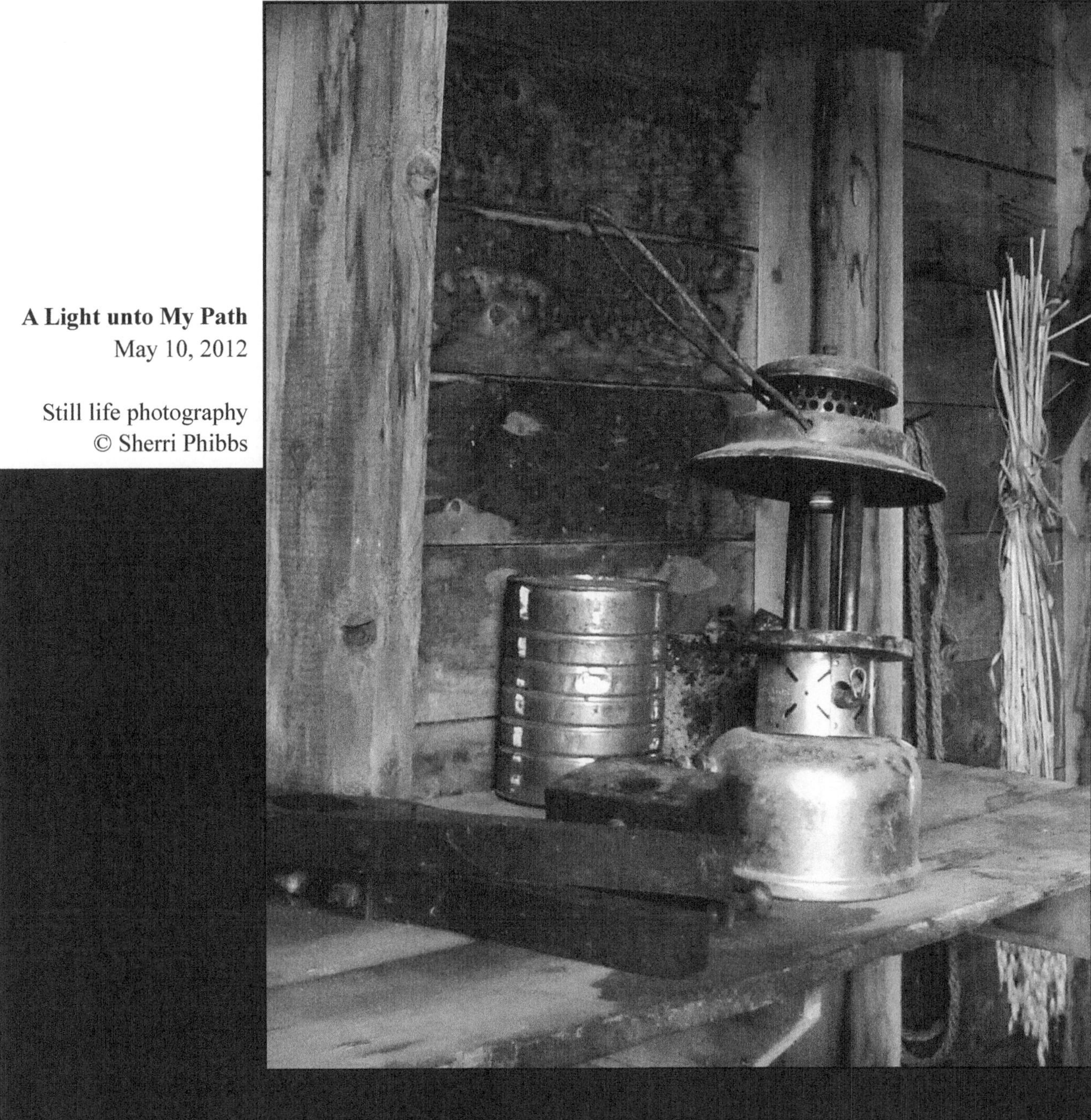

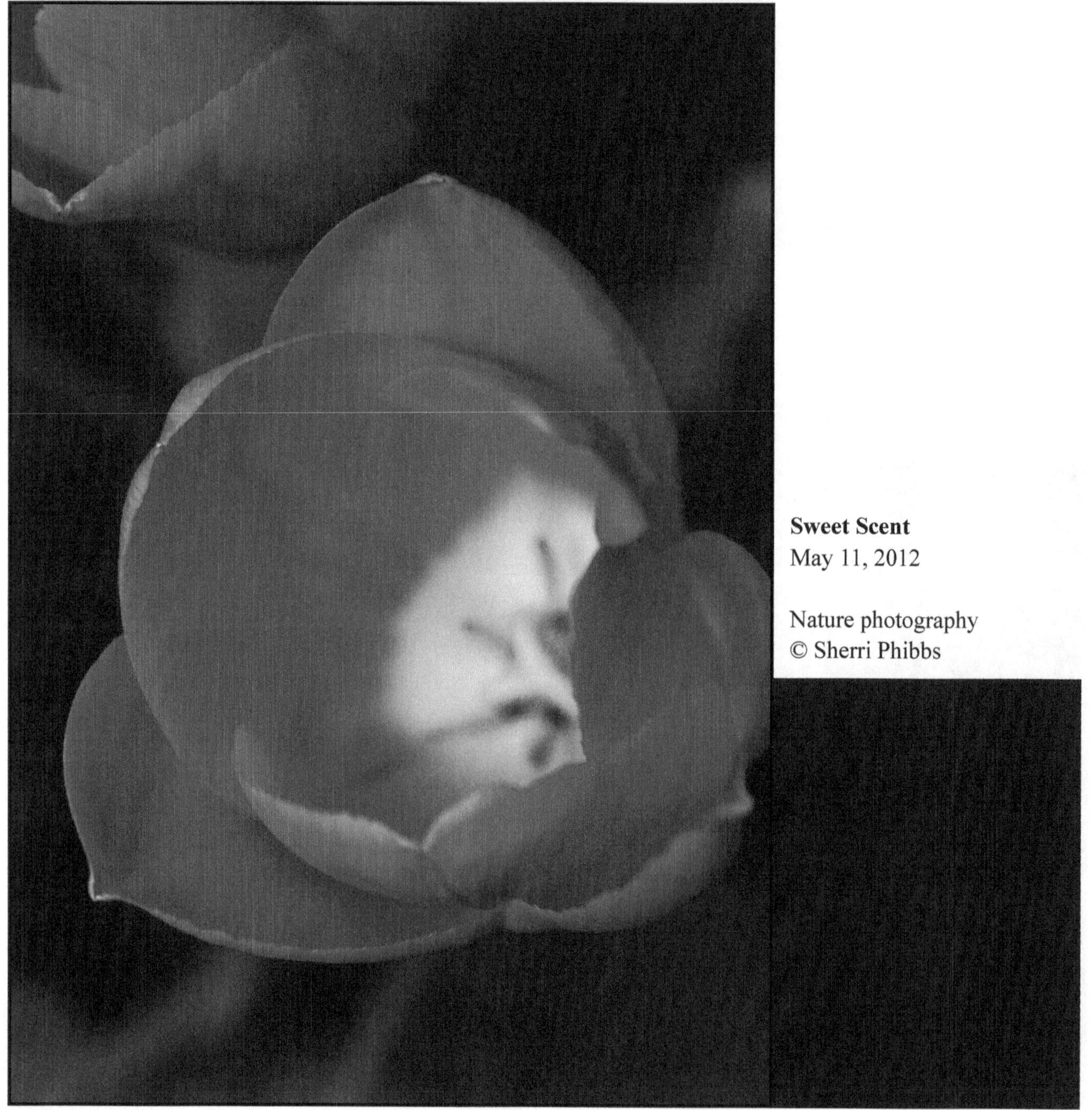

Sweet Scent
May 11, 2012

Nature photography

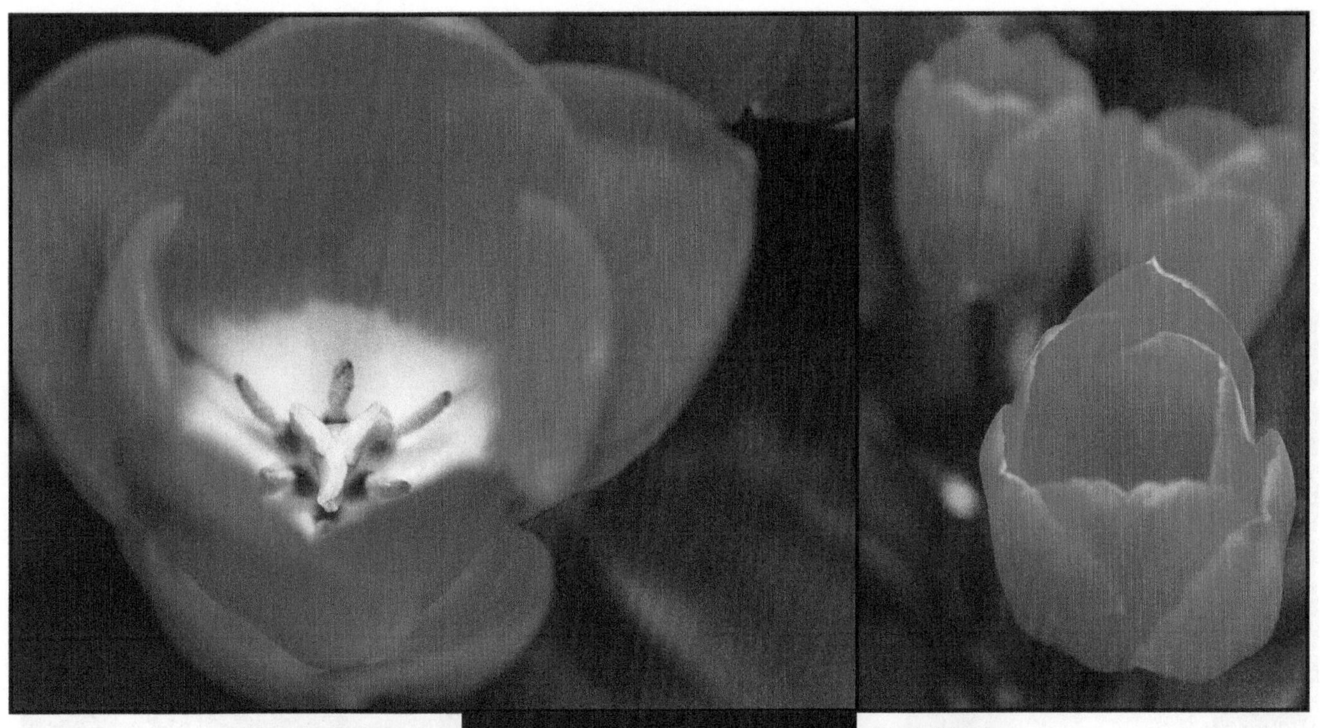

The Sensual Tulip
May 12, 2012

Nature photography
© Sherri Phibbs

The Blush
May 13, 2012

Nature photography
© Sherri Phibbs

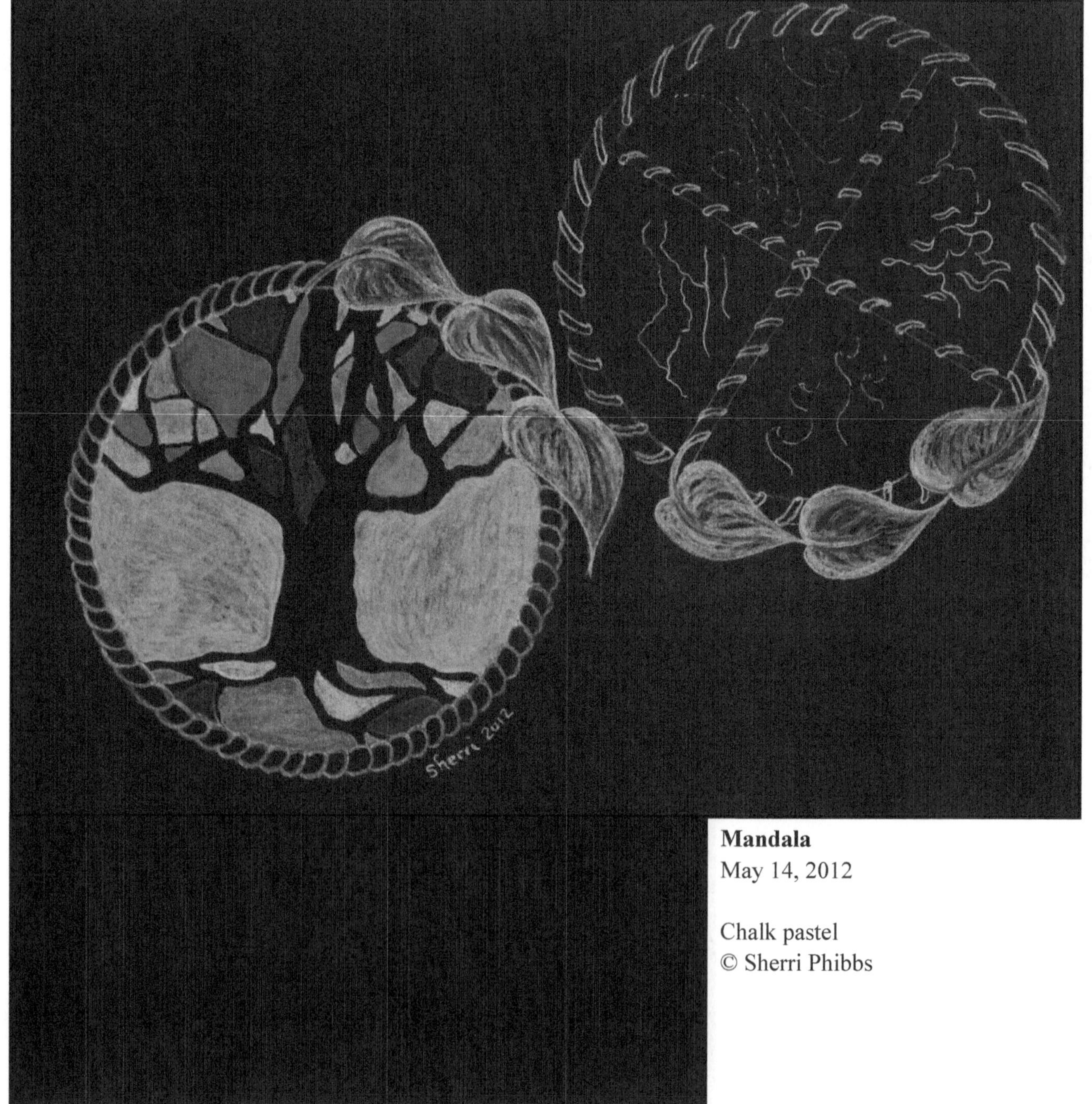

Mandala
May 14, 2012

Chalk pastel

ROOT AND BRANCH REFORM: relating to the natural world and the impact of human activity on its condition

Root and Branch Reform
May 15, 2012

Digital collage
© Sherri Phibbs

Root and Branch Reform II
May 16, 2012

Digital collage

ROOT AND BRANCH REFORM: relating to the nature of the problem

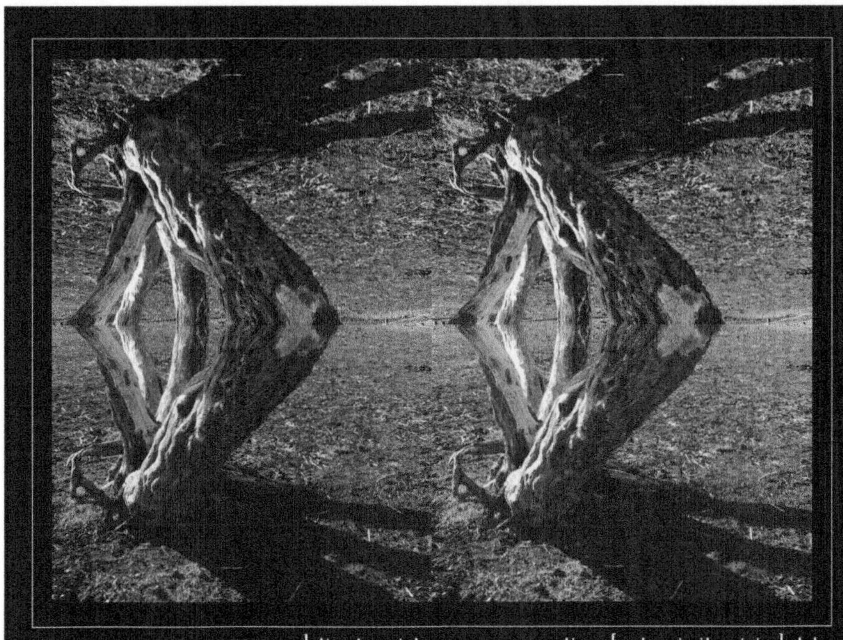

ROOT AND BRANCH REFORM: relating to maintenance or preservation of nature in its original state

Root and Branch Reform III
May 17, 2012

Digital collage
© Sherri Phibbs

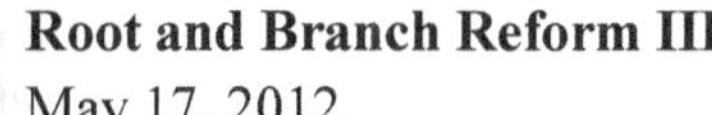

In Pieces (A self portrait)
May 18, 2012

Digital collage
© Sherri Phibbs

Soul Retrieval (A self portrait)
May 19, 2012

Digital collage
© Sherri Phibbs

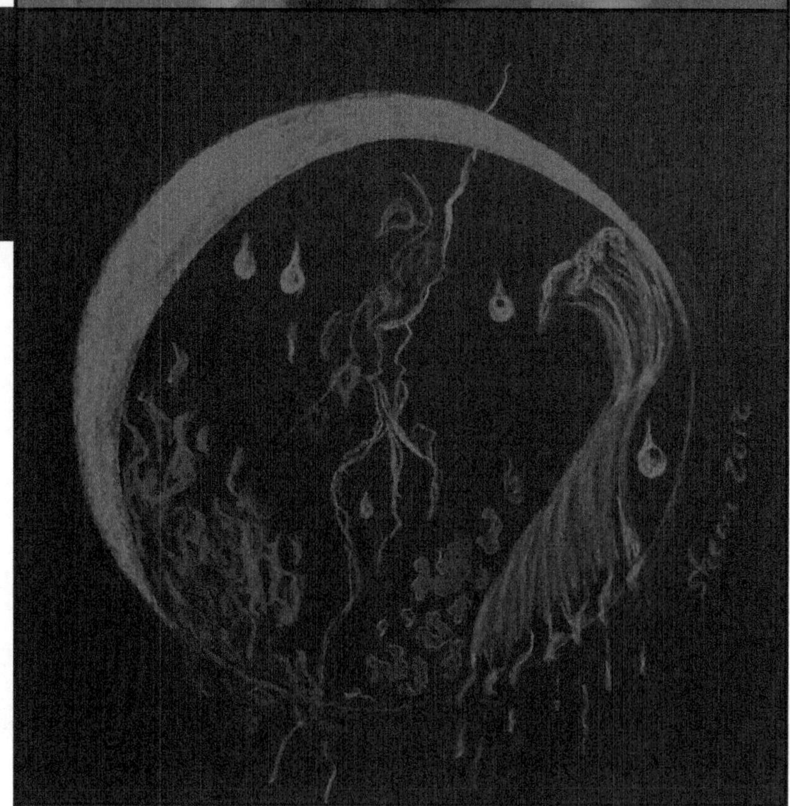

Meditative Mandala
May 20, 2012

Chalk pastel
© Sherri Phibbs

Twisted
May 21, 2012

Nature photography

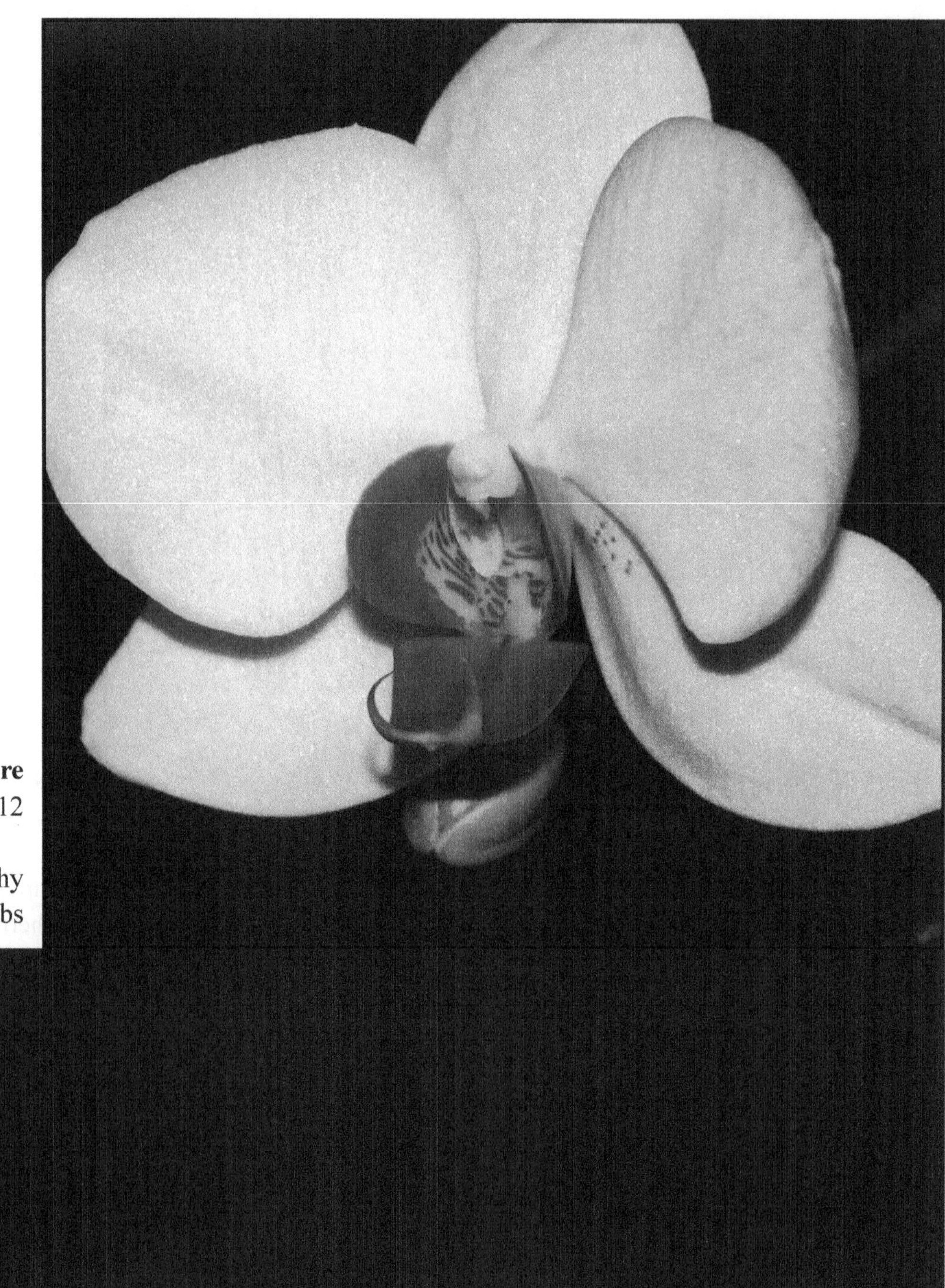

Joie De Vivre
May 22, 2012

Nature photography

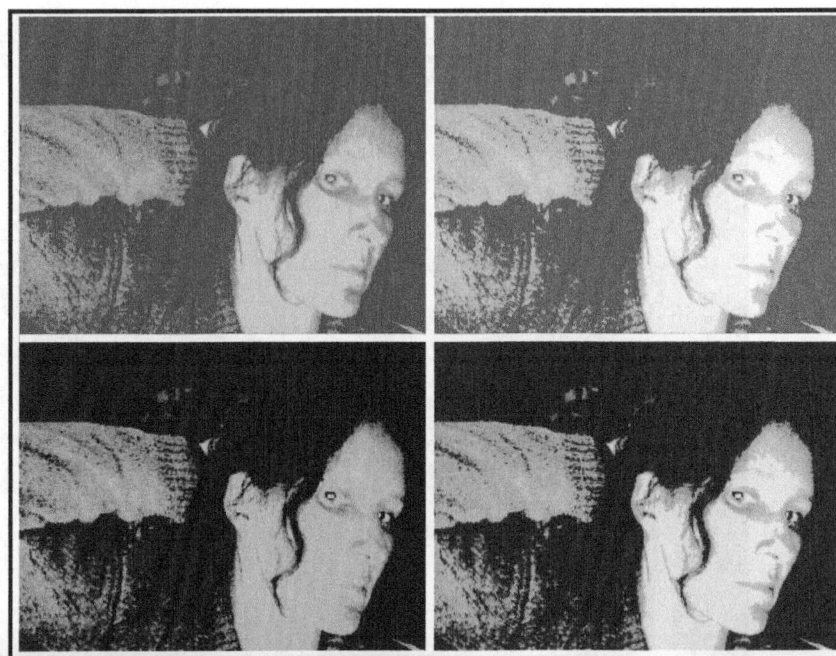

Exposure (A self portrait)
May 23, 2012

Digital collage
© Sherri Phibbs

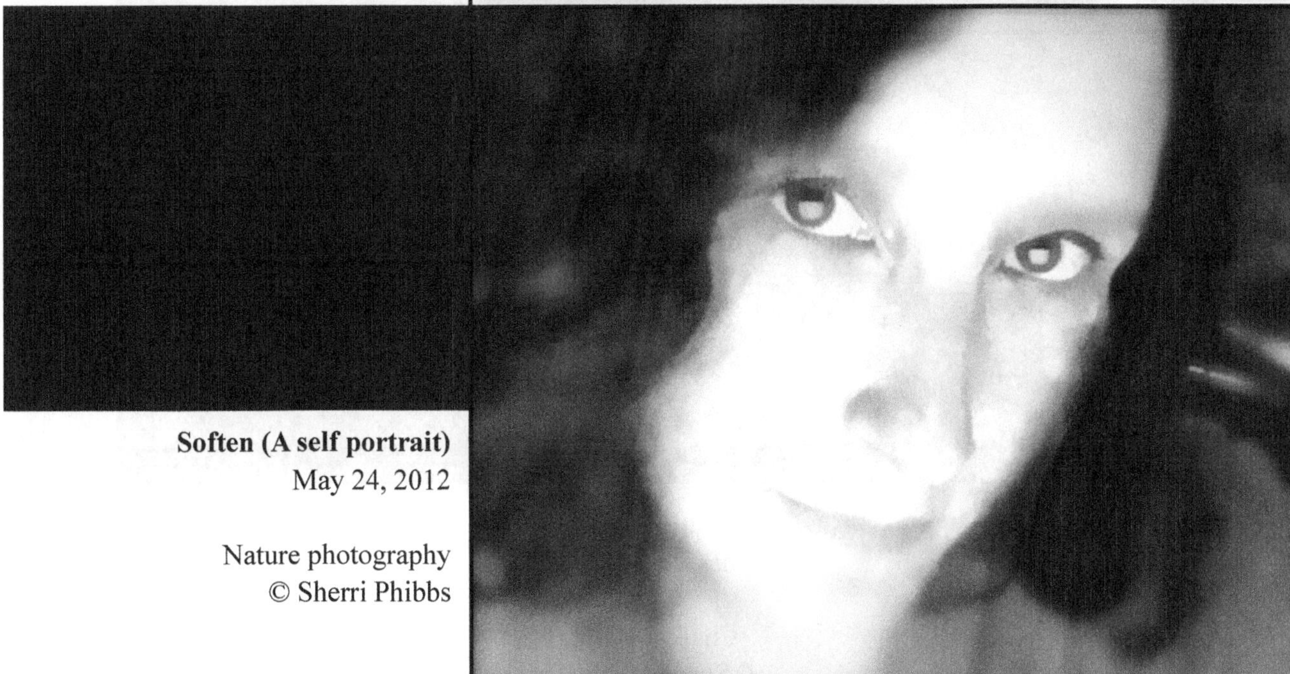

Soften (A self portrait)
May 24, 2012

Nature photography
© Sherri Phibbs

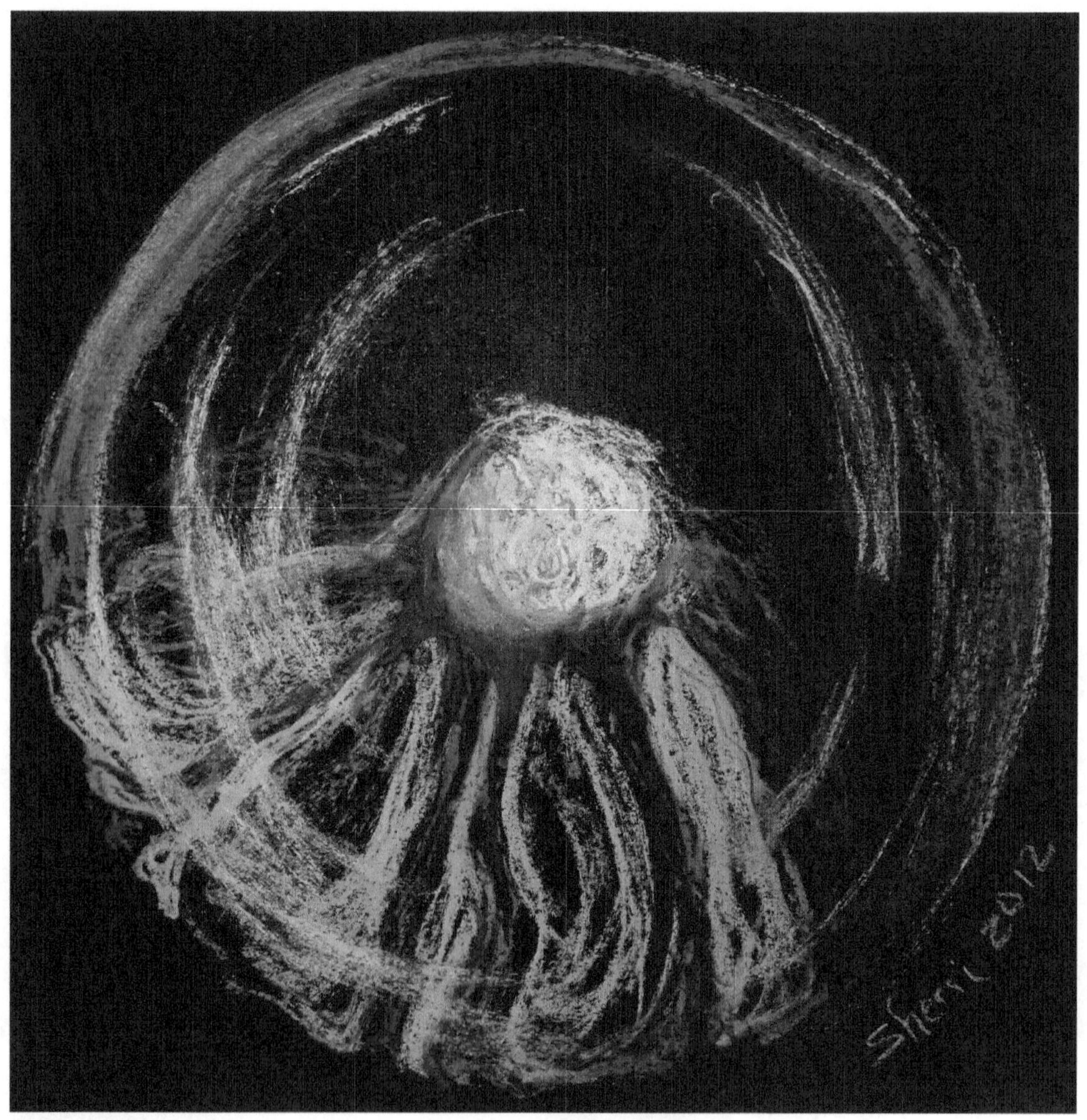

Echinacea
May 25, 2012

Chalk pastel

Cascade
May 26, 2012

Nature photography
© Sherri Phibbs

Something
May 27, 2012

Nature photography
© Sherri Phibbs

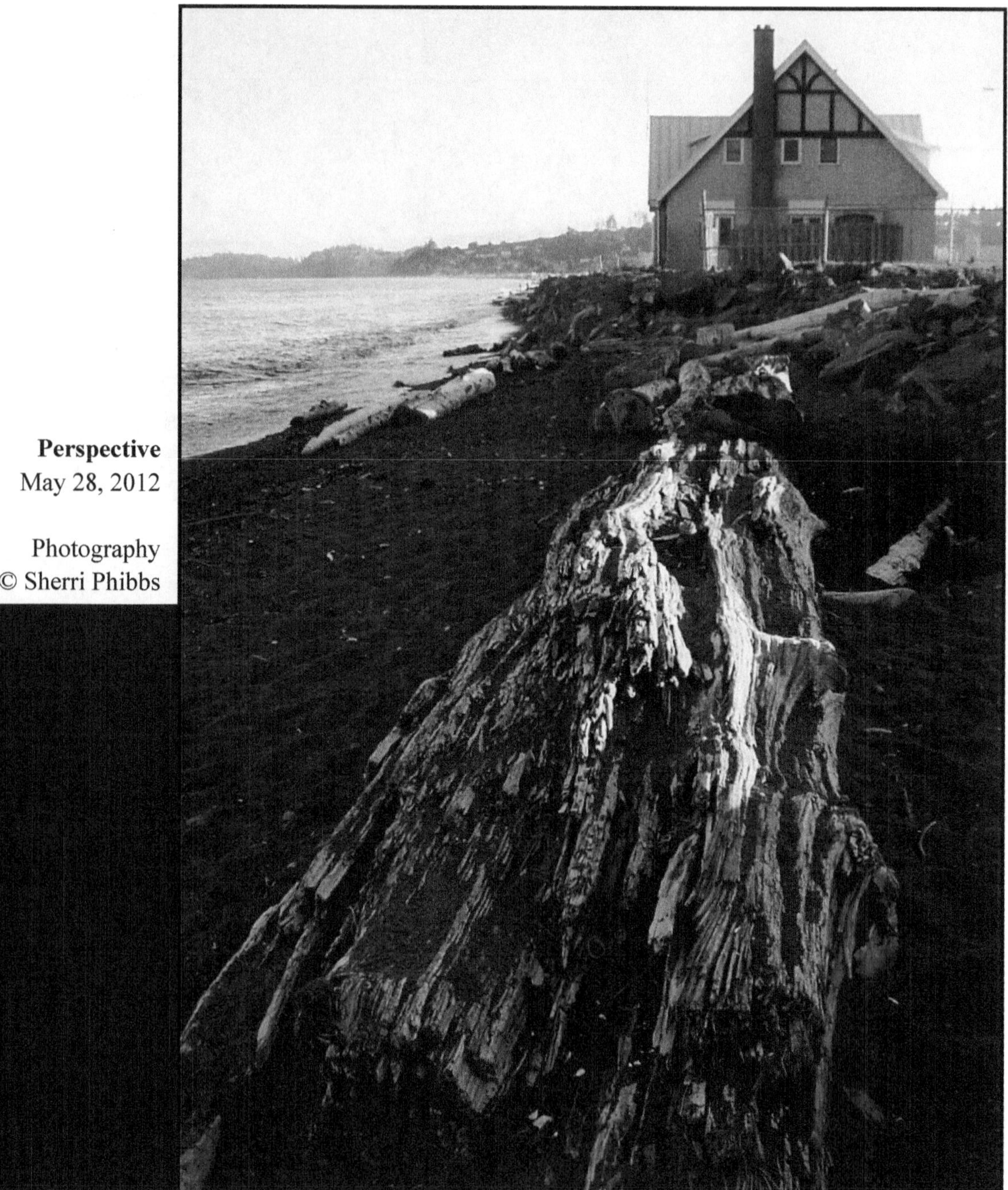

Perspective
May 28, 2012

Photography
© Sherri Phibbs

Emotional Overload
May 29, 2012

Nature photography
© Sherri Phibbs

Changes
May 30, 2012

Chalk pastel
© Sherri Phibbs

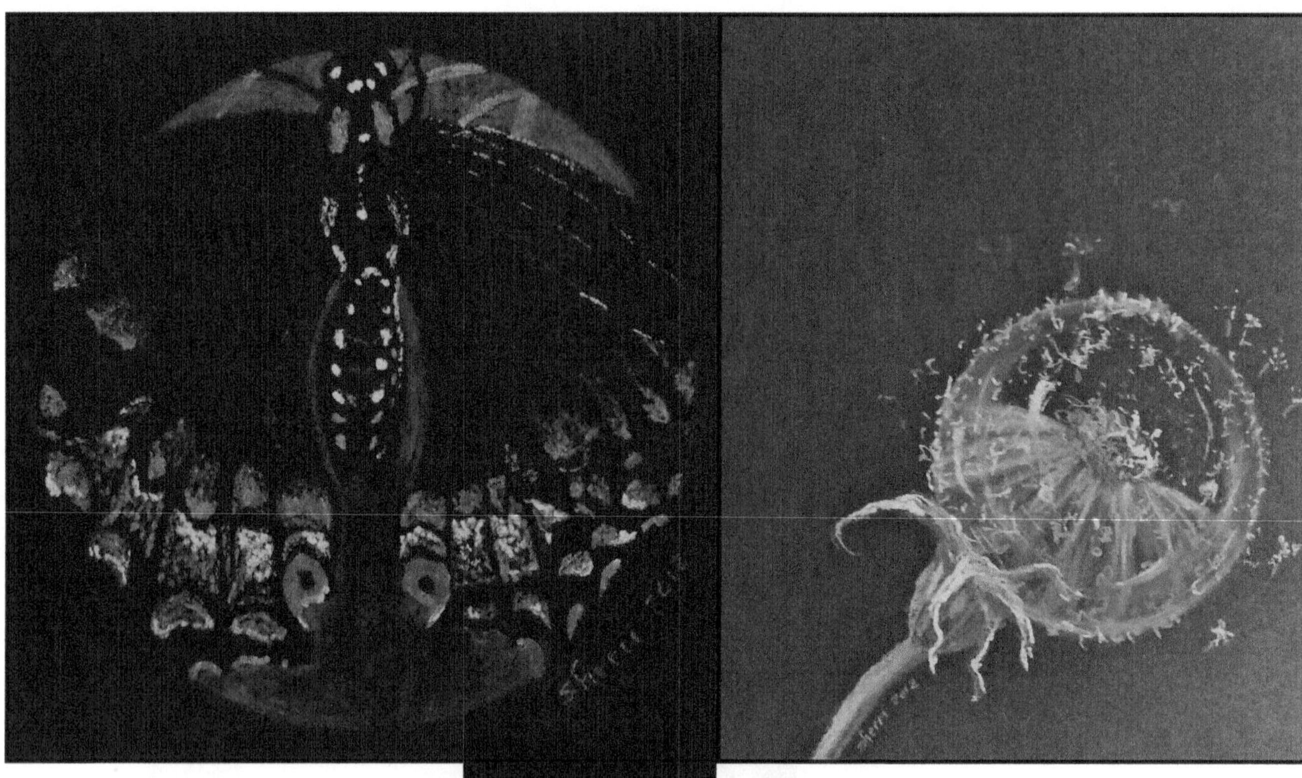

Transformative Mandala
May 31, 2012

Chalk pastel
© Sherri Phibbs

Wild Floral
June 1, 2012

Chalk pastel
© Sherri Phibbs

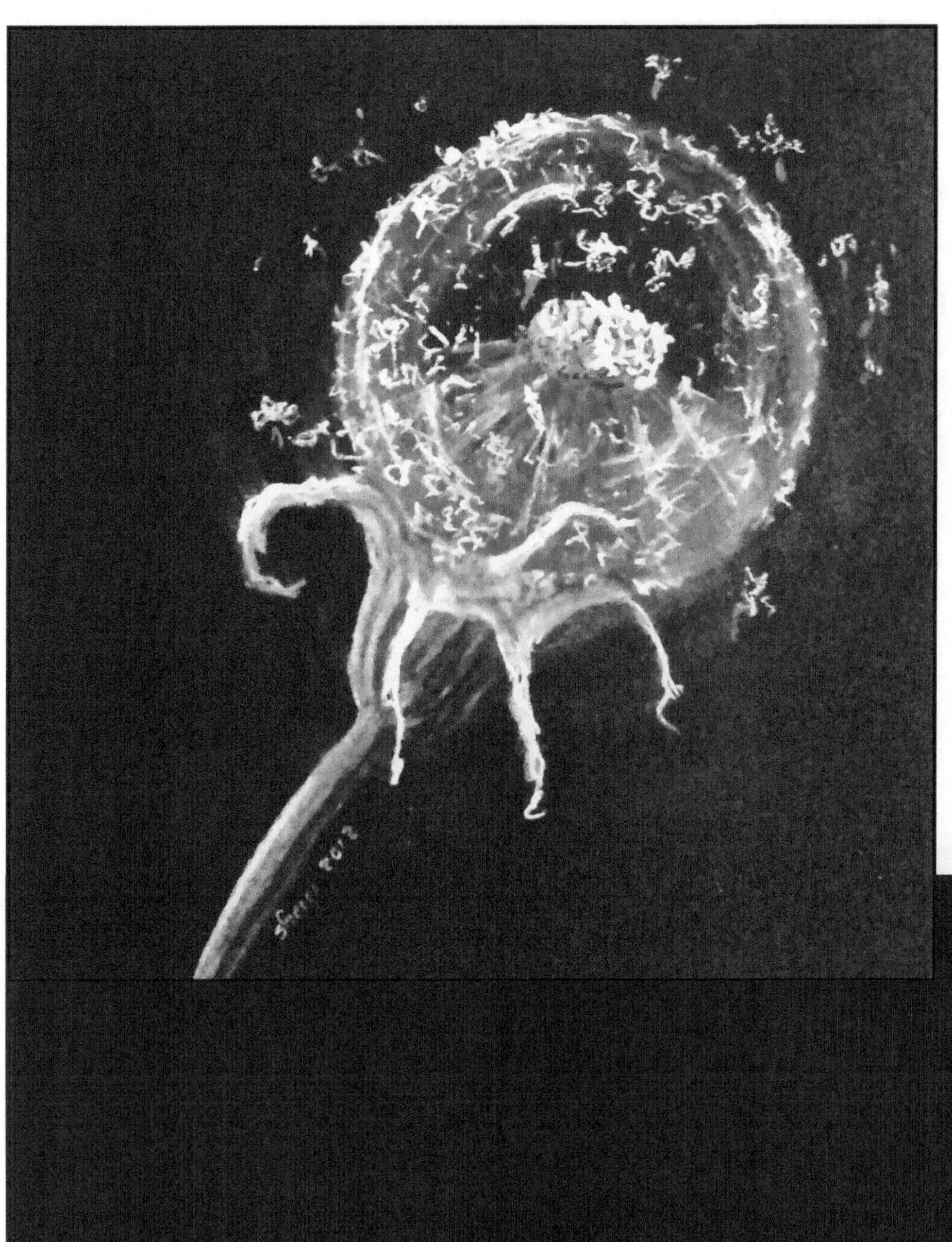

Tiny Wildness
June 2, 2012

Chalk pastel

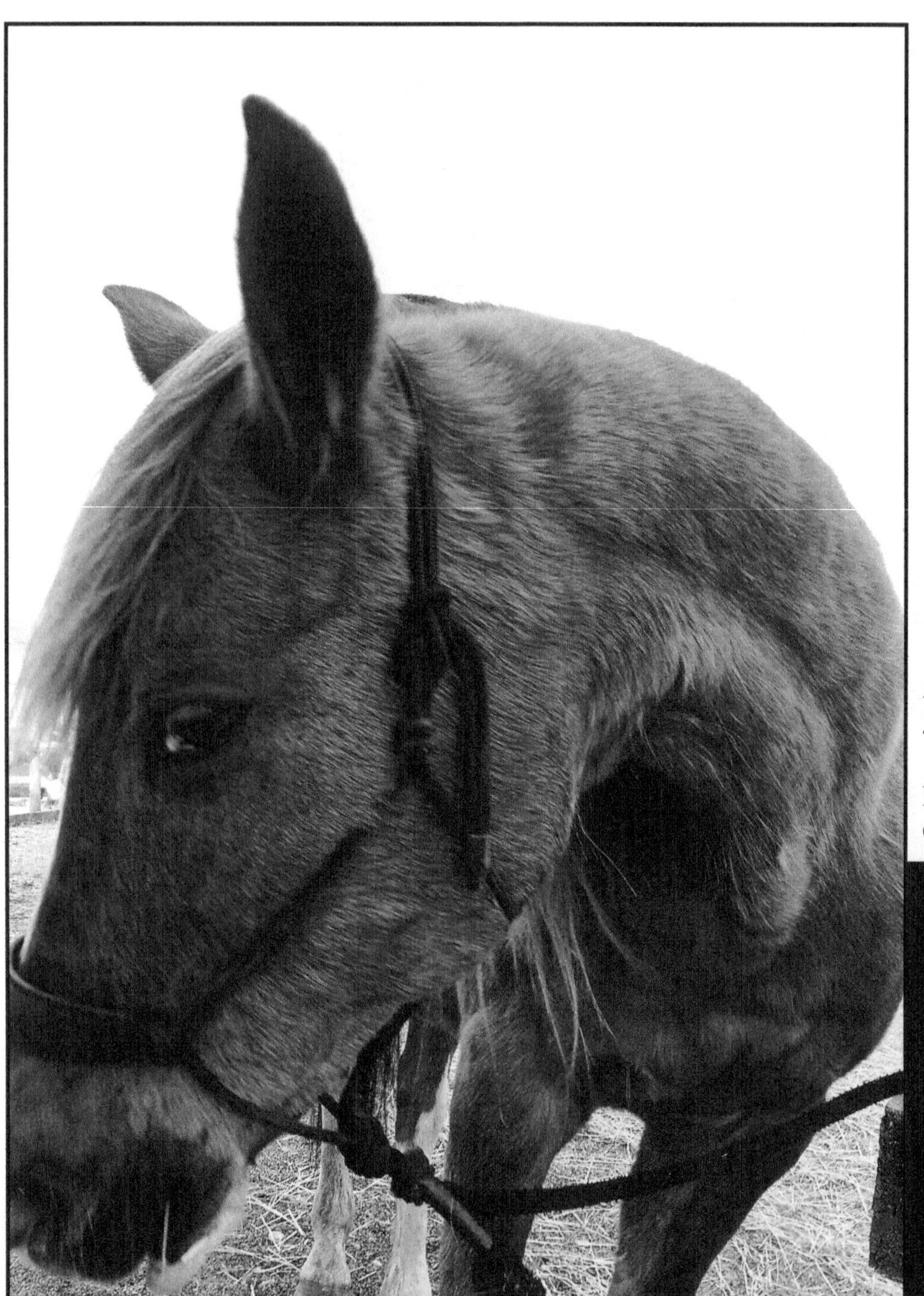

Arch-softness
June 3, 2012

Pet portraiture

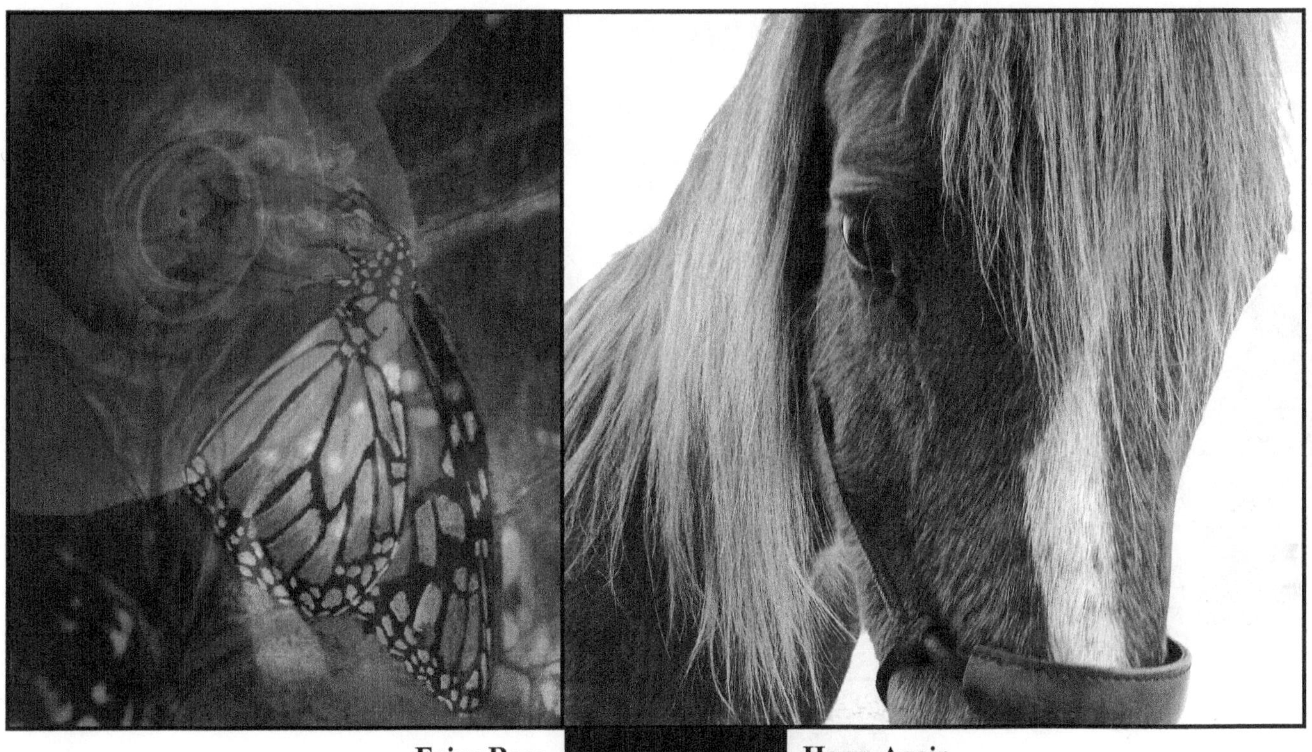

Fairy Rose
June 9, 2012

Digital collage
© Sherri Phibbs

Home Again
June 4, 2012

Pet portraiture
© Sherri Phibbs

A Painting Prelim
June 5, 2012

Nature photography

A Painting Prelim II
June 6, 2012

Nature photography

Living Colour
June 7, 2012

Nature photography
© Sherri Phibbs

Fascination with Roses
June 8, 2012

Nature photography
© Sherri Phibbs

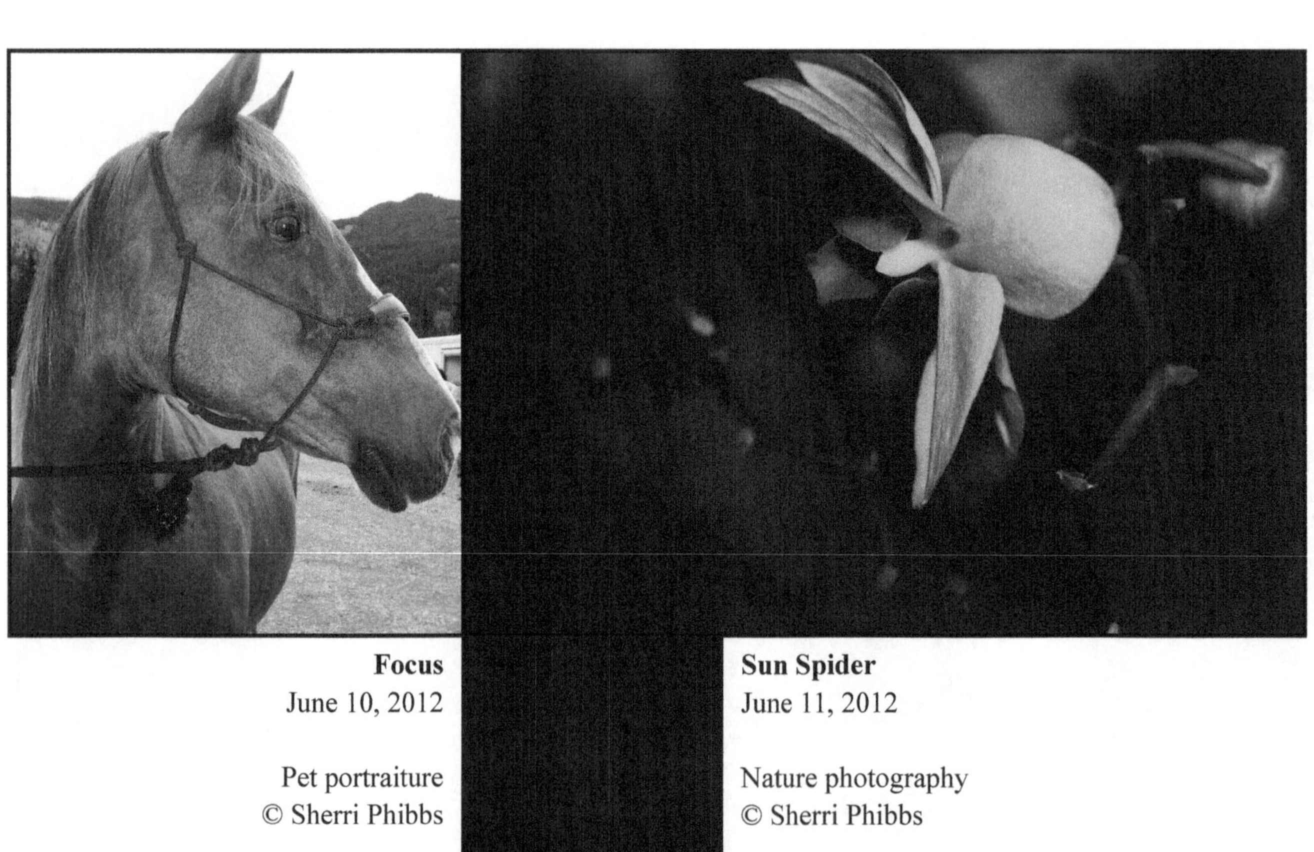

Focus
June 10, 2012

Pet portraiture
© Sherri Phibbs

Sun Spider
June 11, 2012

Nature photography
© Sherri Phibbs

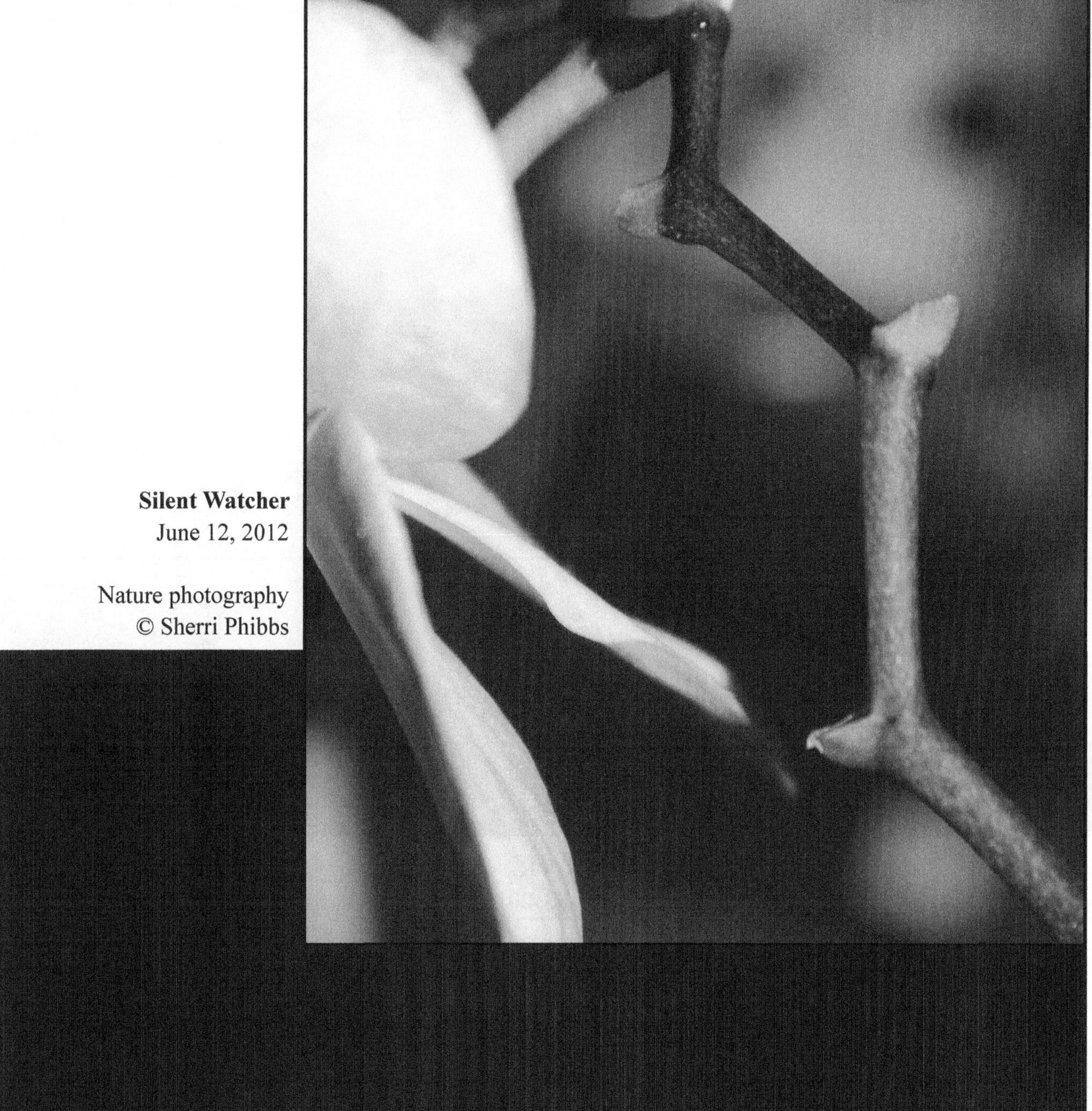

Silent Watcher
June 12, 2012

Nature photography
© Sherri Phibbs

R N R
June 13, 2012

Pet portraiture

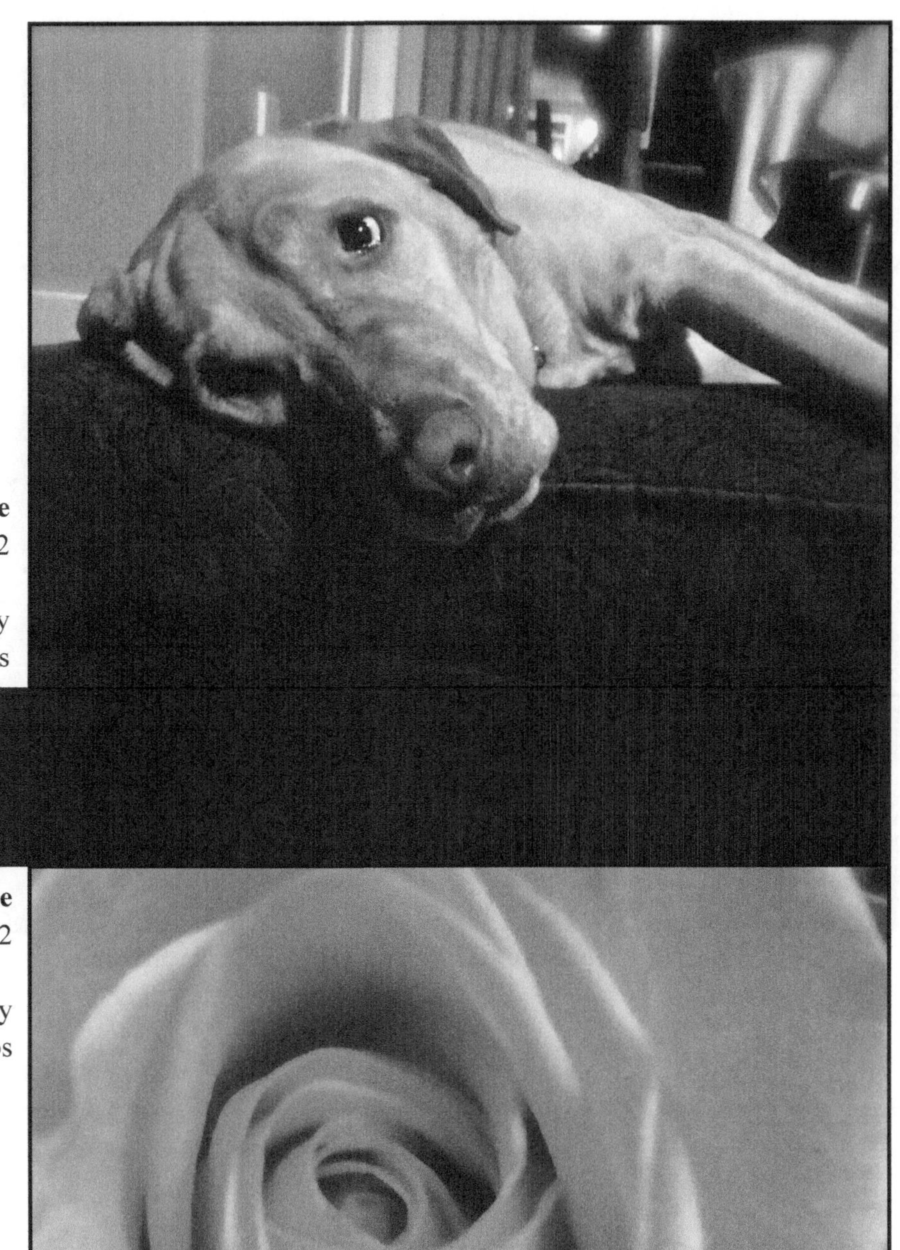

So Tired Only the Eyes Move
June 14, 2012

Pet photography
© Sherri Phibbs

Summer Solstice
June 15, 2012

Nature photography
© Sherri Phibbs

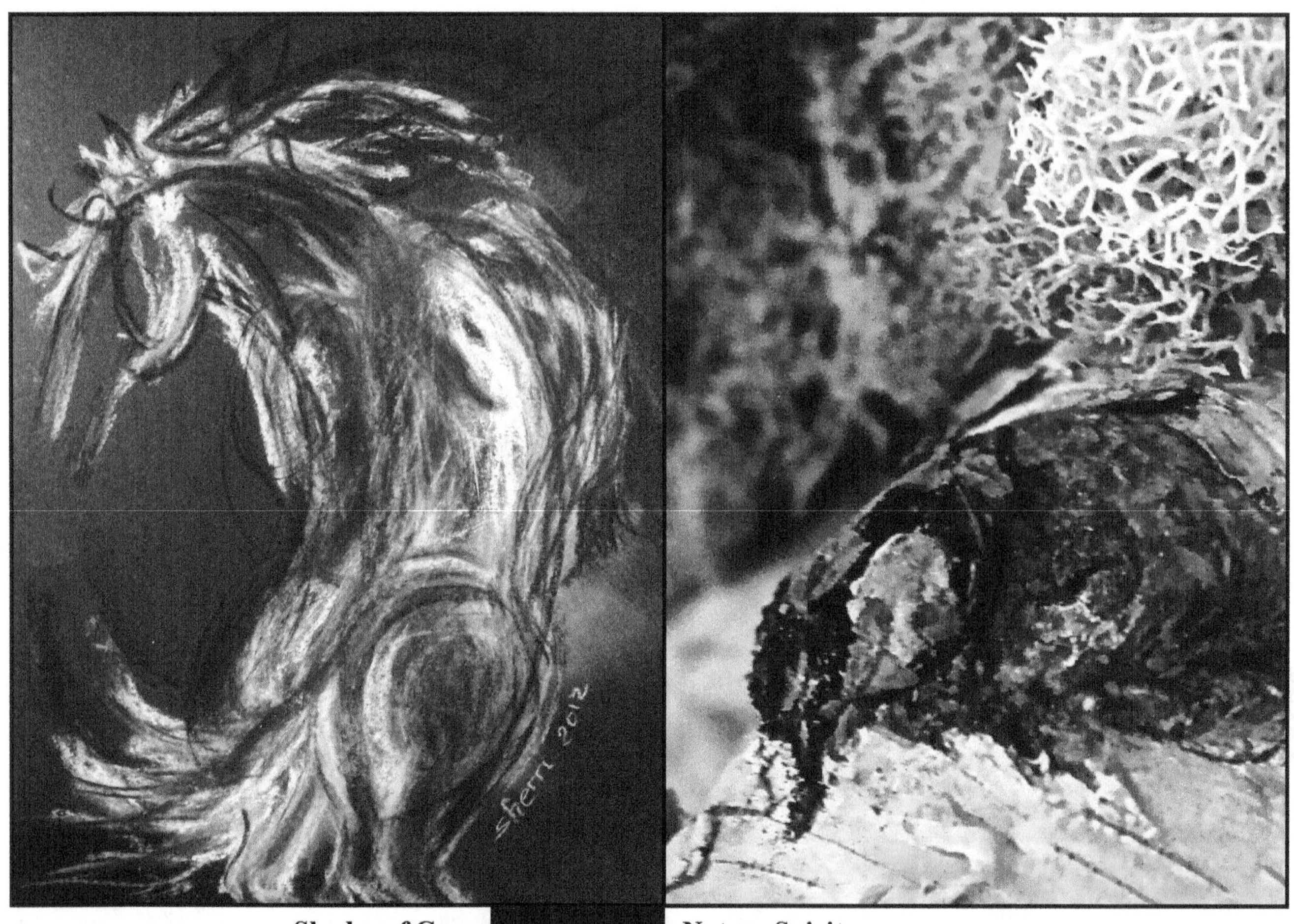

Shades of Grey
June 16, 2012

Charcoal
© Sherri Phibbs

Nature Spirit
June 17, 2012

Nature photography
© Sherri Phibbs

FIRE: The Written Words

Creative Integrity, Bit by Bit

March 26, 2012

A strong pull toward traditional carving led me to this sketch. Strange that I should be drawn to this rather than something more peaceful, as today I was in the presence of a woman with an angelic voice who was singing and playing a cello in the grand and formal St. Mary's Cathedral. During the hour of silence as I listened to her play, I prayed and meditated in my own fashion, with whispers of healing from the inside out and making a consistent daily habit of communing with nature and the divine swirling through my consciousness. (My apologies to the Catholic Church, as I do not know your rituals) It was a startling experience that led me to an exploration of a St. Sebastian, and a day filled with moments of quiet reflection. But it was not conducive to axes. One interesting sentence that flowed through the meditation: You must heal from the inside out as you have much to do. Again, I'm unsure how the ax fits in with this. More reflection necessary, I am guessing!

March 27, 2012

What a strange day. As I've set about the doings of my day, I noticed what seemed to be a heightened sense of agitation; a hyper-sensitivity. The force of my energy even intruded on the grooming time with my horse as he skittered sideways, looking at me wide eyed. He helped me to refocus; I apologized and continued with the brushing, intent on just being and feeling the experience. This realignment with the daily expression of care and love that usually accompanies grooming helped him settle. As I became more mindful, present and centred, his response was my reward, a peaceful, joyful interaction between species. Have you ever noticed that when you are changing to a new way of doing things you feel out of balance for awhile? As though something is just off? That's the adjustment period between the old and the new, the time to persevere. And so, on to the daily artwork! It's time to return to my nemesis, the orchid.

March 28, 2012

If there is a time and place for everything, today was comparable to a confluence of many rivers surging in powerfully and all neatly wrapped up in a bow at the end of this very long day. With great love, I celebrate this day.

March 29, 2012

You know, I thought when I hired a wedding planner that they would, you know, do stuff. Apparently, they make lists of stuff … for *you* to do. Almost every waking moment of my day has been filled with invitation wording, etiquette, seating plans, decor, and believe me, the list goes on. So, I have made a vow to carve as much enjoyment from this process as I possibly can. The formality and solemnity of the occasion will not defeat me. I will not be mired in tradition to the point of suffocation. There will be freedom of expression, there will be creativity, and, OMG … There will be FUN! There, I said it: the F word. With great love and determination, I celebrate this day.

March 30, 2012

Some days, you just hit the ground running until you find that moment, place, or person where everything comes together, and you are at peace within and in harmony without. It's a touchstone of sorts. My touchstone moment came late in the day, but I realize what a blessing is to be had by acknowledging and feeling this peace. All that came before, and all that might still be, are powerless against the joy in that moment. The mindfulness and awareness required to appreciate it are also gifts, gifts each one of us has, and like muscles, can exercise at will. Be the present. When you are, you are a gift to the world. With great love and determination, I celebrate this day.

March 31, 2012

Today I am exhausted. I am drifting off to sleep as I type. So please, forgive my meagre efforts at blogging this evening. I am hopeful that the drum offering of tomorrow will make up for tonight. Wishing you harmony, both within and without.

April 1, 2012

Illustrating a drum as incredibly detailed and complex as this one is probably the epitome of my drum making career. The rich colour and development of the design is an amazing expression of the backside of a natural, unpainted drum. April Fools! I'm celebrating Life.

April 2, 2012

I'm finishing up a last bit of "Peace Ambassador" homework, and I am ready for creativity! Ummm, okay, so where did I put the inspiration? Did I mention I've been working on wedding planning? The invitations are just about complete. I'm only missing the hotel information for out of town guests. That's on tomorrows list. The prototype of the centrepiece is almost complete, so I can show it to the wedding planner. I need some crystals and flower choices for centrepieces, and then I'll be ready to build them. Funny how things I hoped would be completed aren't. It's also interesting to try and sell a house while planning and making wedding decorations. There is a certain messiness that just bursts out of the one process and conflicts with the show home look required for the other. Honestly, do I seem a little distracted to you? No, really? Focus, it's a lovely little quality that is part of exercising the mindfulness muscle. Thank you, Neo (my horse), for acting as my "spotter" while I stretch my self-awareness. And, friends and readers, many thanks and much heartfelt gratitude for your comments, encouragement, and guidance, without which I would be lost. I am humbled by your enthusiasm and care. Great thanks, great peace, and great love, to you.

April 3, 2012

Awesome! Awesome! Awesome! How else can I describe the happenings of this day? The universe reached out, and the teacher was taught, not only the student. I am in awe, and stand humbly in gratitude. Blessed be. Great thanks, great peace, and great love right back at you.

April 4, 2012

There are times in life when lying down for a nap in the middle of the day really doesn't seem like such a bad idea. I know this seems like a no-brainer for a lot of people, but I have assiduously battled with the nap demon since the age of three, and so far have managed to win more often than not. However, that being said, I must admit I napped. I was nappy. Nap-i-licious, actually. The comforter, warm flannel and wool, tucked under my chin, created a delightful cocoon of my own making. Was there any transformation involved in the subsequent emergence from this chrysalis? Maybe not, but, you know, even if I am not a majestic monarch butterfly—instead more like a "dragon"fly today—I will hold the healing nature of sleep more dear for the very experience of it during the daylight hours.

April 5, 2012

Well here we are at a full moon in April, under a blanket of snow; and, I don't know about you, but I am appreciating every glistening moment of it! I spent some time playing ball with Ru, but the majority of the shots were a blur of golden motion. They are very pretty but a little unnerving, so I settled on this one because I love his eyes. That little orange ball, well, that was the sole purpose of his existence. It gives me some insight into the true meaning of mindfulness, completely centreed, and in the moment. The picture of intention!

April 6, 2012

… All the better to eat you with. I couldn't leave this one in the folder without sharing it. The lines in the fur, the stretch of the leg, and the feeling in the expression are very strong. It's a nice roadmap for the eye to follow as it works its way around the picture. This would be a great beginning for a painting. As a lot of my work has it's beginnings in photography, I love to keep reference photos on file, not only as a source of inspiration, but for determining compositions, textures, lighting and line. The strength of character in this photo is what drew my attention, so I'll hold this one close.

April 7, 2012

Egg-shaped creativity + time with family = memories and many blessings. Celebrating life.

April 8, 2012

Oh, am I sick! Uninvited, that flu going around has come home to roost at my place. Between the chills, the fever, and the rather insistent intestinal gurgles, I really have no thought for anything other than ginger ale and sleep, but I will attempt to do the colour touch-up on an egg photo from yesterday and provide an outline of a quaint family custom. I hope you enjoy it. Groan. Egg Wars: A tradition handed down for generations in my family. Every Easter we decorate eggs then have a contest to see who has the strongest egg. Two competitors, two eggs, one small tap pointy end to pointy end, and one small tap round end to round end. The egg that doesn't crack is the champion and takes on the next competitor. The winner is the uncracked egg that is still whole when all others have been vanquished. Hmmm, maybe we should petition for its inclusion as an Olympic sport?

April 9, 2012

There are so many ideas going through my head at the moment; it's amazing what rest will do for creativity! This concept of rest is one I've struggled with a great deal over the years. I'm still learning to listen when my body screams, "Enough already!" I've been repeatedly burned out, stressed out, and exhausted from lack of sleep to the point of collapse at various times in my life. What is so difficult about knowing my own limits and allowing myself the grace to say, "No"? What is this compulsion I have to work myself into the ground? Is it low self-worth? (The "I am never good enough as I am" loop?) Is it as simple as a drive to improve, to best my last best effort? Or do I feel like I have something to prove? (The "I am good enough, just look at this" track?) Does the cause really matter as I work to heal this pattern? Many great healers suggest that naming, forgiving, and releasing are the steps necessary to begin this process. If this is so, may I step forward on this healing path, confident that I am enough, that I will improve and grow, and that I am doing what I love, not to prove something but to be something—me. May my path and yours be lit with the light of love.

April 10, 2012

After a day of expending newly restocked energy, I find myself once more on the exhausted end of the scale. But I feel alright, and I am so grateful. Friends and family are awesome, both the two-legged and four-legged ones. Many blessings.

April 11, 2012

This bout of sickness has lifted up another layer of the onion that is my life. I am an extremely poor patient with an extremely low level of tolerance for boredom, staying still, taking it easy, drinking copious amounts of clear fluids, and eating semi-solids: all those things you are expected to endure in uncomplaining silence while convalescing. So maybe I push the envelope just a teensy tiny bit too far. Yesterday I decided that my symptoms were bearable, so I went to a physical therapy session, then out to the horses. By 6:00 pm I was sick, again, right through until about 1:00 pm today, when, yet again, I decided my symptoms were bearable; in fact, I even felt immensely better! I went out to the horses, then engaged in the evening's lecture for the Peace Ambassador's course I'm enrolled in. I was impressed. Just a little dizziness and some vague sense of dehydration, nothing I couldn't handle. Woohoo! Let's eat! Bad idea. I'm hopeful I've learned my lesson.

Positive thinking, visualizations, and acting with intention are wonderful healing agents if you allow your body time to catch up with the speed of your thoughts. There needs to be some processing time before action. At any rate, I am hopeful for tomorrow. However if I were a betting woman, I would not take any odds that I stay home in bed for the day. Given my past record, I'm sure I'll be fine by, say, 1:30 pm tomorrow afternoon. Just in time to head out, you guessed it, to the horses. They may do nothing for the flu, but they definitely heal my spirit. Why are my eyes starting to water and sting? Oh yes, did I mention rinsing your onion in warm water can alleviate those symptoms? I wonder if a steam shower would work? No, really?

April 12, 2012

Okay, so maybe I am starting to feel better, truly. I did go out to the horses today, in the biggest snowstorm this season. What wonderful snowflakes. I've never seen flakes that large. While trying to catch them on my tongue, I had to stifle the impulse to duck. Yesterday I had the opportunity to set up a still life for my photo shoot. I enjoyed the results and played awhile with the various shots. Today's offering is a favourite. The reflection of the onionskin on the knife surface caught my attention, and there is a catchy rhythm in the way the light and the dark play together through the piece. Just a little bit of fun. With gratitude.

April 13, 2012

Well. That's me. Well. The flu appears to be in retreat, and I'm actually feeling a little bit like drawing something. Let's see where that leads to... carving with colour. I'm loving this! Many blessings.

April 14, 2012

The quiet and formidable presence of the polar expanses whisper on the edges of human consciousness with a stillness that permeates the very molecules, a latent power held at bay by a scant few degrees in temperature. A great inland sea bobbing suspended in its briny berth, waiting. Wow, what a thought. Personally, I'm all over focusing whatever healing energy I can generate toward ecological balance for the highest good of all beings on this planet.

April 15, 2012

There has been a tremendous amount of activity around here today: probably not a great thing for someone who is still a bit queasy. Yet the time at home today has been valuable as I am rapidly returning to full health. I am so hungry! Hunger, a state that somehow or other contributes to creative energy, and hence to creative endeavour. Who knew! At any rate, I discharged a tremendous amount of said creative energy into planning upcoming programs and the attendant advertising flyers, brochures, posters, website updates, etc. Digital Graphic art is art with a practical side. Today also included dealing with the myriad details of wedding planning, from guest lists to master of ceremony guidelines and final detail decisions on decorations and timing and flow. There is only a bit of homework to do for tomorrow. My only issue with today is that I feel regret as I missed a workshop with a gifted teacher and peace worker, Sequoyah Trueblood. May I have the opportunity to meet soon with this Elder. With great thanks, great peace, and great love...

April 16, 2012

"Yesterday I was clever, so I wanted to change the world. Today I am wise, so I am changing myself." - Rumi. I offer many thanks to Maja and Jovan for sharing the beauty of their framed piece. It's gone to a good home. I'm learning to be the change.

April 17, 2012

Here we are, 108 days closer to December 21, 2012! It's been a wild ride so far, with emotional ups and downs in the extreme. I'm finding that continuing with this project is getting more difficult. My sense of commitment is wavering a little, but today I renewed my intent and focus.

There will be creativity daily, expression through art as a way to document this journey through the calendar. With the flu bug behind me and a resolute intention formed, I step forward into the unknown, allowing the path to unfold before me and being on the look-out for some of those inspiration muse-type moments. "Be in the moment," they say. In the moment, hmmmm? I'm at my desk, in my studio and I hear the dry, forced air of the furnace blowing through the vents. "In the moment" may not be the best place to look for inspiration at the moment. So how about the moments recently passed, or those immediately in the future? Can I grab bits of those, bring them to the present moment, and present them as art? Playing with time? Isn't that what art does, freeze-frame moments? I'm getting dizzy! Back to the path, at least that's solid. Isn't it? ;-) Okay, enough. I'm not going to get into quantum physics this late at night. I'm stalling. Every time I pick up a brush, pencil, pastel, etc, I wonder, will I be able to convey what I see in my mind's eye? Will it be good art? It's been twenty some odd years of accepting this personal challenge. Why haven't I given up? Talk about tenacious!

April 18, 2012

Tremendous growth, that's all I have to say. I'm pitching on the emotional roller coaster of life, hanging on with everything I've got, and loving every screaming moment of the ride. It's honest expression. There is no putting on "the face" to be the good, polite diplomatic model of correct behaviour when you are hanging upside down, plunging toward the ground at colossal speed with only the whisper of a seatbelt holding you in the safe zone. This is when your true colours shine through. So what do you do? Scream? Swear? Sweat? Cry? Whoop with delight? I claim all of the above and then some. Bet you thought I didn't even know how! I guess I can also claim that I don't sweat the small stuff*. And I guess most things are small stuff. My life has been a series of roller coasters, and I learned at an early age that finding my centre, regardless of the craziness around me, is what keeps the inner boat on an even keel. When I talk about the importance of being in the moment, connecting with the natural world, being true to who you are, I am not just reiterating the wisdom I've learned from my teachers and mentors. I am relaying hard won, personal touchstones that allowed me to survive repeated events of emotional, physical, and spiritual trauma in a way that has kept me relatively intact and whole, or, at the very least, has allowed me the opportunity to try and build trust in others again. There are still injured areas, reactions that can be triggered more easily than they should, but there is also growth and awareness, tremendous growth. So I whoop with delight as I plunge toward the ground. That's how trust feels to me: as though the ground has been pulled out from beneath my feet, and I just have to hope that little whisper keeps me safe. Honest expression! Crazy lady!

*Quote from Richard Carlson, *Don't Sweat the Small Stuff—and It's All Small Stuff:* Simple Ways to Keep the Little Things from Taking Over Your Life. Published by Hyperion, 1997

April 19, 2012

Have you ever noticed times in your life when you feel like second guessing every action you take? Or is this just me? Perhaps there are times where fence sitting becomes an art. I've discovered that as the longer I sit there debating the right move, the more frustrated and stuck everything gets. Yet as soon as I commit to whichever choice, direction, or path to take, suddenly the ball starts rolling. Events click into play, and synchronicity happens. It's funny, but whatever path you take—good, bad, or indifferent—you are right where you are supposed to be: facing "the learning experience". It's either the feather life lesson or the hammer life lesson, depending on your previous choices. Personal responsibility. Here's hoping I'm approaching enough of a wisdom level to tip the balance to the feather side...

April 20, 2012

It's our one hundred and eleventy-first day of the Art-down! It's time to feel grounded by a visit with my touchstone place in Kananaskis. Meditative Journey: Spring is warming the air in the sunshine, while winter still holds sway further in under the trees. The fragrance of wet stone and earth teases my senses, and I feel centred and rooted in this place. The music of the waterfall plays along the edges of my nerves, soothing and easing the rough spots, the stress spots. I feel the wind in my hair and ears, hear it in the trees, and it speaks to me of winter storms, snowflakes, and icicles. Turning up my collar, I huddle deeper into my jacket, glad for the extra layer. Despite the warmth of the sun on my cheeks, my nose reddens. But I want to stay. The air is crisp and clean in my lungs, the only sounds are those of nature and they touch me in a way that is relaxing and kind. As I watch the light dancing with the water droplets in the falls, I am entranced by the beauty of their play and I melt into the surroundings, becoming part of the whole. Breathe in, breathe out ... be at peace with the spirit of this place. Be at peace.

April 21, 2012

There is a point when seeking to understand the depths of human emotion and response during tragedy where you just have to get out for a bit. During the Peace Ambassador training I am enrolled in, we have focused on healing personal and collective wounds which involves examining the wounding and healing of others in depth. This view of the wounding of others can trigger a reliving of our own wounds: perhaps a ripping off of our own band-aid only to discover not a healed injury as we expected, but, instead to discover a pocket of festering anger at a deeper level. An injury still, just deeply buried until some event shocks us back into that space in a post traumatic episode, and we are laid waste by nausea, headache, depression, flashbacks, adrenalin spiking fear or rage. At times like this, illustrating emotion through art can be cathartic, taking the edge off it. Here is a piece, harsh in colour, dark and brooding, yet tinted with a glimpse of humour and fun. Humour and fun are two of the best tools for creating a peaceful feeling in any situation. It's difficult to hold on to anger or fear when you are truly enjoying a good healthy laugh. It's a play on the dogs of war.

April 22, 2012

Today was the first off-property horse ride of the spring! On the road out to Kananaskis Country, with fresh air, fresh horses, and a good group of riders, what a wonderful way to spend a couple hours on a Sunday afternoon. And it was warm, unseasonably so. Does this mean something important during this portentous year? This supposedly-worst-winter-ever that wasn't, followed by the spring with summer heat a week after the largest snowflakes I've ever seen? Weird weather! Are we humans messing with this somewhere in the world, at this very moment? Hmpfff. Isn't that a given? As we try to modify the earth and its eco-systems to better conform to our ideas of the way it should work for our area, are we forgetting that all is one and that if we shift the balance at one point something else will shift to compensate? It's sort of like a worry ball: when you squeeze one part tight, the other parts balloon outward, slipping through your fingers. It's something I've been thinking about on this Earth Day 2012 after basking in the sun, while on horseback through a mountain meadow. Celebrating life with gratitude, peace and love.

April 23, 2012

More photos! Hardly surprising as I do so love to paint from them. Poor Rupert. He is such a good model, but he just can't sit still very long. The effects of this on slow shutter speed are quite a bit of fun. I've a few shots where it looks like he is being masked by Spirit: the swirling glow generated by his movement surrounds him with an intense energy field and produced some interesting "paranormal" shots. Wishing you love.

April 24, 2012

Okay, this is the last shot of Rupert for a while. I promise! It's just that the energy flow in this shot, like a phantom or fairy dancing around between us, was so intriguing I absolutely had to share this! Although Ru looks relatively stationary, he couldn't stop moving, so the lines of colour in the photo are actually energetic footprints of where he has been, the ghostly outline of his presence in a particular space mere seconds earlier. This technique certainly produces some interesting effects! By playing with the contrast or colour, a wide variety of results are available, from the supremely creepy to the fantastically comic bookish. What a fun way to explore the possibilities! I'd like to try this with a human-type person next.*Insert creepy music here*

April 25, 2012

It's been one of those strange days. An oxymoron at it's finest: wonderfully woeful, brilliantly heartbreaking, horrifyingly happy, and I could go on. The day moved from really, really great moments to tremendously desolate moments. Events, not mood swings people. So, illustrating this strange dichotomy is the starkness of winter trees, black and white, embraced by the subtle and soft whisper of blue velvet shadows on a snow covered foundation. Crisp and clean meets soft and ethereal.

April 26, 2012

Pssst! Is it over? The day, is it over? A learning experience, that's what it is, a learning experience. Honestly, Murphy ought to be strung up and his law crumpled up and stomped all over! With all the upheaval, I have to admit that my horse is so wonderful! Helps me settle and decompress from the pressure cooker of my current schedule, life, existence. I'm so very grateful for his presence and his gentle teaching. He even lets me ride when I'm angry, with just a high-stepping twisty turning reminder at the beginning of the ride to leave all that stuff at the gate. Just be with me, you and me, together, in this moment feeling the wind, smelling the grass, appreciating the sounds of the huge flock of songbirds in the trees and fields. Just be with me. Words of wisdom from my horse, the source of many blessings. Celebrating life.

April 27, 2012

I've spent way more than a bit of time getting this photograph ready for my project tomorrow. I thought I'd share a bit of my process with you while I'm preparing for all that self-expression. Artwork, watercolour in particular, usually requires a fair degree of forethought before a stroke is ever placed on paper. There is composition to think about, contrast, colour, perspective, lighting, etc., etc, but the most important part for me is the story. What kind of vision, dream, tale, does it weave? How does it make you feel? What is it, specifically, that you are wanting to express? Having clarity in these areas can make or break a piece. However, that being said, it is also necessary to sometimes go with the flow of the work. At times, the storyline unfolds with surprising twists and turns, bringing forward something that was previously unremarked. Something wonderful! Watch it bloom on the page under your very nose. Be the startled and astonished artisan. Create!

April 28, 2012

Sidetracked! I admit it; I was completely swept away by the nod of a shy little bloom. My lovely orchid flowered for a second time! The first of three buds opened its petals fully to the radiance of the love I've been sending its way. This flirty little sweetheart captured my heart and attention with a subtle wave and the vibrancy of its presence. What a gift, the second blooming of a captive orchid! I am blessed! So of course, I share it with you, spreading the beauty out into the world. I hope you enjoy it. Back on schedule for tomorrow!

April 29, 2012

The best laid plans... It's bizarre, really; the sheer magnitude of chaos that can erupt in such a short span of time. There seems to be a force of nature between me and the projects I have scheduled of late. As soon as I specifically designate a time to work, within the space of a breath, something happens to throw everything into disarray. I feel as tossed about as a small vessel on a raging river. Things are definitely moving, there just doesn't seem to be a whole lot of navigation involved. This takes going with the flow to a whole different level. So, what to do? Create, maintain focus, continue on, trust myself, and know my limits—excellent plan. I'm sailing my vessel.

April 30, 2012

Follow through. It's important in discipline, sports, life. Art. Even when all is shifting and changing, integrity and perseverance remain a priority. I will create every day until the end of time (aka the Mayan calendar), step-by-step.

May 1, 2012

Young and unfinished, this wild stallion seeks to make his way in life. With rock star dreadlocks and superstar attitude, this horse is all about doing things his own way, carving out a niche and expanding to fill it, competently. He will succeed. Many blessings.

May 2, 2012

There is a story suggested by this hat-holding shelf. I'd love to hear your version!

May 3, 2012

I love taking photos like this one. The storyline is already set, and we have only to fill in the gaps with our imagination. Hear the sound of the cattle outside, smell the branding fire as "Cookie" steps out for a quick break before the frenzy of feeding all the ranch hands begins again. So, on that note, I'm off for a two-day horse ride in the foothills. Tomorrow's work will be posted early in the morning, and Saturday's will be posted late the following evening. I should have some great photo ops, but I'm going to bring along my pastels and sketchbook, just in case I have time. This will be a challenge as I am expecting to be physically exhausted. I'm squeezing in some artwork to document the trip. Hmmmm, let's see if I can do this!

May 4, 2012

Here is today's offering ... Another attempt at a floral in pastel. Can it get any worse? Sigh. You would think I'd stop trying after so many floral disasters, but I must admit to a certain sense of determination. Sooner or later, I am going to get better with flowers! With homework for the Peace Ambassador's course (which, has been fantastic these last couple of weeks! It's moving from communicating peace to managing systems change.), a house inspection, a wedding dress fitting, plus another scheduled horse ride, I'm feeling the pressure. I might just bring the homework on the trip. It can be done. I didn't realize I was missing a lecture Saturday morning due to the horse trip, so I'll be playing catch up. It's always such a great place to be, behind by a nose ... Many blessings.

May 5, 2012

Here is today's offering. What to write about a harrowing foray into an emotional confrontation with death and loss, a bone chilling but rewarding search through unknown forests and trails in the twilight? When the situation is so in the present, how do you reply to the question, "What did you learn from this?" Some twenty-four hours later it comes back to me from this and other events like it. I've learned to take every moment of joy and love as the blessing it is in gratitude.

May 6, 2012

Okay, I'm noticing a theme here. It's one that began before my recent horse trip. It appears that the western photography quartet is about death and loss. I'm not really certain how this came about as in the beginning my take on the first piece was more a feeling of someone having just been there, putting down their hat, and walking out of the room. The second piece gave a sense of being in the eye of the storm. A frenzy of activity just passed, with another one on the horizon about to hit. Yet after the experience of searching for my stampeded horse (as well as the ten others) in a strange forest at twilight, the third piece had a definite tone of grief. Today's piece (and the final of the series), sends a cold chill up my spine. The vacant seat, awaiting the return of the craftsman...and yet, wait a moment... There is hope, bated breath. Mere moments later, and, yes, there is the sound of footfalls. The craftsman returns. Art inspires emotion, or emotion inspires art. Either way, it works for me. Take care, and many blessings 'til tomorrow.

May 7, 2012

The things you see when out exploring the countryside have a way of staying with you long after the return to hearth and home. There's something about the smell of pine and wet earth, the feel of the breeze, the way the sunlight and shadows play through the waving grasses. I can visualize this clearly and putting brushes in the paint, I attempt to capture that feel. There is a sense of connection for the artist when someone else "gets it". A yearning, with each stroke, to vibrate the webstring that attaches us to "place", bringing about a touchstone moment: a memory of belonging and relationship.

Au revoir.

May 8, 2012

Someone mentioned to me on the weekend that Moose seemed to be aligning with me. As I held a treasured bit of moose hide in my hand on Saturday morning, I wondered about all the moose reminders I had been experiencing over the last few weeks. Analyzing the whole, I came to the conclusion that I really couldn't be certain whether it was aligning with me or others who were also present. How would I know for sure who this was for? The question flashed briefly through my mind; noted, then dropped for something more immediate as I went on with my day. Occasionally over the next few days, I'd glance at the moose tuft I'd laid on my bedside table and wonder about it briefly. Then today, alone in the house and on the phone with my fiance, I was startled when my dog started giving out his alarm bark. Refusing to be quieted from a distance, his single, sharp and staccato sounds continued, and I went to see what had him so excited. I could hear the neighbours' dogs across the back, as well as the one next door, also joining in the chorus. So, phone in one hand, I cornered the dog behind the dining room table, and I stood there, dog collar in the other hand. Imagine my surprise when I looked up, and right there, less than ten feet away on the other side of my floor to ceiling dining room window, stood a very big, very dark, female moose. Unhurried by the barking of the dogs, she calmly and gracefully picked her way across my back yard, and I stood there as Rupert squirmed barking and pulling out of his collar. When she reached the pine trees at the edge of the property, she turned and looked over her shoulder at me still standing there, staring in awe. For a few sweet seconds we stood connected, seeing each other. I felt her quiet confidence and strength, her grace reach out to me. What a gift. At 5:45 PM today, I had the answer to my question. Aho. P.S.: Happy 22nd b-day, Neo!

May 9, 2012

Feminine strength and grace, celebrating life.

May 10, 2012

Okay, there was one more western photography piece in me. It reminded me of a verse I memorized as part of the badge work in Pioneer Girls when I was about 6 or 7 years old. Funny how things stick with us for so long and crop up at the most interesting times. I hope this piece sparks a touchstone moment for you also. Take care.

May 11, 2012

Tulips, daffodils, hyacinths, lilies-of-the-valley, crocuses, poppies, hen-and-chicks, hostas: the garden. It's A.L.I.V.E.!!! There are forget-me-nots and daylilies by the pond. Sigh, I'm in heaven! Celebrating life.

May 12, 2012

I'm feeling the scent, the colour, the life; I'm getting lost in the beauty of spring.

May 13, 2012

Okay, I might have to admit that I'm fascinated with flowers, and totally frustrated with incorporating them in art. There have been times in this daily process where I am absolutely not happy about the pieces I have available to post. I take a deep breath to reassure myself that it's the process that is important in this project, the daily commitment to creative endeavour. As I work through these days, I realize that my skills are improving. I am aware of where I need to improve and even have a glimmer of how to go about it. After over twenty years of creative expression through art media, I still find excitement in learning and working with something new. The completion of these "mini-arts" brings a sense of peace, of rightness. I am on the path to something special, and I can't wait to see what's around the bend in the road.

May 14, 2012

As the prelim drawing for a moose antler tattoo (I'll explain in a bit), it is a gift. Every moment of the process is a gift. The symbolism of the Tree of Life is also a gift. Combined with the elements encapsulated in a medicine wheel, the dichotomy of life and death is explored. Conscious awareness and subconscious knowing, sinking into the void and emerging with pearls of creativity and wisdom are all explored here. The Tree of Life in full colour, vibrant and rich, is linked to the stark emptiness of the void with the newly sprung leaflets of trembling aspen. The white line drawing of the medicine wheel and elements is in direct contrast with the seemingly living tree. Here is where it gets interesting. The tree itself is depicted as shadow; the vibrancy and colour are actually coming from the light shining through and around it. The elements in the medicine wheel are tilted sideways but resting in the embrace of the living leaves, as though cradled in the arms of nature, just waiting for the breath of spring to bring it all to life. It's the potential for all creation. As for the moose antler tattoo, I was privileged to pull these designs together as a mock up for possible use in decorating a pair of moose antlers. Centre healing circles for the palmate spread. Many thanks for the opportunity! I hope it helped.

May 15, 2012

This piece speaks for itself. Celebrating life.

May 16, 2012

Environmental activism is a form of peace ambassador activity. It speaks out on behalf of the living, breathing components of an environment that sustains us all. Art has a purpose, a gift and a voice to share with all who view it.

May 17, 2012

Environmental activism as a form of peace ambassador activism speaks out about turning natural systems upside-down and inside out in the name of progress. Art has a purpose, a gift and a voice to share with all who view it. Celebrating life.

May 18, 2012

Looking back over my life with the intent of healing, in my mind's eye I see the bits and pieces that have broken away from my soul laid out before me like the pieces of a complex puzzle with both sides printed at 45 degree angles to each other. Layers or dimensions of experience stare back with a tentative sense of hope. They seem to whisper, "Do you know how this all fits together?" How do we pick up the pieces? We do it one motion at a time. In this moment, I welcome back this blue part from when I was small, to be embraced and integrated into the whole, one piece at a time. It's an exercise in healing. The first step? It's being aware of the pieces. Many blessings.

May 19, 2012

My life is a journey forward through the calendar, punctuated by flashbacks of the past, or memories, or post-traumatic stress, whatever label(s) you choose to use. Taking stock of where I am in the moment, I come to the realization that I have been damaged. I work to repair this, seeking out the injuries with white blood cells, platelets, calcium ... focused intent. It's an auto-response from my body's systems, supported and sustained by the natural systems in which I exist. The fragrance of trees, flowers and grasses tickle my senses. The sight of mated crows in flight, tiny bluebirds establishing territories, ladybugs on the wind, these things bring peace and healing to my soul. Spreading out from my centre to shyly touch those around me, there are ripples of healing on the air. Reaching out, bit by bit...

May 20, 2012

Meditating to the sound of crystal bowls, expressing thoughts and emotion through the creation of image in the controlled circle of a mandala is a soothing and cleansing experience. I feel emptied out and am off to bed. Today it was extremely difficult to show up to make art. With a day filled to the brim with relationship and creative expression, putting it to paper almost had a redundant feel. However, somehow here it is, short but sweet, a quick nod to the creative muse. Blessed be.

May 21, 2012

Have you ever noticed that some days just feel as though the path is twisted? Filled with switchbacks and hairpin turns, navigating the path seems more an effort in avoiding the rough spots than enjoying the journey. One stumble and everything scrapes along the edges of your being. Maybe it's from looking at things in black and white, perceiving life through the filter that is our own judgment and belief structures. If I let go and allow for shades of grey, subtle colours, reflections of light, perhaps then I see the whole picture more clearly. Picking up on other stories, sensing how they wrap around and relate to my own, I can feel the kinship between myself and other beings, and am able to be kinder, less fearful or guarded. Maybe I can explore the connection rather than define the edges? It's been a day of learning.

May 22, 2012

At day 143, I can't help but question where I am going with this project. There is a definite sense of day to day art experience, yet I feel that the personal quotient is maybe lacking a bit. Should I spend more time on the written portion of the day? Is it time to express solely in the realm of non-digital media? How do I achieve balance in presentation? How do I balance the life experience with the art expressions? Lately, I've been feeling a bit of stress, I admit. With the wedding day getting closer and all the necessary preparations taking a bit of my time, I guess I'm falling down a bit in other areas. Maybe I'm not, and I need to relax my personal expectations. It's so difficult to judge. All I know is that Doug and I are really enjoying dancing together. Our practice sessions are the highlight of both our days. We can go into the process grumpy and tired, then be smiling and relaxed when we call it done for the night. We've found a new love. As for the project, I am finding it difficult to go on at the moment. It's time to look for some new inspiration ... But where to begin?

May 23, 2012

This art journey has been a lesson in self-discovery for me up to this point, so why not try to illustrate that just a little further. With wedding planning, house selling, peace ambassador training, volunteering and art making all vying for a piece of me —not to mention important relationships like family and friends—there are moments when I wonder what is it that makes me create these stress levels in my life. Is there a secret piece of the puzzle waiting to be discovered during this journey that will shed light on the "why" of my decision tree? Are there cycles or rhythms of life that are at play in my soul? Perhaps there is an outline of my soul's journey that I may review, where I may know what prompts me to learn my limits through these types of experiences? What is this path I have embarked upon? Does the visible part of my life actually correspond to the "real" me? Or is there a veil over the whole that defies the penetrating gaze of others, only allowing them to see me through the filter of their own life experience and belief structures? A pale reflection or dark shadow of me, depending on where they are in their lives ... That brings to mind the greeting of the native peoples in the movie *Avatar*, I see you. How often do we really see each other or ourselves for that matter? Maybe we should really look.

May 24, 2012

This is the last foray into self-portraiture, I promise! This piece is all about the process, kind of like my life. It's about having the raw materials and polishing away the rough spots, grinding down the sharp edges, mindfully softening the approach. My concern is that I not over work the procedure. If I continue to rub away at this, soften the edges of that, file away, grind away, polish away, it does away with all the things that make me distinctive and individual, interesting. Rubbing it down, all that would be left is the white glow of an indistinct shape. Is this the inner being, the glow of the soul light? Or does it mean I've been muted, silenced, or had my integrity compromised? If I stand in my own power, be who I am at the moment, do I negate the need for growth? What if this isn't growth? What if it is blending? Becoming one with? Do I lose myself? Or do I discover I am bigger than I thought?

May 25, 2012

Well, the wedding planning is ramping up and the peace ambassador training is also drawing to a close, so I am a little strapped for time and very stressed. Meditative mandalas sound like a god-send! Some drums and flute music and a nice quiet studio are a beautiful way to de-stress! And what comes to light, but a North American coneflower! Used in herbal medicine for its antibiotic and wound healing properties, its appearance here is very appropriate with my work on self-discovery, personal peace, and healing. My thanks go to the spirit of the coneflower.

May 26, 2012

These tulips called to me today, probably because I am dead tired, can't think straight, and am looking for something beautiful and perfect that I don't have to mess around with too much in order for it to work artistically for me. The tulips are beautiful. My day was a flow of brightness and colour that radiated through me moment by moment. Bridal shower day... I am blessed.

May 27, 2012

There is something about the interlaced petals of this tulip that suggested to my mind the gentle embracing of something precious. By softening the colour and sharpening the contrast, I was able to present this subtle beauty in a way that displayed its delicacy, its fragile strength. Its layers of love hold dear the centre, a centre which is only partially revealed to us. The mystery of it softly tickles at our consciousness. What a gift.

May 28, 2012

Creating the appearance of distance between objects can be a challenge, but practicing in black and white is a wonderful way to perfect this skill. It's also a great way to check in on composition. It works for looking at other things, too. Events, actions, people all described in varying shades of greys, held on each end by the bookends of black and white values. Hmmm....

May 29, 2012

Today was difficult. Acknowledging illness in two old friends (one human, one equine), letting go of a decade long home-base, trying to balance the big joyful events with the big grim ones and focusing on this moment, the swells and troughs of the ocean speak volumes about this day. A drum ceremony at day's end created a sense of peacefulness, but like the foam on the water in this picture, it has a surface quality to it that is unnerving even while acknowledging its interconnected web patterning. It's a nod to how we hold it all together while the depths roil and seethe just below the surface. Celebrating life with eyes wide open.

May 30, 2012

Peace in the eye of chaos, a few moments of artwork to focus and process the emotional turmoil of the last days. I'm waiting for news from the operating room.

May 31, 2012

Meditative mandalas: what a great tool for growth, peace and transformation, and much needed moments of focus and rebalancing. The news from the operating room was positive, with more milestones yet to come. I'm hoping he will be able to congratulate his son on his wedding next week. We will know more when he is brought out of sedation in the next 24 hrs or so. And funny, but things just go along as they normally would. We do the tasks we've set for ourselves, build and care for relationships with friends and family, carry on carrying on.

Just a quick heads up, I will be away from a computer from June 1st to the evening of the 3rd, so I will post those days' artwork and commentary on the 3rd. Not sure how the drum offering will go this month, whether I will work on it tomorrow or leave it for my full attention on the evening of the 3rd. Honestly, I think that would probably be the best course of action, netting the best possible results. So I'll do a sketch on June 1st and 2nd, with the drum going up on the 3rd. Whew, such angst!... ;-)

Have a wonderful evening. My horse and I are off for a weekend jaunt near Lethbridge. It's sure to be amazing. I'll take pictures for reference and of course for fun. I'll be back in a couple of days. Oh! And stay alert. We will be moving to a new website address shortly (meaning within the next week). I'll let you know when we are ready to make the shift. Bye for now, and many blessings.

June 1, 2012

Here it is, the first day of the ladies' horse riding retreat! What a wonderful experience, travelling with my horse, experiencing the wide expanses of prairie grass, rolling hills, and twisting streambeds, sprinkled with the soft colours of a multitude of spring wildflowers and scoured by the prevailing west winds. Birdsongs of many varieties played a symphony for us as we rode through the vast landscape. We are blessed.

June 2, 2012

Today we were blessed with an aerial display by a flock of pelicans as they rode the updrafts above the hills of the coulee. Synchronized grace! What a beautiful gift. I have to admit, I am exhausted from the riding. I was in bed by 9:15 PM. Now that's unusual! PS: Will play catch up tomorrow, as well. Two entries of work are completed. I'm just too tired at the moment to do anything more on this computer. This is the end of my energy until I get some sleep! Back at it tomorrow! We are blessed.

June 3, 2012

Wow! Sunday already, where has the weekend gone! This morning started bittersweet, as I watched the ladies' group ride off down the road while Neo and I watched from the paddock. It was nothing more serious than an early departure from the retreat for me. (I have a dance lesson with my fiancé this afternoon!) Neo took the time in the pen quite a bit better than he did the last time I tried to leave him alone. There was minimal distress: only a bit of calling and pacing, and absolutely no jumping, or tearing around in a panic. The alfalfa may have helped with this, and the fact that he had his own little red shelter was a nice touch. It was still heart-wrenching to leave him behind when I was picked up. The wonderful ladies at the retreat made sure he was all packed into the trailer and brought home safe and sound. Many thanks!! And as for the dance lessons, we are learning and having fun doing so. It makes my stomach all funny to dance with my guy. Our toes felt funny, too, from all that walking all over each other. Good thing we are learning to give up that habit! We are blessed.

June 4, 2012

Up-to-date, but no drum! I know, I know. What about following through, ensuring quality of product, getting things done and on time? Well, I have a theory about that. The important stuff happens just when it is supposed to happen in the larger scheme of things. For whatever reason, events take place when we need them to, even though we may not recognize the fact until years later. Now it may seem that the drum for June 1st isn't really one of those big things, but maybe by requesting an extension of the due date, I produce something that really speaks to someone? Rather than having a rush job that does no one any good, I am going to request and grant myself an extension on the drum due date. Maybe, I will even donate this drum to a charity silent auction. It must be the full moon! I am learning to forgive myself for my perceived failures. Accept, guilt-free, the kindness I extend myself to complete this project in a fluid and peaceful manner. So events and artwork may unfold with divine grace. Great peace, great thanks, great love.

June 5, 2012

The funny thing about *the* Mayan calendar is that there is more than one. Each charts different cycles, beginning and ending at different times. So what's all the fuss about? Why the prediction of the end of the earth as we know it? This I would love to know. This summer, the summer of 2012, has been designated the Summer of Peace, with events worldwide being organized to promote and celebrate a peaceful humanity. As part of my training as a peace ambassador, I am required to arrange or organize just such an event. Whether it is an action at the individual level or something more community-based or larger, the premise is to do something. What about a drumming event? Sounds of Peace? A workshop to make a drum followed by a potluck get-together of previous students, drum holders, or the musically inclined? The price for the workshop would be the cost of materials only, with a traditional gift (such as sage bundles, sweetgrass, organic cornmeal, crystals, handmade goods, etc. Cash gifts would also welcome) for the elder providing instruction. I'm thinking I'll start planning this after the wedding, along with everything else, after the wedding. Oh yes, the wedding. We are coming down to the final hours of "technical freedom". Hmm, are you wondering what that means to me? So am I! ;-) Did you hear about the honey bees?

June 6, 2012

A nod to the Mayan calendar, I guess I will find out. I am looking forward with curiosity to December 21st, as day by day, the pages of my calendar are peeled away. Unfolding: that should be the name of this piece. As the days of the year pass by, the petals of the rose fall away leaving us closer to the central secret. "And what is that secret?" the petals whisper softly as they return the caress of the seeking hand. Is it the seed of life contained in the heart of the rose? Its ability to recreate itself, to continue on long after the petals of the individual flower melt back into the soil at its root, melting into the earth to feed the future growth? Or is it the feelings aroused in the human heart by the beauty of the rose's expression, the scent, the subtle softness, the breath-taking process of blooming?" Either way, it seems there is communion with the heart involved. Thank you for your comments on the "Sounds of Peace" or "Sounds like Peace" initiative. As soon after the wedding as possible, I'll start the planning process and keep you up-to-date on any developments. I can definitely put you to work if you'd like!

June 7, 2012

Blooming, unfolding, opening, and revealing the insides. I love flowers, and after the wedding I am going to paint up a storm of them. I've been studying the textures, forms, colours and play of light, listening with my heart to the story they tell. It might just be what I needed. And then there is the secret. It's true, we are moving the studio. August 31st. I will have more information available as the terms and site are solidified. Look for mini art retreats, days and weekends! A new web address is also pending. Things are starting to move!!!

June 8, 2012

There are so many things that still need attention that I'm quite certain I am going to dream about them all night. From seating arrangements, to flowers and cake, vows and readings, stones and blessings, and milk for the fairies—it is the solstice, after all. It is all starting to come together. And now, we are shopping for a new home. Oooooh: shirts for the ushers, rehearsals, the order of ceremony .... Did I mention shopping for a new house? And there is a nephew's wedding tomorrow, out of town, of course. Then there are the dance lessons, a horse and dog to exercise and care for, the feeding of the family and the plants, all while attending to a plethora of incomplete wedding details. Did I mention shopping for a new house? There is the homework for the Peace

Ambassador course, organizing a Summer of Peace 2012 event. I like the idea of holding the Sounds of Peace workshop at the new studio space, outdoors surrounded by birds, pine trees, and warm breezes. I'll need to get the word out to see if there is interest, so … "Go, social media!". Plan this, and new website location. It's all good ... Great Peace, great thanks, great love, and great focus

June 9, 2012

Today, we are attending a wedding. We are traveling two and a half hours to be witness to the vows made by my fiancé's only nephew to his new bride. I'm looking forward to a wonderful experience. And yes we are going to practice our dance steps in celebration. Ooops! I forgot to post this before I left for the wedding, so here is yesterday's work! Many blessings.

June 10, 2012

I'm looking for the profound lesson in today's experience, but I'm not getting anything yet! We drove home from the wedding early this morning, and the wind was incredible on the highway so we opted for the back roads. There were whitecaps on the sloughs! Tiny, grey, fluff-ball goslings huddled among the blowing grasses on the banks, trying to cuddle up with their parents to stay above the crashing waves. We were driving, driving, driving: just so we could make it back home in time to do some more driving. drive some more. We're looking for that prime site where we can move the studio/home/hearth. The search took us to the windswept hillside of a wide valley and creek, then on to a forested hillside with a view of rolling, crop-covered hills dotted by stands of trees. Both were private and each charming in their own way with twisty roads and standing water, birds and frogs, cattle, and the shades of green in the variety of trees. Despite the fact that I seem to be oblivious to the teachings of this day, I must admit, Dan Millman is right (author, *Way of the Peaceful Warrior*) "there is never nothing going on". Maybe that's the point, just being aware of the stuff going on around you and making note whether you get the lesson or not.

June 11, 2012

Here we are, ten days until the wedding; yup, ten days. Sitting here shaking my head over the progression of days is not helpful, but it does seem perfectly appropriate. My senses are firing. The senses of fun, panic, and humour are getting a full body workout. Meanwhile, the senses of peace, calm, and restfulness are on hiatus. In this piece, the orchid resembles a spider in its web. A symbol of balance and creativity, let spider encourage you to spin your creative threads in the dark so when your work is kissed by the rays of the daylight sun, it will sparkle with startling magnificence. May you walk the threads of life lightly, easing into the ebb and flow, and dancing with joy to your own creative song.

June 12, 2012

In the background of this photo, an unfocused shape of a face appears to be looking back at the camera, this being regards us in silent contemplation. It's as though the lens has captured the image of a fairy who, unbeknownst to the photographer, was shadowing the whole procedure. Perhaps it's the spirit of the orchid made visible for a brief moment in time. Fanciful reflections to balance out a day filled with practicality. Many blessings.

June 13, 2012

The Dress was ready to be picked up today! On the way there, I was provided with an amazing display of spring weather. It was sunny when I started out, then there were sprinkles of rain, then driving rain, and then hail accompanied by a full piece orchestra of thunder and lightening. Fifteen minutes later, arriving at my destination, all was dry. That is, until I had to take my dress out to the car, at which point the whole sky opened up and poured on me. Happy is the bride the rain falls on! Yes! And it is a good thing I'm not made of sugar. The appointment at the alterations shop took a bit longer than I expected, so off I went afterward, with The Dress nicely wrapped up in its carrying bag and spread gracefully along the backseat of the car. And where does one go with The Dress neatly altered and waiting to hang in my closet? Why off for a 45 minutes drive through the rain, out into the countryside, to feed and visit with my horse, while standing in water and hail! Was there really any question?

My horse has me concerned, which reminds me to do more research on the effects of chaste tree berry powder on a horse's heart. He has a substantial heart murmur. Supposedly, there are no side effects, but I feel the need to look closer. He fell to his knees today, while standing still and eating. Maybe he slipped, but the look in his eyes said he was shaking something off. And when I caught him in the field, he gave an all over shudder. It was not his usual shake; it was really different so I spent some time with him in the hay shed, just watching him eat and grooming him. Every moment with him is a gift. And now more wedding decorations are complete, the last class of the Peace Ambassador Certification program is complete, an offer to purchase another home is complete, and I feel like Rupert looks in this picture.

June 14, 2012

There were many new beginnings and completions today. From August 15 – 31st, the home, hearth and studio will be moving to their new location, 13 acres of beautiful meadows and forest about twenty minutes northwest of Cochrane along Grand Valley Road. What an adventure this will be! The Peace Ambassador Training program is complete, and I have my certification, which is lovely. What an amazing course and group of instructors. I have learned so much! The building I had hoped to use as a studio is apparently sporting rotted out bottom plates, so I am thinking of putting in a yurt and a greenhouse, and building an outdoor classroom with a labyrinth. Oh, the plans!! I can hardly wait to share them with you. There are so many things I have been working on that I can't share here yet. The suspense is incredible. Seven days to the wedding, nine days to finish a project. Oh yes, no pressure.

June 15, 2012

Midsummer's Wedding

Brightest day and shortest night,
Seasons turn with sun's warm light.
Birthing fruit and herbs and grain
Upon the vibrant earth again.

Spirit sparks to feel the bliss
Of the sunbeam's blessed kiss.
Open hearts and minds and hands
Sharing peace across the lands.

Dancing through the wheel of life,
Husband takes a precious wife.
Hand in hand and heart to heart,
A new life they pledge to start.

Blessed with joy and love and peace,
Abundant life without cease.
Married now upon this day,
Grown together they will stay.

June 16, 2012

Wild motion and raw power, the movement of a horse epitomizes the glory of passionate self-expression. Evocative! To temper this uninhibited honesty with softness is a blessing of harmony and grace. Taking time to examine the shades of grey can bring to the surface the myriad facets of a situation, how illuminating and eye-opening. The learning available in the simplest of interactions brings a wealth of wisdom and understanding to our fingertips. An interaction with art, both for the creator and the observer, can bring about the same ah-ha moments. Do you see the figure of a horse or a man?

June 17, 2012

Pulling on the webstrings of my imagination, the little wood sprite in this piece makes me smile. It's fanciful and fun. The spirit of the birch tree makes a shy appearance. It doesn't take much for the imagination to fill in features and personality. Typing is a bit painful at the moment, so I am going to keep this one short. It seems I sprained my finger during the horse ride today. The first and second jumps were fine, but the third ... my bad. At any rate, it was a wonderful journey through the forests of the foothills. Well worth repeating, like say, tomorrow morning. I hope this is the extent of injuries before the wedding. It's a small injury to be sure, but it has played havoc with my plans for a French manicure.

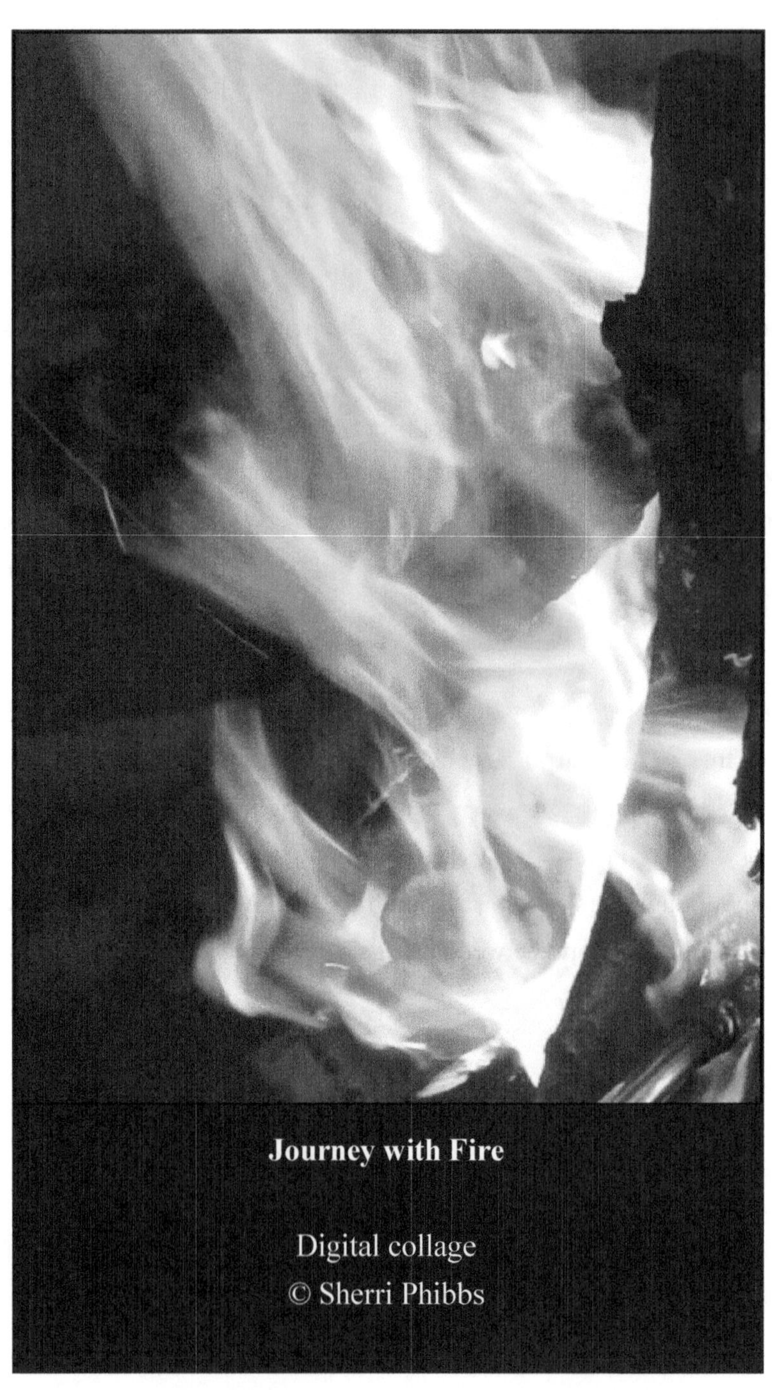

Journey with Fire

Digital collage

The Final Art-Down: WATER

The Final Art-Down: WATER

Sitting on a lawn chair in the middle of the streambed, with feet dangling in the cold, clear mountain water, the artisan watches the light glint and dance across the surface of the quickly moving creek. Captured by the motion of the light, mind completely emptied of all but the sensation of the flow below as it passes soothingly over heated skin, there is no room for the whispers that arise and they are brushed aside.

Yet, WATER is persistent. It will change shape to fill any available course, and so it does.

"I am the Queen of the River Waters", it whispers. "There is something you must do."

The artist extends a lazy hand down into the flow, allowing the sensual feel to sink deeply into every cell. Absorbed and mesmerized in this wondrous moment, just being, the whispers of change are ignored and discounted in favour of staying absorbed in the physical delight. And WATER tries again, with tender spray reaching higher.

"Hear me! Be aware! There is a test."

Still the artisan is caught by surprise as the waves of emotion well up like a never ending tide, and events rush along like rapids in a canyon, shaping and shifting life until solid ground is a wisp of a dream and all that CAN be done is to stay in the moment . . .

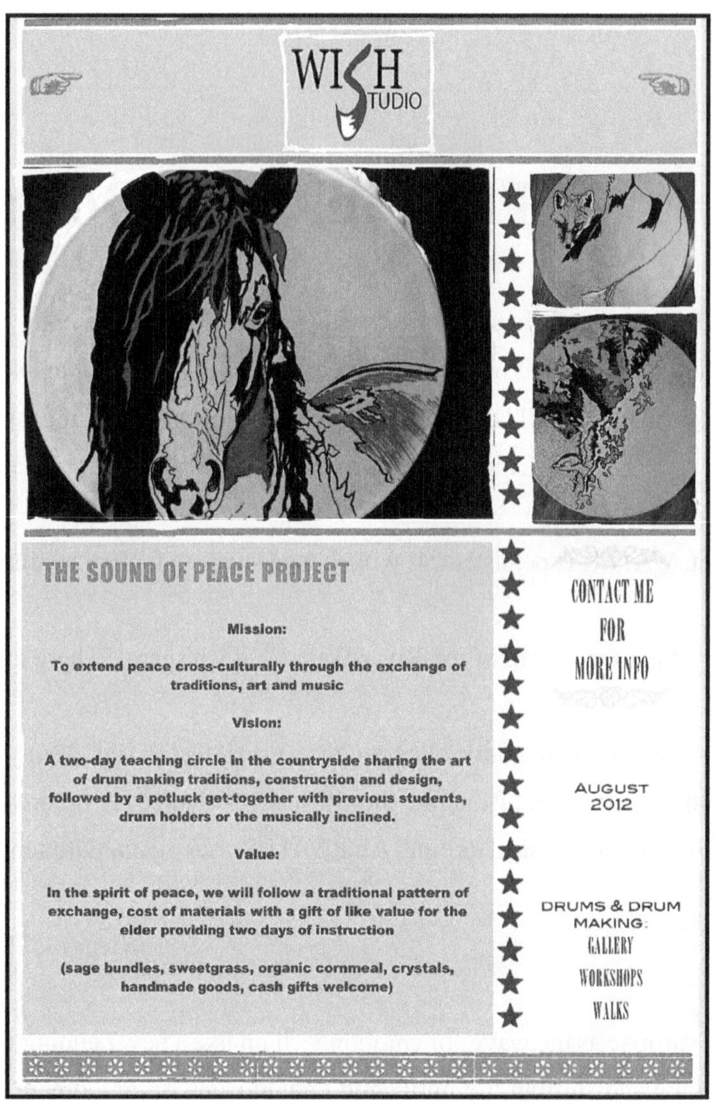

Sound of Peace
June 26, 2012

Graphic design
© Sherri Phibbs

Awareness of WATER

Go to a place in nature where you can feel WATER and sense the power of its flexibility. You may choose a waterfall, a small stream, hot springs, a riverside, a lakeshore or ocean, or even a glass bowl filled with water. Sit next to it, or dangle your feet off a dock. Wherever you are drawn to, take along a coloured pencil and a journal. When you arrive at this place, address the area respectfully, requesting permission to interact. You will know if you received permission as a lightness or rightness that will make itself know in your mind, spirit and body. Honour a negative response by moving on to another area and repeating your request. When you have permission, make yourself comfortable. Use all your senses to track and be aware of everything in your surroundings. Note the sensations in your body. Breathe in, breathe out...with gratitude.

When you are ready, begin to form a request in your mind for inspiration and assistance on your journey of creative discovery and integrity. Pay particular attention to the thoughts that flow through your mind, the images or sounds, and record them in your journal. Also note your feelings and physical responses as you interact with Nature in this way, tracking and recording this as well. Are you drawn in a certain direction? Do you feel excited, tired, inspired, or something else entirely? Is something in the area pulling your attention, and why? Don't know? Then ask it, and track your thoughts. Describe and make note of the experience.

As you complete your interaction with WATER, you may wish to express your gratitude. You may do this verbally with heartfelt sincerity or with an offering of sage, sweetgrass, organic tobacco, or cornmeal. You may repeat this interaction with WATER again and again as a way of getting to know the element, becoming connected to your natural environment, and opening your mind to the experience of this Divine and self-sustaining world of which we are a part.

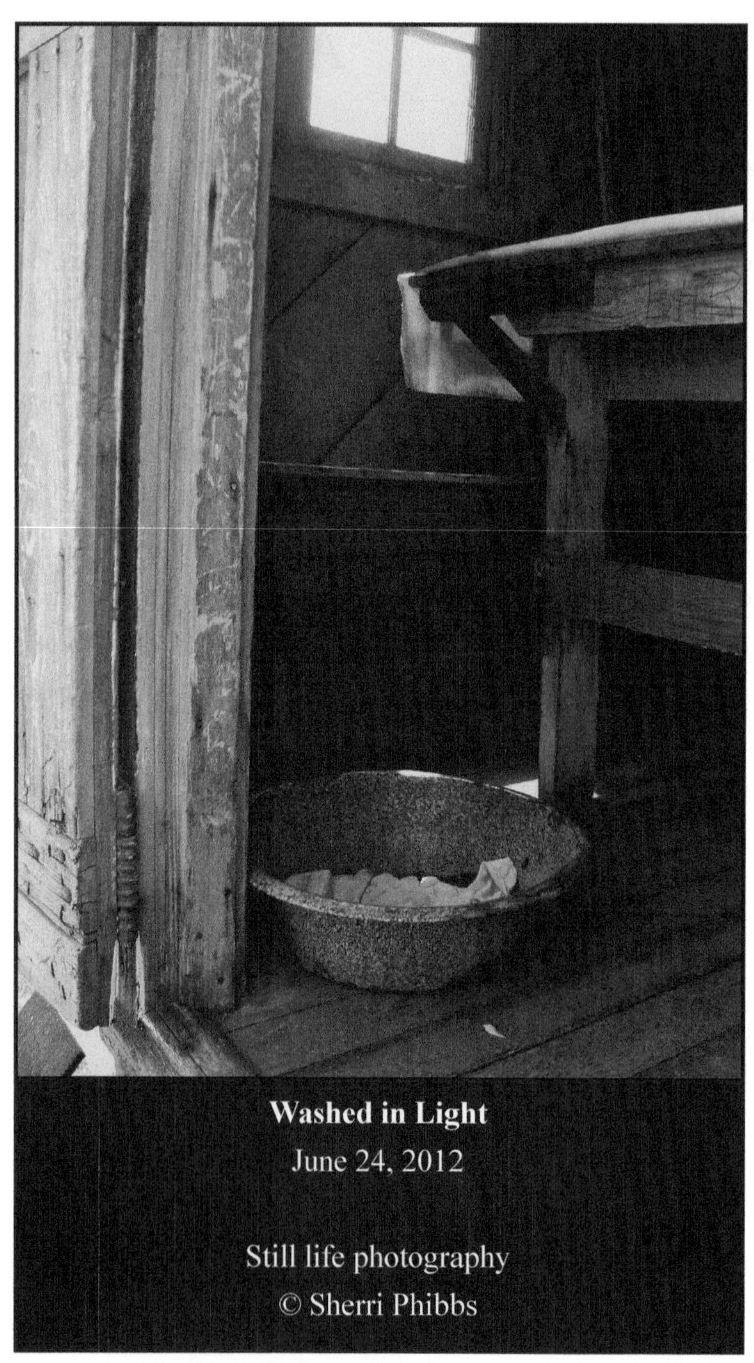

Washed in Light
June 24, 2012

Still life photography

WATER: The Image

This project came to life in pieces, two pieces. The whole, comprised of a written journal of daily life experience matched with a corresponding artistic interpretation, is separated here into its individual parts.

Going with the flow...

The Road Forward
June 22, 2012

Nature photography
© Sherri Phibbs

Beginning the Work
June 25, 2012

Nature photography
© Sherri Phibbs

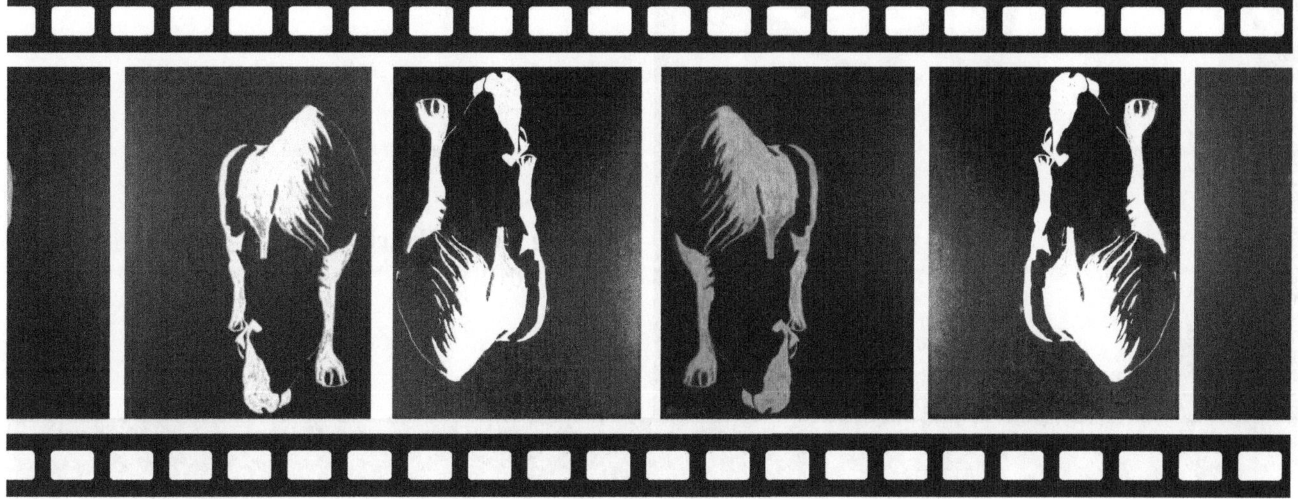

Let It Roll
July 9, 2012

Digital art
© Sherri Phibbs

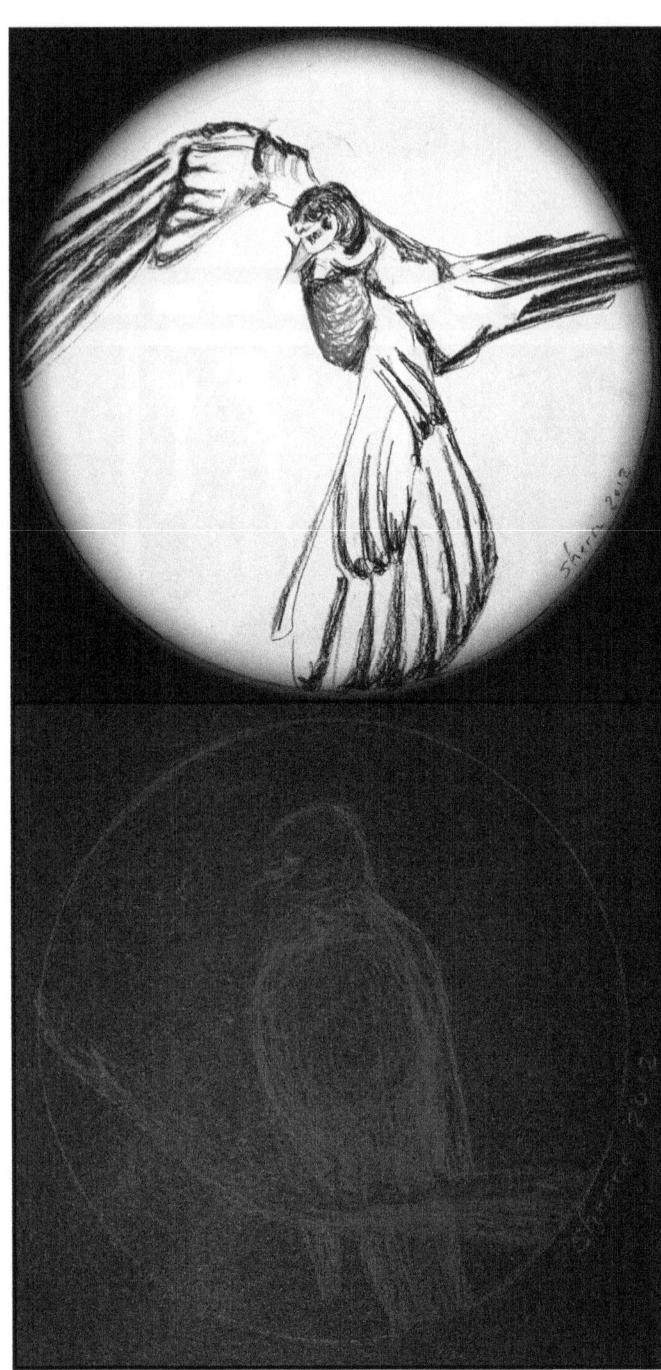

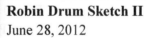

Wedding Drum Sketch
June 27, 2012

Conté

Robin Drum Sketch II
June 28, 2012

Chalk pastel

Robin Drum Sketch III
June 29, 2012

Chalk pastel
© Sherri Phibbs

Poppies
June 30, 2012

Nature photography
© Sherri Phibbs

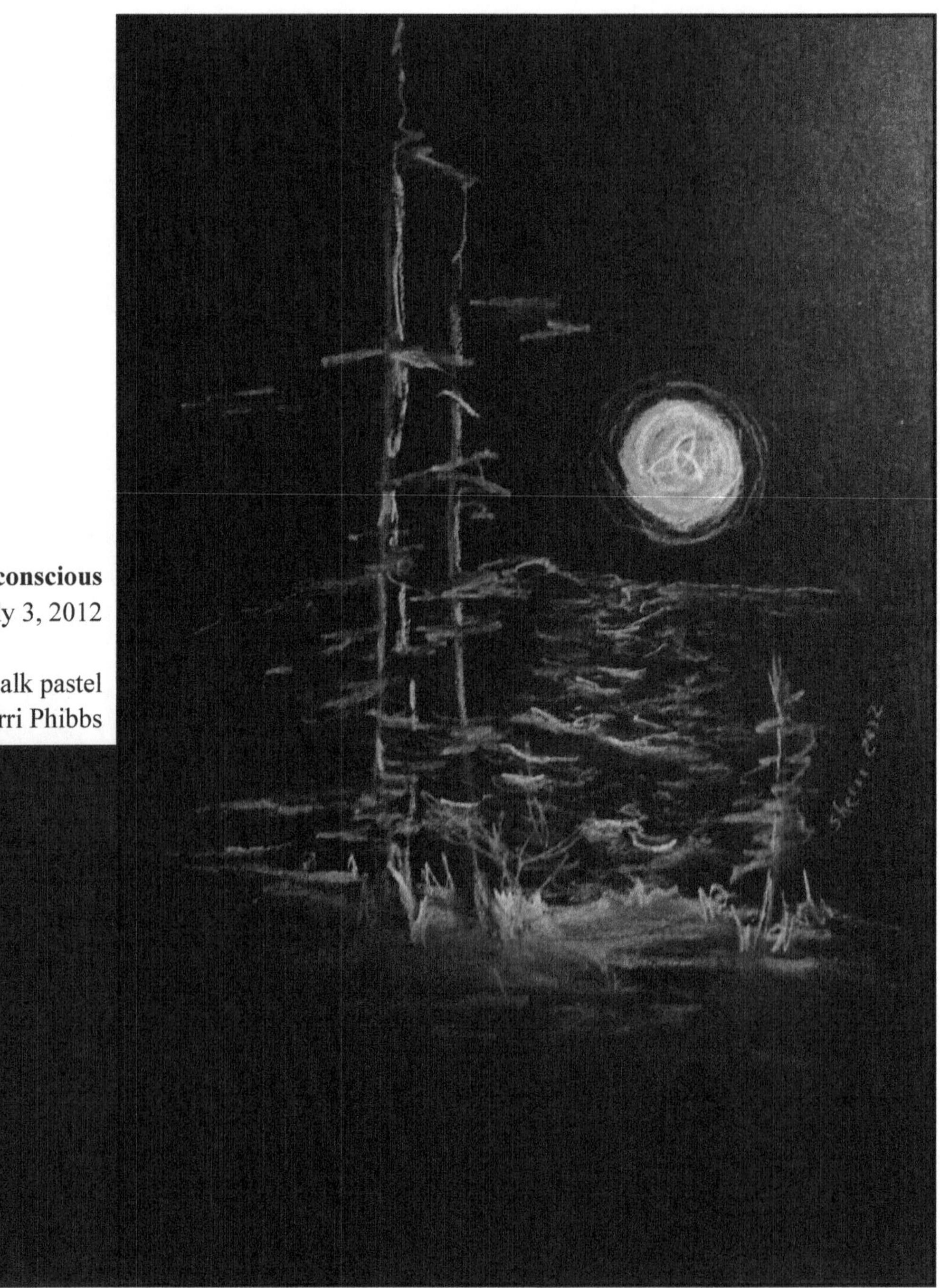

Subconscious
July 3, 2012

Chalk pastel
© Sherri Phibbs

Perspective
July 1, 2012

Nature photography
© Sherri Phibbs

Protective
July 2, 2012

Chalk pastel
© Sherri Phibbs

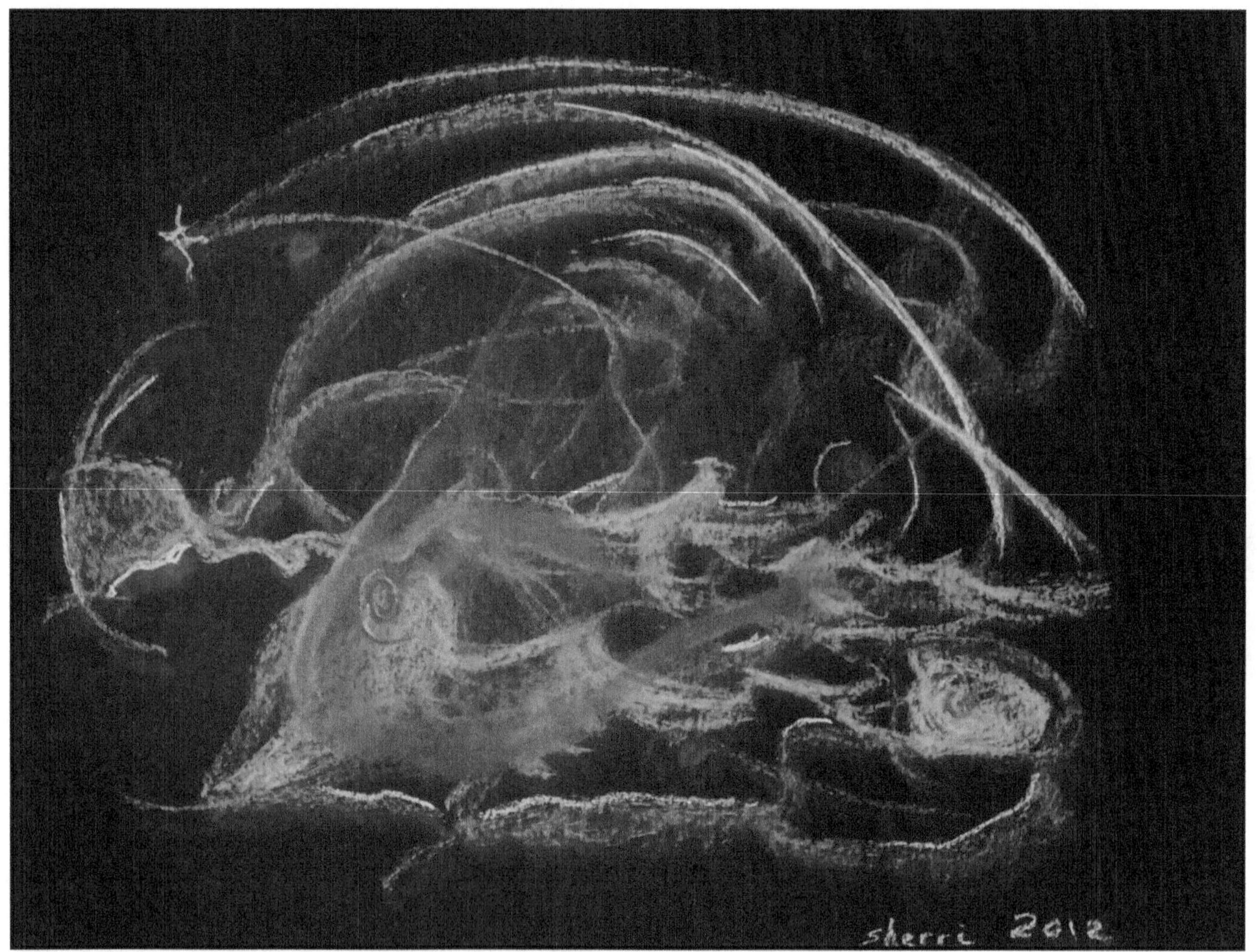

Touched by a Mac
July 4, 2012

Chalk pastel

A Gift For You…

Meditate Mandala-cly!

As you may have noticed, there is a meditative tool that I frequently use when I want to centre my emotions and mind. I highly recommend that you apply this practice to your own creative journey. It will build focus, inspire contemplative thought, and provide a constructive outlet for emotional turmoil.

I have found that creating a mandala with non-fluid media (such as pastel, conté, or inks) to be the easiest to manage during times of stress. The more fluidic the media, the less control there is. This can translate to an over-abundance of the WATER element, meaning a less controlled emotional response to the work. It's a bit unsettling if feelings are running hot, so I prefer the slow release of tension, a release with balance provided by the dry media.

Start with a circle, . . . carry on. ;-)

Red
July 5, 2012

Nature photography

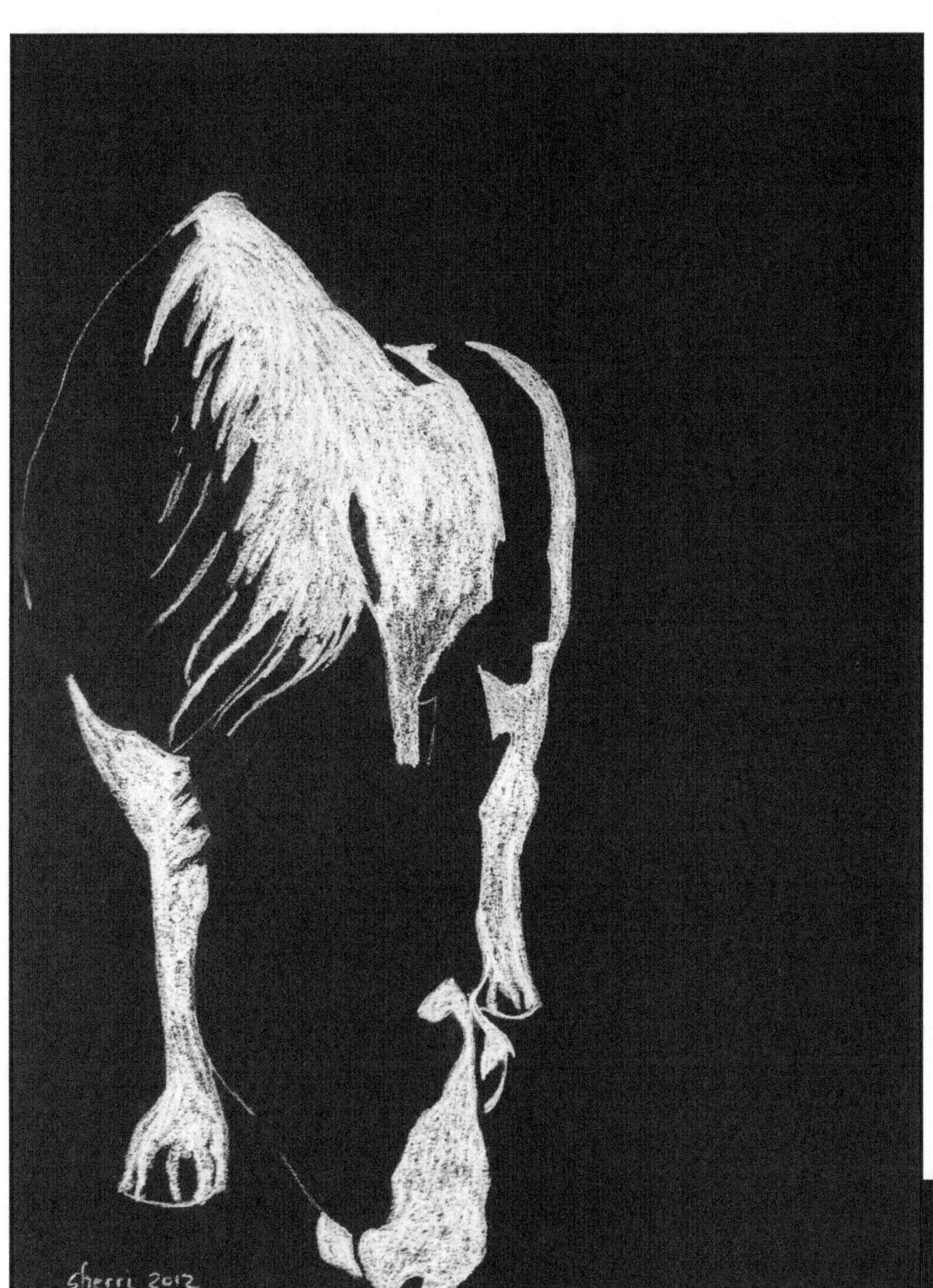

Legend
July 6, 2012

Conté

My Journey with WATER

Emotional chaos! I had a nasty quarrel with a teen and I am unable to sleep, so up I get at 3:00 AM to sit alone in the office and seethe. How can I fix this horrible situation? What can possibly make this better? Unable to release the upset and agitation, I turn to work on my organic eco-psychology course. It's a good time to verify these methods, I think. So I breathe deeply and decide I am not going outside in my housecoat to commune with Nature in the middle of the night. What to do? Looking around for a natural object, the salt rock light on my desk grabs my attention. That's a natural object, right? Working through the exercise, I check in with the rock and feel a sense of rightness about continuing.

Picking up the rock and holding it close to my face, I whisper sheepishly… "Do you have something to say to me? How can I fix this?"

Tracking my thoughts and senses, I notice the rock smells salty. A thought travels through my mind… "Taste Me!"

Alright, this is very strange. I really feel uncomfortable. I look over my shoulder. The street, dark and empty through the window, seems to be watching even though no one is in sight. Sighing, I lean over and tentatively stick out my tongue and lick the rock. The things I do for science. Another thought flits through my mind space, "My salt is on the outside." A pause, then "Your salt needs to be on the outside."

Realization sinks in, and the floodgates open. Tears flow freely as I sob out the trauma of the day. Letting it all go with that lengthy rush of salt WATER, I finally thank the rock, and return to bed to sleep immediately and dreamlessly. The morning arrives fresh and new with no harboured resentment. The gift of WATER washed it away with the tears, releasing the pent up emotions, toxins and dis-ease, leaving only the love.

Watery Vortex
June 23, 2012

Nature photography
© Sherri Phibbs

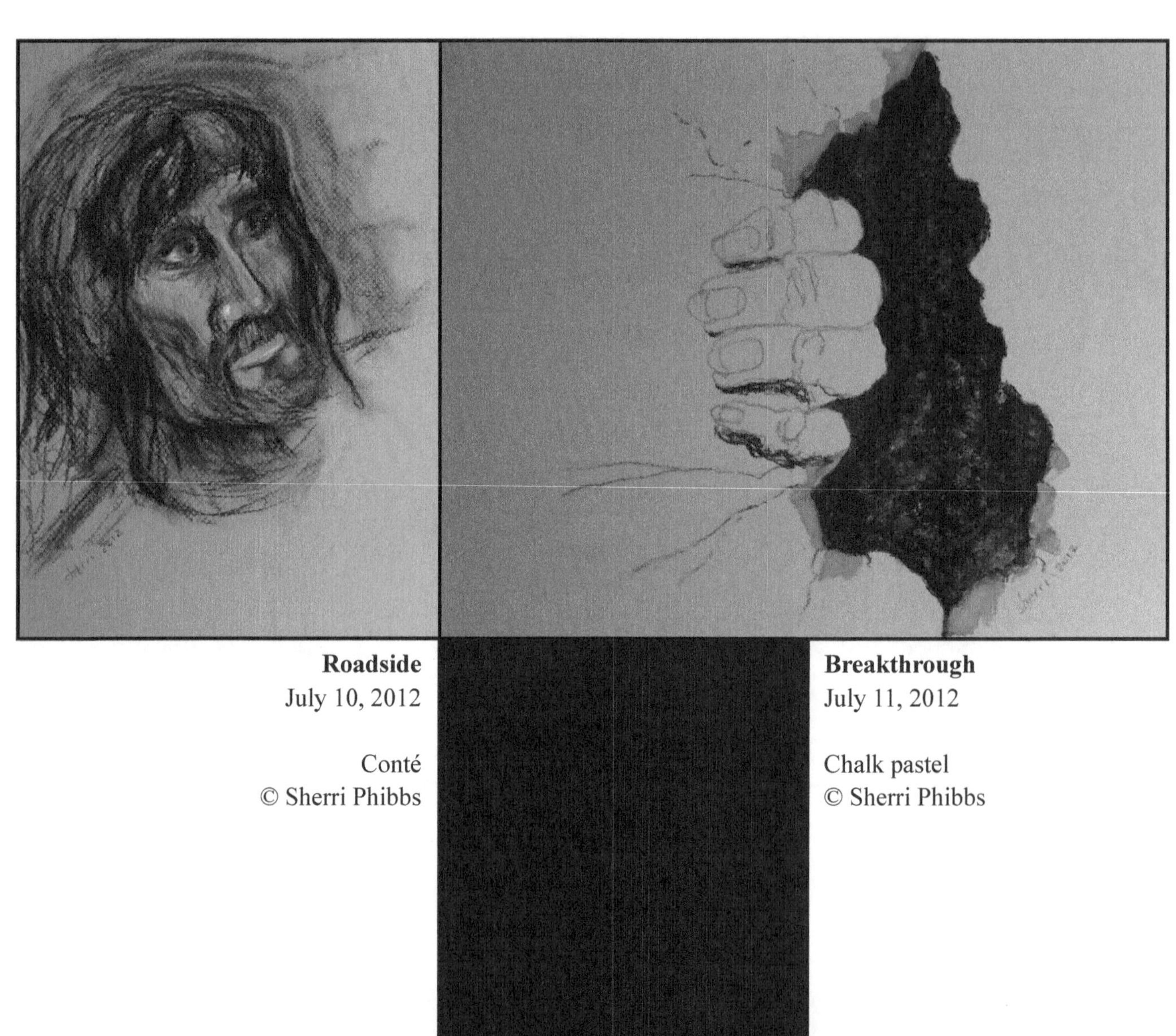

Roadside
July 10, 2012

Conté

Breakthrough
July 11, 2012

Chalk pastel

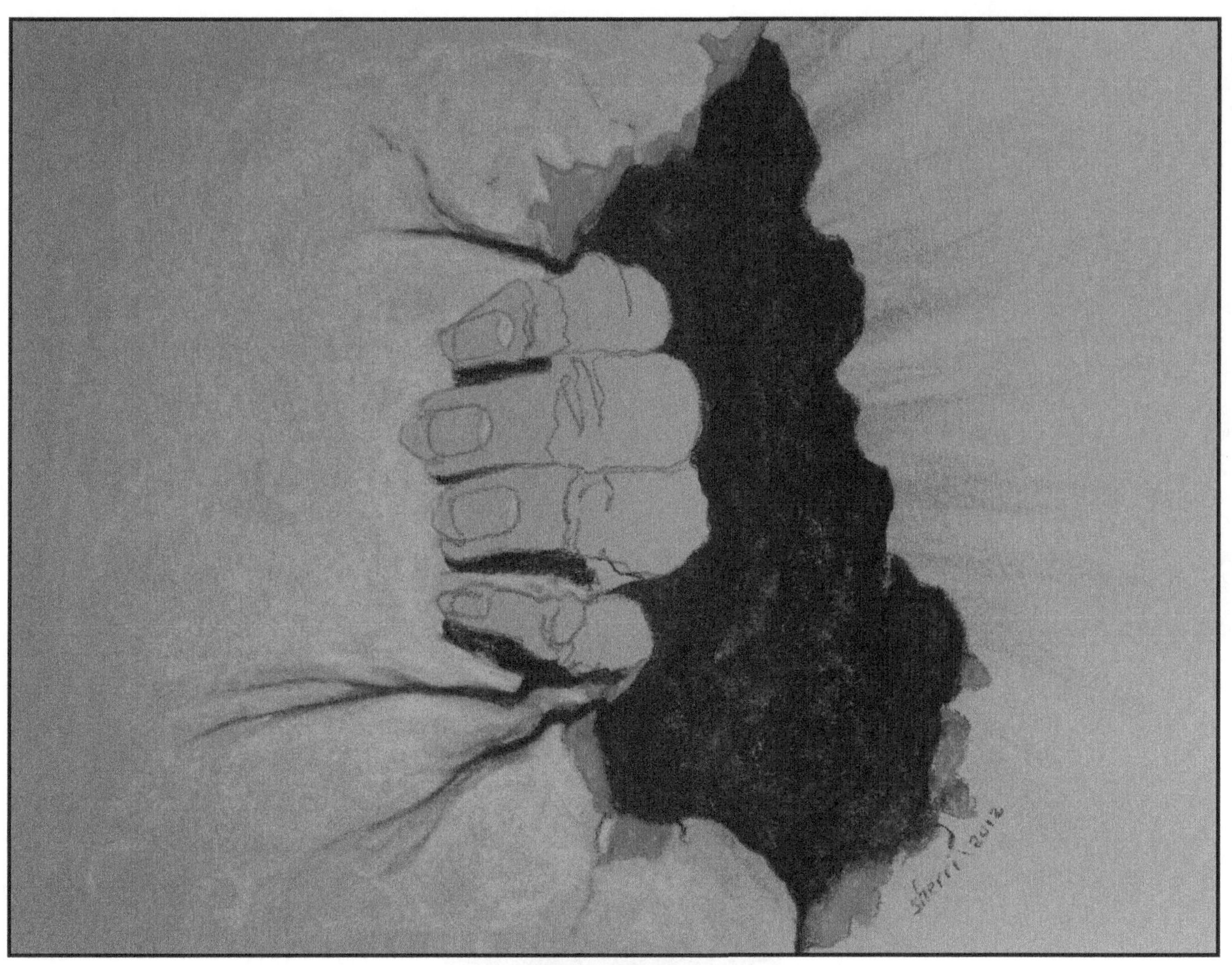

Breakthrough II
July 12, 2012

Mixed media

Signs
July 13, 2012

Nature photography
© Sherri Phibbs

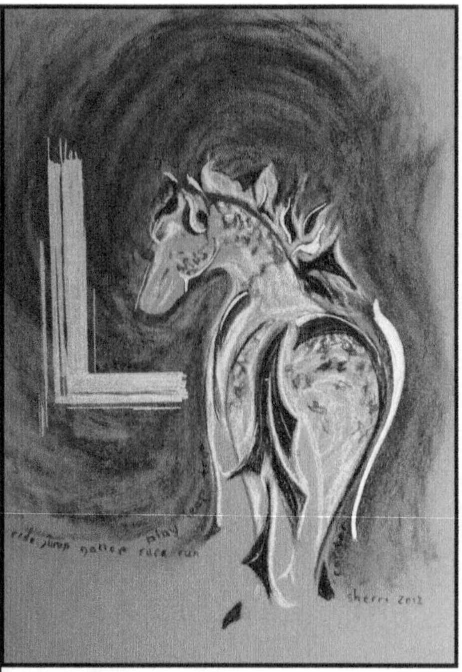

Fires King
July 14, 2012

Chalk pastel
© Sherri Phibbs

This Means Move
July 15, 2012

Conté
© Sherri Phibbs

Fires King II
July 16, 2012

Acrylics
© Sherri Phibbs

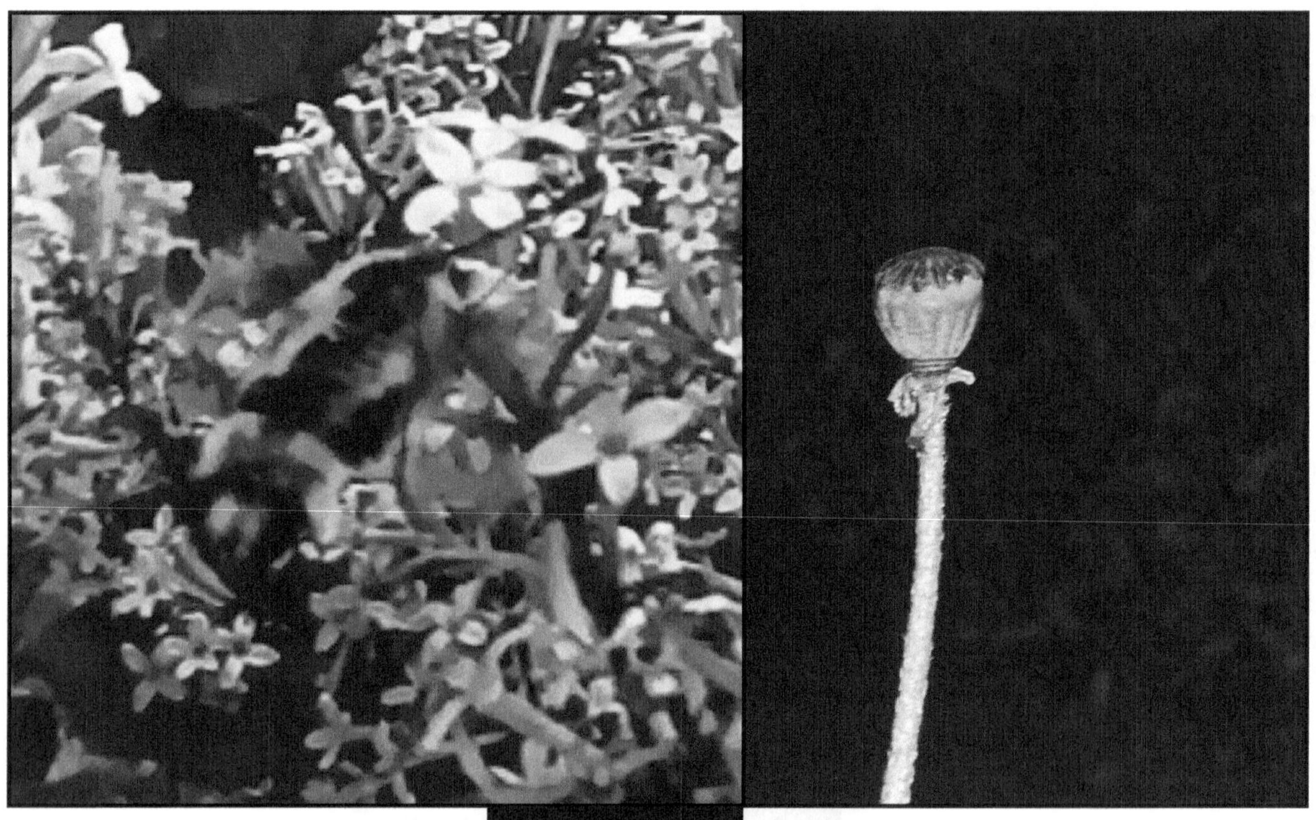

The Colour of Lilac
July 17, 2012

Nature photography

Potential
July 18, 2012

Nature photography

Peek A Boo
July 19, 2012

Nature photography
© Sherri Phibbs

Impression of a Rose
July 20, 2012

Watercolour
© Sherri Phibbs

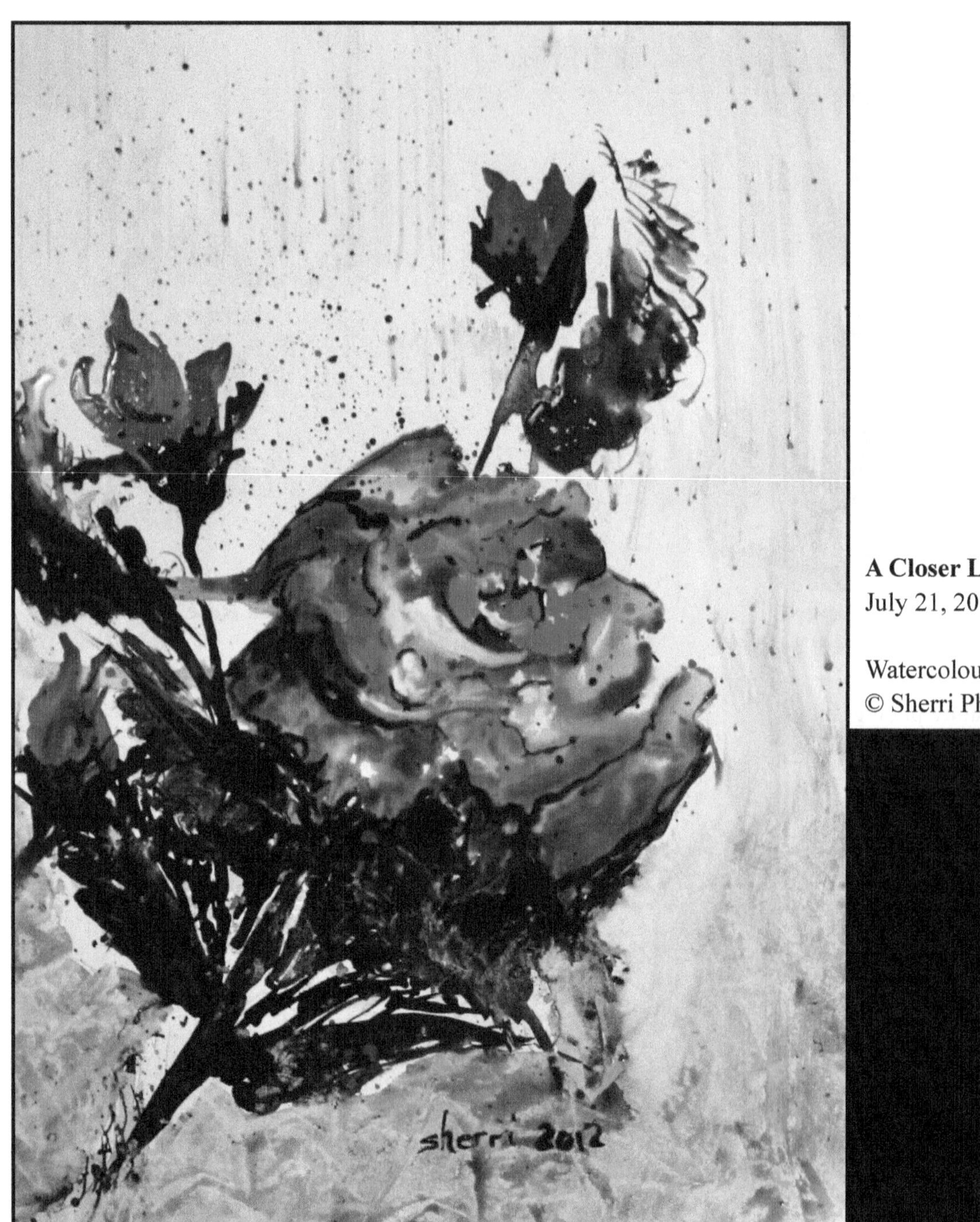

A Closer Look
July 21, 2012

Watercolour
© Sherri Phibbs

Through a Different Lens
July 22, 2012

Digital art
© Sherri Phibbs

Fox in 5 Seconds
July 23, 2012

Conté
© Sherri Phibbs

Fox in 20 Mins 5 Secs
July 24, 2012

Conté
© Sherri Phibbs

Meditative Mandala
July 25, 2012

Ink drawing
© Sherri Phibbs

Meditative Mandala
July 26, 2012

Sepia conté
© Sherri Phibbs

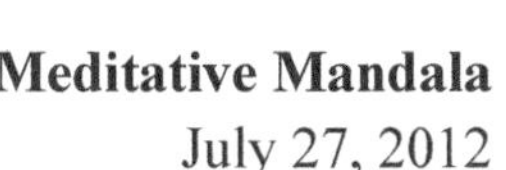

Meditative Mandala
July 27, 2012

Ink drawing
© Sherri Phibbs

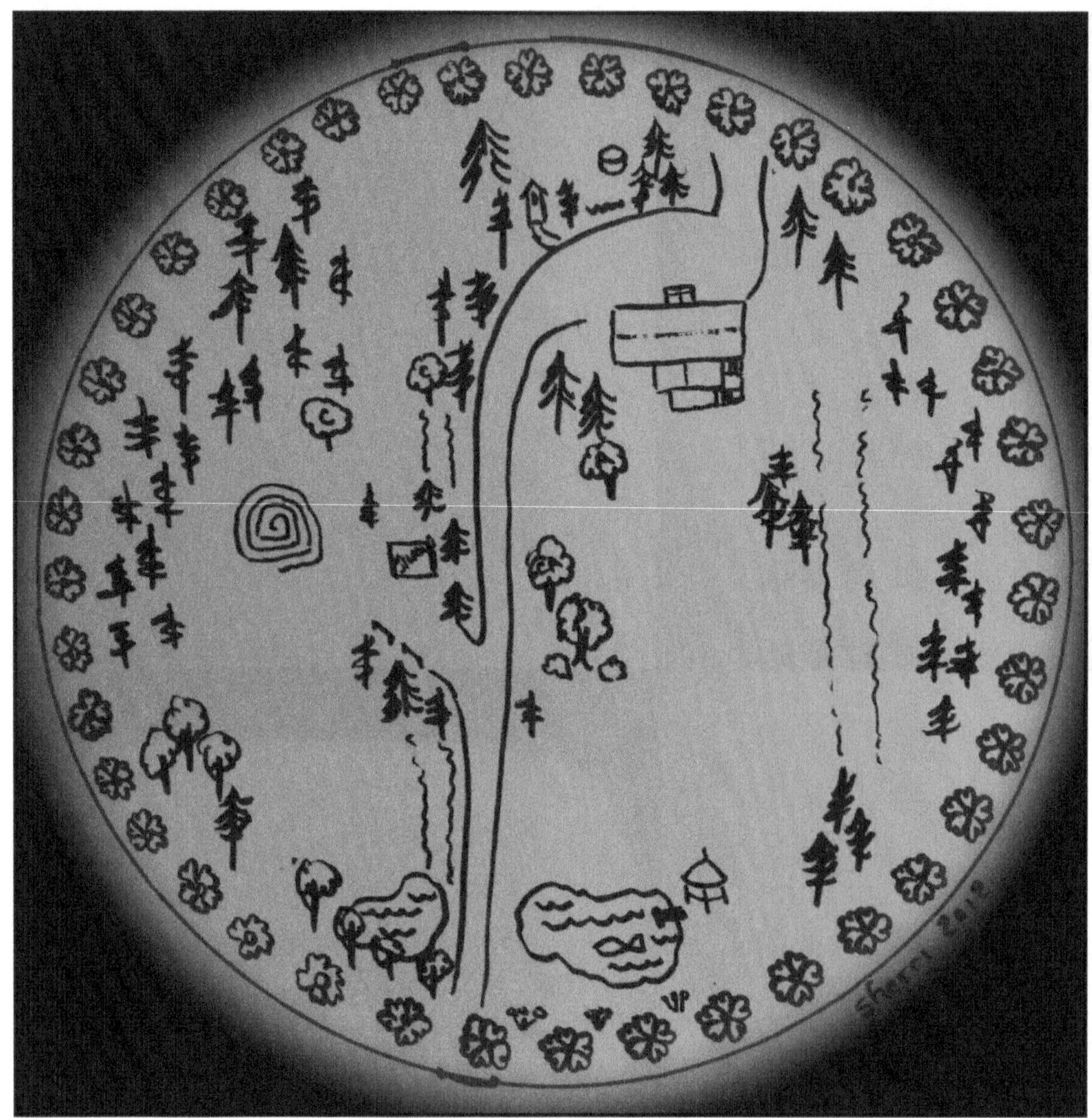

Meditative Mandala
July 28, 2012

Ink drawing
© Sherri Phibbs

Meditative Mandala
July 29, 2012

Ink drawing

Meditative Mandala
July 30, 2012

Mixed media

Meditative Mandala
July 31, 2012

Charcoal

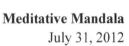

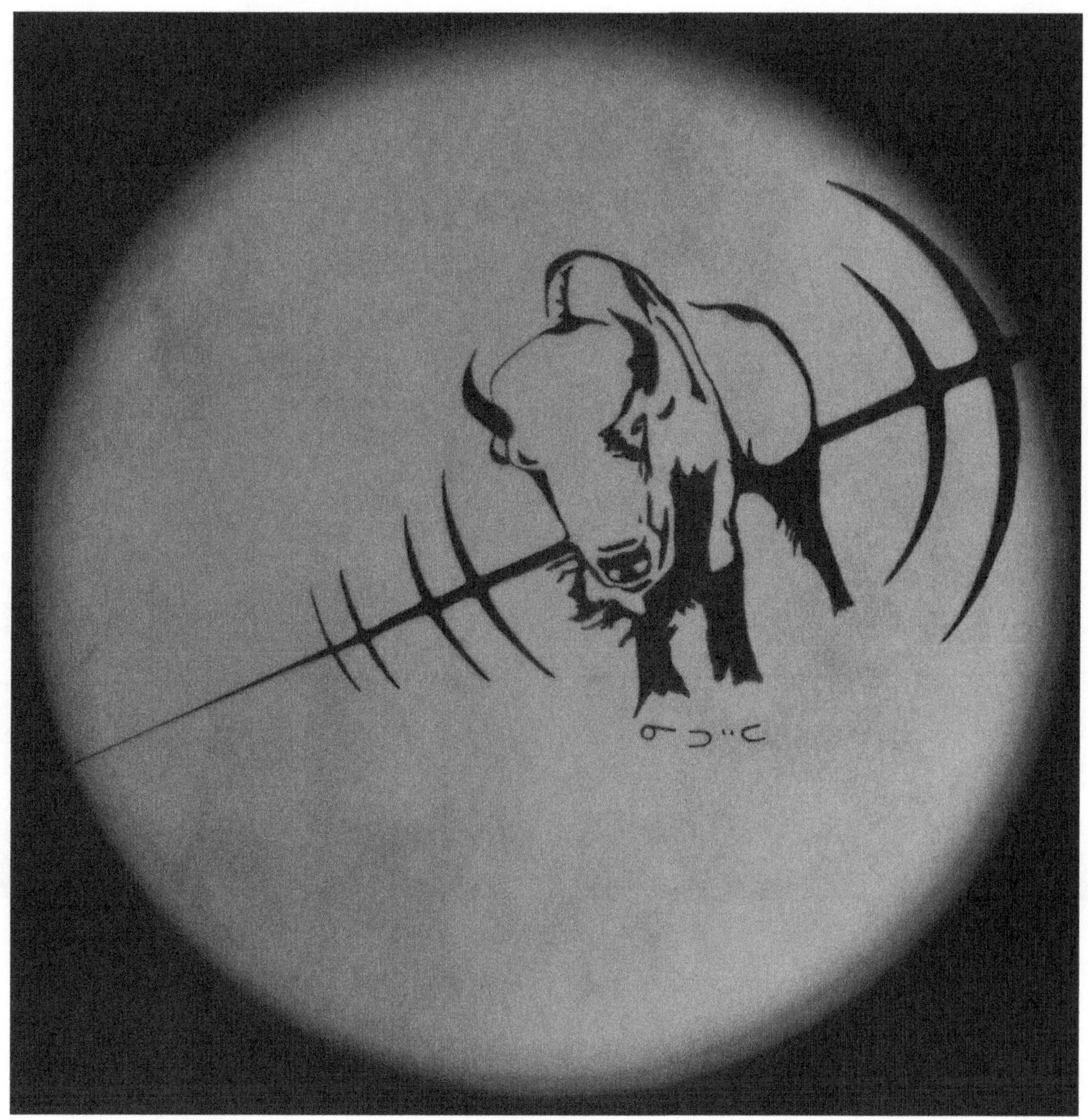

Totem Drum: Nitohta
August 1, 2012

Traditionally hand-made rawhide drum

Simple Beauty
August 2, 2012

Nature photography

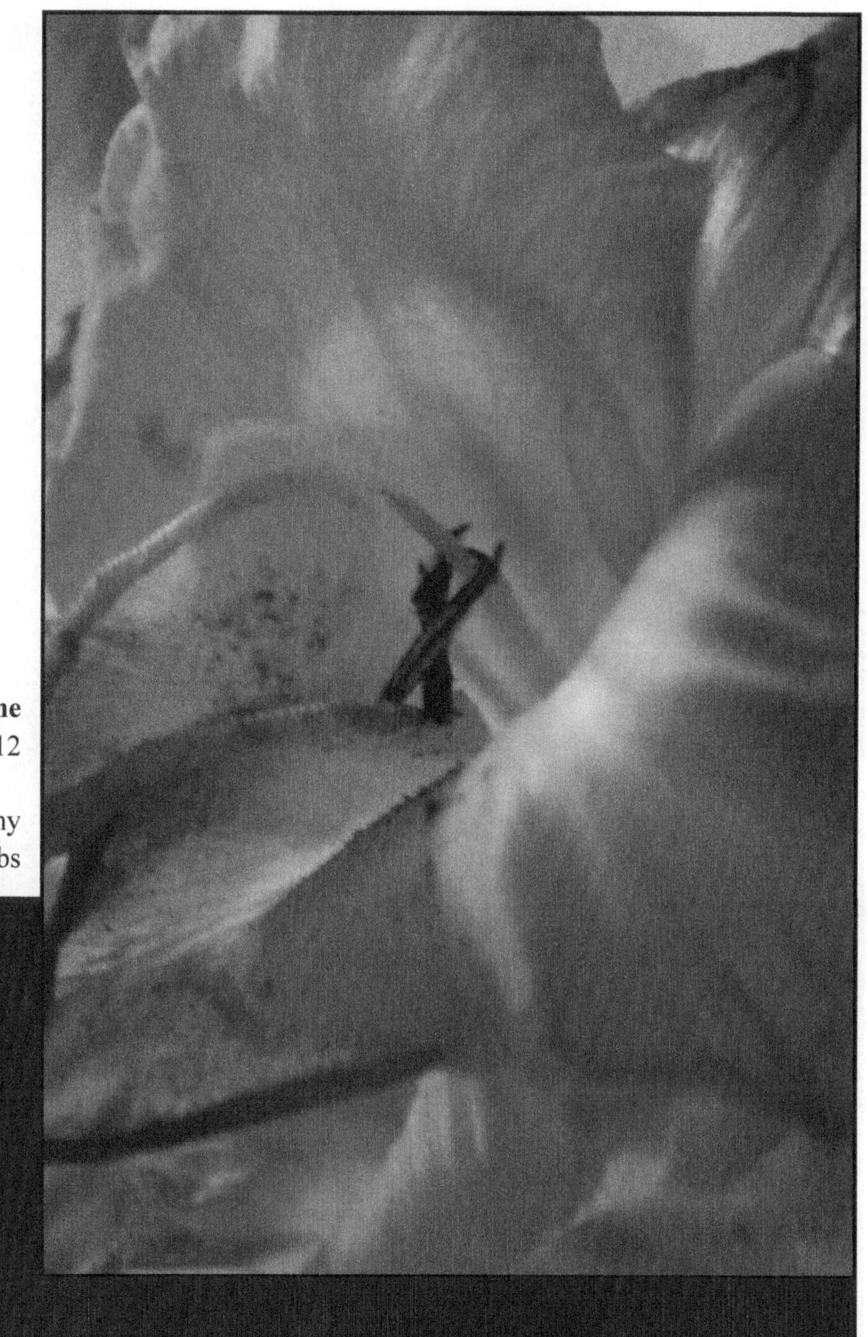

The Decline
August 3, 2012

Nature photography
© Sherri Phibbs

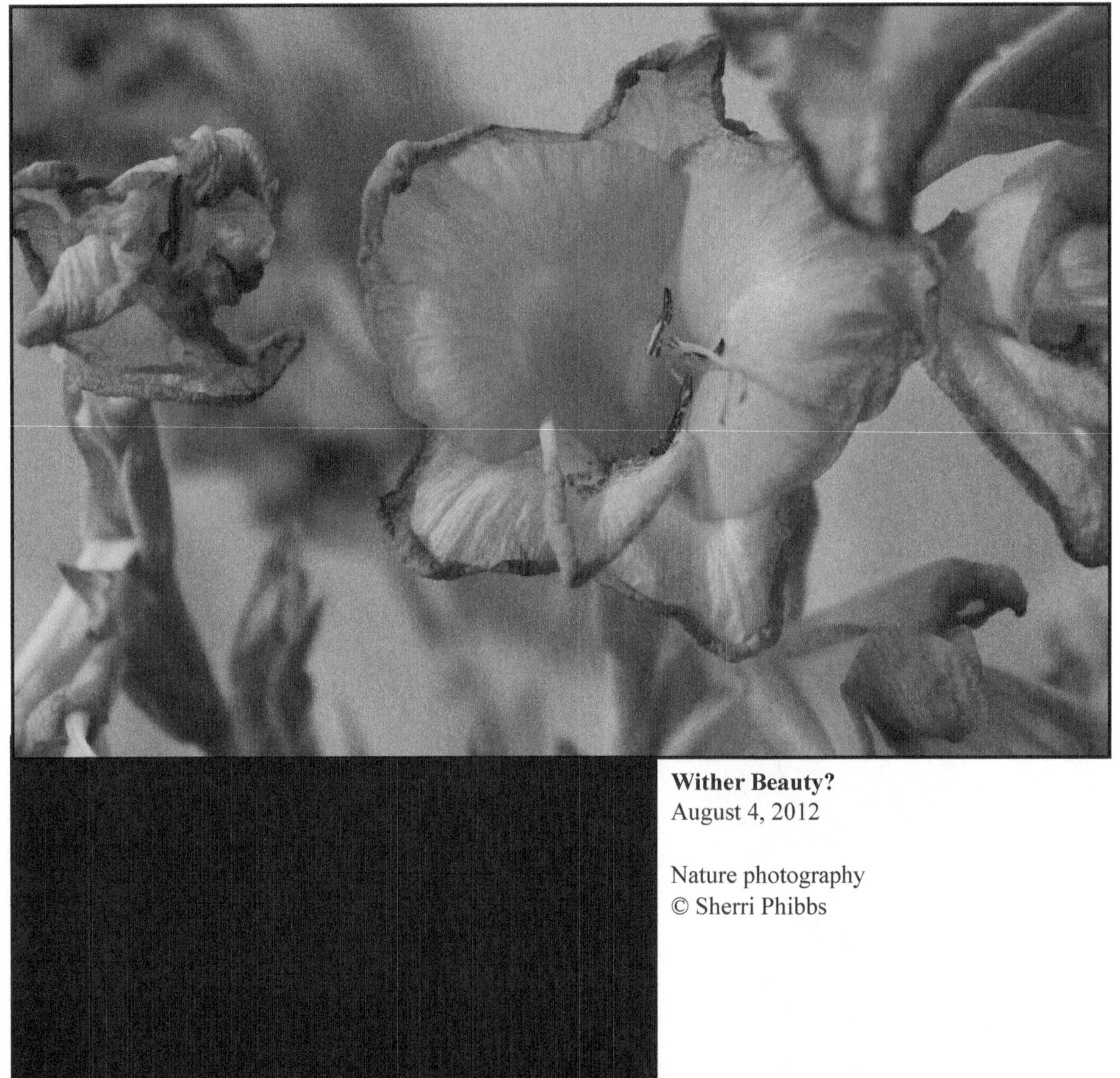

Wither Beauty?
August 4, 2012

Nature photography

A Trip Roadside
August 5, 2012

Nature photography
© Sherri Phibbs

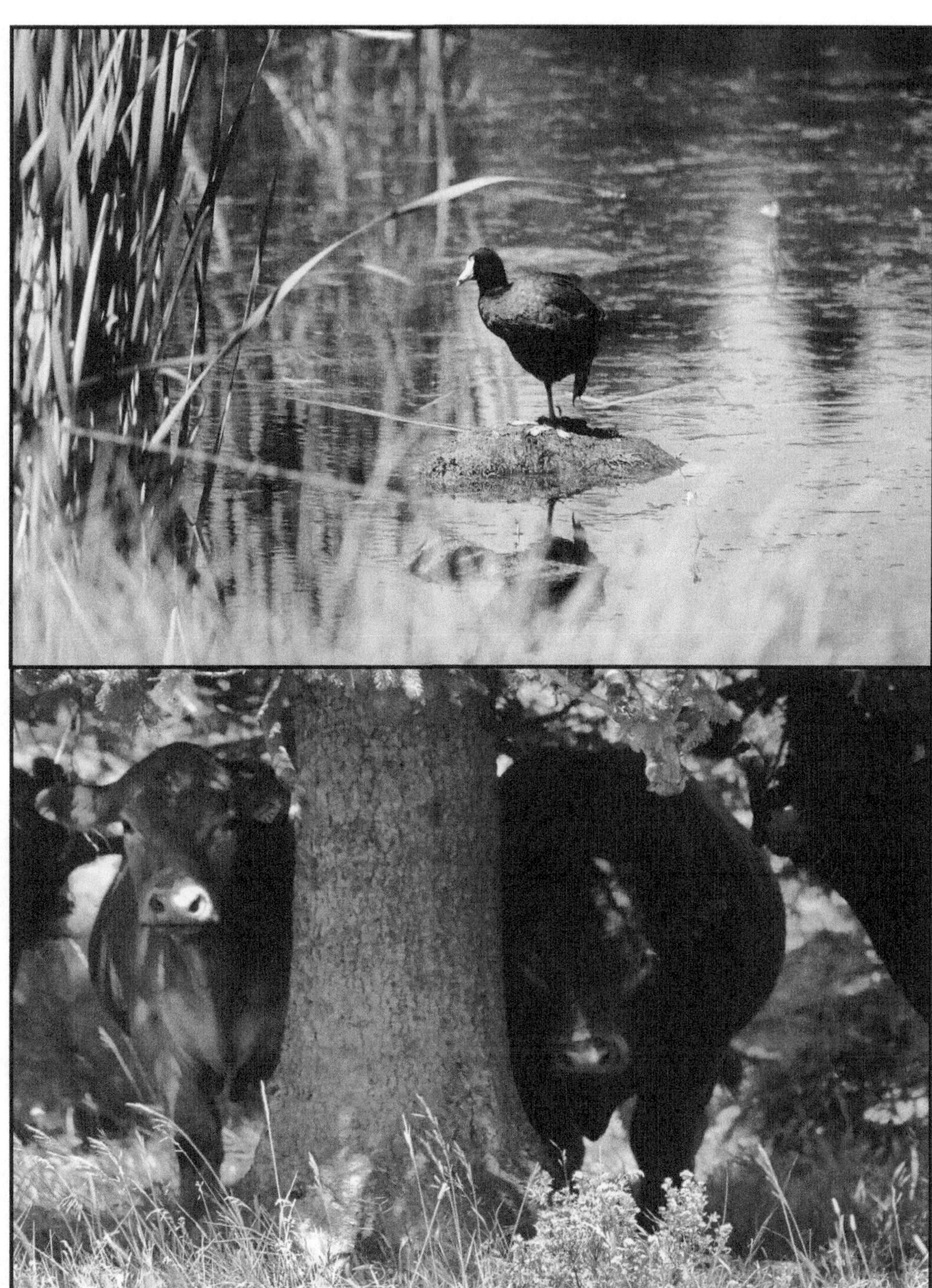

Wha'sup?
August 6, 2012

Nature photography
© Sherri Phibbs

Disconnected
August 7, 2012

Nature photography

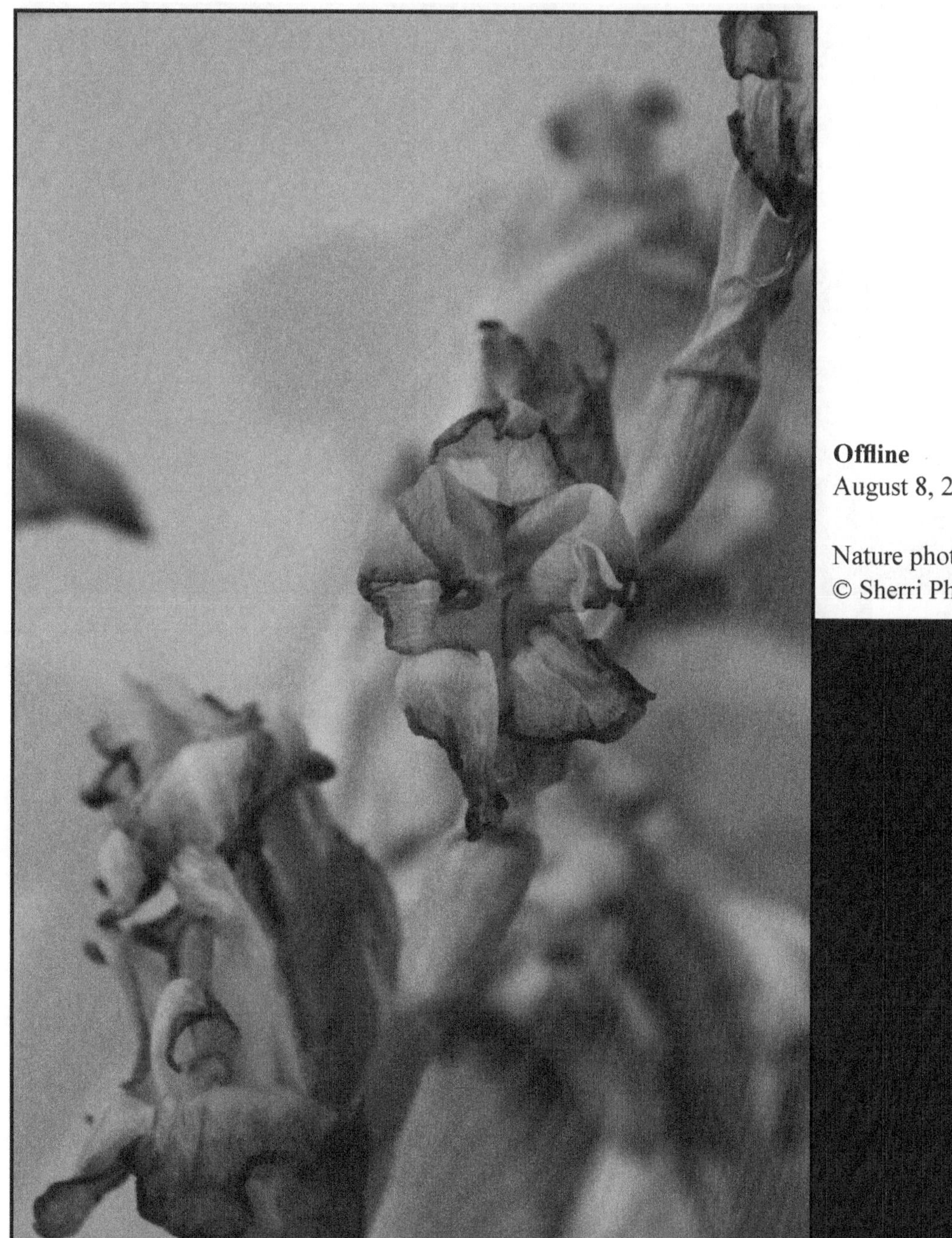

Offline
August 8, 2012

Nature photography
© Sherri Phibbs

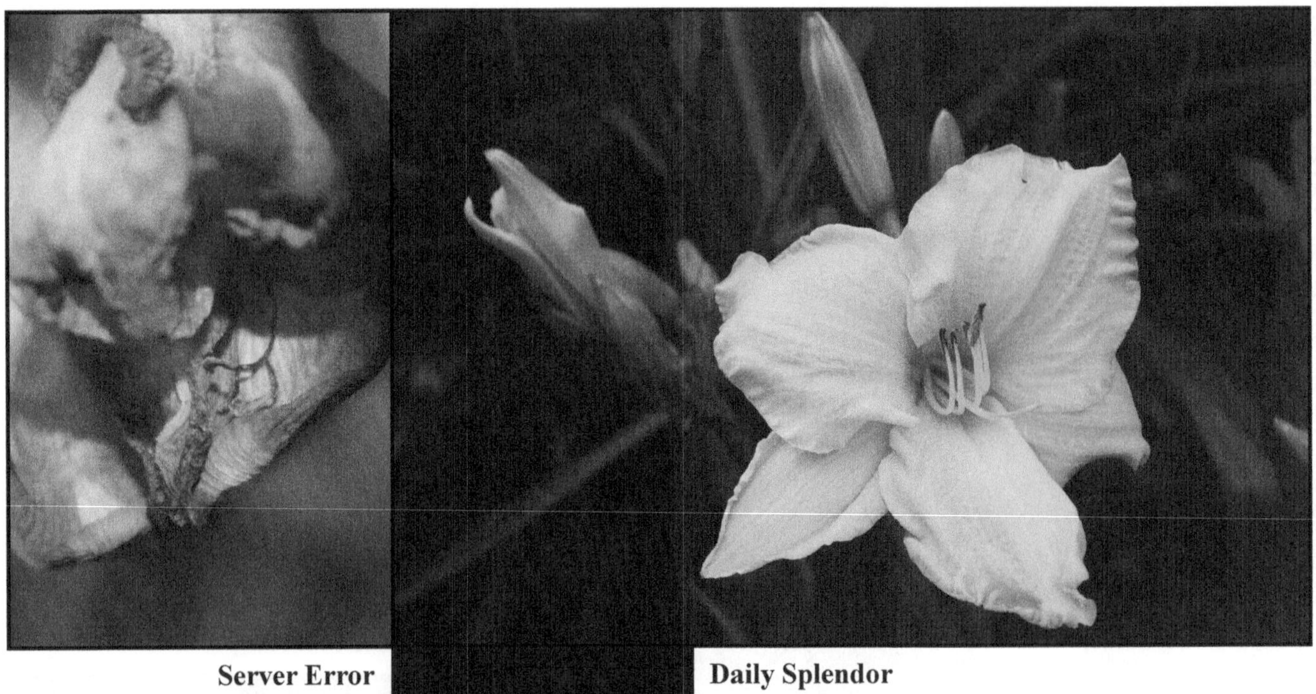

Server Error
August 9, 2012

Nature photography

Daily Splendor
August 10, 2012

Nature photography

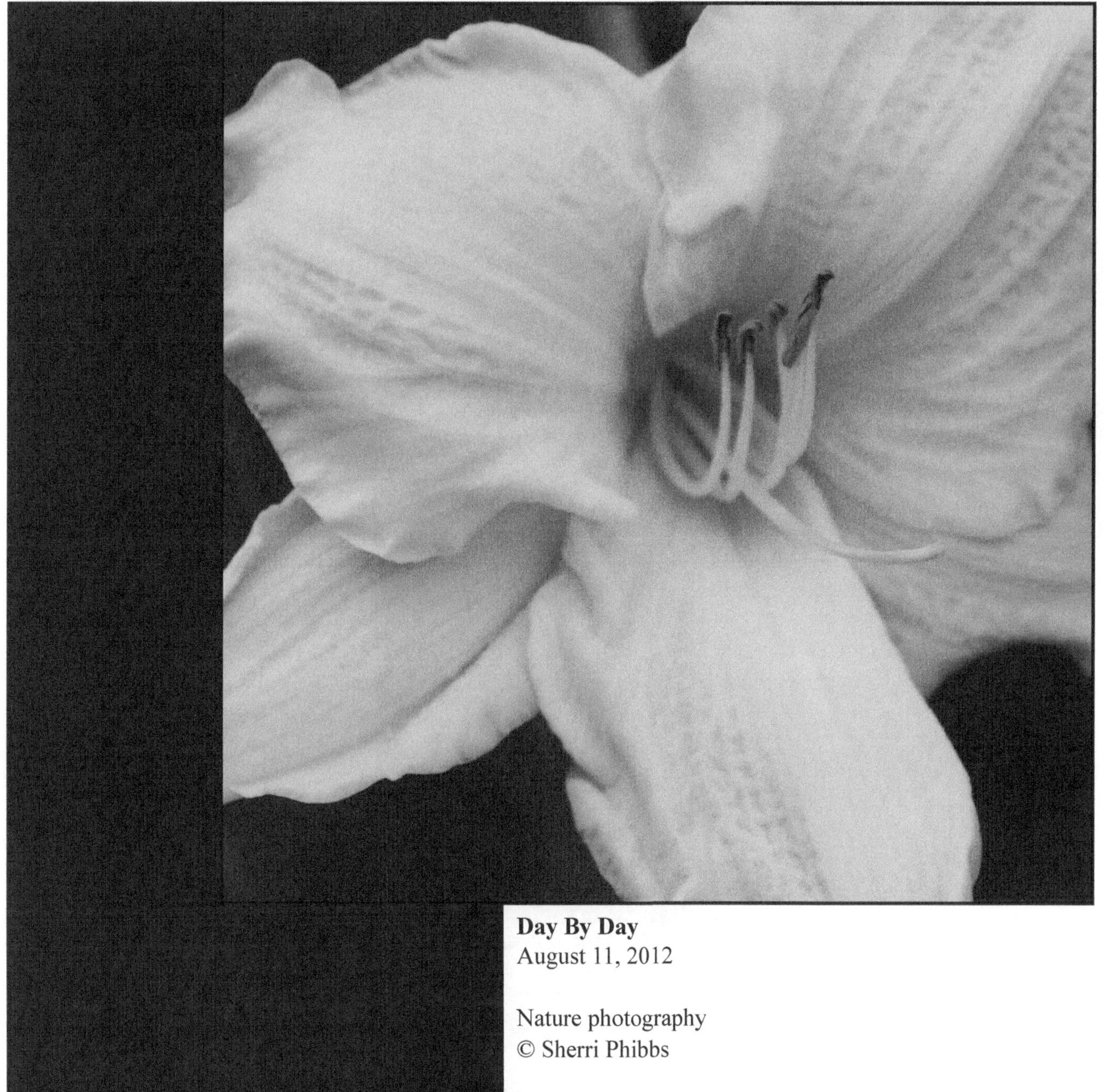

Day By Day
August 11, 2012

Nature photography

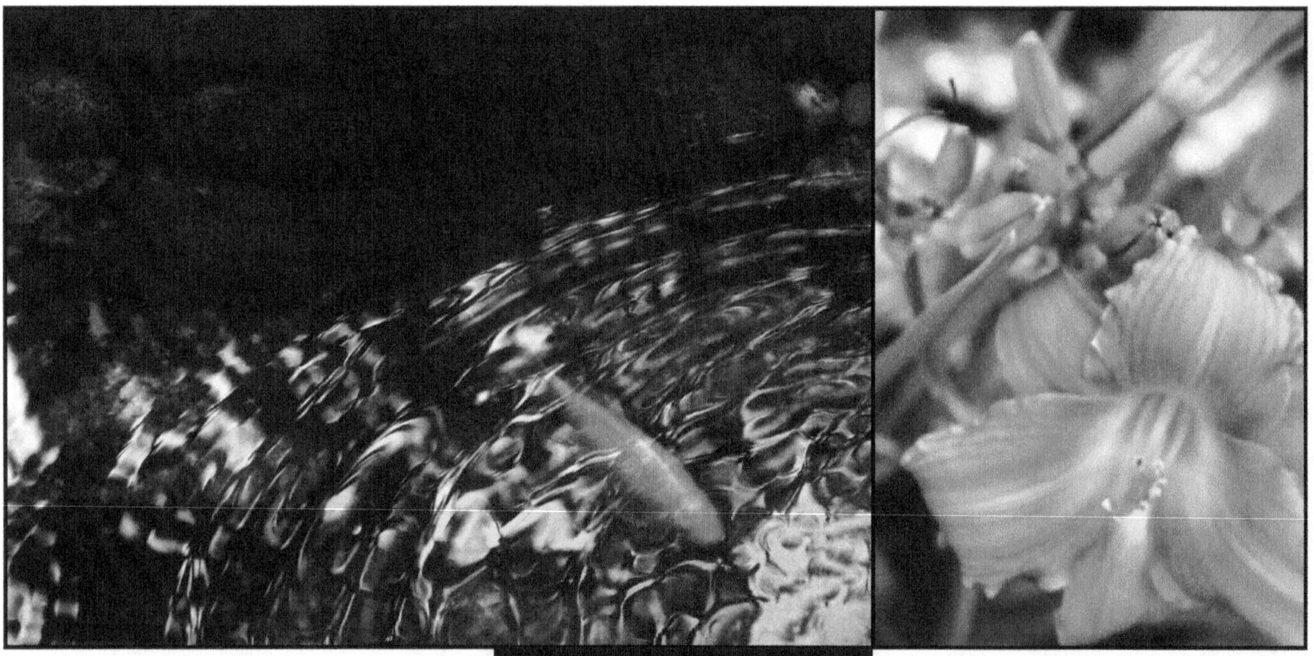

Ripples
August 12, 2012

Nature photography

Seething
August 13, 2012

Nature photography

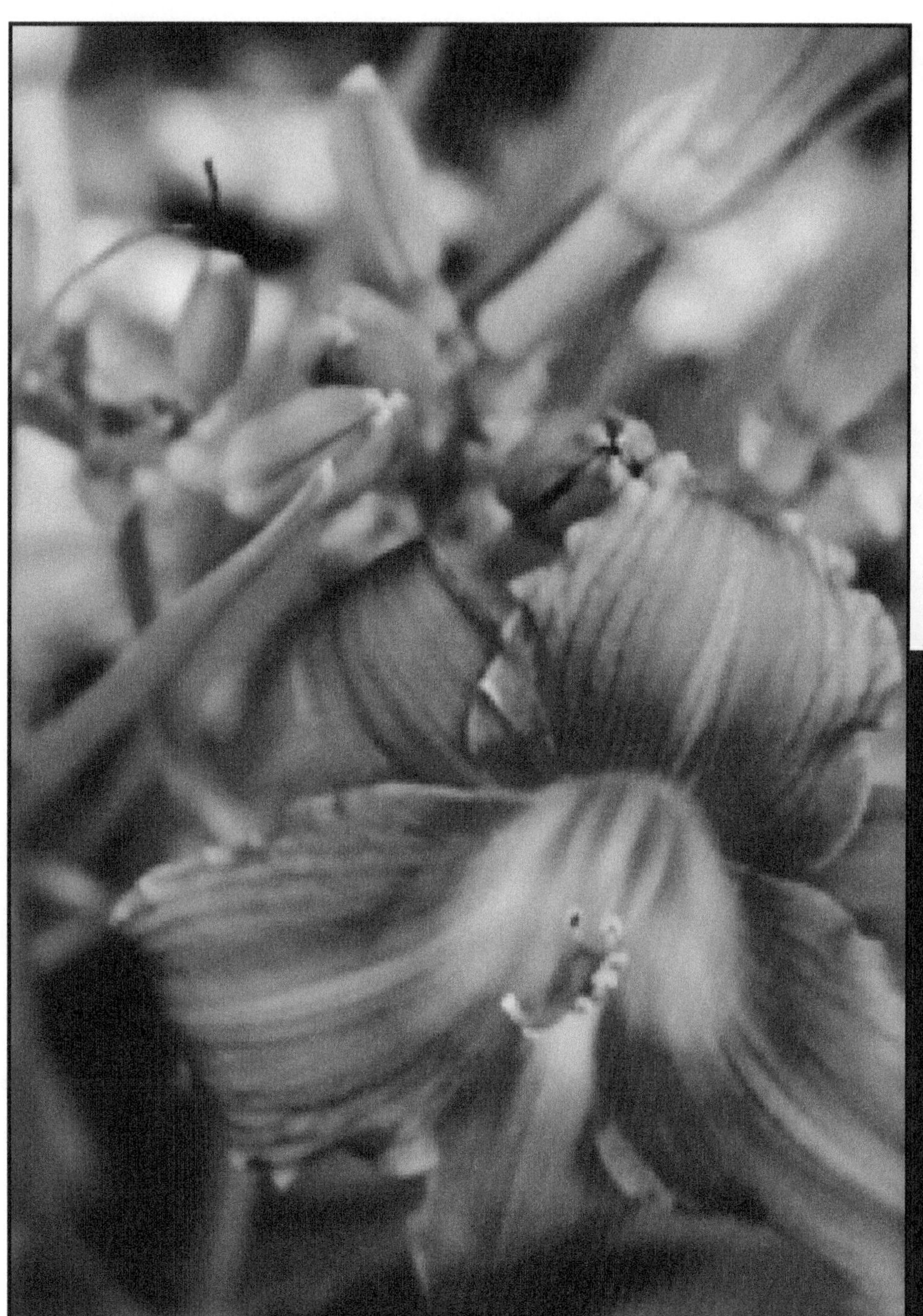

New Outlook
August 14, 2012

Nature photography

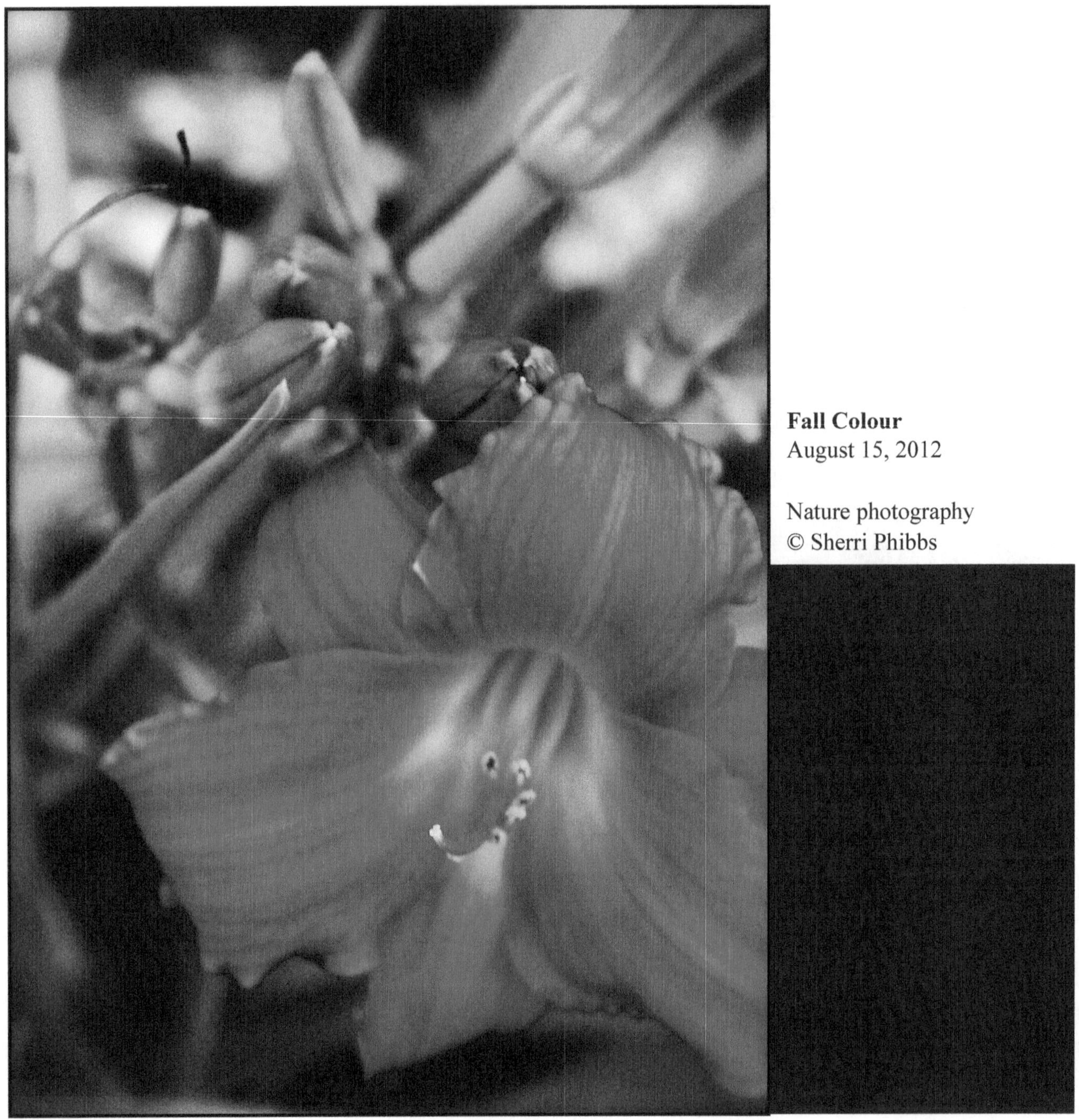

Fall Colour
August 15, 2012

Nature photography

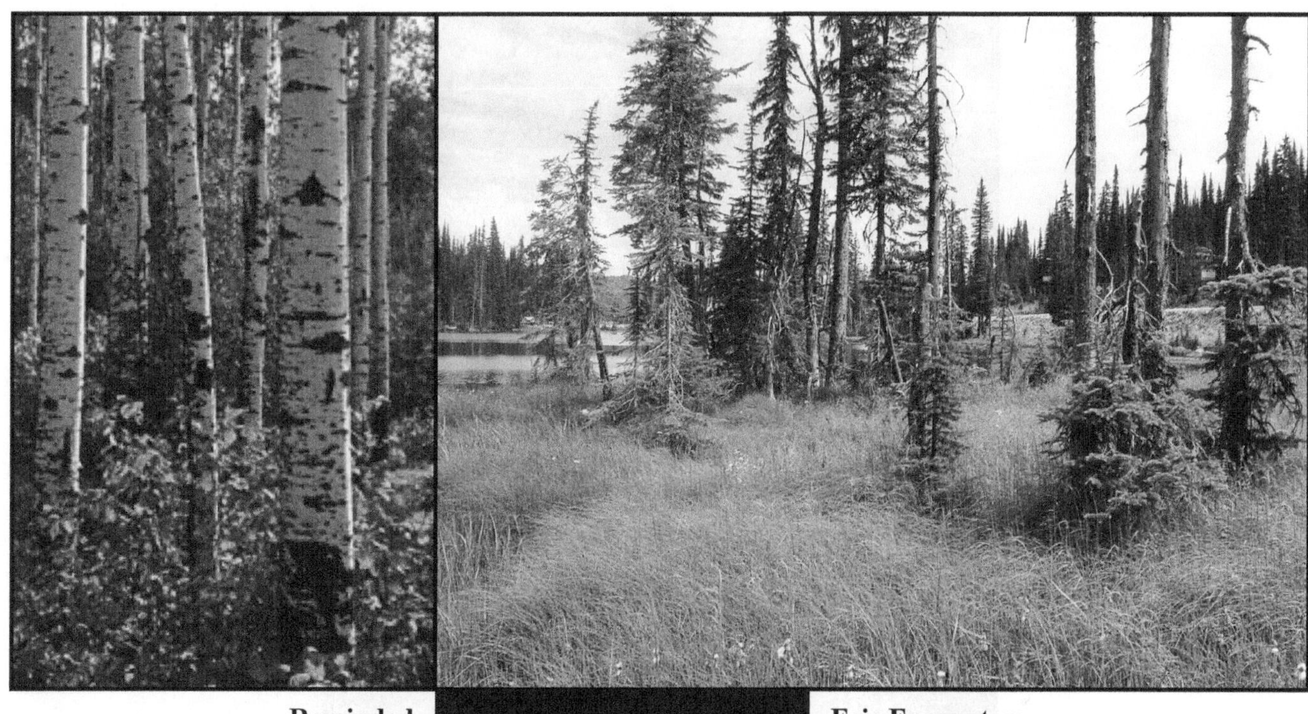

Reminded
August 16, 2012

Nature photography
© Sherri Phibbs

Fair Encounters
August 17, 2012

Nature photography
© Sherri Phibbs

Full Moon Drum
September 1, 2012

Traditionally hand-made
rawhide drum

Aspens@sunseT
September 2, 2012

Nature photography
© Sherri Phibbs

Captured Brilliance
September 3, 2012

Nature photography
© Sherri Phibbs

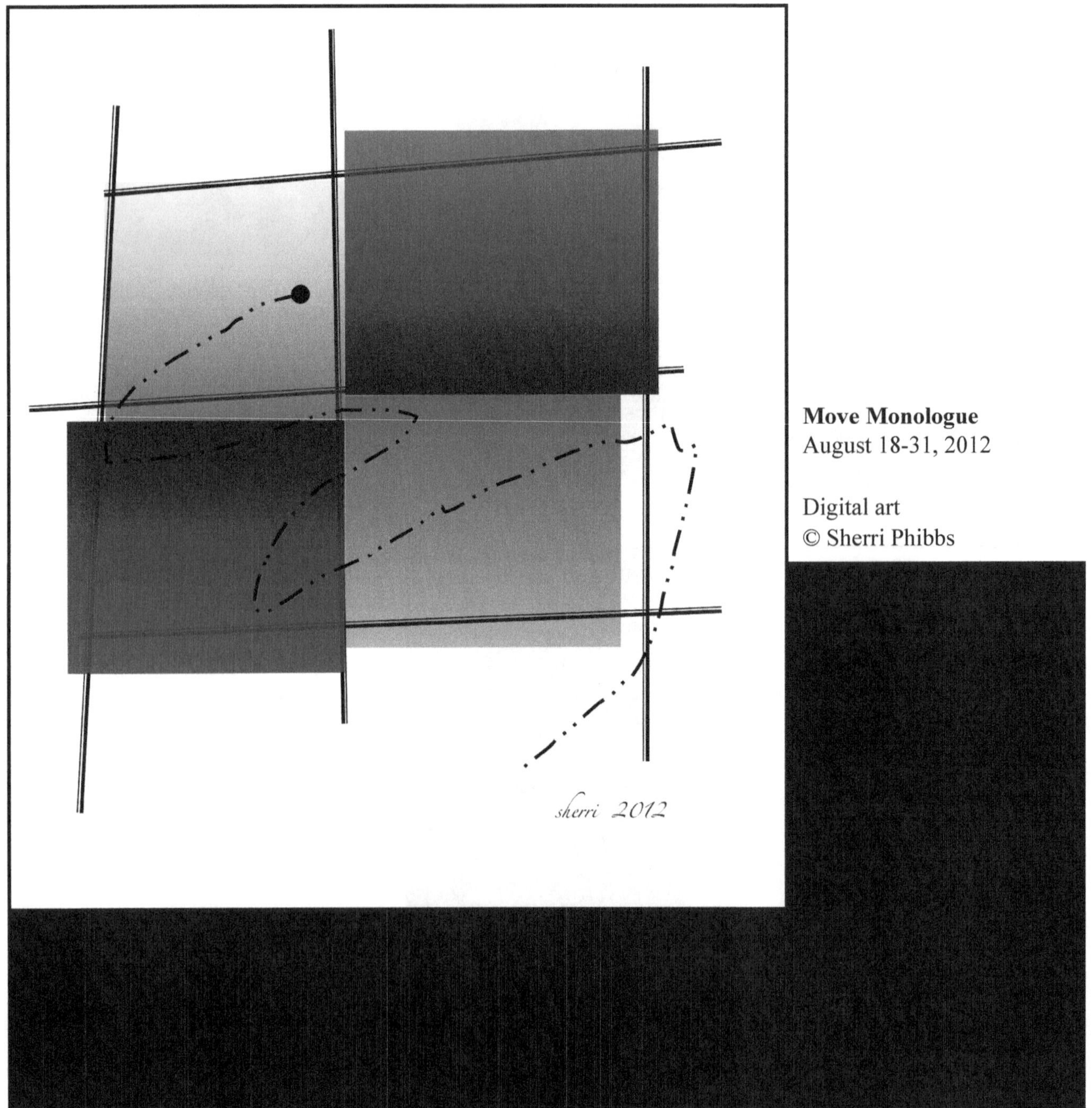

Move Monologue
August 18-31, 2012

Digital art
© Sherri Phibbs

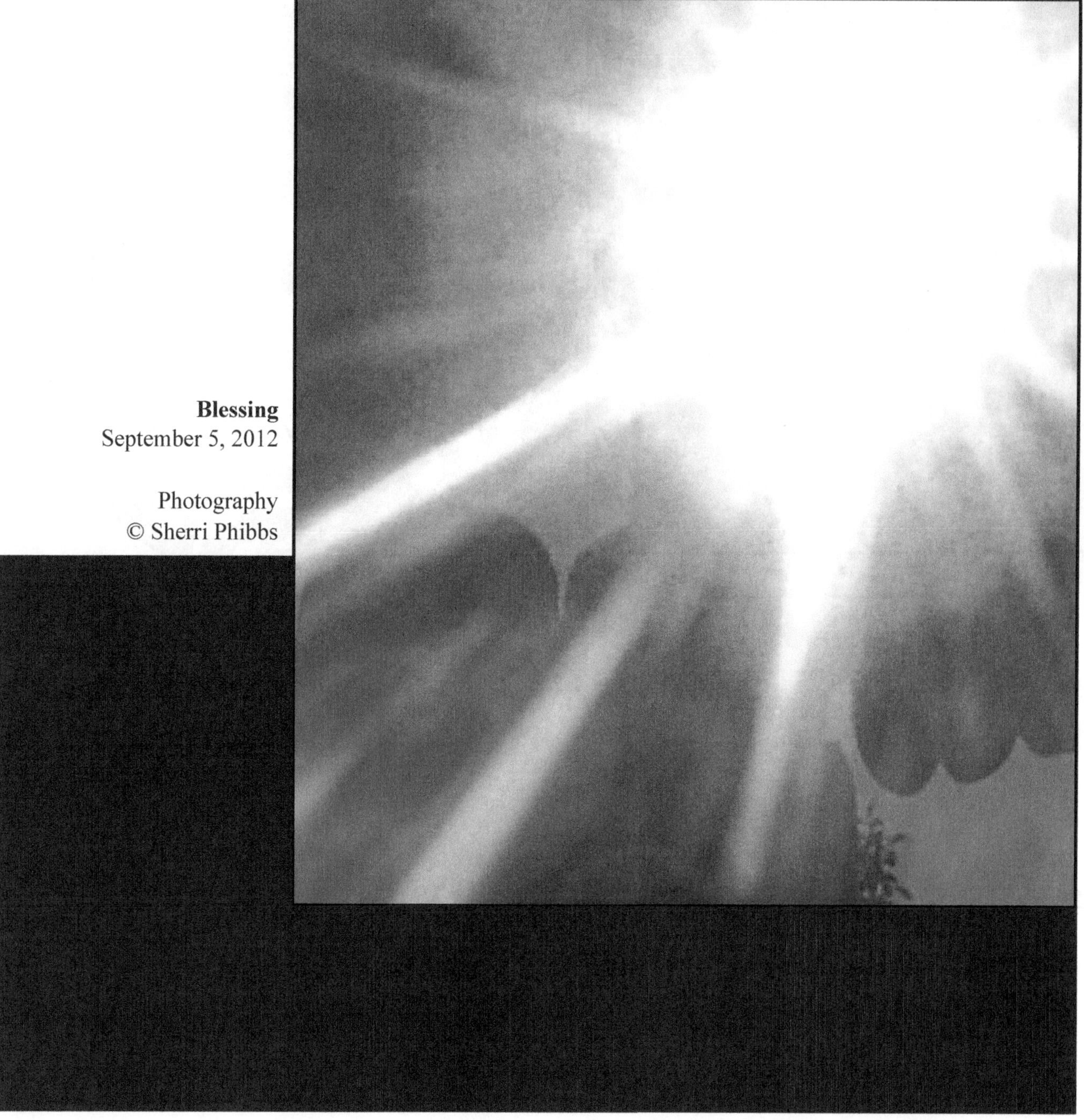

Blessing
September 5, 2012

Photography
© Sherri Phibbs

Lacework
September 6, 2012

Nature photography

Tanglewood
September 7, 2012

Graphic art

Tanglewood Gate
September 8, 2012

Graphic art
© Sherri Phibbs

Tanglewood Gate II
September 9, 2012

Graphic art

With an Autumn Brush
September 11, 2012

Nature photography
© Sherri Phibbs

The Right Path
September 14, 2012

Nature photography
© Sherri Phibbs

Layers of Shade
September 13, 2012

Nature photography
© Sherri Phibbs

Into the Sunset
July 8, 2012

Digital art
© Sherri Phibbs

Into the Sunrise
July 7, 2012

Digital art
© Sherri Phibbs

It's a Sign
September 12, 2012

Graphic art
© Sherri Phibbs

Impressions of Fall
September 21, 2012

Mixed media

Alignment
September 15, 2012

Nature photography
© Sherri Phibbs

Soulfire
September 16, 2012

Digital collage
© Sherri Phibbs

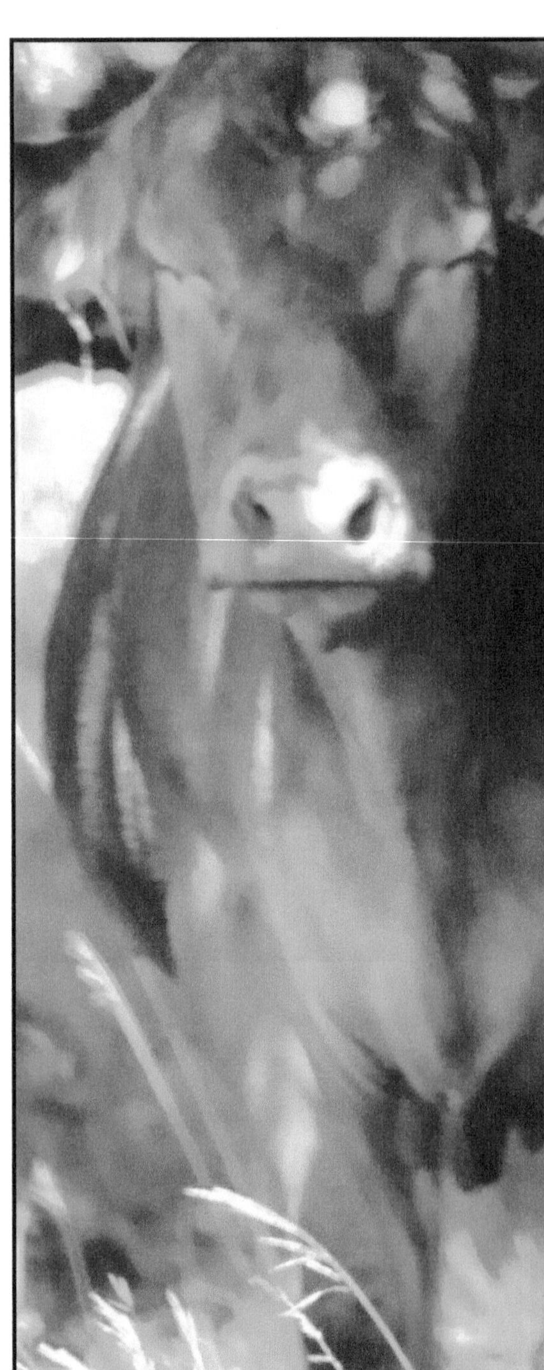

Green Cow
September 18, 2012

Nature photography

Stoo-di-yurt
September 17, 2012

Photography
© Sherri Phibbs

Purple Mule
September 1, 2012

Nature photography
© Sherri Phibbs

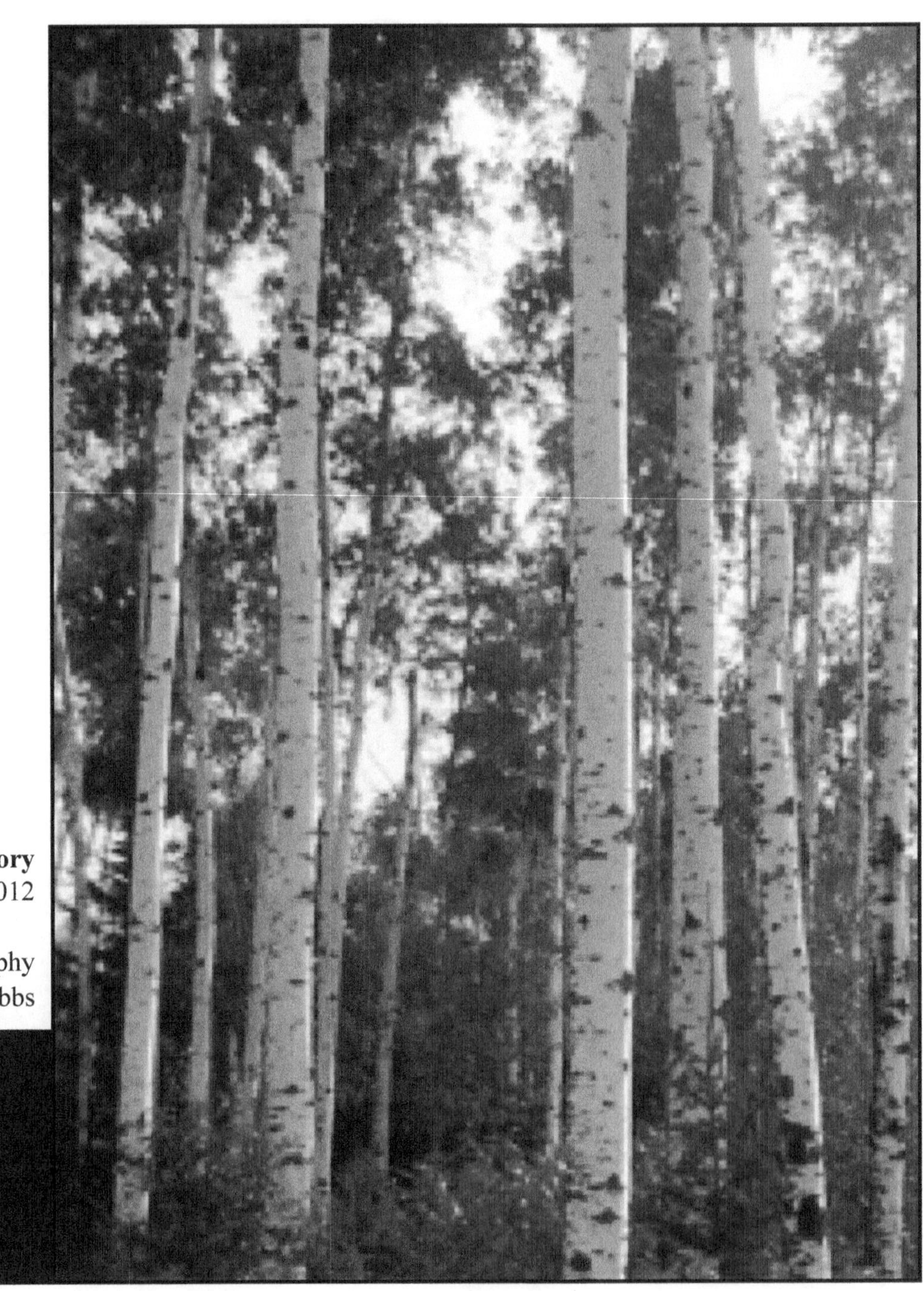

Morning Glory
September 4, 2012

Nature photography

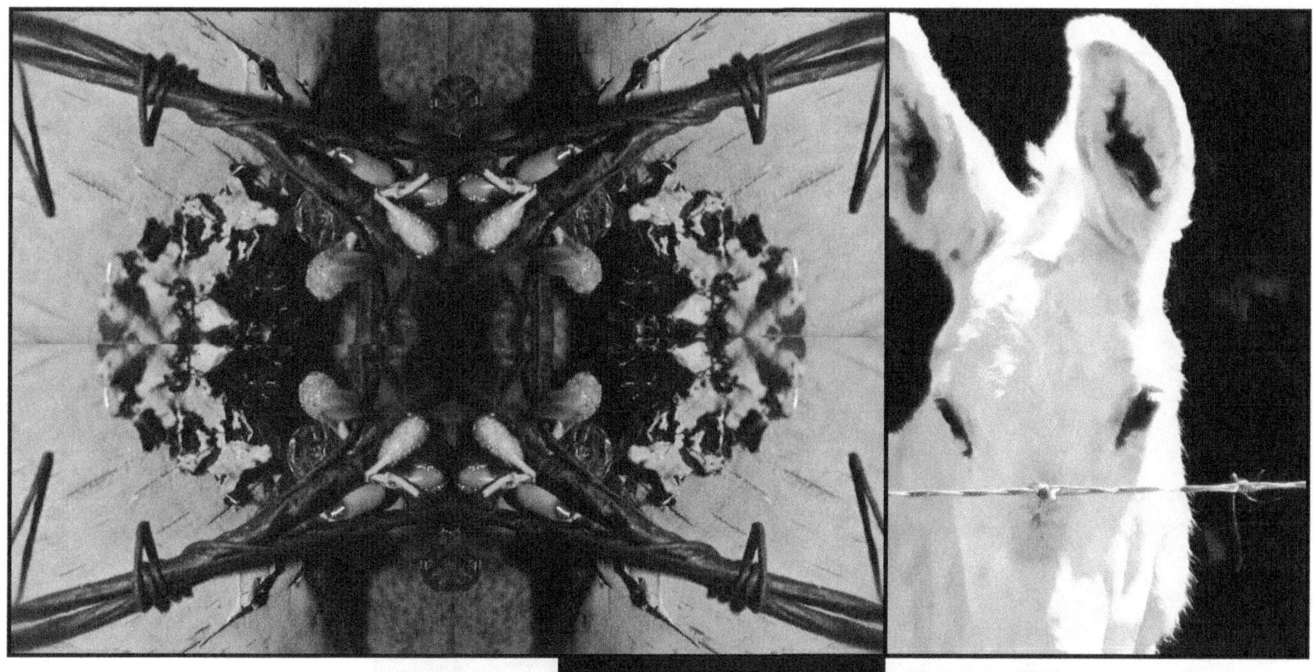

Confluence
June 18, 2012

Digital collage
© Sherri Phibbs

Hair on a Wire
September 20, 2012

Nature photography
© Sherri Phibbs

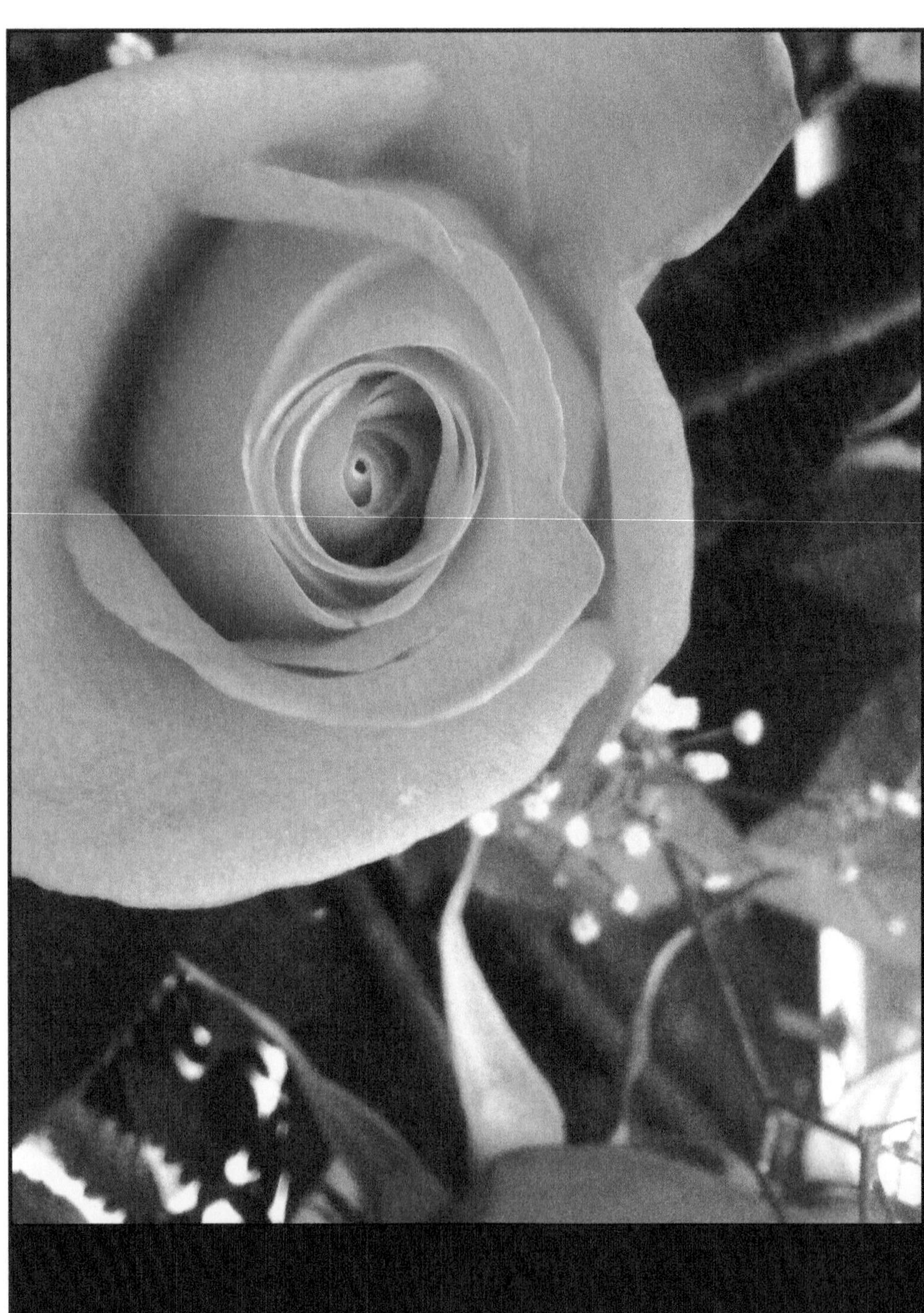

The Rose
June 20, 2012

Nature photography

The Dance
June 19, 2012

Digital collage
© Sherri Phibbs

Homemade
June 21, 2012

Sculpture
© Sherri Phibbs

Added Layers
September 22, 2012

Mixed media

WATER: The Written Word

Blogging along to Creativity

June 18, 2012

Today has been especially busy with a beautiful ride in the trees, creative work on wedding decorations, programs, visiting with riding friends, dance practice, and finally some creative artwork. I believe it might be time to get some sleep! And it starts all over tomorrow!

June 19, 2012

Rehearsal day! Things have come together in a beautiful dance, each note playing off the other in a joyous expression of rhythm that brings tears to the eye. Such beauty! Each friend, relative, and participant, a perfectly composed phrase in an elegant symphony, joined through the dance! Celebrating life and love.

June 20, 2012

One more sleep! Should I run?

June 21, 2012

Wedding Day! What a beautiful evening. Celebrating life with love.

June 22, 2012

The Road Forward

The path laid out before my feet
Unfolding with each step,
Each turning point a place to stand
And choose the way.

The choice is made with careful thought
Intending for the best,

Sending love out down the line
To light the way.

A beacon bright that loving glow
Prepares the way with grace,
And ripples back to trav'ler's heart
Along the way.

Celebrating life with love!

June 23, 2012
Watery Vortex,

Sensual spiral,
Wetly caressing the stones
In musical time.

June 24, 2012

Wow. I'm not sure what happened to my comments section, but as the website will be moving to a new address this week, I hope, this should resolve itself. I love reading the comments section. …Just discovered the comments section of iWeb no longer works. Mobile Me is not hosting websites after the end of the month, and the function is not viable elsewhere. Grrrr! Effective June 25th, the new web address is www.wishstudio.ca. Whew! Please send comments (including final art-down #) via "email me" button at bottom of the page, and I will post them on the page you are commenting on. Celebrating life with love and, I hope, some grace.

June 25, 2012

With the wedding, the planning, the fun, the ... everything … done, I find that I now have a few moments to reflect on the experience, although I feel it will be quite some time before I am finished processing. To begin with, I am so very grateful for everyone who helped make the day so special. These were truly moments to remember and treasure. One such moment was nature's gift of spontaneous joy. Floating across the garden on the gentle breeze, the lilting sound of robin song pulled at our heartstrings as the summer solstice sun set over the hills. We began our wedding ceremony blessed by this lovely bird's presence on the branch overhead. Today I published my website on the "real" web, as my son describes it. While sourcing a web-host, purchasing a domain name, uploading, managing accounts, etc., I'm discovering the need to copy and paste all the comments from the original blog pages onto the corresponding pages on the new website. I've found that my video clips are not working either, they may not make it, especially for a book. Earlier I was frustrated and growly, now I am just working through it all. More processing. The thought of that robin buoys my spirits. If Creation can provide such beauty to celebrate the truth of love, then the remembrance of that beauty can inspire love, truthfully. What an amazing circle I have the honour of being a part of.

June 26, 2012

Here I am, at the half-way point in the project! What a perfect time to promote Peace! And promotional artwork is the scope of today's work. I've been struggling with a project for the Summer of Peace 2012 initiative, and had briefly touched on the possibility of a local peace event offered through the studio. The poster in the art-down space is designed to hopefully spark some interest. This will be placed as a separate page on the website, as an event on Facebook, and a project on LinkedIn; with hard copy posters being distributed throughout my community. My goal is to max out attendance at six people for the workshop portion, with open attendance for the potluck. The new studio will probably be under renovations, so I hope to have this outside under the trees on the acreage! The artwork for the last while has centred on photography and Digital art of one sort or another, so in the next month or so, I hope to re-focus on the fine art of painting! Today will be the last digital offering for awhile. Look for June's drum offering on tomorrow's blog! And thank you for sending in a comment!!! I posted it on Final Art-Down 177 (FAD 177) at the bottom of the page.

June 27, 2012

Hmmm, that little fix of a glitch on the website was a bit more involved than expected! The sharp, stabbing pain radiating from between my shoulder blades is advising me to listen to my body. It started with a small twinge and a whisper but has since turned up the volume in order to make it through my thick skull. Today's artwork is the first step in creating the June drum. As a way of outlining the process, I thought it might be helpful if you saw a working drawing prior to the final drum product. Things just start out messy, then bit-by-bit, the refining process takes hold and a polished and complete work of art appears. Be willing to embrace change, allow the flow of ideas, and make room for the creation to grow. Most of all, have fun with it!

June 28, 2012

I'm not very happy with the shape of the robin in yesterday's sketch. Definitely a re-work is needed, but I have had a headache since last night, and it does not seem to be letting up at all! How to work when the light is piercing my head? Meditative mandala, here I come. Soothing music, soft light, and a conté pencil; does it get any better? Yes, a wedding dance under the stars, a warm puppy, breathtaking horseback rides. I am so blessed! Celebrating life with deep gratitude.

June 29, 2012

Here is a very interesting link to a book excerpt by Richard Louv. His book *The Nature Principle: Reconnecting with Life in the Virtual Age* is thoughtfully presented. http://noetic.org/noetic/issue-twenty-three-june/the-nature-principle/

Spending part of my day immersed in nature, I could literally feel the headache easing away. Perhaps it is as Richard Louv and, the forest medicine scholars at the Nippon Medical School and the Centre for Environment Health and Field Sciences in Japan have discovered. The salivary cortisol (a stress hormone) levels in my body were decreased with the exposure to a natural environment. Apparently, this exposure combined with movement can produce an effect that lasts up to thirty days, boosting the immune system and thereby increasing the body's ability to resist the detrimental affects of stress. Bye bye, headache. I love it when science catches up with and supports what we all inherently know to be true. Being immersed in a natural environment makes us healthier and less stressed. However, this robin sketching is creating stress, but of a different kind, the good kind. The kind of stress that pushes us to do our best, extend ourselves, surpass our previous levels of achievement. I'm feeling that push with this robin idea, so I'm still working it. Let's see what tomorrow brings! I can feel the adrenalin pumping excitement!

June 30, 2012

The garden called to me today. Well, actually Doug called to me, too, while out in the garden, to see how lovely everything looked. How thrilling to see the poppies in full bloom, to smell the completely bloom covered lilac tree, to see all the buds ready to open on the wild roses and the beginnings of berries on the saskatoons. It is lush and full, blooming, blossoming and fully thriving. How beautiful! It is like the plants are putting on their grandest show for us. We walked together in the garden, admiring all the new growth and exclaiming over the delightful new buds on the lilies and roses. The forget-me-nots waved their slender stalks to us as we took in their grace. What a wondrous display, this garden! How beautiful to share it in love. Celebrating life with deep gratitude.

July 1, 2012

Today I had to weigh my priorities; spend time with new husband as he is home for the weekend, or work on a drum this afternoon for the project. I have to admit, although the draw was strong for the drum production, the pull to travel through the national parks with my guy on Canada Day was stronger. However, as I was still creating with the camera in hand, this picture is a cool exercise in perspective. The placement of the camera, the angle of the shot, the lighting, etc., all distort the way we view the size of the objects in relation to each other. The tree is less than one foot tall! Says a lot about how we view the world we live in, if where we stand can affect our perceptions so deeply that an 8 inch tree can look huge. Makes me wonder...

July 2, 2012

As I continue to struggle with the robin imagery, I am taunted by the non-completion of this drum. This is the most difficult time I have ever encountered with a drum. There is a sense that something is taking shape but has not yet reached the defined state where the image is visible to my mind's eye. Quite often when I start a piece, the final image is already complete and visible to me, so this blind process of evolution is a little frustrating. It's as though I am seeing only one small part of the puzzle at a time and I'm required to piece them together as they arrive in random order. The eggs are important. The actions of protecting, caring, and loving are also very strong and deserving of expression. Yet the final outcome is still vague and in shadow. So piece by piece, I carve out the glimmers of the image and wait. Wait for the definitive, ah ha moment. Until then, I celebrate life with deep gratitude.

July 3, 2012

Okay, I'm putting the drum away for a bit. The image isn't coalescing the way I'd like, so back it goes to the subconscious for further play. I'm awaiting the time when it suddenly reappears, coming fully formed to my awareness with a glorious shout of excitement, create this now! The sketch for today was fully formed, but by no means perfectly executed in the short time span. However, this glows with its own light. It's a simple piece yet full of the mystery of the full moon. I won't say more; I'll just let you come into your own story. Hope you enjoy. I celebrate life with deep gratitude.

July 4, 2012

There are times when I just can't seem to find the words to express my experience of a day. Today is like that. But being the persistent, dedicated soul that I am, I am still going to give it a go. This week I've been volunteering in the mornings with a summer horse camp for children, working with a young boy who has autism. My horse and I have had the privilege of being part of his life for about three years now, and I was excited because today was the day we painted Neo. So, just like they did in the "wild west", we gathered up our paint and told our story. After some streaks of paint made it onto Neo's flank, I noticed that they resembled the tail of a comet or shooting star, so I added a star in the appropriate place. This was followed by numerous dots in every colour of the rainbow. At this point, the paint was running down our hands, so we decided to just add more, and a beautiful hand print in purples and blues appeared on Neo's side. We followed up with a ride around the pond where we watched as the wind played all around us, creating waves on the long grass of the hills, and the water in the pond. We watched the windmill turn and he told me about solar power, wind power, and hydro power. Then we listened to the birds, and watched quietly while Neo ate grass. Later in the evening, after summer camp was well over, I had the opportunity to go for a ride. We loaded the horses into the trailer and took off for the country. We rode through the tall trees of foothill forests, up and down long, steep hills, over creaky bridges, rivulets and mud, and waded among tall fields of wildflowers of all colours and shapes. And through it all, I was accompanied by the shooting star and little purple and blue handprint. I celebrate life with deep gratitude.

July 5, 2012

I'm working on other pieces, trying to finalize the drum and get ready for the November show, oh and move! At some point I am going to have to pack everything up and sort and have a garage sale. This picture is a focus on the colour of the day. Red. Blood, life, passion, frustration, anger, love ... vibrantly alive! Celebrating the range and depth of feelings.

July 6, 2012

Pieces of this one have been flitting through my mind since Wednesday night's ride. This is begging to be developed further on a much larger scale. I'm looking forward to exploring the balance in this work; I feel surprised when I look at it.

July 7, 2012

It's interesting how the smallest change can create such a difference. By adding warmth to the colour, changing the perspective and angles, we move from a colder more distant feel in yesterday's work to a much friendlier and softer approach to today. Maybe that is a reflection of my inner growth process as well. Maybe I have had my heart warmed and made softer today, and this artwork is just a reflection of the changes on the inside. Maybe it reflects the vulnerability that comes from relationship with others. Being able to accept and feel emotion essentially requires an openness of heart, mind, spirit and soul. Sometimes we open on our own, and sometimes something breaks us open. The old adage of the feather or the hammer lesson comes to mind ...

Perhaps today was a bit of both. I send out the intention to touch those in my life in a way that brings peace. May you be happy, may you be whole.

July 8, 2012

Timing, it's all about the timing. I've heard this phrase so often that it is almost engraved on my eardrums. Kairos time, things happen right when they are supposed to. The changes in lighting that are created as the sun moves has a magnificent effect on the perception of feelings in an art piece. Where there is a sense of expectancy in early morning light, the gloaming time or sunset provides a sense of wrapping up, or being enfolded in the nightly hug and kiss from the light, the glorious splendour a reminder that all is well. Warmth and sleep beckon.

July 9, 2012

It looks like I'm not quite done playing with this one! Must admit that I am having quite a bit of fun. The model touched my heart years ago, so every chance I have to work this in somewhere makes me smile. And here we have it, pop art meets western imagery! Who knew my journey would uncover such quirkiness. Quintessentially Albertan, its rural roots are being pulled up, presented and modernized by both the film and art industries, as well as through the efforts of the Calgary Stampede's 100th anniversary program. It's the modernization of western culture, presented through today's lens of marketing, economics and viable investment potential. Perhaps it's a social statement of the times? Hmmm, I am so confused! What is it we are trying to say? Is it really all about the money?

July 10, 2012

Art can make statements. Sometimes on our journey we encounter others who are lost, drifting souls on their own paths, parallel or at the very least simultaneous to our own. We see them, but do we really SEE them? Are they in our path to stimulate action, or are they there in our field of vision as a reflection of the lost parts of our own soul that need or needed healing? By addressing or dressing our own broken places and wounds, we are able to move past the "it's all about me" stage of healing, and move on to the "it's about us" stage of healing.

I see you. I see the brokenness in you because I have seen and dealt with the same in me. Now what can I do about it? Art makes statements.

July 11, 2012

These high temperatures have me melting like a Dali clock. Yet despite (or maybe because of) the intense heat wave, I have had a break-through, a moment of insight, self-discovery and clarity. I am absolutely terrified by the idea of self-promotion, either artwork or business related, and it all boils down to a lack of confidence in my presentation skills. So, here I sit, unmoving, surrounded by the plethora of today's marketing genius: SEO's and PPC's, networking and social media. Galleries, art clubs, corporate event promos are all things that require face time with another living, breathing human being who will judge me as worthy or not based on a three sentence elevator pitch. No wonder I have approached this with trepidation! I'm evaluating my intent. I intend to be found by an image consultant who can see my potential and will enthusiastically and sensitively develop it. I'm coming across with my halter and rope all fouled up in the wrong hands, tentatively asking, "Do you think maybe you might see, possibly, a bit of value, maybe in this bit of a ... kind of a ... team building thing I have designed... maybe?" Ummm, I should stand in my own power, yes? On that note, I'm looking for a business that would be interested in participating in an "at cost" six person, two-day team building event in September or early October. This event will be filmed and developed into a promo video for corporate team building event planners and then placed on YouTube and various other social media platforms, as well as my website. I'd love to talk about this and how your company could benefit from it. Contact me at sherri@wishstudio.ca .

July 12, 2012

Maintaining integrity and remaining heart-centred through the promotion process will require a great deal of focus and strength of purpose! How do I not get caught up in my own hype? A wise friend of mine provided a word of caution: There are those who will think you are golden and saintly, and those who will believe that every word uttered is supreme b.s. and you are going to h*ll. Always remember you are neither of these: you are balanced, humanly, somewhere in the middle. So throughout this process, I will live heart-wise, checking in for integrity, balance, harmony and peace. My direction may change, I may experience personal or professional growth, be wounded or reopen old wounds, heal or clear out the chaff. Things happen. And yet, as I focus on being heart-centred and authentic, I am heartfelt, true, and sincere. Bee yourself! (Groan.)

July 13, 2012

One hundred and sixty days to go to the End of the Age, and if humanity hasn't been destroyed by the catastrophic eruption of a mega-volcano, I am going to take up the suggestion of having this work put into a book. It will be a peace offering of sorts, with a percentage of all sales to be donated to a local charity, promoting healing and harmony from the grass roots up. Honestly, as I sit here at the end of this Friday the 13th and approaching the Mayan end of the world as we know it, I feel excited. Are there signs of a transition? If so, what are they? Am I missing them? Is there a change management process in effect? What about process charts, a map? What if ... we shift to a higher level of consciousness, as some expect? What if ... we experience spontaneous evolution, as some others expect? What if ... nothing happens? What if... something does? What if... we move away from destructive patterns, personally, socially, environmentally, globally? Would you be excited?

July 14, 2012

Dancing the Journey: Listen. Dance. Fly...

"Really be alive," the Spirit of All Horses whispers to the heart of man, "I am of spirit and of soul. I am in you and around you. Listen. You are whole; you are alive, so live like you are! Listen... and be." Celebrating life with love.

July 15, 2012

The shaman's walk has come to mind repeatedly today, so perhaps I can share a little bit about it here. I must admit I am a bit hesitant to get into these skills in a blog, but here I go.... There are those who approach shamanic practice with religion in mind. What's interesting to me? I approach shamanic practice with science in mind. There is no worshiping during journeying or ceremonial cleansing or meditation practices, only a deep connection, love and acknowledgement of our natural world, creation. A natural world that doesn't dictate what or how we worship, or what we believe. The main caveat for all work is that it is conducted in the highest good of all involved. So with the disclaimer out of the way, and not very comfortably on my end I must admit, let me tell you about a shamanic walk. Have you ever done an exercise where you hold your hands together like they are encasing a ball, then push together until you feel the energy of the ball pushing back? Holding chi? A shaman's walk is like that on a larger scale, using your senses (all 53, thank you for your research, Dr. Michael Cohen, Project Nature Connect) to feel the energy of other push against your own energy. How close do you come to a tree before you feel the energy of the tree meeting yours? How close to the rock, the dog or the horse? There is a process for learning and experiencing this meditative walk that I'd love to share with you and will try to illustrate with today's artwork.

July 16, 2012

It's been a long day what with all the paperwork, etc., on its way for The Sound of Peace Project, the material inventory checks complete, the visits with amazing people, and the beginning of the purge in preparation for the move, all in between the feeding of horse, dog, fish, and family. As the song goes, what a wonderful life!* Hope you enjoy today's piece as much as I enjoyed making it! Take care until tomorrow.

*(Elvis Presley, 1962 song lyrics, *What A Wonderful Life*, from the album *Follow That Dream*, soundtrack from 1962 musical of the same name, Mirisch Productions).

July 17, 2012

Today began with the rescue of a vole. Yes, I can hear you. ... why would she rescue it rather than trap it? Well, I couldn't trap it; that felt so wrong. It fell into the basement window well and was scrabbling against the window trying desperately to climb back out. After watching this cute little teddy bear hamster type being frantically searching for a way out, I couldn't *not* help it. You see, I've had mice die in there before, only to find their sad little bodies days later. I knew if I left it, this one would die, as well. With my deeply ingrained sense of respect for all life, I was determined to rescue the little beast. I went out to the garage and grabbed a branch, pruned from one of the yard trees earlier in the spring, and propped it inside the well, hoping it would serve as a ladder for the little one to climb to safety. I must admit I had horrifying mental-pictures of it swarming up the stick and onto my arm, so I was rather abrupt in the stick placement. And since it was 2:45 AM, pitch dark and very quiet, I didn't hang around to see if it worked. I remembered the little one when I woke this morning and went out to check. Expecting an empty window-well, I was dismayed to find that the stick I'd chucked in there in the dark had landed in the middle of the well, and of course voles travel along the walls.

Poor little one, I thought, you didn't even see the escape route! So more carefully this time, I gently placed the end of the branch along the wall, directly in front of the panting furry body. I remember wondering if it had sustained any injuries in the fall. Once again, I left hoping to return to an empty well. Around noon, I returned from my morning appointments and went directly out to take a look. There was the poor little furball, all curled up as though it was completely devoid of hope, just laying down to die. I was horrified! No way, little one, are you going to give up when I have made such an effort to provide you with an escape route! I realized there was no water down there, so I filled a small rice crispy square mould and placed it in front of the ball of fur, who perked up enough to come over and check it out. It looked up at me, and when nothing happened, it just seemed to sink back into itself and huddle back down into a ball. Again I was thinking I have got to get this little creature out of this hole! So I grabbed buckets and brooms trying to gently coax the cute little hamster type fur-ball to go into the bucket so I could lift it to safety without it scrambling onto me. No luck. It was so despondent that I could lift the little back end up with a gentle push of the broom, but it would just plop back down in place.

Finally, I said to myself, "Sherri, you are going to have to stop worrying about what could happen and just reach in and scoop it up, lifting and trusting that it won't move around and fall off or scramble up your arm." But what should I lift it with? Thinking, thinking. Finally, I had an "ah-ha" moment. I have a big round flat strainer spoon that's used for stir-frying veggies but it has no sides. What if I tip it? Taking this spoon (which is about a foot and a half long with the handle) out to the three foot deep window well, I realized I was basically going to have to lie down and stretch in order to scoop up the fur-ball with the spoon. Gingerly, I knelt in the wet grass in my dress pants and white shirt, stretched down and gently tried to insert the scoop under the little pink feet. It was like the vole knew I was trying to help. It calmly looked up at me and stepped onto the makeshift elevator, sitting motionless while I raised the platform. Twisting to the side, I swung the scoop with the traveler over to the bottom of the lilac tree, nearby, and the vole stepped right off. Then the most beautiful thing happened. Rather than scampering off in a panic, this little, furry beauty turned and took a few very purposeful steps back in my direction, stopped and looked up at me for a moment as though to convey deep gratitude. Then the little darling turned and went off into the foliage. Talk about feeling the love.

July 18, 2012

Day 200 draws to a close, and I contemplate direction. What do I hope to accomplish? The mission of this studio is to effect change in the world, one piece of creativity at a time. Mine, yours, the amorphous others.... I have been going over something that I was told by an interesting person that I met yesterday when I was checking out galleries. He said something about how when we were young we were all bright and forward thinking, how our art was going to change the world. How sad it was that the big companies downtown are liquidating their collections, to the detriment of all of us. How our bright, shiny dreams are dimmed by "reality." This evening I had a reality check, as well, on enthusiasm and joy. Apparently I sound like a teenager when I am exuberantly discussing something I love. Grow up, Sherri. Don't you think you should be more serious minded? You are aging, you know. What is it about our culture that thinks we need to be depleted of joy, exuberance, and enthusiasm for the things that we are passionate about just because we reach a certain age? Being "silly" is just plain enjoyable sometimes. Being light-hearted and enthusiastic is a joy rather than a sign of immaturity. So, what's up with this? Are we just supposed to be so sophisticated, jaded, blasé —seen it all, lived it all—that there is no longer anything that gets us excited? Are we supposed to live in a grown up, serious world without any rose-coloured glasses, where all reality is harsh and devoid of passion? Hmmm, I will do my solemn best to continue to look at life and the world around me with the joy and wonder of a child. I solemnly promise to smile and bubble over with enthusiasm and passion when I feel called to express it. I will seriously commit to owning my creative potential in every phase of my life.

Living life, wonderfully.

July 19, 2012

It's been quite a day! The poppies were nodding their heads at me on the way up the walk. It's such a whimsical feel, as though each flower is a little fairy slipping out from behind the veil to share a giggle and a smile. Reciting Shakespeare, *A Midsummer Night's Dream*, "I know a bank where the wild thyme blows/Where oxlips and the nodding violet grows/Quite over-canopied with luscious woodbine/With sweet musk-roses and with eglantine."

July 20, 2012

After a day filled with reminders of my grandmother and aunt, my daughter and cousins, and my women friends, I stand in awe. The core of feminine grace flows with a strength and beauty that is honoured here in this artwork. To the Rose's in my life, ... *Nayeli*. This is a Zapotec word that means I love you. Today is the first time I've heard that word, yet it sent shivers of joy and light through me before I even learned the meaning. So I share it with you. Nayeli.

July 21, 2012

Reviewing yesterday's entry, I found that the photo taken just didn't seem to reflect the feel of the piece very well. So with some adjustments to the white values and some cropping and sharpening, this version of the work appears to be in a different mood. It's so easy to use this experience as a metaphor, my own dear metaphor. Here it goes…with some looking on the bright side, not getting caught up in extraneous details and focusing on what's important, our whole perspective on a situation changes. I do so love metaphors, and clichés, too, apparently. But no matter how you express it, the core of truth rings out like a crystal bowl, singing and reverberating in ever widening ripples of joy.

July 22, 2012

Finding a balance between the natural world and that which is man-made is not a simple task. I find myself being lost in the trembling of the aspen's leaves, the fall of water, the colour green, the kiss and heat of the sun's rays... A hummingbird visited our deck today, hovering outside the living room window with an eye for our new cherry trees, I'm sure. The bright red fruit would be a splendid lure for the little creature while these beautiful trees sit in their pots, waiting to be planted at the new acreage. These "fruitful trees" from our wedding ceremony have already given up some cherries. It's interesting that the hummingbird is often associated with Faeries. Hummingbirds are a symbol for doing the seemingly impossible or being aware of the miracles in our lives.

I am touched by the stories, experiences and care of those around me, changed by them all. How could I not be? The blessings of divine creation surround me, and I am bathed in them daily, from the robin's song and the buzz of hummingbirds, to bluebirds at the window and voles in the grass. And then there is the glimmer of the sun's rays as it sets over the mountains and the stirring of the cool, evening breeze as the first stars begin to cast their light across the deepening indigo shadow of the night sky. I breathe in the scent of the sunset and know that it is unique to this moment, like the laughter of a child or the freedom and joy in a woman's heart. Living life, wonderfully.

July 23, 2012

When I went to post this last night, my server was down. It's funny how a few months can change my reaction to this event. No panic, no freaking out ... just calmly deciding to post in the morning. So here it is. Most of the day was spent researching service providers for rural internet, TV, and phone. There is quite a bit of information available to sort through. I guess the most difficult part was the realization that marriage does change some things. A bit of compromise on my part was in order. Being quite an independent soul, I found the need to confer with another on the decisions rubbed me the wrong way. Does marriage mean I am no longer capable or trustworthy enough to handle such a simple decision on my own? Am I suddenly demoted to "the little woman"? I was in facilities management for a multi-billion dollar corporation, and now I am "not allowed" to make an independent decision in my own home? Is this the case? We are a couple; respecting each other's approaches, our way of being in the world, is part of the deal. As I struggle to deal with his innate need to slowly and methodically sift through every minute detail, he struggles to deal with my need to view the synopsis and form a gut feel. He is dedicated to doing it right after due processing time, and I to doing it right, but right now. Each of us want the same thing but we are coming at it from different directions. It's a good thing we can meet in the middle! After dealing with the initial emotional fall out, I realized something; I am being cherished. He is dedicated to taking care of things to the best of his ability, and so am I. We are trying to take care of this the best way we know how. We are working together toward a common goal, co-creating.

July 24, 2012

Day 206. What an amazing thing, carrying this project through so far. Many times I've wondered whether to continue with this project, and the supportive comments and care I get from readers, friends new and old, and family have proved to be such a blessing in moving forward with this. I quite honestly and humbly admit I couldn't have gotten this far without you. May you always feel as blessed by others as I feel when I think about all of you. There has been a change in how I come to the easel with this artwork. I come to the easel with a renewed sense of confidence, vision, and commitment. There are times when studio time has been the last thing on a long list, yet carving out the time for this has healed me in a way I hadn't expected. Having a voice, standing in my power (which means self-confidence), and being the change (thank you, Gandhi) are all important parts of this process. If I hope to send ripples of creative expression out to the world, then consistency is paramount. Effortless effort is required; joyful, effortless effort. I think Mark Twain had it right: "Choose a job you love, and you will never have to work a day in your life." Living life humbly and with feeling.

July 25, 2012

The ride tonight was fantastic. We went to Forget-me-not Pond in Kananaskis Country, and did some river crossings and a couple of hills I would not have done on foot! Many thanks to the beautiful horse who carried me places I'd never get to on my own. The views were stunningly lovely; the smell of the pines and the mossy ground were tangy and sweet. The company of riders was talented and experienced, joking their way through tough spots, like the veterans they are. What a way to spend an evening! And now it's time for some creative effort! I'm thinking of doing a meditative mandala to let this evening's experience settle in a bit. It's unusual for a lion to show up in my mediations, so off I go to research this. I'm feeling the creative flow.

July 26, 2012

Here's a link to Mayan calendar information: http://soundofheart.org/galacticfreepress/content/what-mayan-elders-are-saying-about-2012-25-july-2012. When I started the Final Art-Down in January of this year, the main focus was to lighten the energy of all the hype around the end of the world for my family and friends. Filled with nature and heart-centreed artwork, this project has developed in unexpected ways both challenging and rewarding. The above link is an update by members of the Mayan community which addresses many of the concerns regarding the prophecies and predictions currently circulating as well as shedding some light onto the transformation expected this December and how our actions can affect the outcome. Here's a challenge. Everything we do matters. May we take heart-centreed action where we can and be clearly focused on peaceful transformation connecting with our natural world, respecting the planet that sustains us.

July 27, 2012

I decided to follow through with another meditative mandala. They are such a wonderful way to gather my thoughts, bring clarity to ideas and just explore with no thought to the product. There is a great sense of freedom in this approach. The Sepia inks are really interesting to work with; I love the feel of the different lines. Today's opening ceremony of the Olympics was beautiful and a great source of inspiration not only for the athletes. I found the "tree of life" symbolism and the flower petals of the cauldron especially meaningful. John Lennon's song "Hey Jude" performed by Paul McCartney was also fantastic. There was a subtle nod to "Give Peace a Chance". I loved seeing the Queen skydiving. This artwork probably has a feel to it that may be reminiscent of the Games, a true summer of peace.

July 28, 2012

The sense of being at peace generated when meditating by creating mandalas has been a wonderful gift during this time of turmoil. Moving has a way of shifting everything, not only the belongings on the outside but the memories, beliefs and fears on the inside. As we all work through the feelings this transplanting has brought to light, I find that the greatest gift from this is a reminder. A reminder that home is about the people who inhabit a place about their memories, hopes, dreams, and loves, that which lives within the walls not the walls themselves. Although we have lived here for awhile, the roots have not gone deep. This bothers me a bit, as I wonder how to change this. How can we put down lasting roots, ones that will generate a future for the children, the grandchildren, and so on. Is there something I can do to care for the earth and create a space for my family? I am determined to try. Having done some research (ha ha, of course), some seriously old traditions have come into my hands. So I intend to see what can be done with the Creator's gifts. Who knows what we will be capable of... I'm feeling the creative flow.

July 29, 2012

The beginning is near! The birth of a new cycle of the Mayan calendar is coming soon. ;-) The meditative mandala series I've been working on has started to take on the look and feel of a drum for me. Perhaps the design for one will evolve from this process and bring with it a message fitting for the project. We'll just have to wait and see what develops! The process for the mandala is simple, really. You need some private space, possibly rhythmic sound or music although quiet works just as well. Then without any planned thought, just make marks in the circle as they surface in the mind/heart. It doesn't require any subject or design, only the contact of the instrument with the page. An exploration, if you will. Free flowing.

July 30, 2012

This is a prelim drawing for an upcoming work on watercolour paper. The quick sketch is just an outline of what's to come. As I worked the colour here, I felt the solidness and groundedness of the piece. This feel is what I hope to transfer to the final artwork. It's much like what I am working toward for the new home studio: a solid, grounded feel that sends out ripples with clarity and warmth. I know that there will be mistakes along the way, learning experiences, or growth potential. Yet to never begin because of the possibility of failure is not an option for me. A wise man once said to me, "Sherri, if you try and fail half the time, you still succeed the other half. If you don't try at all, well, that's a hundred per cent failure rate." So in fine cliché form, here I go, shooting for the stars. And if I miss? Well, there is always the moon.

Many blessings.

July 31, 2012

Listening to the sound of the raindrops as they splash against the gravel outside the window, it's reminiscent of the night of the vole. ... maybe I should go look. Whew! It's just the rain. It's time for sleep. We were up at 4:30 AM, sending my son off on a 10-day trip to Montreal. Sleep will drift in at any moment. This is a re-edit of a previous piece. Adding the sepia tones has created a drum feel to the artwork that I particularly like. The glow of the background provides a sense of either sun or fire light shining through rawhide. With some border work added, this could be an interesting possibility.

August 1, 2012

Finally, a drum offering! Here we are at August 1st. It has come along so quickly that it seems as though time is slipping through my fingers. Only 141 days to the change of the age. When I began this project, I was optimistic and committed to doing the best I am capable of to illustrate my journey. As the tides of life have raised events to the forefront of my attention and eased them away again, I have both struggled and shone with creative inspiration and projects. There are pieces I wish I didn't have to post here, and those that I'm going to frame later. Pieces I will stick in a drawer that will never again see the light of day. There are other wonderful pieces that will hang on the walls of the studio, my home, an art show, or gallery. Like the tides, the will to create ebbs and flows. There is a time to rest and a time to do. Working through the rest times is where I struggle. What is the purpose of doing art when I don't want to, when I know there is no flow, when the ideas just don't work? Does it build character? Skill? Discipline? Possibly. It builds self-confidence, surely. Feeling a lot like the little engine that could, I think I can has turned into I AM! And I am grateful for the experience.

August 2, 2012

Watching the Olympics these last few days has been such an inspirational experience, cheering on dedicated athletes from all around the world, and witnessing the wonderful sportsmanship shared between competitors. I couldn't help but wonder how any of us human beings can sanction killing each other in war and conflict in the face of such a vibrant celebration of human possibility. I've just read an e-mail that has shocked and saddened me. A young man's life was tragically cut short in a car accident this evening on Highway 8. I'm searching for words of condolence and kindness, yet everything seems hollow in the wake of such loss. To lose a son while the world celebrates theirs at the games can only make this more difficult. Please everyone, drive safely this long weekend. Turn the phones off and leave the alcohol untouched when you get behind the wheel. The photograph for today's artwork was taken in low light with a Rebel T2i camera. Warmth and beauty seem to explode off the screen in this close-up rendering of an old-time favourite. Reminiscent of grandma's garden, its fragility and ephemeral display are a testimony to the shortness of our summers here. We emerge, grow, and bloom with abandon, only to be covered once more with the cold of winter's snowy blanket. Acknowledging the beauty of a life.

August 3, 2012

Once again the ephemeral beauty of the cut flower is presented. Yet here we see the beginning signs of deterioration. The petals' integrity has started to fade. Folding in on itself as though protecting the sensitive core from the inevitable chilling breath of death, the once delicate edges of this softly glowing bloom are curling and drying. Changing before our eyes, we stand witness to the decline.

August 4, 2012

The beauty of this time-sensitive process is self-evident in the shining glory of this fading blossom. There is such sensitivity, a vulnerable depth that astonishes the inattentive. "What am I seeing here? Aren't all withered plants supposed to be ugly," we whisper quietly in our thoughts. Well, apparently not. This study of daily change for these gladiolas has uncovered something stunning. Each stage has provided a gift, a beauty inherent in each moment. A metaphor? As this project continues through the days of the countdown, I look at each moment and whisper quietly in my thoughts, "What beauty exists right now? Do I see it, or am I inattentive? Is this a reflection the world is sending back to me?" What am I seeing here, and what does it mean for me, for you, for mankind or the Earth? Acknowledging the beauty of a life.

August 5, 2012

What a wonderful day we had exploring the backwaters of the Rocky Mountain foothills! A day filled with sunshine, ponds, wildlife and trees. It was a great day to be outside!

August 6, 2012

Yet another spectacular day! Time well spent listening to the sound of the horses' footfalls on the trail, the swish of tails, the scents from the dense underbrush, the breeze in the treetops! All I can say is Wow! This is a beautiful world! I'd like to share another shot from nature. Here's some personality...

August 7, 2012

The server is down; I am disconnected. Cut from the living body of the plant, this stem of gladiolus immediately began to wither and decay. Although the cutting is a gladiola, also it is not. When removed or isolated from the living web, the vital life force of the greater plant is missing. That which nourishes it is no longer there, a revitalizing flow of energy that keeps these flowers in a healthy balance is missing and they fade. Like us, the whole is much greater than just individual bits and pieces added together.

August 8, 2012

The server is still down … I'm wilting … I'm wilting. This is the last of the gladiola series. The plant has completed its expected descent into ruin. The disconnection from the living force of the Earth has produced the predicted results; this piece of the plant has died with no possibility of procreation. I offer many thanks to the Spirit of All Gladiolas for sharing yourself with me. Your beauty brightened my life for the time you were here; and for that, I am deeply grateful. Acknowledging the beauty of a life.

August 9, 2012

Okay, the server is still down. One more gladiola seems to be in order, disconnected from the life-blood of nature; broken off, disenfranchised, isolated and deprived of access to the source. Hmmm, some things just aren't pretty. Acknowledging the beauty of all life, afterlife, beyond and before, as well as everything in between.

August 10, 2012

Finally! The server is operational and accepting updates again! This time of year I spend a ton of effort compiling reference photographs for potential paintings or sculptures. It's unusual for me that the majority of them seem to be floral this time around! Until now, I have always gravitated to landscapes, animals or people. Perhaps it is just time for me to honour the life-sustaining flora of Earth. I've been furthering my study of sacred plant medicine this last while, and as a result I have developed a great respect and understanding of the mostly unacknowledged gifts that plants provide for our livelihood every day. There are multiple layers of interconnectedness wrapped around us in an elaborate web of sustenance, without which we, and the planet would become extinct. Trees, the teachers of the law, are the lungs of our planet…when injured, there are plants that come to repair the damage. Certain types of lichen attach to trees to help with respiration, as needed. If the damage is greater, a species of mistletoe moves in to assist with healing. Plants are not only available to heal our ills, but also the ills of the greater eco-system. The depth and intricacy of the web is breath-taking.

August 11, 2012

This is a continuation of the photo shoot for reference pictures. The delicacy of the day lily calls to my heart and soul. The plants in my backyard are late blooming as they are not in direct sunlight but rather sheltered. Yet the display, for all its late start, is stunningly beautiful. Unfolding in majesty day by day, the spectacular show is breath-taking as though in a rush to make up for its tentative start. . I stand in awe. Acknowledging the beauty of all life.

August 12, 2012

There was a time, awhile back, when I looked at the surface of water as though gazing through the veil to see a familiar face peering back at me ... grief. Just yesterday, I stood in the place where the loss occurred and felt for a moment that closeness, that touch of spirit to spirit. A soft whisper against the soul like a ripple in the cool surface of a pond ... I am the wind. Acknowledging the beauty of all. PS: Three more days 'til we own the new acres!

August 13, 2012

Today my emotions are roiling, seething, just waiting for a weakness in the wall to spill forth with vitriol and venom. This picture (when you see the whole) is a writhing, twisting expression of line and shadow, a sense of too much going on to be able to grasp what is being seen. Only with close focus and attention to the detail of the thing does the pattern become visible. With love. PS: Two more days 'til we own the new acres!

August 14, 2012

With just a slight change in colour, the whole feel and experience of this piece morphs into something soothing and peaceful. The tension and edginess of yesterday's work has dissolved away leaving only calm and gentle beauty. I always find it so amazing how a simple thing like colour can both reflect and stimulate human moods. Oh, to keep this in mind, as we choose the paint for the new house. It's paramount to select colours that will assist us all to feel comfortable and at ease, welcome and appreciated. Oh, help! With love. PS: One more day 'til we own the new acres!

August 15, 2012

Oh the stress! Moving day is looming. Painting, flooring, and ensuring lighting changes are complete at the new home prior to the move date is the goal. Time to apply the colours! On your mark, get set, ... go!

August 16, 2012

I was standing on the new deck wondering what the first wildlife I'd see would be and an owl flew by, in that exact moment. Then a few moments later, another owl perched in the tree just fifteen feet away from me. We chatted for a few moments, with the owl making saw-wheet sounds and me talking about how this is our new home. I invited the owl to please stay and continue hunting mice, gophers, and rabbits whenever the need arose. The most astounding thing during this encounter was how interested the owl was in meeting me. It was very curious, very intent in its regard. It even moved to a closer tree in order to get a better look. So we chatted a bit more, and I saw how beautiful and strong its wings were when they were stretched out in the tree. When I started getting chilly, I bid the owl adieu and explained that I was going in to warm up. I think we will meet again. And it is to be hoped that I will have the camera in hand!

August 17, 2012

What an amazing day! Painting the new house is fantastic! We spent all day at this task, and I must admit I am tired but supremely satisfied. Only occasionally did I think about the horseback riding trip to the Badlands that I am missing this weekend, only occasionally. Okay, probably about ten times today. However, I had such a wonderful experience working with my new husband, feathering our nest. I even came to a momentous bit of self-discovery. I do not wish to ever be a painter, ever. Hats off to those who do! I believe I will stick to artistic expression, exploring creativity and motivation, maybe even some sculpture and carving. Leave the building painting to the building painters. Oh, and I had another animal encounter today! A red fox made itself known with a flash of bushy tail along the side of the road. What big eyes it had! Again, no camera! What is with that? I am continuing my exploration of the new environment with the camera, and I'm finding it interesting that the wildlife stays out of sight while I have it in hand. In the chaos that is moving, my studio is in a shambles and I find that the collection of art reference pictures is holding my attention for the moment. The movers are coming to collect me on the 20th, so I may be offline from then until the 22nd while the satellite dish is being installed. Wish me luck! With so many stressful events (all good, just stressful) this year, my stress meter should be hitting into the red zone. So what is it that is keeping things on an even keel? Nature? Horses? Artwork and meditation? Absolutely, all those and more ...

August 18, 2012

Exhaustion, thine aspect is blue. Another fine day of painting, followed by an encounter with a large buck possessing a pair of velvety covered antlers of quite a remarkable size. Again, no camera!

August 19, 2012

Wow, it feels incredibly strange to be without a computer! I'm just going to have to transcribe this later when monitor and such have been unpacked and hooked up. I feel naked!! Nakedness aside, watching the packers attack our considerably down-sized and de-cluttered belongings was an awe inspiring experience. They arrived en masse at 9:00 AM, and with considerable waving and signing of papers and waivers and boxes and newsprint, so began the process of enclosing our lives in little cardboard boxes. I hovered, feeling decidedly inadequate next to the speed and efficiency of The Team. Within three hours, ten years and two households' worth of stuff disappeared into the maw of the cardboard beast. Quaintly labeled "Kitchen" or "Upstairs Hall", the impressive mound of boxes rose to intimidating heights in the centre of the main floor, all with surprising ease. As I regarded the mountain, I suddenly envied my son's ability to pack himself into three small boxes. What are we? Hoarders? Oh, dear! Fluttering from room to room, ... thoughts of "Oh, that was my grandmother's", or "Ooo, please pack that carefully!" popped into my mind, but mainly I reminded myself to ... "just let them do their job, Sherri." And now as I look around, I see the beauty of their efforts. There on the counter ... two forks, a knife, and cup. Smiling, I call to my husband,. "Would you like to order in a pizza?"

August 20, 2012

Right on time, the two big white trucks arrive at our doorstep to begin the transfer process. Oh, to be able to say, "Beam it up, Scotty." And so it begins. Watching and joking with the moving crew we hold our breaths as our lives, graciously packed in the belly of the cardboard beast, are stacked, shifted, crammed, and otherwise crushed into the seemingly endless black hole of the trucks' cargo space, only to emerge hours later, fully formed (just add water). It seems like everything was shrunken to fit, then reformed on arrival. I offer many thanks to the great humour of "The Team", who responded with quite a sense of fun. "Oooops" is not a word you want to hear from someone holding your favourite stained glass lampshade. Ha ha! And thanks, also, to Doug's brother Jerry, for traveling miles to help with truck and muscle. We salute you! And we will send chocolates. :-)

August 21, 2012

I am grateful that I did not see my beloved piano being disassembled and packed into the small truck it arrived in. The crew was wonderful, efficient, and incredibly rushed ... couldn't even wait for a cheque. The mover's baby was captured on film today, and he was hurrying to meet wife at the ultrasound clinc. He promised he would be there. Bye, gotta run, will call for payment later! And out the door he flew! Colour me shocked! Next came the satellite installer. "It's always the cable guy...." No, wait, I've viewed way too many episodes of Criminal Minds. He was a very friendly, helpful, talkative sort. "Oh, no, we only run to the one point, if you want outlets in the house, well then you will have to look after that yourself." WHAT!!!!!!! Sniff, sniff, ... no internet for me today. :-(But on the bright side, I can paint! Now, where are those studio boxes? Okay, I will go feed my horse. I did unpack and organize thirty of those neatly labeled "kitchen" boxes, some time with my 900 pound fur-ball is a necessity. Oh, I can smell the hay already!

August 22, 2012

Awk!! What do you mean we have a slight thistle problem, one that requires immediate and numerous hours of attention? After a quick analysis of said problem, I am impressed by the enormity and density of plant growth. It takes some doing to produce three to four foot high plants in six foot wide x four acre long rows like that. Cudos to the Creator. And yes, they are all in flower and basically overflowing with abundant life. You know the kind? The "oh great, it's going to seed", kind? So off my work / painting crew goes, armed with bug spray, the dog, and leather gloves to the elbows. Returning many hours later, they are completely in awe of the magnitude of the job. Meanwhile, back at the ranch ... the unpacking continues. Thankfully, the monotony is broken up by a fantastic ride at Little Elbow. What a marvel, my horse. At one point we are faced with two extreme obstacles. We could either go straight up a hill at more than a 45 degree angle, or through a thigh deep mud bog. Hmmm, decisions, decisions. As he has refused them both, I gauge his reaction and decide to try the hillside. Just as I feel him shifting to the side, someone at the back calls out to me and tells me there's another path. Glad of the alternative, we head back and around. It's safer for my horse and I am happy!

August 23, 2012

"This place is great! Gotta go. Do you know where the camera is?" And so, off she goes with my camera for the weekend. I finally get the internet working, and I have no camera to take pictures of proposed creative expression. "I love your horse. Of course I will look after him. Any special care required? No problem. Have a great trip, drive safely." Am I nuts? No. Maybe. Hmmmm, I don't want to go down that path; it looks like train tracks with a light at the end. Honestly though, I love being available and able to help. Many years ago during the darkest night of my soul, the care of my children pulled me out the other side, and I am grateful to see the sun rise on a new day.

August 24, 2012

I admit it. Today for the first time in my life, I “skipped out”, “played hookie”, “cut class”, “ran out”. I completely ditched all responsibility. By nine in the morning, I was on the road to the farm, off to play with my horse. “I’m getting his hooves trimmed today, honey. Gotta go!” Waving vaguely at the stack of boxes, paint cans and mounds of thistles...I am so outta here! I spent time talking to the farrier. Beautiful, healthy feet on my boy! I was grateful to hear. My horse is on chaste tree berry powder for pre-Cushing’s symptoms. Did you know this powder is also good for menopausal symptoms? No, Really! My greatest interest in this is how anyone ever made this connection to menopausal symptoms. (Man talking to the Vet: Oh yes, I’m using this on my gelding, and he’s growing less hair, losing weight, gaining muscle tone, and has a happier outlook. Pause for thought, calls to wife: ... “Honey, I want you to try this new herbal remedy...”) I’m laughing so hard that tears are forming in my eyes. And then I went for lunch. WITHOUT CALLING!

Many thanks to the lovely family at the stable who braved the chill and the storm to blanket the shivering beasties. My heart is full to overflowing with gratitude, and I know my horse feels the same way. My daughter’s horse is probably very grateful to Lorraine who agreed to take his blanket off again after lunch. He wasn’t really shaking like my poor fellow, and was likely feeling overly warm. I’d like to express much gratitude for Lorraine.

August 25, 2012

Today I am so sad. First my husband and painting/cleaning/unpacking partner was called in to work on his vacation this morning, which completely disrupted our plans for the day. Then when I arrived to feed my horse at nine-thirty in the morning, he was the only horse in the field that still had his blanket on and it was so warm already! Yesterday’s near zero temperatures with driving rain had changed to a balmy, shorts-wearing day by mid-afternoon, and unbeknownst to me, an error in communication had prevented him from having his blanket removed. So now everyone who saw him out there sweating in the heat with a blanket on thinks I am the utmost idiot who is so controlling that she can’t allow anyone other than herself to take the blanket off. Sheesh! Where did anyone get the impression that my control of an issue is more important to me than the health of my horse??? Never in a million years! I am crushed that anyone would even think this about me. What a misunderstanding. I am so hurt. When my husband arrived home, I was ready to just have some down time from unpacking and stewing, and relax over a dinner out. He was game, so off we went, headed for the lights of the big city. Over hill, over dale, we were chugging along and watching the bars appear and disappear on our cell phones. (Oh where, oh where, do we get coverage?) Then it happened. Ding, ding. The engine light came on. Awk! What's that smell? And there we sat. The engine had overheated. The lady at the AMA was helpful. The tow truck driver was efficient. The taxi driver was sensitive and quick. The car went to the city without us, and we went home to pick up the work truck and follow the car into the dealer to secure the keys. There are no night drop offs at our dealership. Who knew? By this time it was quite dark and late, so we decided to pass on dinner. Welcome Cheezies and pine nuts. It's 11:30 PM, and I am ready for sleep. My husband, my horse, and my car all overheated in one day. With great thanks, great peace, and great love, I'm crawling off to bed to pull the covers over my head.

August 26, 2012

A new day, thank God! I am even looking forward to cleaning the old house. We feed the horses and head to the city in the work truck. RRR RRR RRR, shake and rattle. "What's that, dear? Did you say something?" Falling out of the high seat of the truck, I land on the driveway in my typically graceful dismount. Yes, of course I meant to do that, and off into the house I go. I hate cleaning house. I know it's a necessity, and I do it anyway, but I really loathe every moment. Tomorrow will be a better day. I have a dentist appointment. A new crown and two fillings are bound to be better than this. And yes, I sincerely mean that! With great thanks, great peace, great love.

August 27, 2012

At three-thirty in the morning I was awakened by a coughing, hoarse growl outside my window. Cougar! I heard the sounds of pursuit, choking, and fluids. It took awhile to go back to sleep. There was no blood around the house in the morning, but all of us were watchful for signs today! Whew! Then it was off to the dentist. It was a simple one hour appointment. One hour and ten minutes, then, one hour and fifteen minutes goes by. After one hour and thirty minutes, the receptionist came in to inquire how much longer I would be as my husband was waiting for me. (Remember the rattling work truck?). One hour and forty-five minutes? No. A full two hours, and no crown yet. It was back to the lab with you, oh, wicked instrument of torture. Did I mention I've been on antibiotics for a tooth infection since the thirteenth? No? Well, apparently it is being stubborn. This is the second course of apo-something-or-other, so the in-and-out-again two-hour crowning ordeal was a bit of a stretch for me, as it is that particular tooth that is sporting the infection. Next? Back to the house for, you guessed it, more cleaning. I love the smell of napalm, oh, sorry, I mean soft scrub, in the morning. It was a poor war movie reference, I know. Please forgive me. Oh, and there is still no car but they did get it in to be assessed. And they did service the drive-train and transmission, and, no, they don't know why the engine light came on. Perhaps it's because it overheated, we suggest.

August 28, 2012

And there's more cleaning. I'm doing a complete spring-cleaning in the fall, with heavy gratitude for no furniture to move about or dishes to remove from cabinets. Some times I wish I wasn't such a perfectionist, but I can't seem to leave any dust bunny (or stone) unturned. It will be perfect. Our reputation will be upheld. We're home by noon, and off the crew goes to denude the scenery of the dreaded thistle. I look at the walls and grab a paint roller. You are so mine. And I do it. I owned it. I *am* a painter. And then it's off to feed the horse. Rattle, rattle. I am absolutely sans car. The engine has something going on. It's been referred to the shop foreman. They will keep us posted. While the rattle trap, I mean work truck, is being employed in the service of horse trailer repair, I sneak by on my horse and escape to the front forty. We trot and canter to our hearts' content, nibbling grass and hiding behind the hay shed at the far end. No one will find us here. Sooner rather than later, my conscience prods me into going back. I am filled with a delightful sense of mischief. I am riding without my helmet, and as I trot the motion is knocking my barrette loose. My horse stops and turns his head back to look at up at me. I just laugh, take the barrette out of my hair, and stuff it in my pocket. We continue off at a fast trot, wind blowing in my hair. Now, this is wonderful! And he of the rattle trap was so happy and busy, he didn't even notice I went AWOL. With great thanks, great peace, and great love.

August 29, 2012

Rattle, rattle, rattle, and off to the big city they went. It's the final clean-down. The carpet cleaner arrives and the race begins. Who will complete their task first? Parts of the a/v wiring hit the floor, the smell of tile floor cleaner fills the nostrils, and then the revving sound of the Chem-Dry truck fills the air. The a/v equipment is dismantled and tagged, there are miles of tile shining brightly, and the carpet cleaner still wins. So after a lagging finish, we hop into the work truck to head for the dealership. You see, the word is in. The car is dead. They performed CPR, but only a transplant will save it now. Oil and fuel must not mix, and cracked heads are bad. We were guaranteed a rookie from the minors would be able to stand in and handle the job. Go, Rent-a-truck! Or more accurately, go rent a truck. Punctuation is so important. You may have noticed that the pictures for the last week are unchanging. That would be because the cord connecting the camera to the computer (You know, the one that uploads the data?) is still packed away in a mystery box, somewhere. Did I mention that the two does with their fawns are now one doe with two fawns? Darn cougar. Yes, I know it's the natural cycle of life. And somewhere, on some level, I am all right with that, but the surface is currently at a slow boil. Hmmmm, I wonder if I am feeling stressed? Ha ha ha. I am sure I have a slightly crazed look in my eyes. All work and no play, makes Jack a dull boy. All work and no play, makes Jack a dull boy. All work and no play, makes Jack a dull boy*. What are you doing with that hatchet? Who's Johnny?

(*Thank you, Stephen King, author, *The Shining*)

August 30, 2012

We are another day closer to saying the final good-bye to our old house. At noon tomorrow, it is officially no longer ours. The fish are staying to welcome their new humans, and most likely the goldfinches and chickadees will serenade them from their waterfall bath place as well. It is very strange, but the new house is more like a home than the old one ever was, and we have only been here two weeks! It's less formal, more relaxed.

Blue jay, blue jay
sitting on the deck rail,

flashed it's tail and
flew off toward
the eastern pines.

What a treat! It's the first blue jay I've seen in my whole life. What a pleasure. Great thanks to everyone for their patience while I've dealt with the realities of moving to a rural area. Satellite internet and TV? Piece of cake! Long drive down a winding road, hmmm. And how is that a problem? Stress? More painting. I'm glad the property transfer is settled tomorrow! It's time to celebrate, and it's a full moon. A blue moon, actually. It's the second full moon of the month, and there it will be, hanging large in tomorrow's night sky. It's perfect timing. I've decided to continue with the Move Monologue until the end of August, so stay tuned for the finale tomorrow evening. It's late, really late.

August 31, 2012

Well, it's official. The old has made way for the new and this new comfort has proven to be immeasurable. They are moments to remember, surely. I am blessed. With great thanks, great peace, and great love, I bid goodnight to the Move Monologue.

September 1, 2012

This was an amazing day. As the full harvest moon hangs pregnant with possibility in the indigo darkness of the autumn sky, the earth seems to hold its breath waiting for the coming of the first killing frost. With my tomatoes under cover, I too wait for the coming of the frost. There is a coolness in the night, silent and still, hovering in the air with a sense of expectancy. I let the breath of the earth seep over me, and I am held in friendship, companionship, love. Tomorrow, I start work on the studio design. The goal is to be operational by the 15th of September. And so, life continues. The drum offering today echoes the light and feel of this evening's moon, providing a warm glow and the potential for reaping what is sown. With great thanks, great peace, and great love.

September 2, 2012

The aspen grove at the end of the drive has been calling to me since I first saw it. What an opportunity for reveling in colour, texture, and majesty. There will be many happy hours spent working to capture and understand the images of this place. Here the moodiness of the lighting has been played up to create … Feel. I have an understanding of the watcher in the woods with this piece, a definite feeling of foreboding or danger. And yet, there is also a sense of expectancy. Is it sunlight or fire and smoke? This just might be soul-fire.

September 3, 2012

The group coming out for the Sound of Peace Project on September 15th & 16th are in for a treat! The temporary studio space has been pulled together and it will be a gracious host site for the two-day event. I won't say any more about it, so you will just have to experience it for yourself. After much debate and site examination, the decision has been made for the new studio space. With an order to be placed tomorrow, we should expect to see the building kit arrive before mid-October. The goal is to have it all snug and cozy before the first snowfall. Surrounded by a meadow with an abundant mix of wild strawberry, blueberry, yarrow, timothy and many other herbs and berries, the site is ringed by pines, aspen (My beautiful grove in plain sight.) and willows. The placement will allow for great light and wonderful views. What is really cool about this space is that it's portable. The construction will cause little to no damage to the environment, and will, I hope, fit seamlessly into the scenery, being one with rather than intruding upon. I am so looking forward to the above-ground space and big windows!

September 4, 2012

It was a less than glamourous day. I have been reminded that in order to heal, the body first must release what it's been holding on to. Mine has done that, so today I am resting and recuperating. The stress of the last couple weeks has culminated in a dramatic need for downtime. It was an amazing day. Everywhere I looked beauty shone out with a special intensity. The light in the tops of aspen trees, the gently waving heads of brome and timothy, the reflection of cattle and blue sky in the pond, and the kiss of the setting sunlight glowing on the mane and dappled body of my gentle and kind horse were all a gift from creation. It was a great day, filled with the support of family, friends and new acquaintances. Humour and love surrounds me, and I am at home. It's been about fifteen years of feeling lost, and now, I am home. There was a picture forwarded to me on Facebook the other day that said it just right: "Sometimes you find yourself in the middle of nowhere, and sometimes in the middle of nowhere you find yourself."

September 5, 2012

I rode the fearsome horse today. With fearsome eye, and hoof, and mind. He softened some, and then he gave the best his heart was able. We loped so smoothly. We trotted some. But mostly, we ate grass. And he was content. My horse who walked beside was smiling. Getting glimmers of amusement from the change, he watched side-eyed, and ate grass, too. And then the sun hit the horizon mark in the quickening of its descent, and the whole world changed! The layers of the land between the sun and I were demarcated with glowing wisps of mist and light. Layer upon layer of softening mist-shrouded depth until finally the whole shone white with the brilliant blessing that is the sun. My, how it filled my soul, my heart, and my mind to overflowing. The beauty was too much to hold even in the mind's eye. I overflowed.

September 6, 2012

The darkness of this piece is a simple reflection of the intricacy with which we can weave our webs of worry, moving the focus away from the light filled areas and onto the patterns we create in our mind's eye. Even though the light shines through, around, in front of, and from behind, that lacework of darkness holds the eye, the mind, trapped. Yet, if I soften my vision, if I reevaluate where I put my attention, I see only the lightness and I smile, feeling the warmth and the glow through the leaves. What an effect this change in focus on a picture can have. I imagine how this type of shift would feel on a larger scale, and I work to bring it to life.

September 7, 2012

I was looking for something that would work with the name we have chosen for the acreage, Tanglewood. Of course, the tree of life, I thought. It's nothing new, the tree of life. It's been around for centuries, ha ha, chock full of meaning and cross-cultural symbolism. How can I go wrong with that? But how do I incorporate such a symbol into a meaningful reflection of this specific place? The trees here are a grove, an interconnected collection of beings sharing the same space with us, enfolding us. Rather that than a single tree, then, it will be a grove connected above and below, in a circle to symbolize embracing the whole. A welcoming embrace. The whole thing has been done a thousand times or more. My mind whispers, "But you haven't done it yet." So I do. Whittling away at the black background with my white shapes, I chisel out a form resembling the grove by the drive, tangled above and below ground level. I plunk in the name, and, voila, a gate medallion. Hmmm, I think it needs some refinement before I send it to the metal workers. I'll get this cut this out of copper plate and allow it to weather to a beautiful verdigris finish. I like it better with this adaptation. And I'll grind the edges so they are curved rather than sharp cuts. Softer, I'm liking this, too!

September 8, 2012

I love this. I was measuring and walking the area where the stoo-di-yurt will go, and what did I find? An antique treasure for the studio! It's an old homestead signpost! There is no longer any sign, but it is topped with the cutest little birdhouse. I'm going to move this over to the studio access road and hang out my shingle! Now I need to design one. We also found an old wagon wheel, but I'm not quite sure what to do with that yet. I spent part of the day designing the gate to go with the medallion from yesterday. I think I've got it, so I sent it off for a quote. We will see. A practical application for artistic endeavour must have been on today's agenda.

September 9, 2012

Okay, so sometimes I can't leave well enough alone. I kept working on this, and changing that, and suddenly realized I didn't really like the previous version. It just didn't seem like us. I'd been working to impress with a gate worthy of being commissioned, and that's what it looked like. This one is more relaxed and casual. It's definitely a better fit all around. Being able to reuse the old gates to create this would be a wonderful bonus. Here's hoping it's possible. I'm waiting to hear from the metal workers.

September 10, 2012

Today I assembled bits and pieces, drew a little, and had some fun. Technically, it's not really art, but it slides under the wire as creative play. I'm starting to feel the anticipation of the upcoming Sounds of Peace Project. Details, details ... You know something? Heating has never been an issue before, but it has to be addressed for this project. And what about light? Ambience? It's coming together nicely, yet there are still a few loose ends to tie up. I'm looking forward to the weekend!

September 11, 2012

Have you ever noticed how beautiful the smell of the forest is in the morning? I had a few things to do at the studio this morning, and I took Ru along for the kilometre long walk to the front of the property. There was a thick frost on the grasses and road gravel. It crunched underfoot and lent a crispness to the air that wasn't there yesterday. And the scents that filled the air! It was a feast for the senses! Later in the day, I stopped by the aspen grove to pay my respects to the trees. Their tall, slender trunks waving gracefully in the wind made their leaves tremble with flashes of yellow and green against the brilliant blue of the sky. They are so tall that the sunlight only glistens on the top ten feet, and the shades of colour deepen as my gaze travels slowly down the beautiful whiteness of their trunks to their blackened and corrugated feet. The place where the roots enter the earth is sheltered by clumps of freeze-dried brome, standing over two feet tall and waving gently in a mirror image motion of the larger grove. What wonder, this dance! I am honoured to be a part of this.

September 12, 2012

Only 99 days to the end of the Mayan calendar! What to do with the remaining days of this age? I could make a sign. One that would hang from that cool old homestead signpost found in the woods, which I've raised in a precarious place in the hope that there will be no wild winds this evening. The bird house is still on the repair list following that last gale that went through. May there be peace in the air tonight.

As I was turning onto Grand Valley Road, headed toward home, I noticed an unusual sight in the bright light of the day. It was a splash of brilliant red-orange wiggling around on the high side of the ditch along the road. A flash of white, and the squirming mass became a fox. There she was in broad daylight, brazenly rubbing her face among the tall grasses tail waving in the air, completely unconcerned as I stopped the truck and watched. In a leisurely fashion, she sat for a moment. I can tell exactly when she observed me watching her, and with quick eye contact she acknowledged me. She's decided it's all right. She continues doing her thing, sniffing the air, marking her territory, and then looking right at me over her shoulder, off she walked to be about her fox-like business. She was confident and sure of herself.

September 13, 2012

What is it about me that encourages total strangers to confide their lifes' challenges to me in the most unusual places? There on the side of the road, out in the middle of nowhere, while I was stuck behind a number of large pieces of paving equipment his company is moving, he spoke to me for quite some time. He then went on to suggest that perhaps I might have a single daughter he could meet? He laughed and slapped my arm gently as he said "just kidding", but we both know he wasn't. There were moments during this conversation when I wasn't sure how to respond appropriately, so I just let compassion guide me. Never mind the social niceties or prescribed topics of conversation, today the heart ruled. After a moment or two, the young man realized how much he had shared with a complete stranger. I could tell he was a bit embarrassed so I gave him a bright and gentle smile, and watched his shoulders soften. May he go forward in Peace. The work today is a reference photo, as all of mine are. I'm keeping in mind textures, rhythm, shapes and intensity, all with an eye to incorporate whichever piece of fine art calls out to be created. How does this tie in with the conversation of earlier today? I'm not certain, but maybe it is about the layers of shadow, being able to see them, draw them out and perhaps through doing so, allow the experience of peace. Peace in observing the rhythm of the artwork. Peace in releasing the wounded energy. May there be peace in the air tonight.

September 14, 2012

Most importantly, the only thing we really need to be concerned about is the moment we are in. All paths are the right path, right for whatever learning experience we are here to garner. Some paths may be shortcuts, some more difficult, some may be full of obstacles while others are smooth and straight. It is just a path, and the only moment we can affect is now. The past is a memory, already gone. The future is just a dream. But in this moment, I can choose. And I choose love. And with that, I step forward on a path.

September 15, 2012

Today was all about yin and yang: the dichotomy of light to dark within the soul, the spirit that requires focused attention to maintain a healthy sense of balance between the two. Both serve their purpose, as there would not be one without the other. The old story of the grandfather and the wolves comes to mind. A grandfather tells his grandchild that sometimes he feels as though he has two wolves fighting inside him, one good and one evil. The grandchild asks, "Which wolf inside you will win, grandfather?" "The one I feed," replies the old man. I feel the flow of a dance rather than a fight, more a feel of one shifting steps to mirror the other, keeping things aligned and in harmony. Balanced around a central point, perhaps, at that point of equilibrium, there is a feeling. And perhaps, its name is peace.

September 16, 2012

There are rare moments in my life where I feel energized and at peace simultaneously. Today happens to be a touchstone moment like that. I'm filled with the fire of peace. Calmly activated and actively peaceful, I walked through the hours of the day in a "fire when ready" state, waiting for the spark of compassion to set everything in motion. Let the healing begin. Merci! And to my ancestors, great thanks, great peace, and great love! To the members of The Sound of Peace Project this weekend, I am honoured that you allowed me to share this time with you. May you go forward in peace. Aho.

September 17, 2012

Exciting times, today. Today's creativity centreed on designing spaces. The new studio is on order (See the sample photo provided courtesy of Yurtz by Design.), and we will have a space to go with the "Narnia"-style lamp post in the meadow. I'm not certain how I feel about it. A number of years ago, way before I had a horse to focus on, a business-guru friend of mine suggested I build a yurt to build my business. Along with the need for an image consultant and an "accept all invitations" advice, the yurt idea from her list has stuck in my mind for these many years. It's come up again and again, and has been referenced by others in ways that were completely out of context to what I was working on but always as a reminder. I feel almost like the guy in the movie standing in his cornfield, yelling "What do you mean build it and they will come?*" At the very least, it will be termed Sherri's folly, and it will be a wonderful guest house for family and friends. At best, it will reach the potential my friend the business guru foresaw. I will even prepare my famous "monster spray" for sale, just because of you, Margot M. Many blessings to you. Something else to add is that we are going to try to establish this studio as an eco-friendly, low environmental impact space with solar panels, etc. Wish us well in our efforts, please.

**Field of Dreams*, 1989 film directed and written by Phil Alden Robinson

September 18, 2012

Okay, I love this one: the softness of the colour, the blending of the edges, the quirkiness of the subject. And it is so peaceful. Is there anything more peaceful than a green cow sleeping in the shade? As I sit here in my life of abundance, I wonder if it is not easy for me to spout off about peace and being at peace. I have a roof over my head, food to eat, water and warmth when needed. It might be a different story if I were struggling to gather the basic necessities of survival. Do humans become less philosophical and more harsh and brutal, do we lose our humanity when under pressure like that? I know there has been a ton of studies done and theories postulated, much speculation and scientific measurement, but I can only approach this question from my own perspective. There was a time (about 5 - 6 years) when I was a single parent, alone and struggling to make ends meet with two small children and no outside support. I was terrified, unsure where the food and necessities were coming from, and yet I gave to our church: I gave both my time (as a Sunday school teacher and program facilitator) and the small amount of money I was able to donate. I was ultra-stressed, and still I volunteered with children's programs and school events. Even overwhelmed with fear, at the point of collapse, and with financial ends hardly meeting most days, I was willing and able to give love. It brought me a measure of peace and held me together. Recently, however, I have been confronted by people who view their own experience of low income in a different way, they are victims. They have been victimized and are handicapped because of the circumstance of poverty. They give up, believing there is no way out so why bother trying. Maybe a change of perspective is needed. Maybe when you are down, the best way to get up is to give of yourself. If I can give love, then I have an abundant life, regardless of circumstances. Maybe abundance is a state of mind, more so than a set financial outcome. Perhaps it has to do with that much overworked, and often quoted "feeling of inner peace". Maybe it is about how we express compassion and love? Maybe it is about the blending of edges and a quirky sense of humour? Perhaps? Go, green cow.

September 19, 2012

Rereading yesterday's entry, I must admit to a certain degree of embarrassment. How judgmental I sound! Everyone journeys through life in their own way, and who am I to judge whether it is better to take one path over another. Each path's teachings are valid and necessary for those choosing to walk them. How smug and self-righteous! And now, I am judging myself harshly. Wow! However can I drop this current tendency? May I move forward with compassion, and a loving heart. A purple mule might be just what is needed ... Whimsical and light-hearted, she seems to be saying something. What is it? "I see the truth of you. And you are beautiful," she whispers.

September 20, 2012

I'm heading off on a three-day horse ride. I'll be back with new entries and art on Sunday, September 23rd! It's all in the details.

September 21, 2012

Hurrying to set up camp last night before dark, there was not much of a chance to appreciate the beauty of the environment, but this morning the grandeur swept me off my feet. The time it took to catch the breath from one spectacular vista was barely enough to restore mind functioning before being blasted with another equally delicious sight. Day Two: The best part of the day was following leaf dotted trails through towering aspen and poplar forests, the softness of the light playing across the equally soft bend of the grasses at their feet. And while we admired the soaring trunks, the wind raced through their branches and cast their leaves out on the air in a shower of glimmering delight. Gold leaves, flakes of gold, absorbed in their aerial play captivated our senses as we passed through their domain. Packing light for artistic expression, I had at hand exactly six watercolour pencils and a pen. Here is a quick sketch just to put the colours in place.

September 22, 2012

Day Three: Sometimes things are not what they appear to be. Added layers of information, interactions, or interpretations can provide surprises of such magnitude that they rock the foundations of your belief structures and knock you off balance emotionally for awhile. Whether it comes at a spiritual or more mundane level makes no difference. Here's to learning experiences.

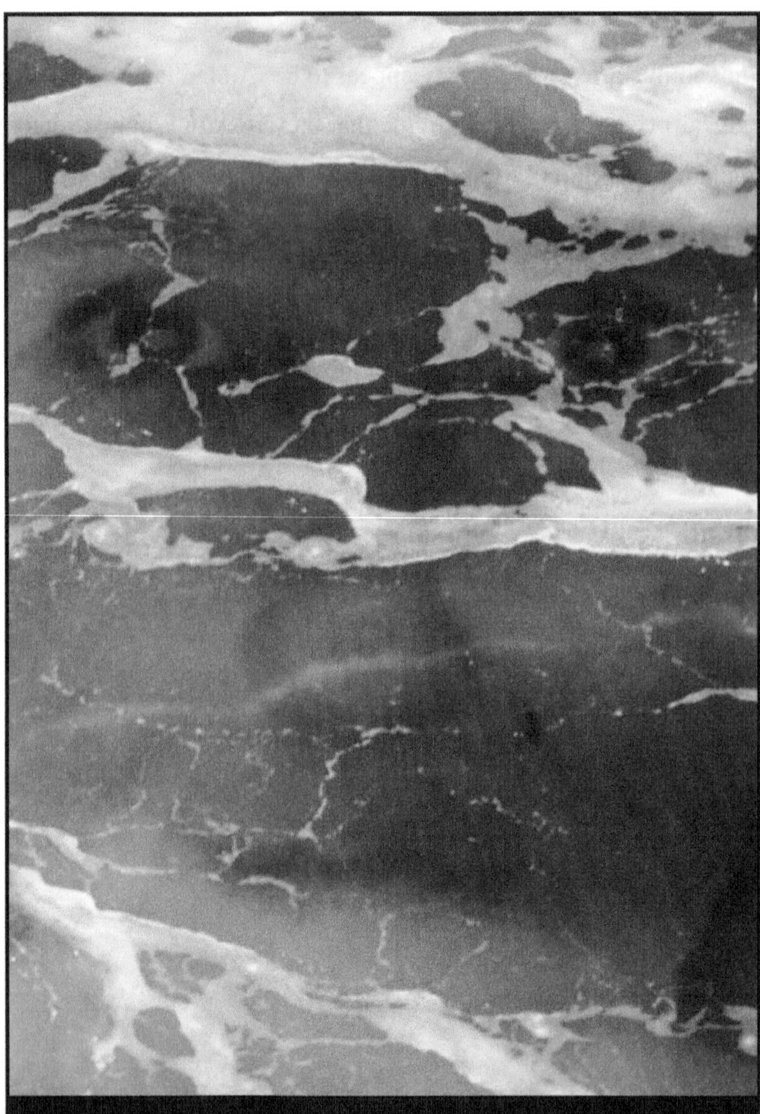

Journey with Water

Digital collage

The Final Art-Down: EARTH

My Journey with EARTH

I see a path with a map to a new life in a magical world that matters. I see the Traveling Stone.

The stone teacher, this travelling stone, this rock that came to me was not the easiest, nor the first available "pick me" voice to make itself known. That first stone voice later revealed itself to be a decoy, and it did so with some glee and personality, actually. It was as though it was purely delighted to be performing this task, a fact which quite annoyed me at the time. What was the need for a decoy? What was this all about? And yet, when hearing Native American folk stories or even folk stories in general, the decoy is actually a common occurrence during the travels of the protagonist through the various plot twists. The evil or often mischievous antagonist who tries to divert the main character from their mission or vision quest could be considered just such a decoy.

So here we have the mischievous one sitting at my side. "You need to go into this no further, no deeper. Pick me. Pick me." Well, I think to myself, perhaps you are, and perhaps you are not the teacher, let us check. I'll just cover you with my jacket so I know where you are and take a quick stroll down the riverbank to explore the possibilities. With that action, that choice, suddenly a whisper plays along the edges of my mind.

"I am not a river rock," it sang. "I am here by mistake."

Following a sense of rightness, I move toward the shore away from the water. Perhaps, just perhaps, there is something here for me to find. I'm not sure how to go about the search, so I allow my intuition to guide me. By focusing my attention and my senses on my surroundings, I notice that my arm feels warmer on one side. I also notice that this warmth is not related to the direction of the sun. The sensation changes as I move, the barest prickling of energy along the surface of my skin seems to orient me toward a pile of wreckage pushed up almost against the bank. This did not look promising, what could possibly be waiting for me in this stack of refuse?

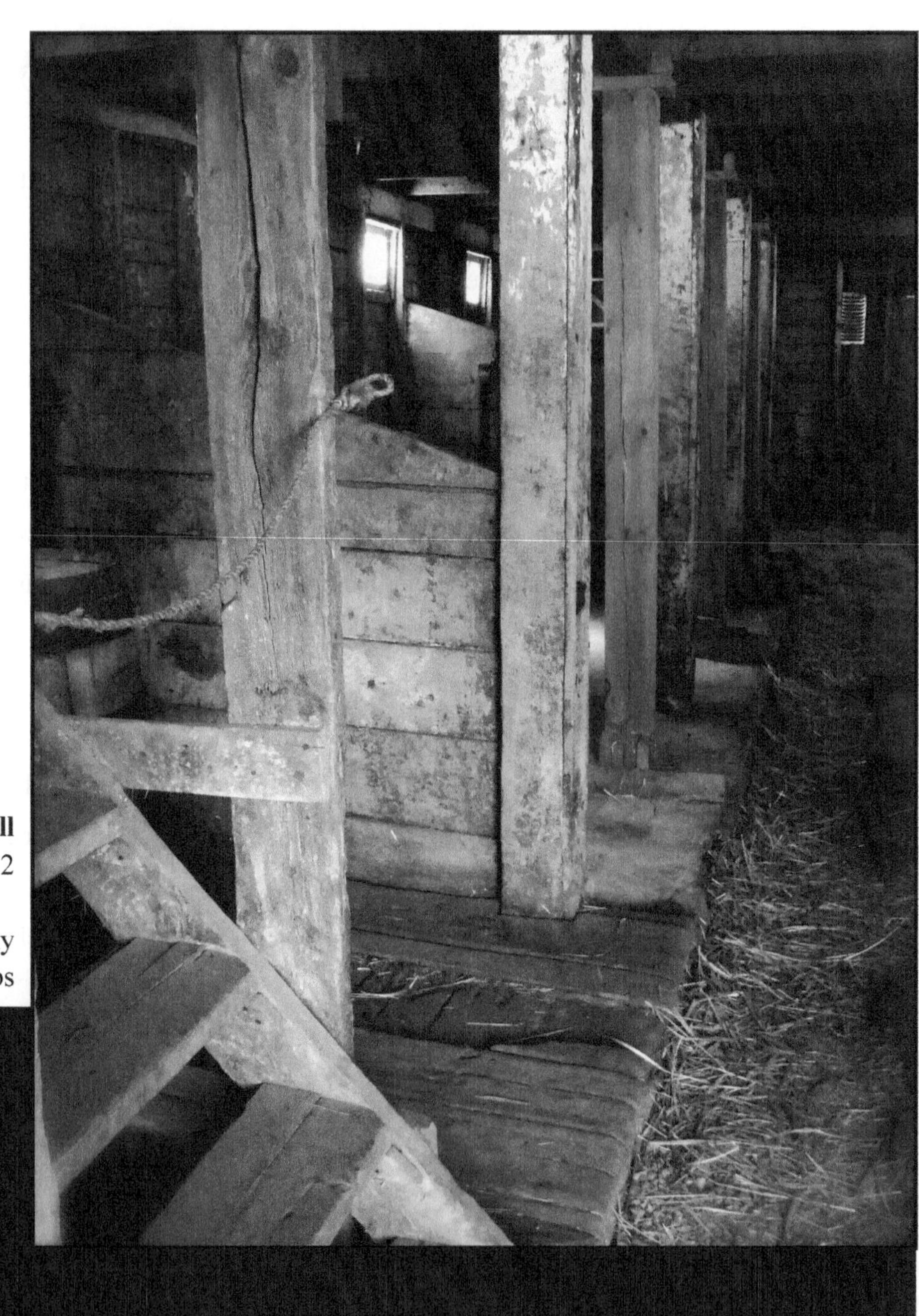

The Empty Stall
December 4, 2012

Still life photography

Yet something prompts me to trust, to hold out my hand palm down. I am rewarded when a ripple tingles across my palm. I move my arm away, and the tingle vanishes. I swing my arm back and forth, watching the rocks below. Where is that energy coming from? Narrowing the field of the swing, I focus on one area. There you are! Resting amid the wreckage of human construction, nestled over what appears to be a rusted tangle of broken bridge railing and the mangled remains of an aluminum truck body, pressed with a quilted square pattern in the metal, lay a good sized stone. It was not smooth or rounded like the other river rocks scattering the bank. I look at it, feeling a bit surprised, but then again, not really.

Sitting next to the stone, I touch it with the palm of my hand. "Will you go with me? I do not know where we are going, or what we will do, or what will happen." I ask.

"That is all right. I will go with you," it sang. "Drum for me?"

Feeling extremely self-conscious, as I am not a gifted drummer by any stretch of the imagination, I retrieve the drum from the circle, and sitting back down with the stone, I quietly begin to send out a rhythm, sending out the deep sound to vibrate deeply through space and time. Surrounded by plants growing new, moss growing old, and driftwood breaking down, I sit with the stone. This year's grass seedpods tickle my shoulder as I move close to my ... my what?

"Do you have a name you wish me to call you?"

"Ti-tan, Ti-tan, Ti-tan," the stone seems to say. This reminds me of the Greek myths about the Titans imprisoned deep in the Earth, massive and moving like the tectonic plates. Watching the stone, I see a glimpse of a shadow, like the top of a totem pole, play across its surface, and I hear the sound of horse's hooves behind me. I turn to look, and behold, no horse. It's time to pick up the stone. As I begin to remove it from its bed, a couple of spiders leave it for me. A sense that this stone really wants me to move him slips vaguely across my mind. Walking to the river, I allow the cold, running water to wash over the pulse points in my ankles, and the current of the wind to run through my hair, caressing my skin. I am cleansed. I open my arms wide with joy and exhilaration. Then I move to the river's edge and find a rock to sit on. There is a heart-shaped pebble in the water that catches my attention, and I pick it up.

With my back straight, palms up, pebble clutched in my left hand and feet firmly planted in the earth, drums cry out, and I close my eyes. I feel the drum beats and suddenly my hands spring open, palms up, the pebble heavy in my hand.

"I am ready to receive,." my heart cries.

I feel the air rush through me, as though through the body of a bird in flight. I take a deep breath in, release it and the drums stop. Apparently there was an eagle and possibly a hawk right overhead. I did not see either, as my eyes were closed. I carry the heart-shaped pebble back with me. It is one of the stones for a burden basket. Writing "surrender" on the back, I place it in the basket. Then I return my attention to my rock that is not a river rock, my travelling stone. I love the smell of this stone.

"Why have you come to me?" I ask.

"Escape. My spirit sings and flies. I feel the song of the air rushing through me. I see the water, cold, icy spears. Deep, deep drumbeats, pulse of the Earth. I bring you a message. It is time to move. I found a way, so can you," It whispers.

Moving my stone to a nearby table I create a line drawing of this stone teacher, add shading, really see the stone. What patterns do you see, what speaks to you ... I ask myself. Taking a good hard look at the stone is revelatory. It looks like a topographical map of Alberta, complete with a flat space that could denote the prairies in the southwest corner. An image or symbol comes strongly to mind. The design is a circle with a cross through the centre, which I then paint on the stone in turquoise blue. I am urged to put my thumbprint in red in the middle, which I do. Pulling my thumb back, I realize I have the perfect replication of the Christian cross, emblazoned in blue across my red thumb. The following thoughts go through my mind.

"My circle is a starting place. A safe, protected ending place. Explore, transform. Begin, and end, and begin, again and again. I am always with you, and with all things living, breathing, pulsing, beating."

****

Who knew rocks could be teachers? Imagine the amazement of experiencing this first hand, and for the first time in a controlled class environment. What a phenomenal opportunity to safely explore the cultural teachings that are part of my own genetic code. I have not felt so free to be who I am since I was a small child.

So I take my rock home with me, and place it on the table. My husband examines the stone, then glances at me with a sort of perplexed look on his face.

"What do you see when you look at it?" I ask, curious to know whether he gathers the same impression.

"Well, it looks like a topographical map of Alberta." He says. "I wonder what's in that circle?"

Intriguing, but that's another story.

At Sandy McNabb
October 26, 2012

Mixed media

Earth: The Image

This project came to life in pieces, two pieces. The whole, comprised of a written journal of daily life experience is matched with a corresponding artistic interpretation. It is separated here into its individual parts. So the journey continues towards its end...

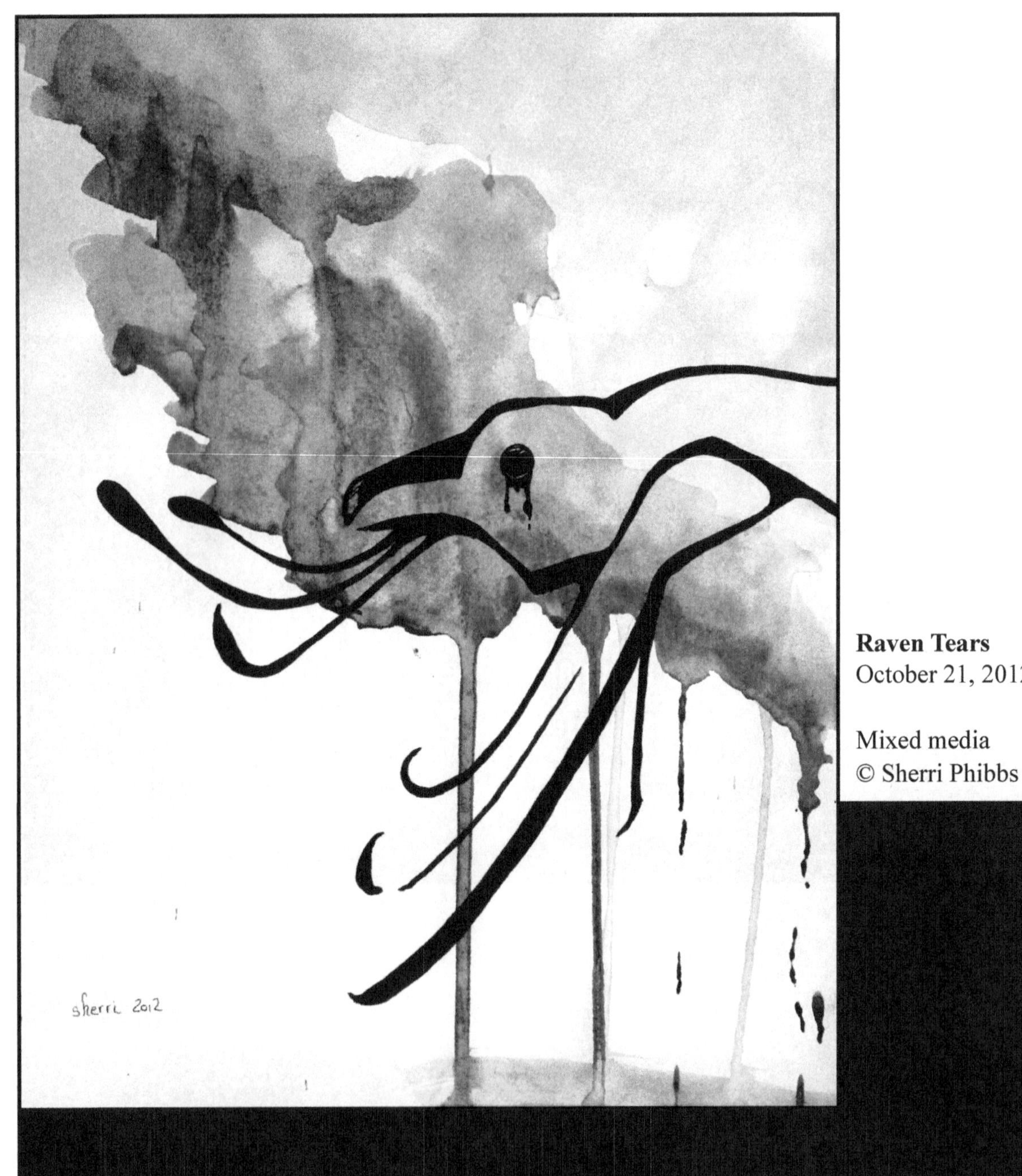

Raven Tears
October 21, 2012

Mixed media

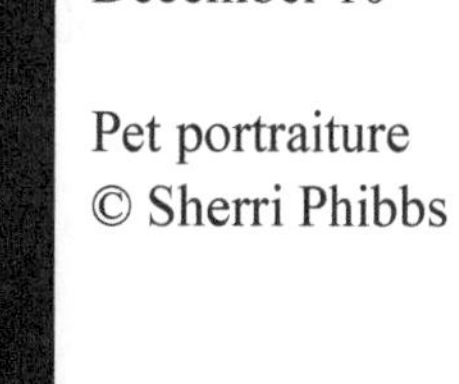

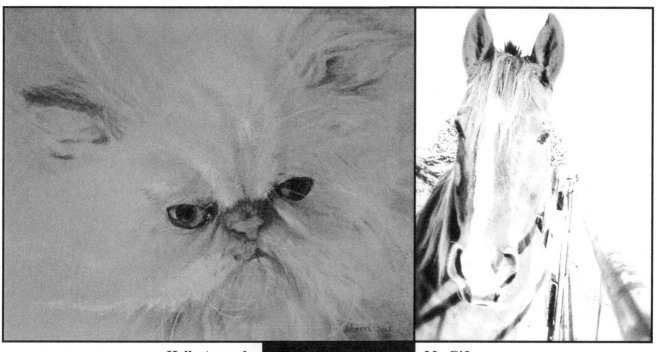

Hello Amanda
December 2, 2012

Pastel
© Sherri Phibbs

My Gift
December 10th - 12th, 2012

Pet portraiture
© Sherri Phibbs

Powerful Flow
September 27, 2012

Sepia ink
© Sherri Phibbs

The Big Picture
September 23, 2012

Mixed media
© Sherri Phibbs

Shades of Gray
September 24, 2012

Digital collage

Change of Perspective
September 25, 2012

Digital collage
© Sherri Phibbs

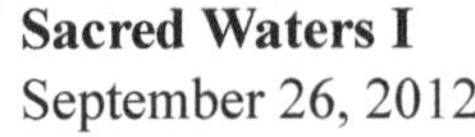

Sacred Waters I
September 26, 2012

Sepia ink
© Sherri Phibbs

Stained Glass
November 13, 2012

Mixed media

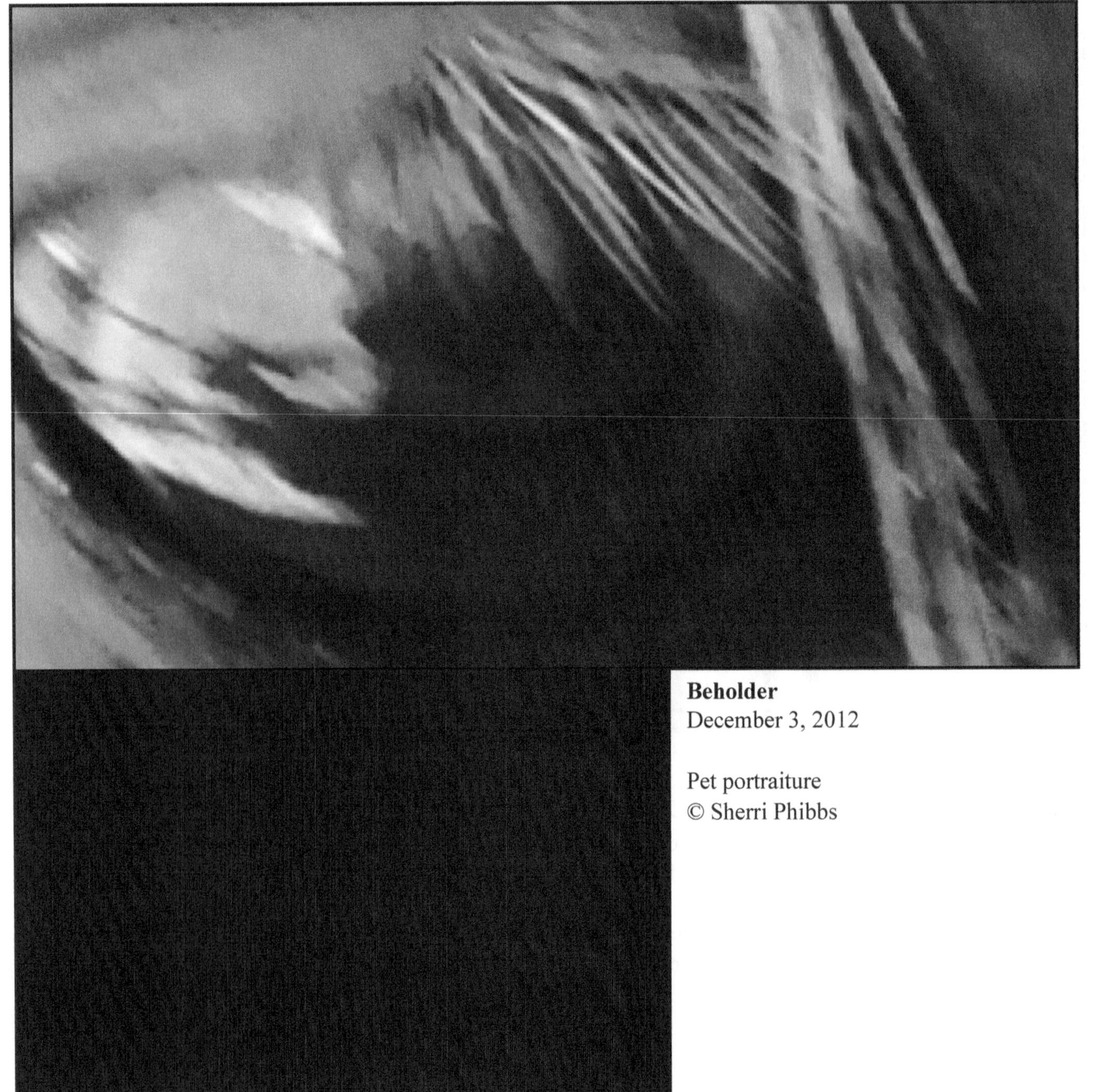

Beholder
December 3, 2012

Pet portraiture

A Gift For You…

A Story Continues or The Journey Proposal

Upon closer examination of the rock that is not a river rock, and crosschecking reference points on a guide map of the area, we discovered an ancient rock monument stands at this circled spot. The Sundial Medicine Wheel has been dated as being older than Stonehenge, and is the only known, archeologically verified double circle medicine wheel in Alberta. Needless to say, another journey began right then.

Gaining permission from the landowner, we were able to hike to this fascinating site, and arrived at noon on the day of the summer solstice. High on a vast wind-swept ridge, rich with flowing waves of natural prairie grasses and overlooking a wide, winding river valley, the stone circles beckoned and a man and woman answered, together. It was a humbling and spiritual experience, one I invite you to explore as you engage in your own journey of discovery.

Negative Space
October 7, 2012

Sepia ink

Sacred Headwaters III
October 8, 2012

Sepia ink

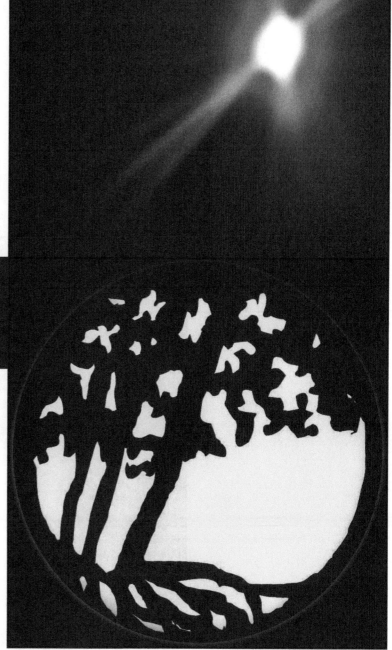

Angel
September 29, 2012

Photography
© Sherri Phibbs

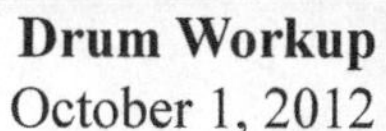

Drum Workup
October 1, 2012

Graphic art
© Sherri Phibbs

In Motion
October 2, 2012

Photography

Time
September 28, 2012

Photography

Northern Light
September 30, 2012

Photography
© Sherri Phibbs

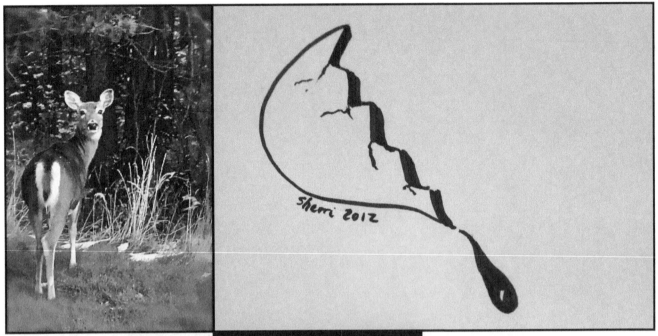

Postcard Art
October 4, 2012

Digital art

Ancient Ruins
October 5, 2012

Sepia ink

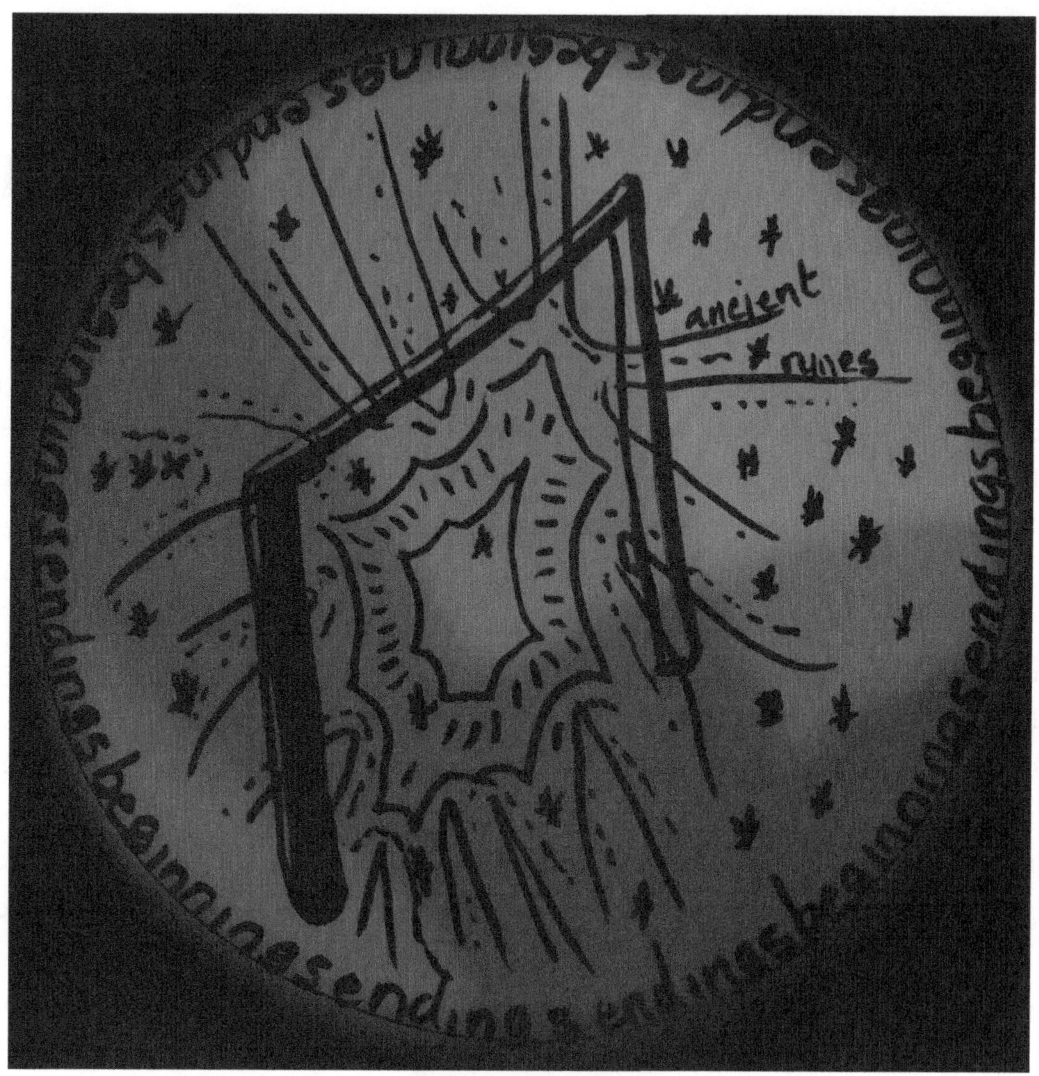

Meditative Mandala
October 6, 2012

Mixed media

Awareness of EARTH

Picture yourself surrounded by the natural world, in a place where you can smell the earth and sense the deep roots beneath you. It may look like a mountainside, a rock outcropping on a hilltop, or an open field or prairie, but it will be a place where you feel a personal connection to EARTH. Give yourself permission to go, physically, and remember to take along a coloured pencil and your journal. When you arrive at this place, address the area respectfully, following the method for connection outlined in earlier chapters. When you have permission, make yourself comfortable. Use all your senses to track and be aware of everything in your surroundings. Note the sense of being grounded. ..breathe in, breathe out, ...with gratitude.

When you are ready, begin to form a request in your mind for inspiration and assistance on your journey of creative discovery and integrity. Pay particular attention to the thoughts or images that flow through your mind, and record them in your journal. Also note your feelings and physical responses as you interact with Nature in this way, tracking and recording this as well. Are you drawn to a certain direction? Do you feel excited, tired, inspired, or something else entirely? What about this area draws or speaks to you? Is there a message? Describe and make note of the experience.

As you complete your interaction with EARTH, you may wish to express your gratitude. You may do this verbally or with an offering of burnt sage, sweetgrass, or organic tobacco, or you may leave some cornmeal. You may repeat this interaction with EARTH again and again, as a way of getting to know the element, becoming connected to your natural environment, and opening your mind to the experience of this Divine and self-sustaining world of which we are a part.

Sacred Headwaters II
October 3, 2012

Sepia ink

Peacemaker
October 9, 2012

Mixed media

Blue Star Prophecy
October 10, 2012

Mixed media

Sleep-ish
October 13, 2012

Ink line drawing

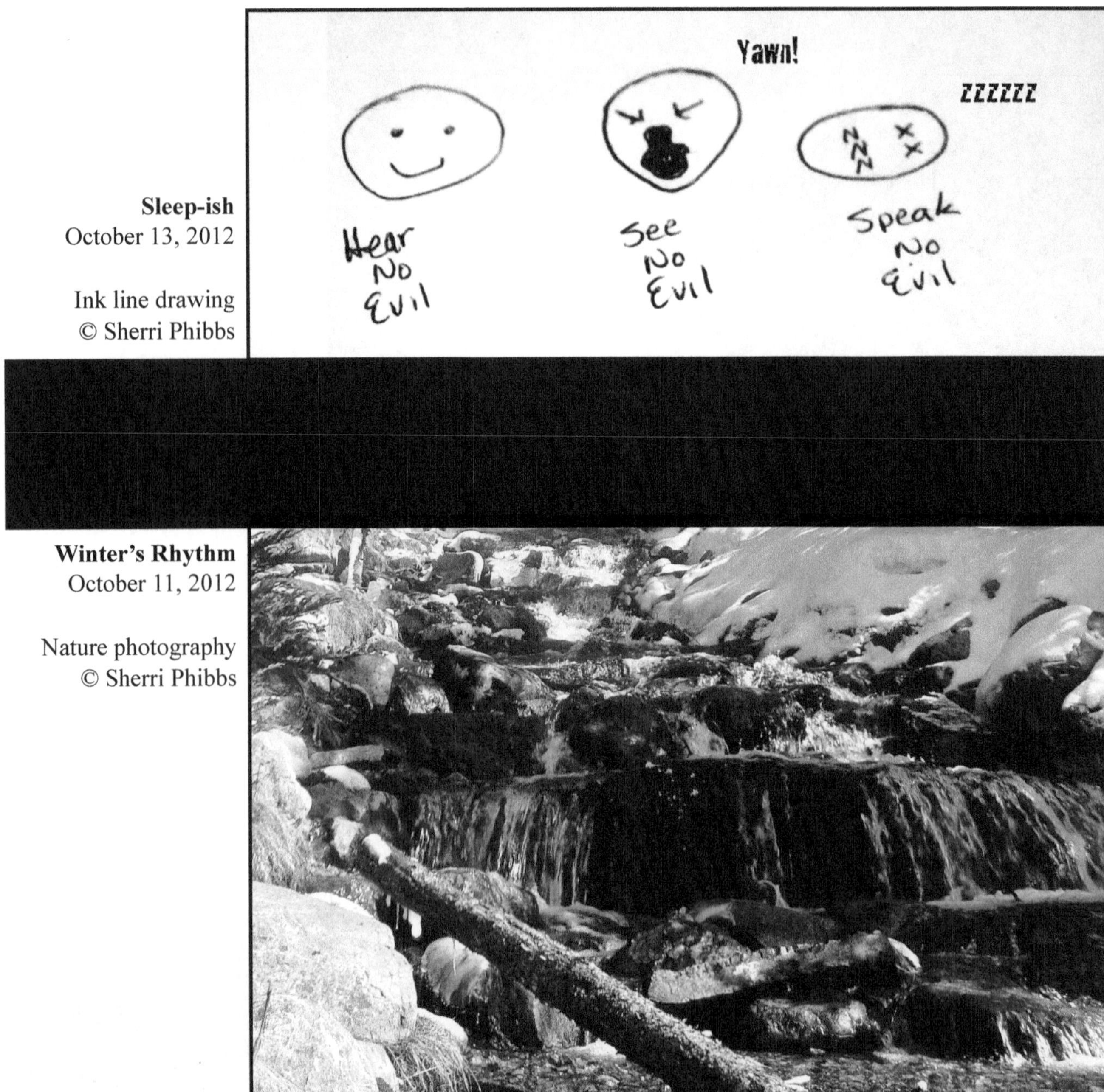

Winter's Rhythm
October 11, 2012

Nature photography

Sacred Waters III
October 12, 2012

Ink line drawing

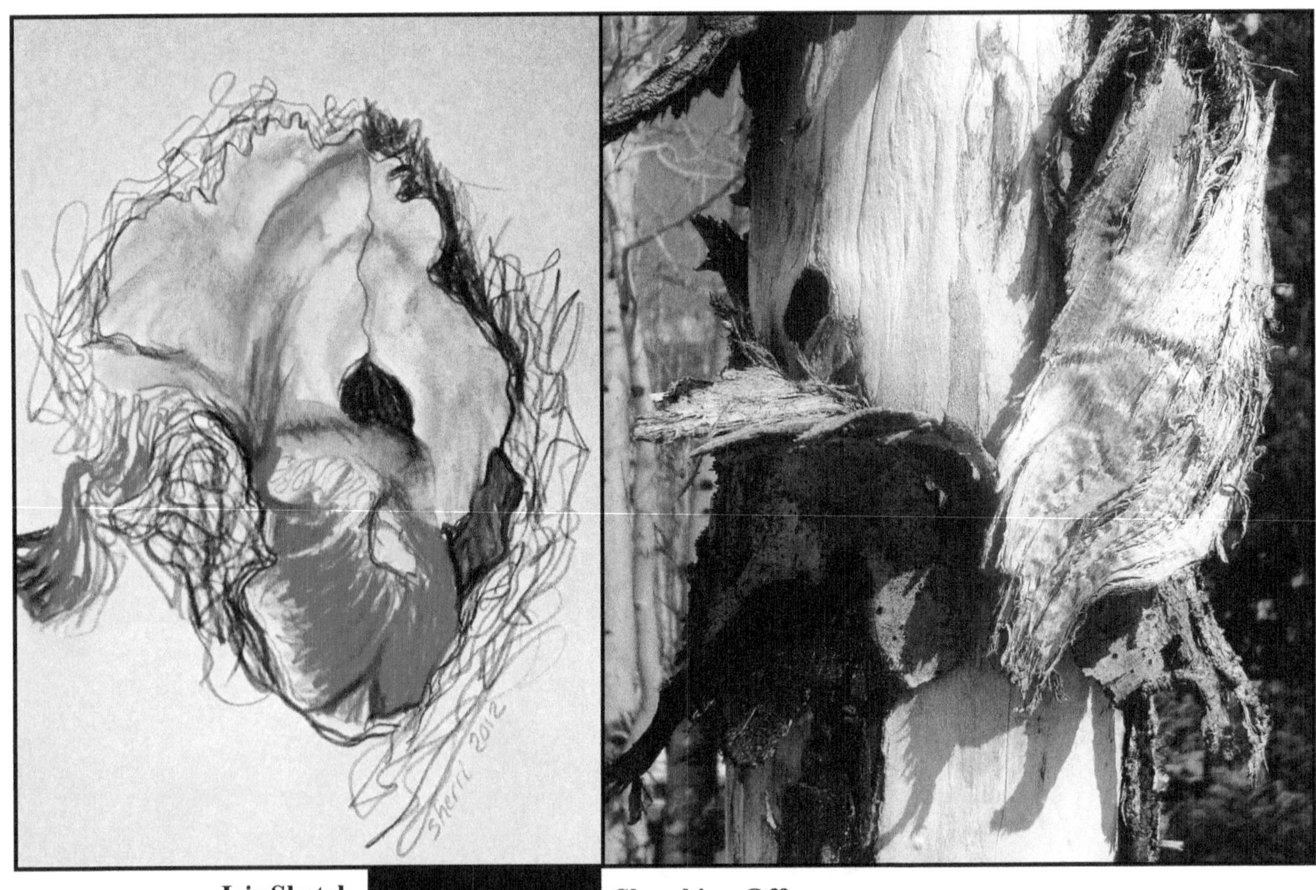

Iris Sketch
October 14, 2012

Chalk pastel
© Sherri Phibbs

Sloughing Off
October 15, 2012

Nature photography
© Sherri Phibbs

Mama & Baby Moose
October 16, 2012

Nature photography
© Sherri Phibbs

Added Layers
September 22, 2012

Mixed media
© Sherri Phibbs

Meditative Mandala
October 17, 2012

Ink line drawing

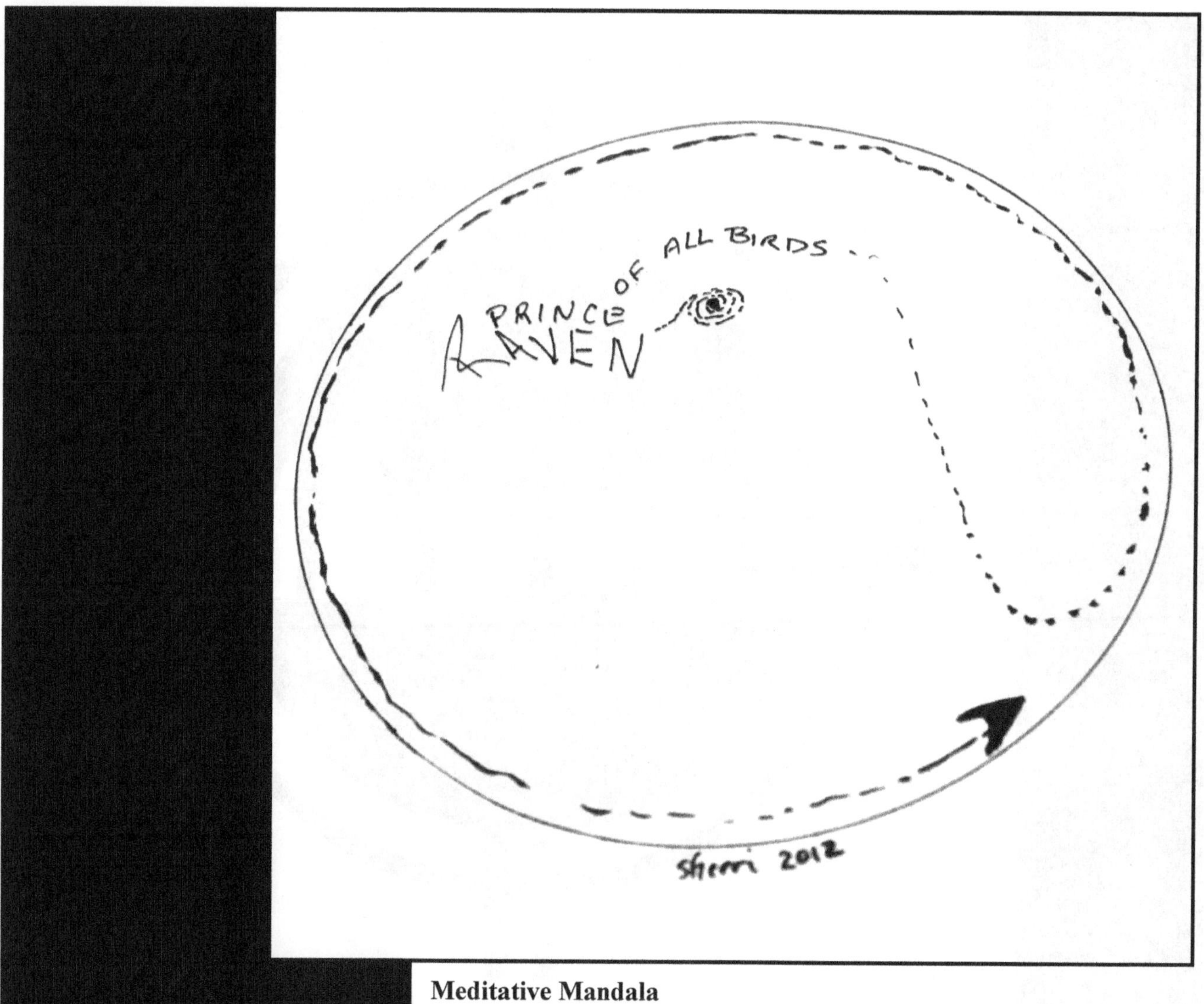

Meditative Mandala
October 18, 2012

Ink line drawing

Gate Logo
October 19, 2012

Graphic art

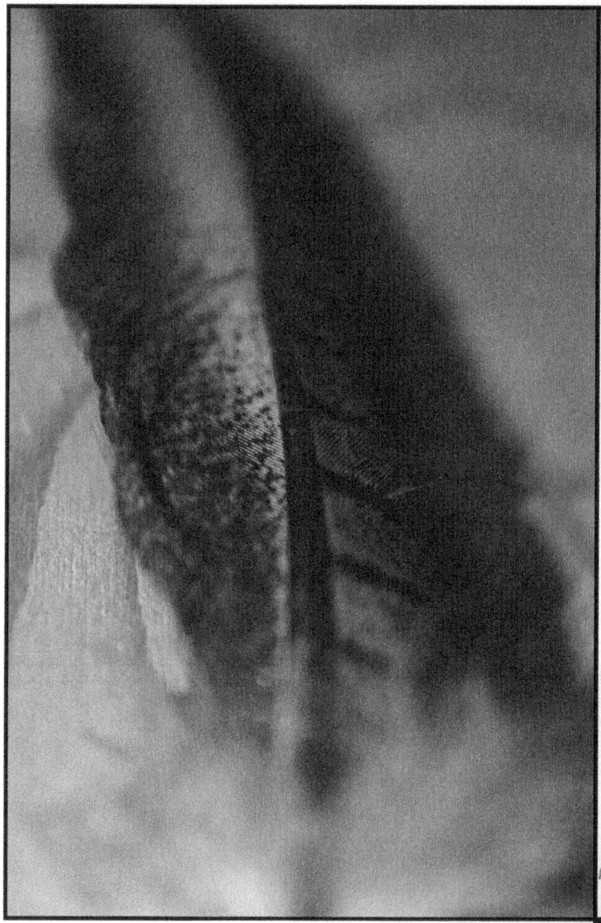

Out of Alignment
October 20, 2012

Still life photography
© Sherri Phibbs

End of Days
October 22, 2012

Mixed media
© Sherri Phibbs

The Ridge
October 23, 2012

Nature photography
© Sherri Phibbs

The Ridge II
October 24, 2012

Nature photography
© Sherri Phibbs

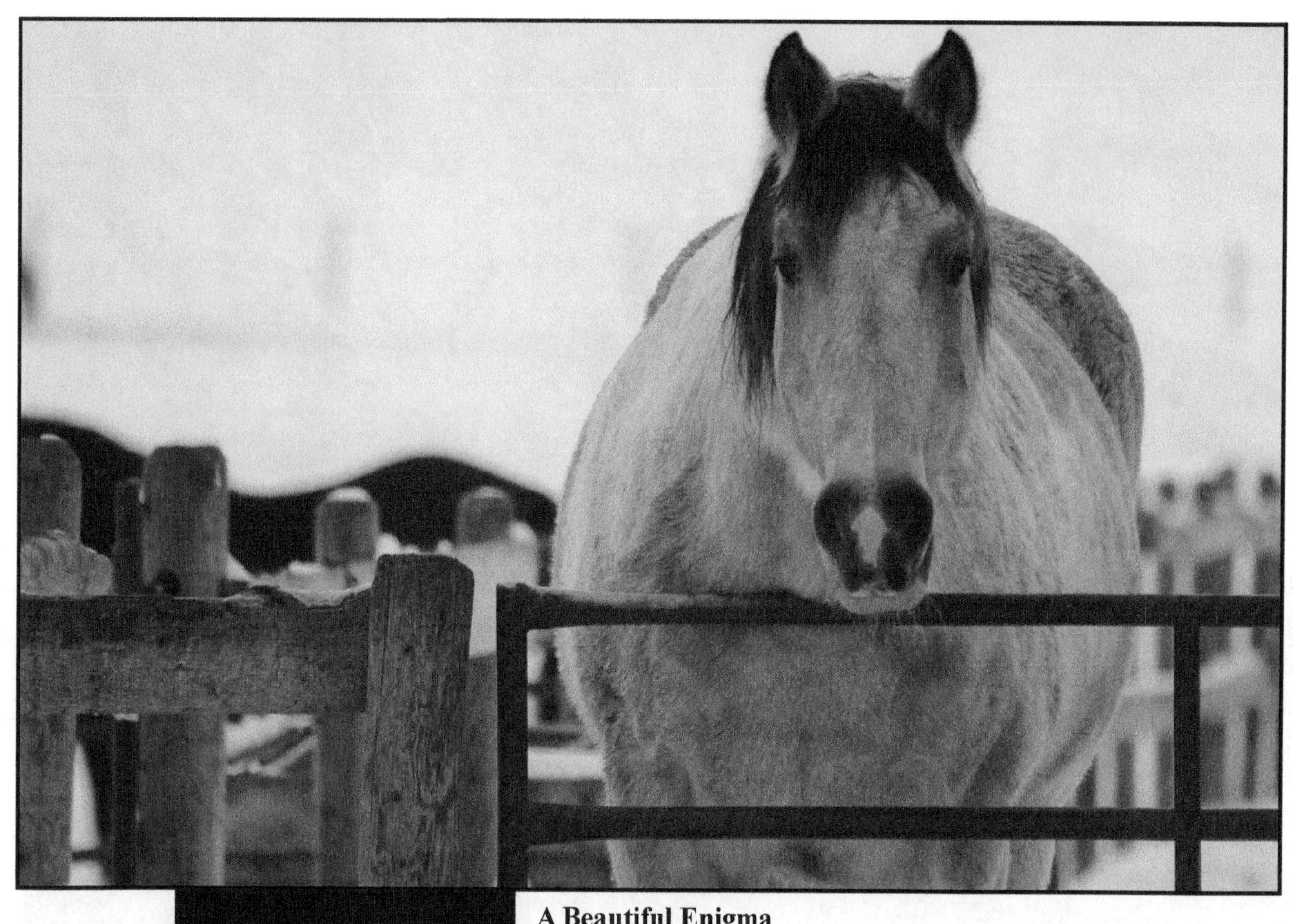

A Beautiful Enigma
October 25, 2012

Pet portraiture
© Sherri Phibbs

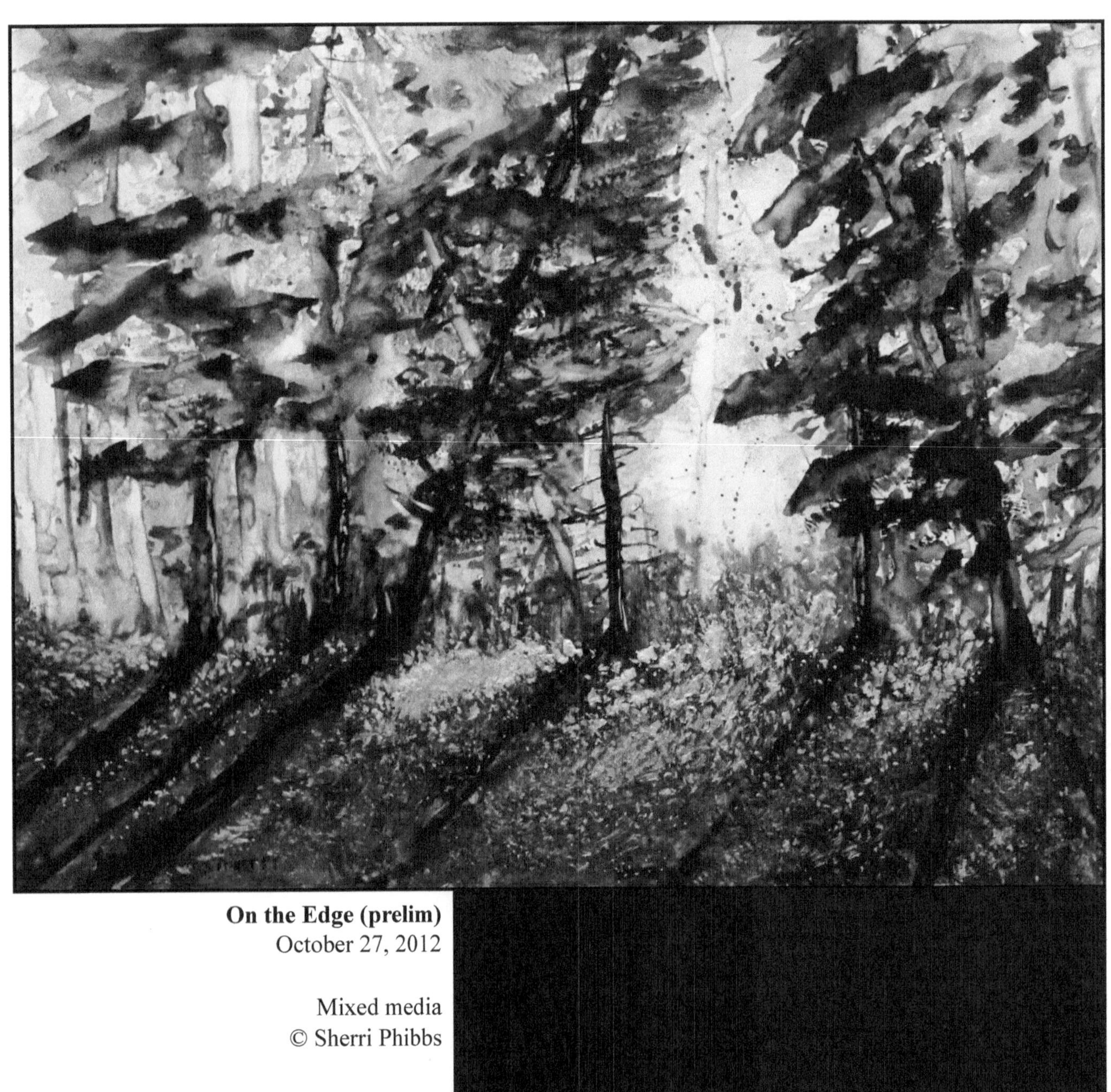

On the Edge (prelim)
October 27, 2012

Mixed media

Sleeping Beauties
October 29, 2012

Nature photography

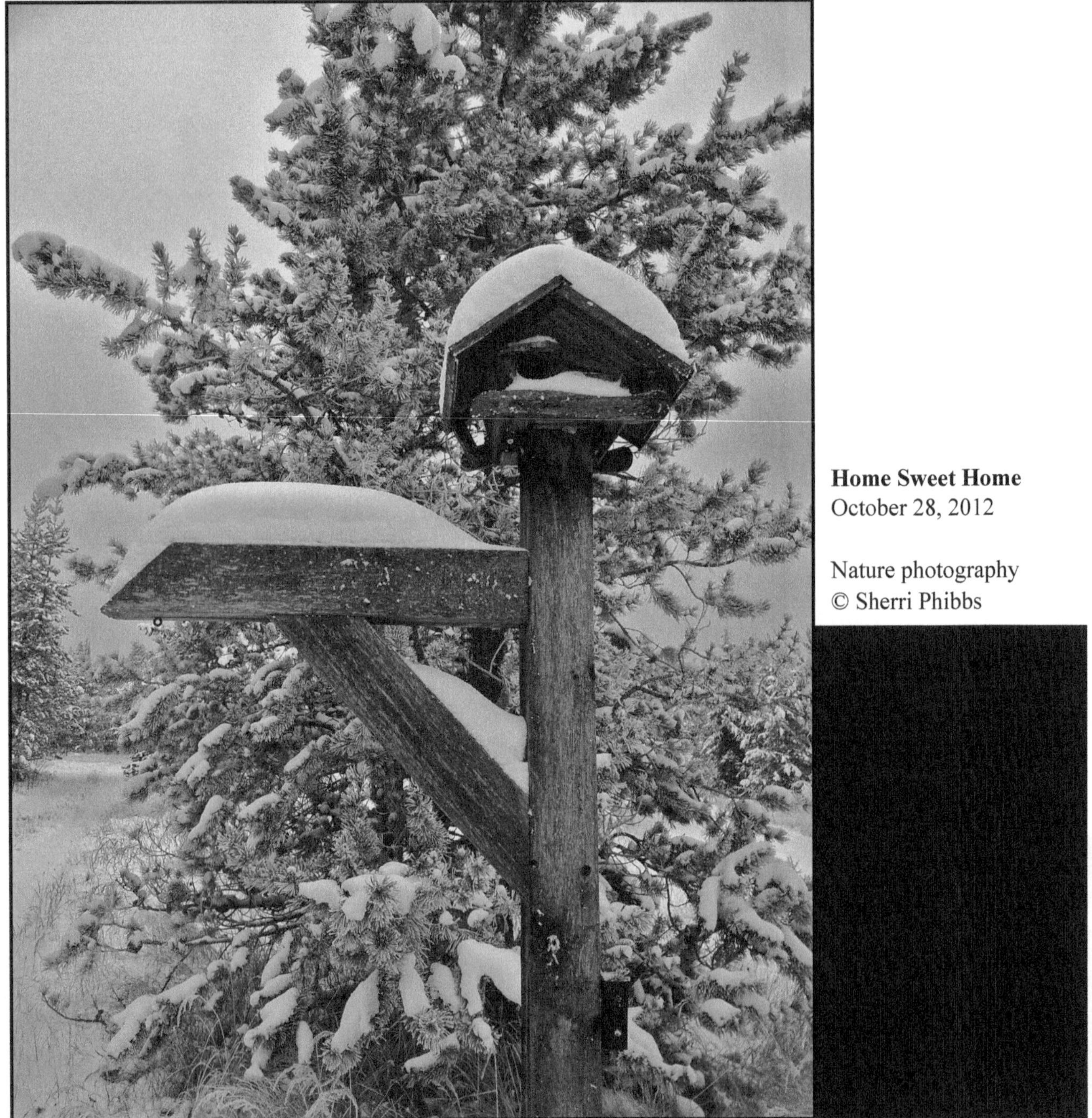

Home Sweet Home
October 28, 2012

Nature photography

Dawn Hunting
October 31, 2012

Nature photography
© Sherri Phibbs

King of Hearts
November 1, 2012

Pet portraiture
© Sherri Phibbs

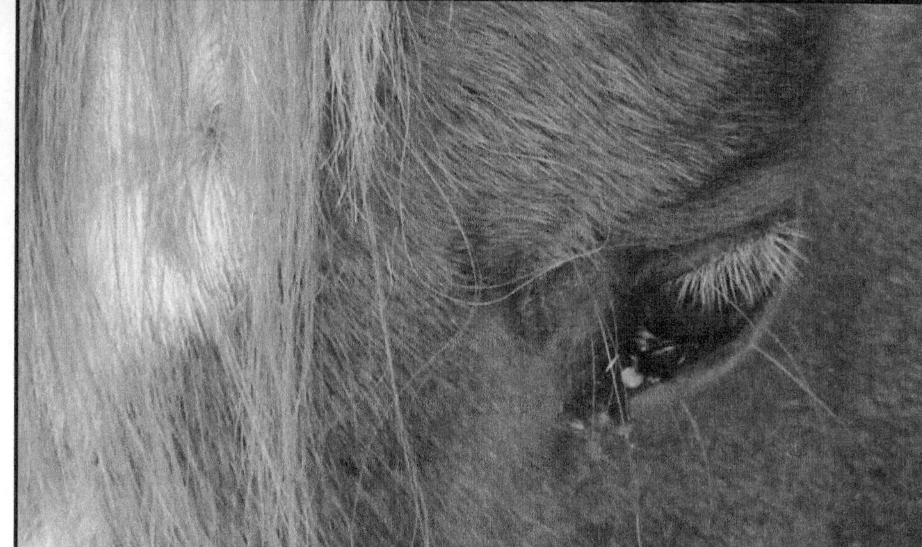

Background Work
November 2, 2012

Nature photography

Moonlight Ride Prelim
November 3, 2012

Mixed media
© Sherri Phibbs

Wild Wood
November 4, 2012

Mixed media
© Sherri Phibbs

Neo
November 5, 2012

Pet portraiture
© Sherri Phibbs

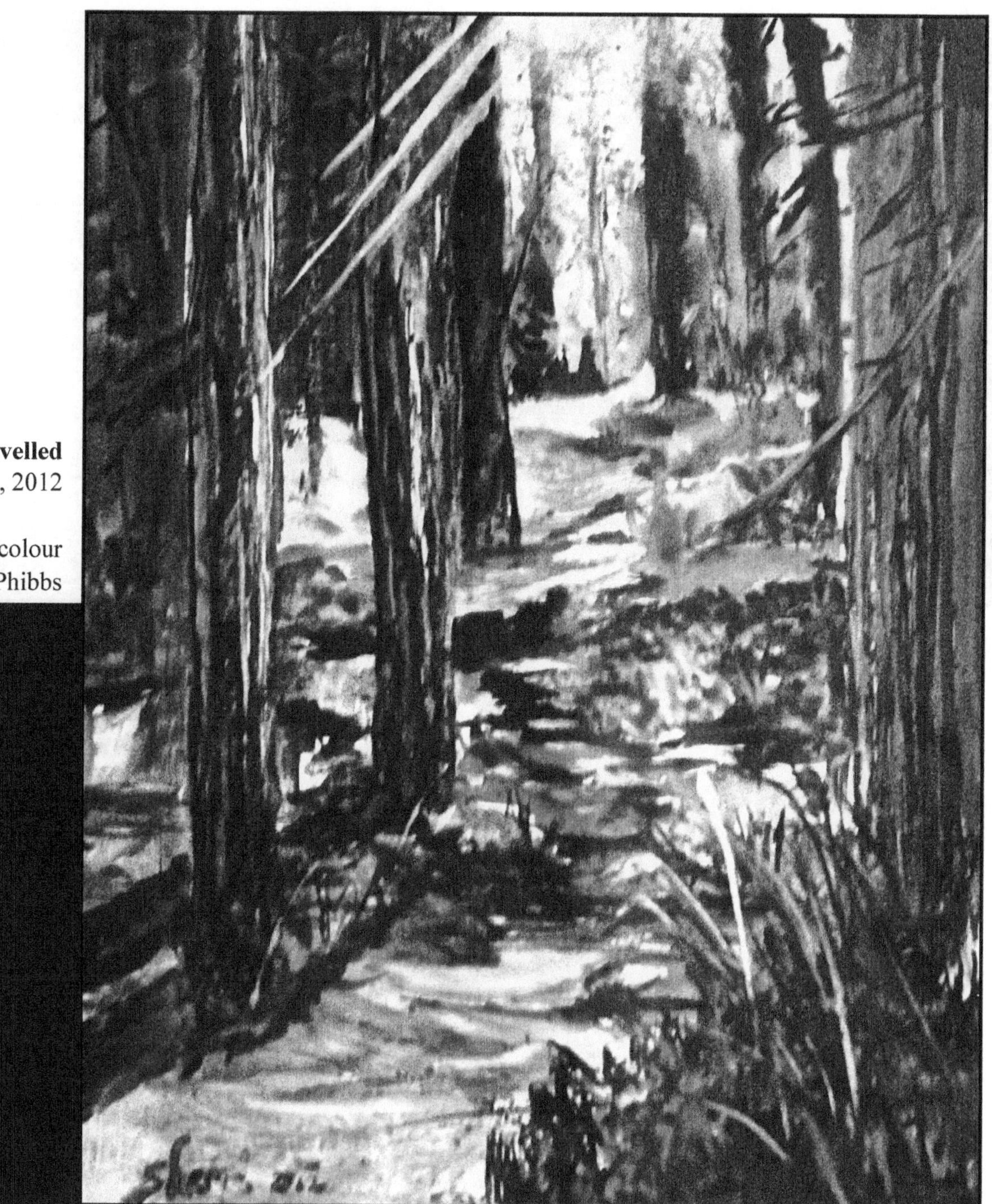

Trail Less Travelled
November 6, 2012

Watercolour
© Sherri Phibbs

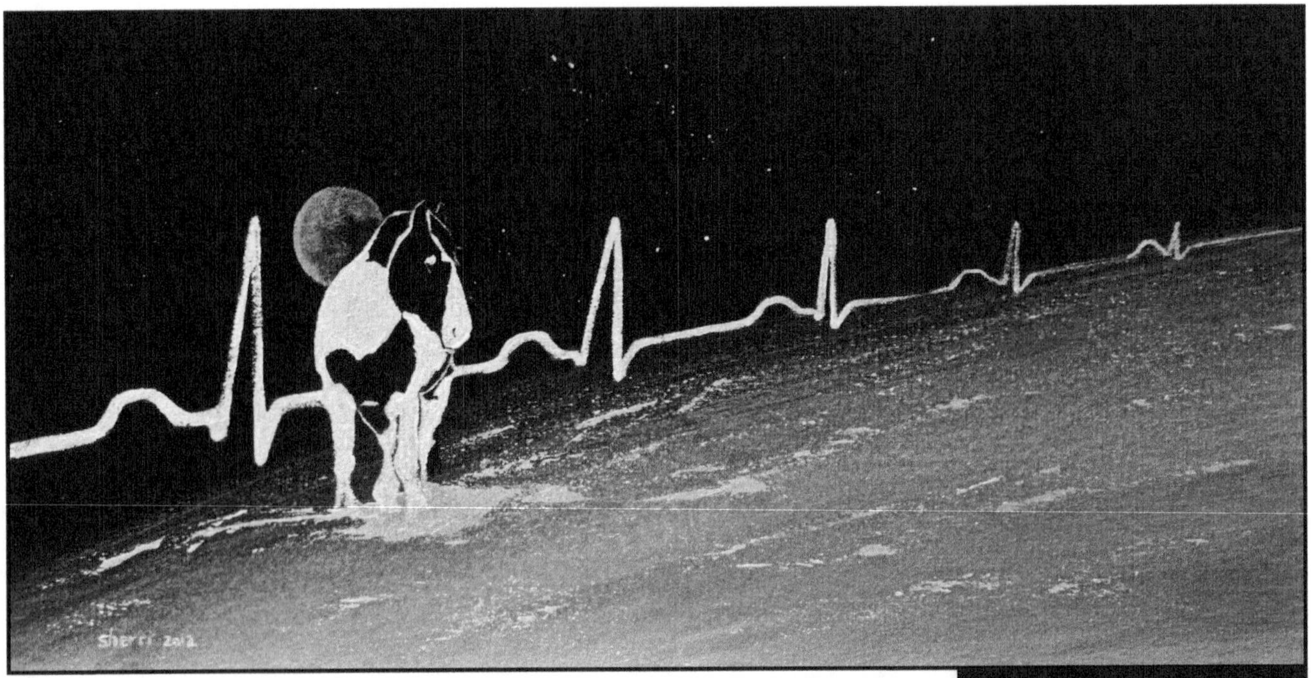

Moonlight Ride
November 7, 2012

Acrylics
© Sherri Phibbs

Sacred Waters IV
November 8, 2012

Ink line drawing
© Sherri Phibbs

Promise
November 10, 2012

Photography

Poppies
November 11, 2012

Photography
© Sherri Phibbs

Meditative Mandala
November 14, 2012

Chalk pastel
© Sherri Phibbs

Meditative Mandala
November 12, 2012

Chalk pastel

Lawn Ornaments
November 9, 2012

Nature photography
© Sherri Phibbs

Meditative Mandala
November 15, 2012

Ink line drawing
© Sherri Phibbs

Grandfather Time
November 18, 2012

Ink line drawing

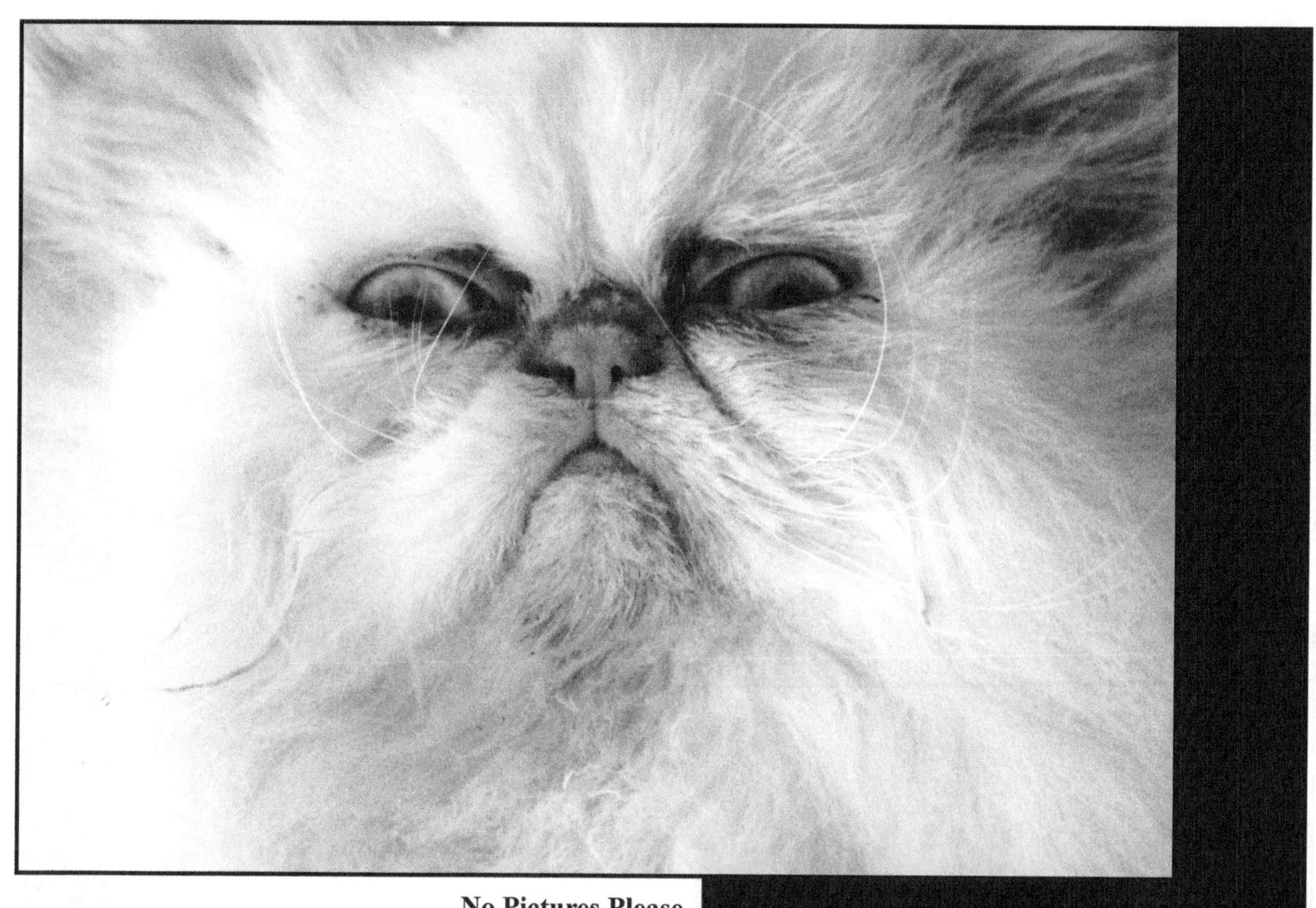

No Pictures Please
November 17, 2012

Pet portraiture

Windows
November 18, 2012

Pet portraiture

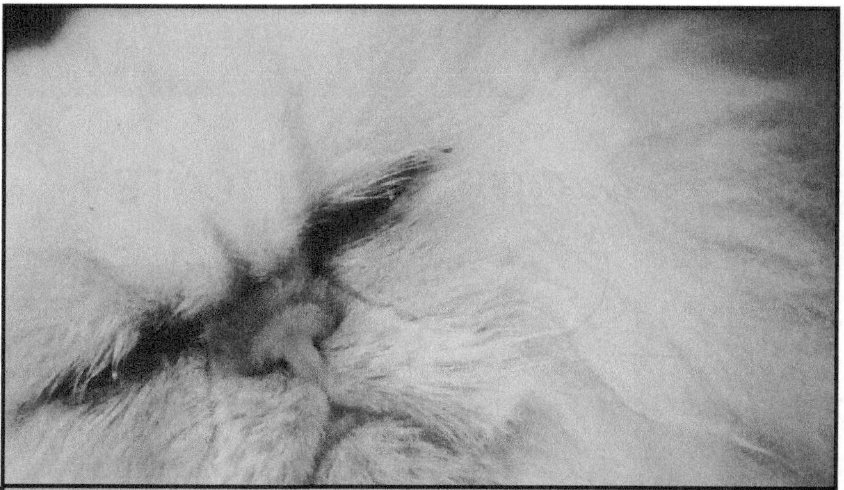

Theta State
November 19, 2012

Pet portraiture
© Sherri Phibbs

Worry
December 1, 2012

Ink line drawing
© Sherri Phibbs

GIFT CERTIFICATE

EXPIRES: DEC 21, 2012

This certificate entitles the holder to a 45-minute Complimentary Rhythm of Relaxation Session with Psycho-Educational Expressive Artist, Sherri Phibbs. Sherri, author of the forth-coming book *"Journey to the End of the World, The Final Art-Down",* supports her clients goals for creative wellness by sharing over 25 years experience in watercolour painting and the arts; as well as her unique perspective and methods for creative inspiration. Your session takes place at the studio–in-the-round, located on 13 acres of woodland delight in the foothills of the Rocky Mountains. Call or e-mail today to get scheduled!

Sherri Phibbs
Psycho-Educational Expressive Artist
www.wishstudio.ca

403-478-4349
sherri@wishstudio.ca
10 Pine Meadow Lane
20 Minutes NW of Cochrane, AB
T4C 1B2

Gift Certificate
November 23, 2012

Graphic art

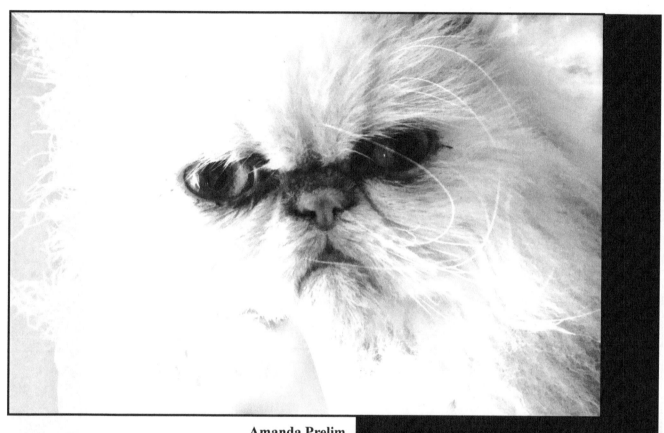

Amanda Prelim
November 21, 2012

Pet portraiture
© Sherri Phibbs

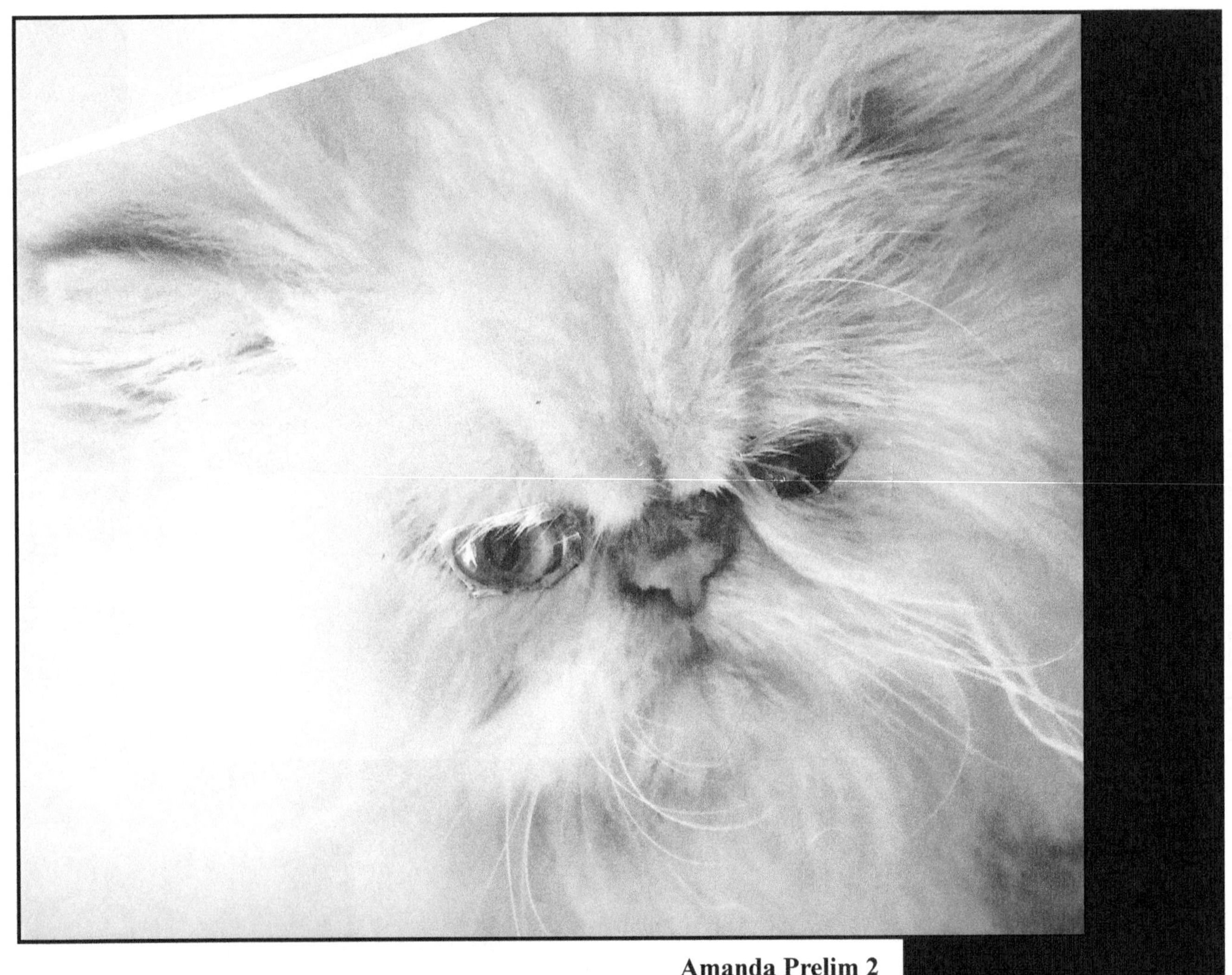

Amanda Prelim 2
November 24, 2012

Photography Collage

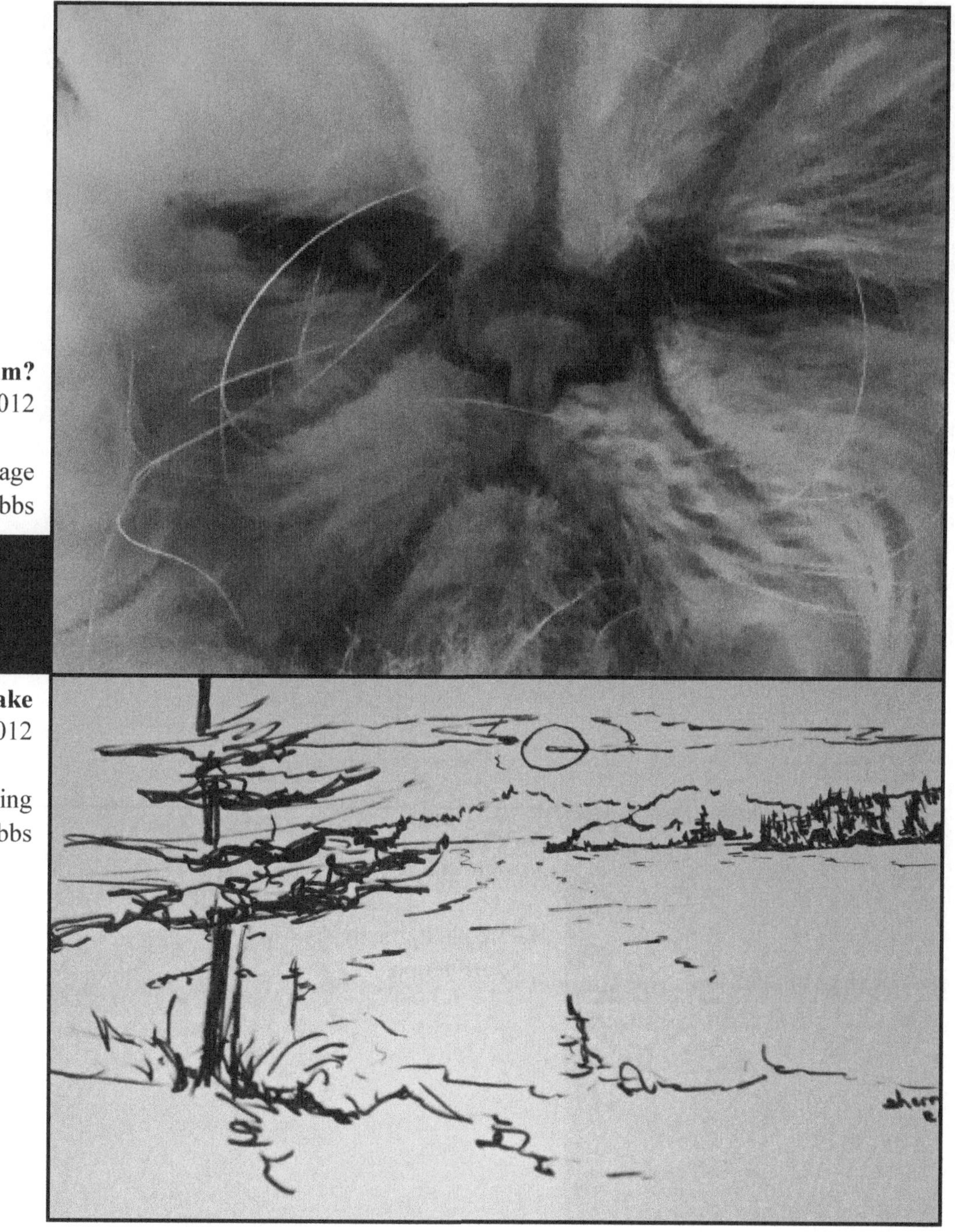

The Next Drum?
November 20, 2012

Photography Collage
© Sherri Phibbs

At the Lake
November 22, 2012

Ink line drawing
© Sherri Phibbs

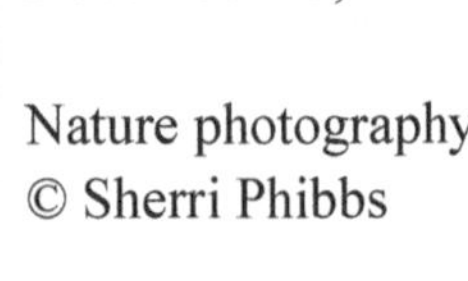

Mooselet
November 25, 2012

Nature photography

Baby
November 26, 2012

Nature photography
© Sherri Phibbs

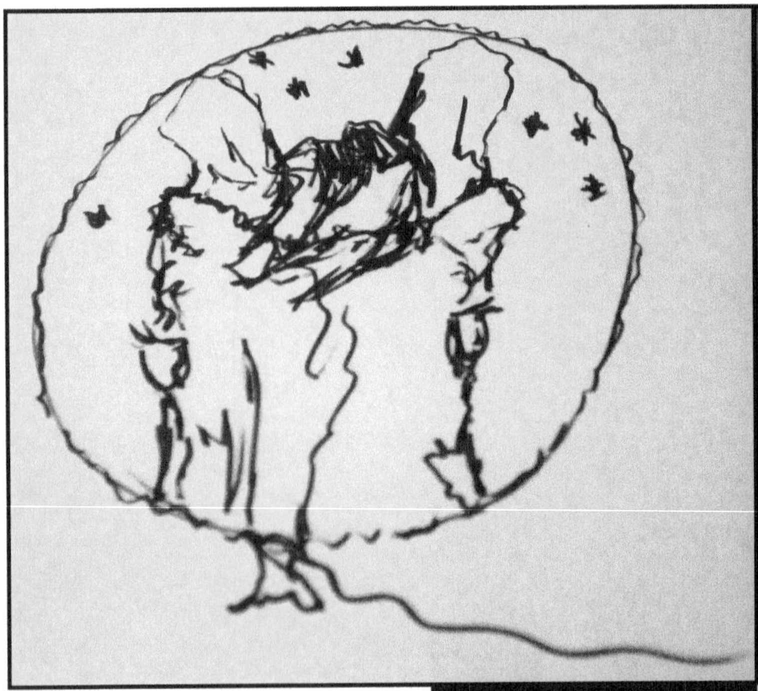

Meditative Mandala
November 27, 2012

Ink line drawing
© Sherri Phibbs

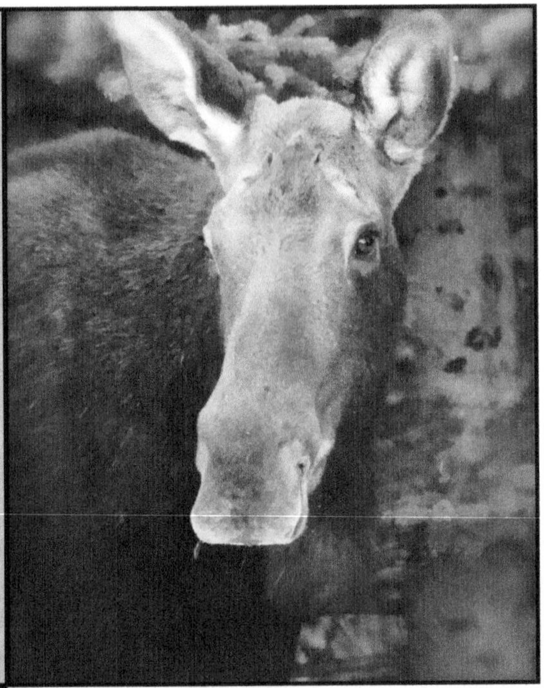

Possibility
November 28, 2012

Nature photography
© Sherri Phibbs

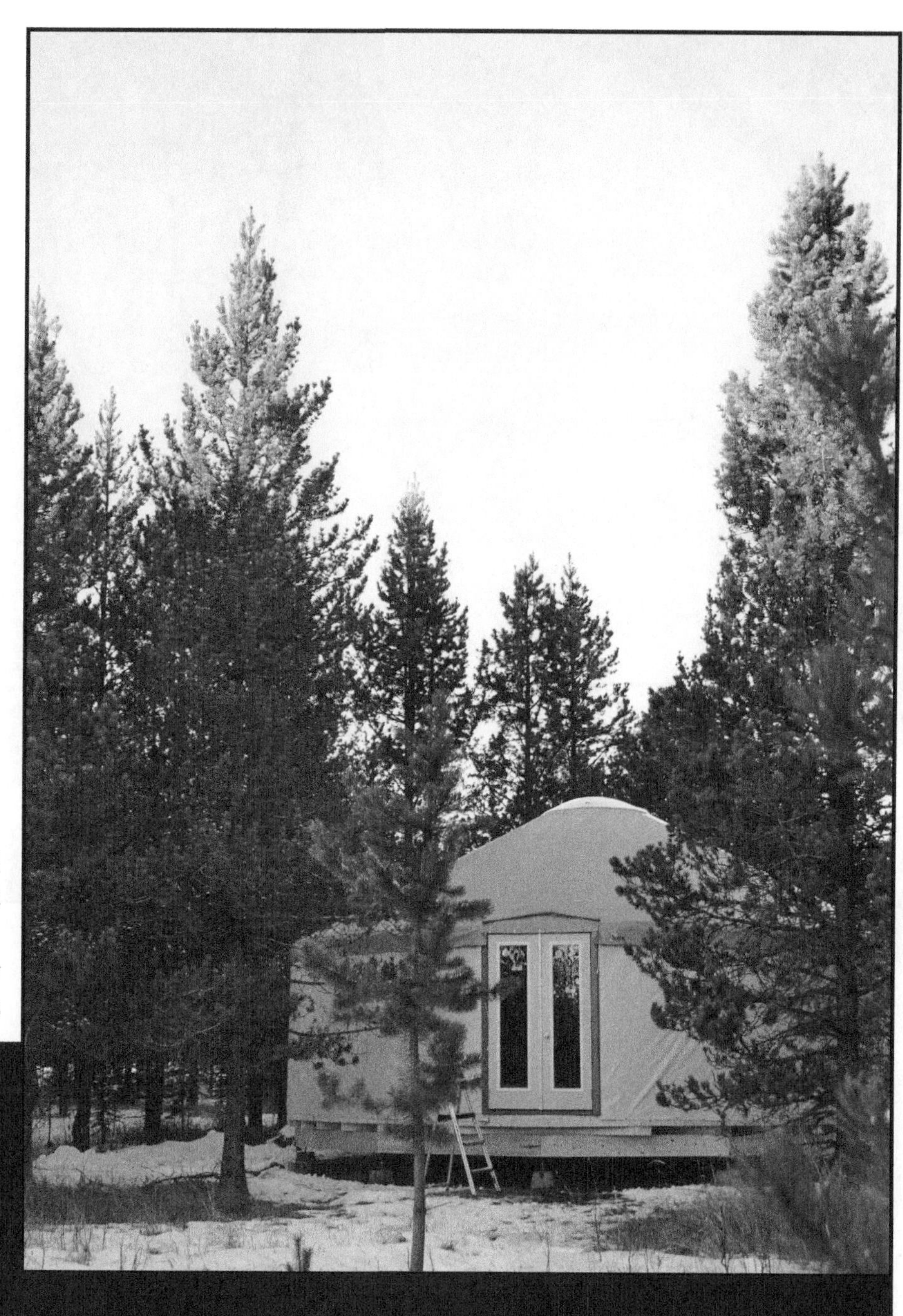

Studio-in-the-round
November 29, 2012

Nature photography

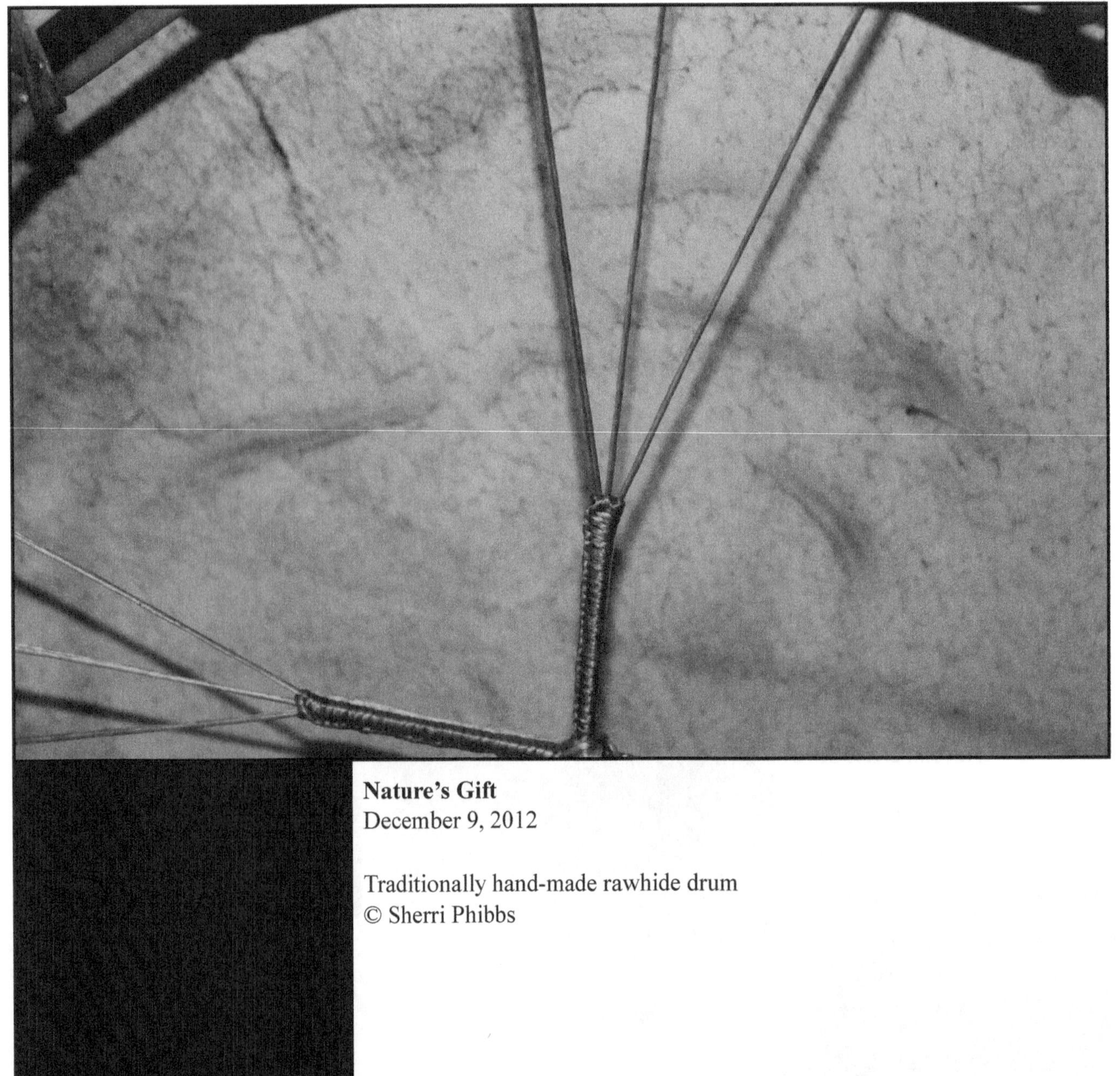

Nature's Gift
December 9, 2012

Traditionally hand-made rawhide drum

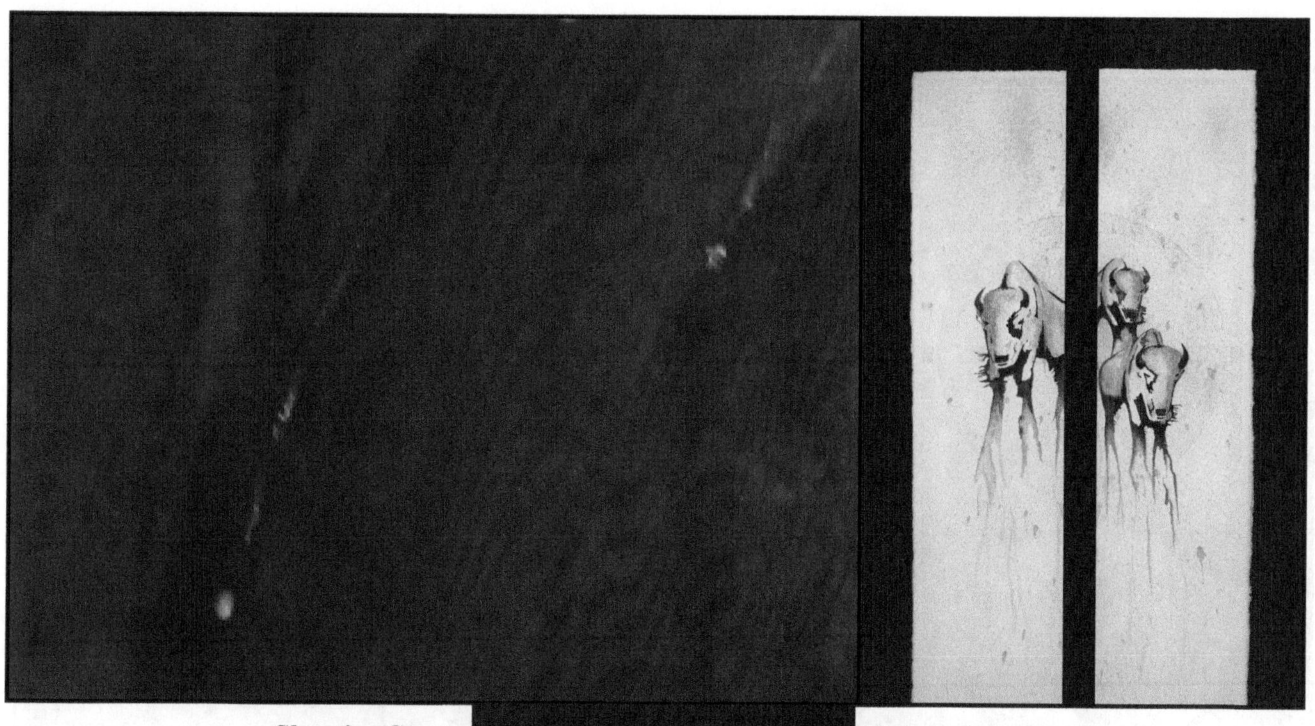

Shooting Stars
December 8, 2012

Acrylics
© Sherri Phibbs

Spirit of the North
November 30, 2012

Watercolour
© Sherri Phibbs

Golden
December 5, 2012

Pet portraiture

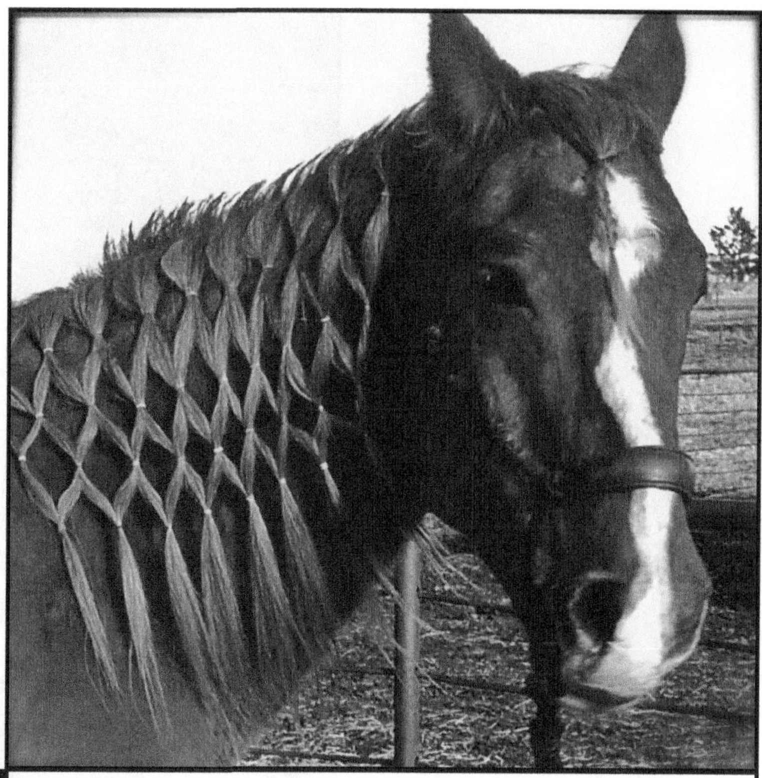

Paint by Neo
December 7, 2012

Pet portraiture

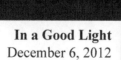

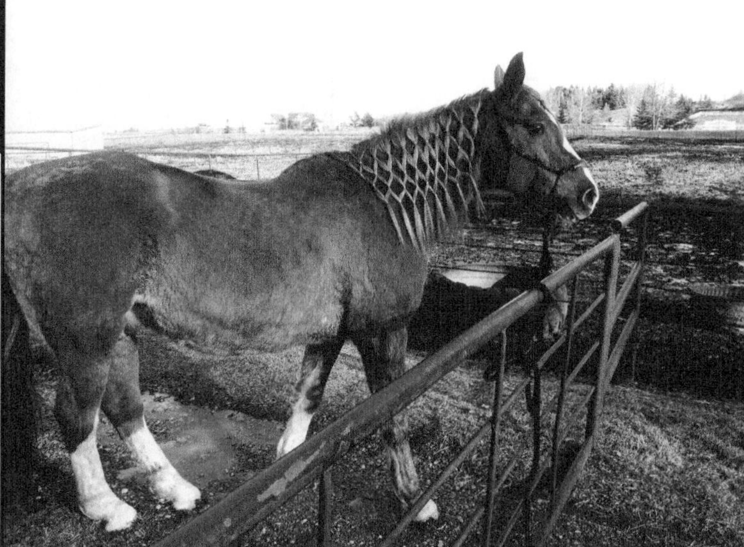

In a Good Light
December 6, 2012

Pet portraiture

Prayers for Neo
October 30, 2012

Pet portraiture
© Sherri Phibbs

In Memory of Neo

Dreamer of dreams,
Where is the night that my waking eyes may
rest?

Deep beneath the tree of life,
Springs eternal
Twining flood.
Feed the roots,
The tree will bloom.

Rest weary one.
Hear without hearing,
Be without being,
Do not be afraid.

- Sherri A. Phibbs

Hiding Out
December 16, 2012

Nature photography

In Community
December 17, 2012

Nature photography

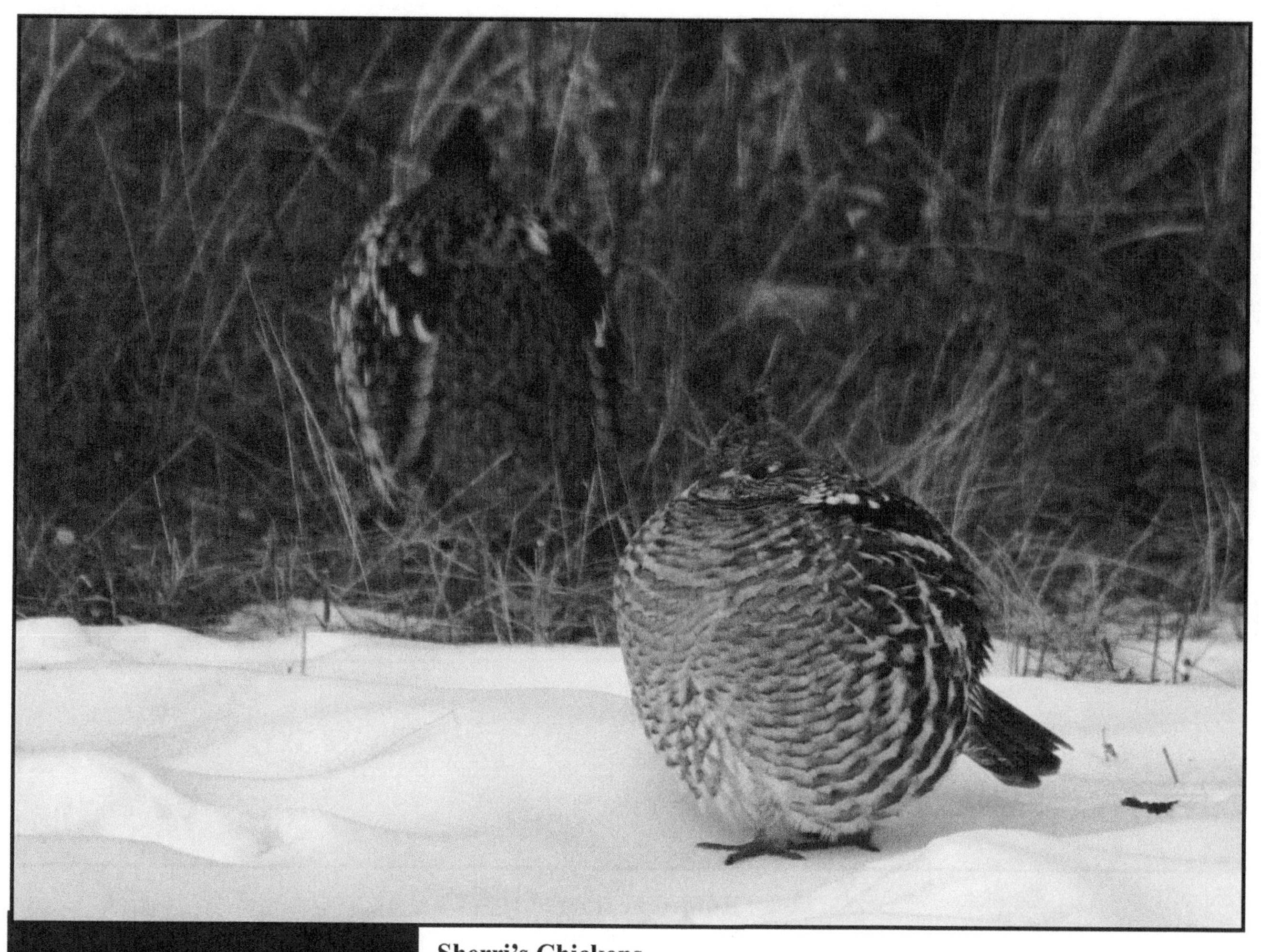

Sherri's Chickens
December 15, 2012

Nature photography

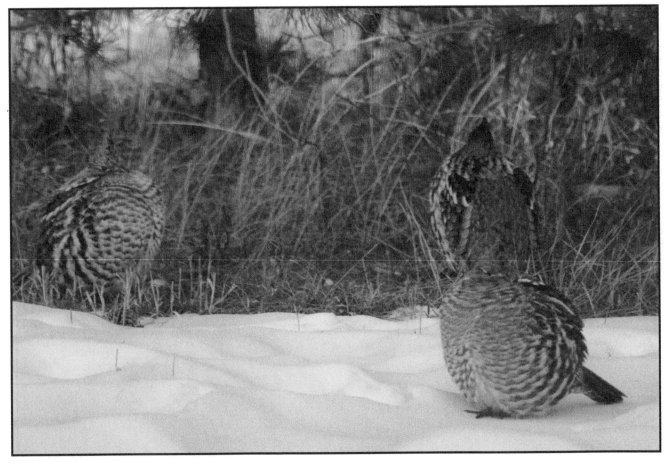

Ruffled Feathers
December 18, 2012

Nature photography

Earth: The Written Word

Creative Integrity One Syllable at a Time

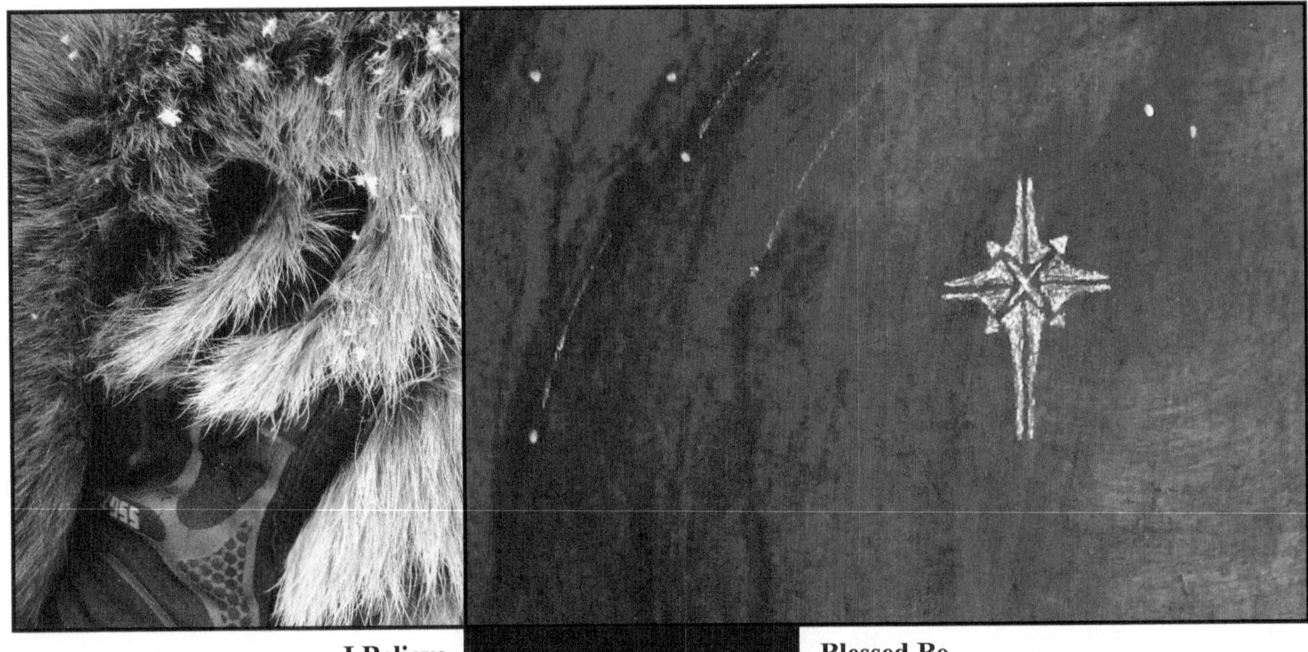

I Believe
December 19, 2012

Still life photography
© Sherri Phibbs

Blessed Be
December 20, 2012

Acrylics
© Sherri Phibbs

September 23, 2012

Home again, home again, jiggedy jig. Celebrating life with love.

September 24, 2012

One of the interesting things about self-examination, or navel-gazing, as a cool older gentleman tossed out to me today, is that you have the opportunity to change things: big things, like limiting belief structures and such. It's rather odd that in an effort to stave off self-judgment I broke into nursery rhyme yesterday. This is a specific self-help tool for changing unconscious patterns of belief. And change is needed. For if we do not move from the mind space we occupy when we create the problem, we will only become embroiled in a never ending loop, a kind of "*groundhog day" of learning experiences that reinforce our self-defeating behaviour. So by changing how the pattern works, I can change my being. And if I change my being, I become the change, re-patterned, as it were. What's a great way to effect this change? Make yourself laugh. Who I am being is way more important than what I am doing, being the role model, the mentor or teacher, being child-like and trusting the feel. Here's to being the ripple that mindfully promotes and creates a culture of harmony, peace, and understanding between humanity and the natural world, one artistic expression at a time. PS: Coyotes ...what's up with all the coyotes today? I'm seeing them everywhere. If you research animal symbolism, you will discover coyotes are a symbol for shape-shifting your life.

(*reference to the 1993 film, *Groundhog Day,* directed by Harold Ramis, written by Harold Ramis and Danny Rubin) ;-)

September 25, 2012

Only 86 more days to go! Today started with a note of hilarity. I was taking the dog for our morning walk through the woods (I love this place), and I turned the corner to find the back end of a male elk. I was eye level with the tip of the tail. He rattled his antlers in the tree and grunted. Rupert and I? Well, we turned tail and ran for the house. Standing on the front porch, I looked back, the dog was cuddled behind me peering around my legs, and the elk rattled again. Okay, it was a short walk. I have to laugh when I contemplate how that must have appeared. Walking, walking, walking. La la la la la ... Spin! Running, running, running. The sound of elk rattling moved slowly off to the northwest, through the thick brush. Rupert didn't even let out one bark. Smart boy! Soon there will be a visitor's page on the website. My darling hubby has posted game cameras on the property to catch all the activity, and I will share the candid shots as they come in. Thought for the day: Notice who you are being, and laugh at yourself.

September 26, 2012

You know, the best thing about these blogs are the comments section. More than anything else, the sensitive mentoring, questioning and living stories are what is truly important. It's that little note that says "I See You". So I want to give my heartfelt thank yous to those of you who have kindly shared your thoughts and opinions. Thank you: Barbara, Julie, Carlann, Catherine, Jan, Ash, and to those anonymous souls who came to me personally. I am so honoured that you would take the time to read my blog and share your thoughts and feelings with me and the other readers here. I am sincerely grateful to you for sharing your wisdom, your joy, your sorrow. There really are no words to say how you have touched my heart. May this collection of "living story" touch the heart of anyone who sees it and may it change the world for the highest good of all beings.

September 27, 2012

Something has happened! There is this relationship thing that has come unknotted. With a sense of potential and excitement, I feel my way along the relationship rope, checking tentatively. Yes it's true! The knots are gone. Honest confrontation and open communication swept the knots away in a shockingly powerful moment in time. The bold steps taken this year have created something much better than my best scenario mind-picture ever illustrated. I sit here with my heart cracked wide open, tears burning behind my eyes in utter gratitude. Commitment and focus, both to projects and people, have ripples that reach out to others in unknowable ways. I knew this, and yet I am astounded. Knowing something in your mind and knowing something with your whole being, are two completely different things.

September 28, 2012

I'm having some difficulty bringing my thoughts into focus tonight. The moonlight is so beautiful across the meadow in front of the house that it absolutely takes my breath away. When the poets say "bathed in moonlight," this is what they must mean. Incredible. With great love.

September 29, 2012

Today was bittersweet. I attended the going away party of someone very dear to me, and I must admit that I am a little torn up as I feel the loss of this. There is a piece of my heart that will travel along to the coast of Vancouver Island, a piece that leaves an ache somewhere in the middle of my being. I know it isn't goodbye forever, but as I sit with this pain I need to remind myself of this repeatedly. Your physical presence will be missed, but know that I will visit you in my thoughts often, my angel. As always.

September 30, 2012

Here it is, we're at the end of September already, and with this passage, another ending and beginning. A wonderful horse-friend is leaving my life on his way to great adventures and white rail fences. Bye, Echo. I hope you enjoy your new stable! On a happier note, the build site for the yurt is fantastic! The trees are in a natural circle and will hold this tent like a hug, protecting it from the wicked northerly winds and the unyielding heat of the south sun. Views from the windows will be lovely, and the natural light will be steady from the north windows and warm from the south. Taking a walk around the property today, I discovered a variety of vegetation and topography. Moss covered hills with tall, dark pines meet up with grassy meadows and aspen forests that meld into long gravel roads. It's a perfect place for a walk or a ride. I'm grateful to be here and glad I can share.

October 1, 2012

Eighty days. Are you planning anything special for the end of the age? A birthday party for Earth? Or maybe a celebration of creation? The above sketch is about connection, both above and below the surface of things. So in my not so subtle way, I suggest that perhaps an outpouring of love and joy and gratitude for our beautiful planet might be in order. We know that the ripples of our actions reach out to others in ways we can't even begin to imagine. Taking this further, the ripples of our joy, love, and gratitude may be felt by all beings, not humanity alone. Envision this: As you inhale, you breathe in the world; as you exhale, the world breathes in you. Wishing you well-connected.

October 2, 2012

Have you seen the new studio page? I spent part of my creative time yesterday and today developing the ideas and pulling together the web pages. If you have a chance to take a look and give some feedback, it would be appreciated.

And as for life, except for a bit of a worry about my mother's state of health and upcoming tentative plans for Thanksgiving, in general, things are brilliant. We've worked out plans for the new studio, we're starting to get things settled in the new home, and relationships are smoother than they have ever been. Love surrounds me and I am feeling so blessed. As I sit here trying to compose this blog, I glance down and there at my feet is my gentle giant of a yellow lab dog, stretched out under the desk snoring softly. A warm puppy. With deep gratitude.

October 3, 2012

I've sketched the Skeena watershed with much more turbulence in the water than was photographed. This more accurately represents the disturbance and anger aroused by the thoughts of decimating this incredible area through mining, forestry, and other "economic" ventures. Here, these sacred waters are churning their alarm. "Wait, you need us whole and healthy. We sustain you," they seem to say. This sketch is part of artists for: http://tidescanada.org/support/skeena-watershed-fund/

October 4, 2012

This style of work brings up memories of childhood trips to the national parks. I'm feeling such a sense of nostalgia and reminders of the romance of the journey. I remember one trip to Jasper where we stayed in a cabin. The trees were tall, and the scent of pine has stayed with me to this day as a touchstone for beauty. When we walked through the pine forest, everything was so crisp. We found a fossil of a leaf in a fist sized stone and had to back slowly away from a black bear on the path. It was g-r-e-a-t ! May our children and grandchildren have the experience of forests, bears and fossils many times over. May the scent of real pine needles bring them joy, and may they know the sound those needles make when the path is covered with the ones that have dropped in the wind.

October 5, 2012

When I was growing up, I often wondered about other families, especially at holidays like Thanksgiving or Christmas. For a while, we would spend time with extended family like aunts, uncles and cousins. I really enjoyed those times visiting family I'd never see between the occasions, especially my grandmother. My mother's illness made it difficult to maintain relationships as there was a constant state of rage, resentment and accusations. Up until a year or so ago, I never really understood how people couldn't just brush off her "symptoms" as part of her illness and just forgive and forget. Unfortunately, as her circle of relationships has become smaller and smaller over the years, I have found myself at the receiving end of the rants with greater and greater frequency. Two years ago, one of her rants broke our relationship. I had been hanging on to the remembered good times from childhood, the confidence and love I thought had surrounded me. I felt it break, my heart. It is so sad to come up on these holidays and feel the loss of my mother. Even though she is still alive, it is as though she is already gone. I remember helping her make burgundy meatballs for Christmas one year, and cabbage rolls and perogies another. I remember working in the garden and watching her at her easel as she did her oil paintings. I remember water fights in the summer and trips to the lake, playing board games and reading together. At holiday times like these, I am lonely and miss family. It has been many years since those memories: years filled with memories of my own children, my former husband and his family, and more recently my new husband. I'm aware that this melancholy is quite a common occurrence during the holiday season, but somehow that doesn't make it any easier to bear. May I be peaceful.

October 6, 2012

What a day! It's been a day for endings and new beginnings, yes? My mother decided she did not want to visit me for Thanksgiving after all, so at the last moment that stress was both eased and a place left empty. It's good, though. I did the right thing, inviting her and offering to pay her way here. I feel good about my decision, and she feels good about hers. Win, win!

So I'm off to pick up the traditional bird in the morning. Ummm, do turkeys come small enough for only three people? I think not. I will make pumpkin pie, however, and maybe even some mashed carrots and sweet potatoes. What about a duck? I will definitely check out the fresh duck. I know, it's not traditional, but, hey, why not step outside the box. You have to admit this is barely putting a toe over the line. I do like traditional Thanksgiving and Christmas meals. I hope everyone is enjoying the long weekend. I'm off to sleep, with visions of cranberries dancing in my head. Groan.

October 7, 2012

It's funny, but in this sketch it's what's not there that holds the viewer's eye in the piece. All that empty space is just waiting to be filled but with what? Wouldn't it be amazing to find out? Such potential, there.

October 8, 2012

I'm letting it all sink in. The feelings around the watershed, the smells of the pine forests, the softness of the moss underfoot, the inexplicable draw that's pulling me to this area. This place speaks to my heart in a way that defies description. And I know, in my heart, that timely action to protect these areas is the correct path to set my feet on. Pure water, clean and effective eco-systems, these keep us alive. They keep our children and grandchildren, and our descendants through the ages healthy and free from disease and catastrophe. This is a given, a fact. Who in their right mind would mess this up? And why?

October 9, 2012

Sometimes revisiting old artwork can be very rewarding. Providing renewed vitality with updated imagery and symbols, building a more current feel with glazing and shading brings a power to this piece that was not present in the original watercolour. The depth of life lived in the intervening years perhaps plays a hand in this transformation. A great deal has changed in my outlook and presence in the world since this painting was first created, and the boldness and confidence in the newly added lines and shading speaks to this. When laid end to end, an artist's work provides a visual roadmap of where they've been emotionally, intellectually, spiritually, even physically. This art-down project is just a small sound bite of the larger scope of my life. During the elapsed time recorded here, there are days when things are boring, frustrating or monotonous, and others where passion sparks and whatever media is at hand just flies across the surface, leaving a dramatic mark, an illustration of a psyche alive with inspiration. Creativity has a definite ebb and flow for me. Yet I've discovered that being on hand to experience that ebb and flow has made all the difference. By that I mean showing up to be creative: committing to do the work, being at the easel, sometimes just making a mark. Maybe it's like how I've learned to live life; show up in the moment and live it to the fullest, even when there are obstacles, pain or sorrow rather than the joy and peace I so love. Maybe it's a lesson on being present, opting in, celebrating life.

October 10, 2012

Again, a power from the past. I'm finding the stark and apocalyptic feel of this piece says a great deal about the struggle between the dark and the light mentioned in the Hopi Blue Star Prophecy. It's a struggle in which mankind hangs in the balance. There is strength and peace in this old face, an acceptance of destiny and a sense of bravery. I will not go quietly into the dark. I will sing my death song and meet whatever comes with the heart of a warrior.

October 11, 2012

The last week or so has seen a few things become finalized on the event calendar for the coming year. I'm excited about hosting new classes and art shows, about the new studio going in, and most of all about being able to help people find their connection to our natural world and let the joy of that experience shine out through creative expression. It has been such an honour to communicate with you through this blog space since the beginning of the year. Here we sit with only 70 more days to go, and I'm turning over the idea of the book again: a complete package of all blogs, art works and your comments and interactions, so it becomes not just about my journey through the year, but yours as well. I hope this is something you would like to see, as I will need to remove the blog space once the project is completed, and would like to see it commemorated. I've got it on good authority that blog spaces are not the way to go for business development. Go figure. However, there may be something else, perhaps a Facebook page. There are certainly times throughout this year when I've wondered whether this project is something to continue with, but then it's never really been about marketing. It's been about a personal commitment to complete creative work on a daily basis. Integrity. It's about self-forgiveness in the face of failure or mistakes. If I can do it, so can you! It's about finding inspiration in the most unlikely places, connecting and communicating with "the resource pool", our environment. It's about walking the talk,. Who knew the Earth was there waiting to connect with us? It's been about helping people approach life by being in the moment, and living fully day by day, building relationship with each other and the Earth. It's about discussing the Mayan expiration date and making plans for beyond it. So, as far as the initial goal goes, I must deem this project a success since it has met the criteria laid out at the start. I hope you're enjoying it as much as I am!

October 12, 2012

Sixty-nine days left, and the art-down continues. Inspiration and life experience saturates my senses almost to the point of over stimulation! The snow melting in rivulets that were running off the roof top woke me, along with the sound of blue jays beneath my window this morning. Bright, crisp sunlight poured through the windows and I felt refreshed. The day continued in this manner, bright, crisp, and refreshing, so when I opened the door to go feed my horse I wasn't surprised to see a small herd of deer practically on my doorstep. They casually turned their heads toward me as I descended the stairs to the car. They were completely at ease with my presence, even when I called out good morning to them. What a delight! And at the end of the day, I checked a rune stone for inspiration on human interaction and cultural healing. The rune talks about wholeness, about letting my divine nature be fulfilled, and maintaining my focus. It talks about divine energy being available to do this. I can't wait to see how this plays out!!

October 13, 2012

I'm so tired I actually dozed in front of the TV. Now that's a first! It must be all the fresh air and exercise from working on the studio site today, measuring and checking plans, walking and walking and more walking to measure. But it is wonderful and scary to see it starting to come into being. The dream of this new space is wonderful because it is becoming tangible and solid. It's terrifying because it's becoming tangible and real. So risky! It makes my heart quiver, or is that my stomach. At any rate, it is amazing fun and something that has been a dream for so long that I am still shaking my head in wonderment, or maybe fright? But I am so very tired, and I ache all over, so I am taking my exhausted self off to sleep. Have a great day tomorrow! Celebrating life, one yawn at a time, presently.

October 14, 2012

Another day closer to the end of the age, and I can't help wondering what will be in store for us, if anything different at all. I wonder whether there will be new stars appearing, the nine stars we haven't had over the Earth for almost 30,000 years. There are so many theories and the Mayan writings are chipped in a strategically located place, as though to allow room for all our speculation. What does this calendar mean? On the home front, we have been surrounded by bear droppings at the yurt site and all around the house. That's one very busy black bear! And it's elusive. We have yet to catch a picture, so we are relocating the cameras yet again. Determination! We did catch a couple great wildlife shots just north of the house and I've posted them in the visitor log on the new studio page. One looks like it may be a wolf (or a very large coyote)... care to take a stab at identification? Today's artwork took a turn to the flora rather than fauna. I hope you enjoy this multi-media sketch. I really am going to try tackling some florals this season. Wish me luck as I am so outside my element. Thank you for being there.

October 15, 2012

Okay, so today I woke up already behind in everything. I tore out of the house to make it the stable for this morning's ride, only to miss them by ten minutes. So my horse and I went for a leisurely ride around the property by ourselves. His winter coat is coming in, and he is all fluffy! While at the stable, I missed today's installment of the marketing course I am taking. It's a good thing it was recorded and I can listen later today, right? Hmmmm. I arrived home just in time for lunch and a chance to participate in yurt platform building. Okay, no course yet. Five o'clock and it was back to the office to work on a grant application. And The deadline for application? Midnight, tonight. Working, working, ... Arghhh, the program is not working. I stopped to cook dinner, oh, and eat it, too. Then it was back to the online application. 10:00 pm ... da da da ... 11:00 pm ... 11:30 pm. Finally, all the paperwork is assembled, the artwork portfolio completed, along with the updated resume, references, yada yada. I submitted it at 11:45 pm. At 11:50 pm, I received confirmation of application. Success!! I need some water. I'll be right back. Oh, and I forgot to mention, yesterday evening I stubbed my toe so badly I think I sprained it, possibly even broke it. The purple bruising, swelling, and pain are not so nice. I think I'll do my course work tomorrow morning, and just do a quick sketch tonight, all right? No? How about a photo op?

October 16, 2012

This morning began with a whisper. A tentative one, since I am known to be quite grumpy when I first wake up. My daughter, brave girl, tapped on my door at 7:30, which seems late by some standards but when you go to bed at 2:00 AM it is darned early. "Mom! Mom! Do you want to see the moose?" Bing! Photo op! I'm awake! There she was; the moose I'd been trying to photograph with game cameras for two months. With her was her yearling calf, calmly eating grass just north of the house. And I mean just north of the house. "Do you think I should wait 'til they move off before I get in my car," she asks. Hmmm …let me get my camera first! Snap, click, focus… "They can be aggressive, right." she says. Click, click… Grrrr. Wrong lens!! "They can be. Where are you parked?" I finally respond. It turns out she was parked right by the house, with my car separating her from the cow and calf. So grabbing my remote start, I gunned the engine on my car. The moose barely raised her eyebrow. I honked the horn, once … twice … and again, still nothing. I contemplated hitting the panic button, but decided against it. There was no sense freaking out the sweet little mooselet. "I think you'll be okay. Just get in calmly, quickly, and drive away." And you know what she said? "Okay. I'll just tell the moose that I'm not going to hurt them." And she did. They were fine, and she was fine. All is right with the world today!! I am keeping my telephoto lens on my camera at all times from this point forward.

October 17, 2012

I am struggling with resistance to artwork today. After an inspiring visit with a friend this afternoon, I later realized I was a bit disheartened by some of the realizations I'd made during the conversation. She asked me if there was anything she could assist me with, like a check-in on accountability, or a way of tracking progress toward goals, then she mentioned that she thought I seemed to be on top of everything. I remember saying that I felt as though I had the ends of many strings in my fist, and she wondered how that felt. "Powerful," I said. "I feel powerful." That started the mind going. Here are all these grandiose dreams, and how am I ever going to get there? I really don't know. I have a picture of what the end product looks like in my mind, but the process for getting from here to there is definitely fuzzy. I feel sad about it, but I am determined to work through this. As for the art today, I believe I'll do a meditative mandala as a way to focus and centre my mind. Let's see what comes of it. Fulfillment is indicated. Share your good fortune.

October 18, 2012

With all the classes, goals, courses, and building going on, I'm forgetting to play! I was reminded just now how important it is to take the time to just jump for joy! Send out the energy of love and appreciation in huge waves to touch all that is. While riding my horse today, I met Raven. A Prince of the Ravens, actually. He preened and strutted, instructing me on the proper manner to address such a royal bird as he. I tipped my head in his direction, and he tipped his head to look up at me from his territorial perch above the gopher hole.

His feathers were shiny, healthy was he.
Prince of the Ravens, We chatted
did we.
Distracted, I looked at another nearby
Are you a prince too?
"No! Only I..." cawed the first, "Only I"
It was clearly a touchy subject.

October 19, 2012

I'm on a quick tour back to the Graphic art discipline and working to discover, uncover, the name of this new home place and put it into art for our gate. The symbolism in this piece is quite attractive to me. We have a double circle medicine wheel, the points of the directions, the grove of trees, the Tree of Life, the circle of the roundabout at the front of our drive and the roads leading off it to the neighbours and community. There is a sense of groundedness, as well as a sense of new possibilities. I like the feel of this.

October 20, 2012

The ice and snow made for an unusual day today, as all plans for yurt works were put on hold until the snowstorm passes. Instead, I found myself looking at lumber and mini-excavators, visiting with a herd of horses east of Okotoks, and finally making my way out to take care of my own horse. That was a lot of traveling on roads in a snowstorm. However, it did allow me time early this morning to work on some of the homework from this marketing course I'm taking. This week carried a ton of information on how to change who I am being; how to break patterns, habits or ways of being that are not helpful or no longer serve me. New ways of becoming more centred and more fully me float through my mind, leaving little sparkling trails like fireworks across the indigo of a soft night sky. I can see the paths they light, yet they are elusive, moving too quickly to grasp at present. Reminder: there are meteor showers tonight!

This evening I will fix in my mind the vision, and ask, "How can I make this easy and fun?" As part of this exercise, I turn to Nature,and find I am drawn to a feather. At first I thought it was the eagle feather; however, once I grasped it and pulled it closer I found it was a pheasant feather. The markings have two sides or perspectives: one striped horizontally, the other speckled. I run the barbs of the feather between my fingers, smoothing and joining everything to create the look it is designed to have. Everything is working together in harmony and in the same direction. I notice the stem has some tiny indents about a third of the way from the base. At first I was sad that it was damaged, but then I realized that it is just part of the whole, the greater design. The marks remind me of the lines I put on the doorframe to measure my children's heights as they grew. Milestones, rites of passage, or growth rings, like a tree. I realize that I am a lot like this feather, and that if I adjust all my "barbs" to work smoothly together, I will create the being I am designed to be. There may be dents or marks along the spine, but it still stands strong holding all the pieces in place, and they are my growth rings. This makes me smile and I'm not sure why. PS: The experience with the feather is an example of the method described earlier in the book to connect with the elements. Please note that this process ancient and proven, step-by-step nature connection process passed down by word of mouth for countless generations may be used with any natural object or place.

October 21, 2012

Today is about the artwork. As always, a quick creative work to fill the calendar day, meet my commitment, and hopefully inspire others to pick up a brush, a pen or whatever, to just begin... Raven Tears turned out to be more than just an exercise in creativity. It is an expression of grief. Often symbolizing Creator, the Magic of Creation, or Bringer of Magic, here Raven is depicted almost hiding the tears in the rain. Or perhaps the tears are the cause of the rain?

Inner world made clear,
Reflected in Raven's tears
On wing through the storm

October 22, 2012

Hmmm, there are less than two months to go, and I wonder where to focus my attention today. I'm looking at yesterday's Mixed media piece, and I am in love. I'm contemplating having this printed as a g'iclee. A g'iclee is an archival quality copy on canvas created through a complex fine art printing process and can produce myriad sizes of a piece. Wouldn't it be lovely in a larger format? Or maybe I'll just redo this on yupo paper, big! I have a few pieces ready for the upcoming art show and sale, and a couple of them will need frames so I'd better get moving. The section of the marketing course I am on unleashed a ton of stuff that sat with me until this morning's class. I'm feeling isolated and alone, disconnected and maybe even ostracized. It's all welling up from a past I thought was long healed. But even when we work through things, often we will need to confront it again on another level later on. Wounds are layered, and healing moves through these layers like artisans cleaning a renaissance painting, patiently and persistently. Before it gets better, the deep and buried stuff needs to be shifted, shrugged off. Carrying this scar tissue around does not serve the highest good of all beings, and it does not serve me. Today's artwork is a twisted version of yesterday's grief: the

apocalyptic, worst case scenario of feeling wounded. It's odd that a shift in how one looks at things, the lens looked through, the filter used, affects feelings. I don't like this piece. The dark, broody feel, the hopelessness and anguish touched a part of my inner being that resonates on just that frequency. I let it shift with a song. Here's the link:
" Give Me Just a Little More Time" by Chairman of the Board

October 23, 2012

Wow! What an exciting turn of events! A local reader has taken up the Art-Down challenge in her own exciting way. A fantastic chef and experienced entrepreneur will be sharing authentic Mayan recipes on the blog space as the final couple months of the Mayan calendar countdown continues. The entries are posted in the comments section, starting October 21st. Make sure you check out the Mayan Hot Chocolate!! Seriously, could it be more perfect for our current wintery weather? Being out on horseback and coaching in horsemanship in this weather was amazing. Breathing in the scents carried on the crisp wind, touching the icicles in my horse's mane, hearing the crunch and squeak of the hooves on the snow, make this a marvelously sensual experience. At one point, we were blessed to watch three flocks of trumpeter swans overhead, flying south. The horses pawed at the snow, uncovering patches of frozen clover and still green shoots. A treat that was appreciated, given the intensity of their focus. The art bit for today focused on the contrasts, the shapes of trees and grasses laid out against the all encompassing white of the snowstorm. What stunning beauty! I feel blessed to be a part of it all.

October 24, 2012

Here we are, just after midnight, and I have so many things to do yet, for this upcoming art show. Also, a reminder to myself about another piece that *will* be done by Sunday! This marketing course is definitely brining up "gremlins", as our instructor calls it. It's more like ripping painfully at the still healing flesh of the wounds, then lancing into the depths of the pain and discovering festering pockets of rot! Grrrrr.... Who knew I was still this fragile? But I am determined. Today's piece reflects the starkness of my current mindset. The reds and yellows are the sharpness, the flare and flames of the woundedness; the greyed-greens are the sentinels of hope that life will spring forth in abundance. Things are not black and white; they are filled with nuances of colour and shadow, stark and true, but vibrantly alive nonetheless. May I be peaceful, may I be happy. May all beings be peaceful, may all beings be happy.
With great thanks, great peace, and great love.

October 25, 2012

While reviewing my work since I've been out on the "ranch" without a studio, I have come to the conclusion that the yurt can't go up fast enough. Fear of getting paint or pastel dust in the house has kept me relatively confined in my expression for these daily mini-projects. Work on the house, the yurt project, the marketing course, and the upcoming art show has all but sapped my energy. So where to go for inspiration? Okay, so I've been playing around with photography during the summer, getting my yearly reference shots for textures, lighting, effects, etc. What would happen if I seriously worked on photographic composition as portraiture? In need of more reference material for a piece I'm working on, I went to the horses with camera in hand and this thought tickling the back of my mind: What about doing a real horse portrait. Well I get to the Herd, go out and I am promptly mobbed by my favourites. Snapping shots left, right and around big, black necks, I manage to get what I need for the painting. However, ... Okay, I'll give it a try. One portrait. Okay, one more. Wow, this is like eating potato chips, you can't just take one! Here's the best of the day. I hope you enjoy them.

October 26, 2012

So it's back to the watercolour. Oh, how I've missed you! Indigo and cerulean, yellow ochre, and umbers, all... Hello brushes, water bowl, and paper. I've pulled them out of storage. I can't stand it any more. I... have ... to ... paint. Here's hoping I don't spatter the house, the carpet, or the floor! Inspired by the incredible scenery encountered during a September horse trip to Sandy McNabb campground in southern Alberta, this piece brings the feelings of wonder and awe back into focus. I hope you check out the complete piece in the art-down album, as this thumbnail doesn't quite give the full effect. The trees aren't quite to my liking yet, so I may play with this one some more. May you be happy. May you be peaceful.

October 27, 2012

What a marvelous day! On the way home from this morning's visit with my horse, I had to stop at least ten times to just take in the scenery (and take pictures). Spending the evening with a friend and a Harry Potter movie marathon just topped off an already wonderful day. I'm looking forward to working on the yurt space tomorrow. It should be ready for delivery next week! Woohoo! May you be happy. May you be peaceful.

October 28, 2012

Ooo, I am sick! Blaaahh. Off to sleep I go.

October 29, 2012

I lost an entry! Weirder and weirder. The picture is on the Art-Down Album, but somehow the blog entry went away. I'm definitely still sick.

October 30, 2012

Is it a coincidence? My horse is sick, too. Please send loving prayers, energy, thoughts his way, to assist him as he fights off pneumonia at the vet hospital.

October 31, 2012

It's difficult to be creative when concerned over another's well-being. This picture was taken from my deck yesterday morning, just before I took Neo to the vet hospital. This owl was a visitor the first night we were here, and to see him the morning I was having the vet come was a bit of a surprise. This noble bird and a doe with fawn were morning visitors to the acreage. The light wasn't great and I had the wrong lens on, so the photo is a bit grainy, but it is more to commemorate the moment than anything else. As an affirmation of life, Neo had his hooves trimmed today, as well as going for a short walk and a small roll in the snow. The cough is less severe and his spirits are brighter. Both he and I are responding to antibiotics. It's odd that we are both so sick at the same time. Anyway, off to sleep I go.

November 1, 2012

I'm starting to feel stronger and more in my body again, and so is Neo. He is quite certain it is time to go home, so when we went for our walk today, he headed off in the right direction. I had a bit of a conversation with him to convince him that it was a good idea to stay at the vet hospital until he was just a little bit better. I'm not certain that he entirely buys into the idea given that he is confined to an indoor stall alone when he is used to having the run of 50+ acres with a herd. Tomorrow, I commit to going back to the painting. I owe this journey a drum for today. And all kinds of ideas have been playing through my mind, as well as a number of others for paintings, so I'd best get at them. As for the course work, I am a bit behind this week and still struggling with an in depth examination of my belief structures. It's amazing how we limit ourselves by what we believe to be true without ever really checking the veracity of the belief. So I look at the countdown, 49 days to go, and I wonder what belief structures have I overturned to complete this project. I am humbled and amazed to find that a vision from years gone by has come to pass.

November 2, 2012

So, how do you know "truth"? Is there a simple test you can apply, one that flashes a bright light overhead with a marquee? Blink, blink, blink ... This is true! Are there indications like chills, sweaty palms, shallow breathing, or a sense of awe? Or is it more like a total body relaxation, a feeling of rightness? Does it need to have outside signs or affirmations from others? Or is it simply an inner knowing? When examining a personal belief system, we often aren't even aware if we have a giant obstacle holding us back or blocking our progress, so how do we even recognize that there is a problem? For me, one indication is a definite "Hey, wait a minute, that should have worked" surprise. Do you know the kind? You get all the ducks in a row, everything just so, and something happens that blows your ducks right out of the water! Now, is it some random outside act that has nothing to do with me whatsoever? Is it because I draw to me situations that are in line with my belief structure? Or is it learning experiences set up for my spiritual development by the hand of the Divine? With so many self-help books, programs, teachers/mentors/gurus/experts, all providing their perspective on this, how do I know what needs to be done to clear a block, or even whether it is possible to clear it? There is fate, after all... I can't propose to have the answers for anyone else, but I have found that using my senses while interacting with the natural environment, or components thereof, has provided me with a few breakthroughs over the years. As I struggle with deep shifts in my values, my assumed true beliefs, my inner knowing gets quite dramatically involved. I feel fragile, brittle, and on edge, as uncomfortable as can be when stretching the boundaries. So I sit reciting poetry to my sick horse, I walk in the wind, or I pray or meditate with a crystal in hand. I put a question out there, and I listen for an answer. Today's artwork is a background for a painting of an animal or bird to be tucked in to this wealth of texture and warmth. I listened to the wind play across the tops of the grasses, smelled the wet pine smell of the trees, felt the crisp air in my lungs, and heard sounds sharp to my ear. I feel a sense of belonging. Welcome back, you are home. With deep thanks, deep peace, and deep love.

November 3, 2012

A visit with the vet today has shaken me to the core. There is a strong possibility that my Neo has leukemia. There is a round of tests pending: ultrasounds for tumors, samples from the trachea and GI tract. I will know more on Monday. Right now, we have given him some "horse advil" to assist with the fever and pain. I read to Neo today. He likes poems about trees, and Robert Frost's poem "The Road Not Taken." It's time to contact the herbalist.

November 4, 2012

There is one more day until the last tests are done for Neo. Most of today was spent with him at the veterinary clinic. He didn't cough at all, but seems to be swallowing with difficulty. He is still eating well, though. I am exhausted and drained, and so is he. There is still a fever despite the antibiotics. However, I am going to continue with this project. I worked a bit this morning on the painting from yesterday's sketch. I had hoped to have it done tonight, but I feel as though I am broken. I also worked on a prior piece that wasn't quite "right". With a little tweaking here and there, I am satisfied and like the work. I find it helps me to work; it is a distraction from my grief and worry.

November 5, 2012

After a day of tests, my horse Neo was ready for some rest. Me, too. He's been started on steroids with fingers crossed that he responds. His heart is being taxed with all this, and the murmur is more severe. There are so many symptoms. I won't go into it all here, but suffice it to say he is quite a fighter to make it this far and still be so interested in his feed. With an art show coming up this Friday and Saturday, I am struggling to get everything in order for framing, selection, and for some pieces ... just to have them finished. I hope Neo is feeling better and is back at home by then. With deep thanks, deep peace, and deep love.

November 6, 2012

We're waiting for test results, and Neo's temperature has finally come down. Everything that is being done at this point is to help him be comfortable as his body deals with recovering from the pneumonia. I must admit, I am not handling the wait with grace. Burying myself in isolation, I share updates but try to avoid contact with humanity. It is such a thin, taut thread that is holding my heart together. So I paint, and rework old pieces like the one in today's art-down blog. In September this year, Neo and I went on a four-day riding trip to Sandy McNabb Provincial Park.

Toward the end of the trip, we found a stretch of path that wound through old growth evergreens and underbrush with a stream along the left side. There were cattle along the trail, and at one point we had to wait while they were gathered and moved back behind us. Neo had no patience for this, and we paced and circled, calling to the other horses. And then, when the time was right, we took off at a fast trot uphill for what seemed like miles through these old trees, on the dark trail strewn with leaves and scented with pine needles and moist undergrowth. We were in heaven, moving in perfect unison and enjoying the amazing beauty of the experience. At the top, we found a meadow that opened into aspen woods streaming with sunlight that shone gold on the autumn colours. I remember thinking about creating a painting that would capture that...what a masterpiece! I breathed deeply in awe of Creation. What a journey!

November 7, 2012

Today's piece is the culmination of experience and expression. Horseback riding in the snow on the night of a full moon is an amazingly beautiful and awe-inspiring way to breathe in Creation. It's one that I highly recommend you try if you haven't had the chance yet. I hope you enjoy this one. I'm still waiting for the test results, but Neo is responding to the steroid therapy. No more fever, no more "horse advil". With deep thanks, deep peace, and deep love.

November 8, 2012

It's the day before the art show, the day of the test results, the day of missing four big trees when I slid off the road. A day of deep gratitude! First things first, my horse is going to live! It isn't leukemia, just a very rare form of pneumonia. The vet is trying to source out reference materials so we can ensure he doesn't have a relapse. It was touch and go for awhile, but it looks like he is on the mend and may be able to go home on Monday! He'll be wrapped in a blanket; he's naked. They shaved his sides for the ultrasound and his neck for the trachea scoping. All his responses to the tests were atypical, so the vet has dubbed him a zebra. I'm going to buy Neo a new winter weight blanket in zebra stripes when he goes home. I knew he was one of a kind. I was smiling so hard after I heard the news about the test results that my cheeks were hurting for hours! I was still smiling when I turned into the vet hospital, and in the process of moving over to avoid an oncoming car, both cars skidded into the ditch on opposite sides of the roadway due to the deep snow cover on the icy drive. Unfortunately, my side had these huge old poplar trees standing in a very long line down the driveway. I managed to not hit anything and pull back up to the road before hitting the spruce at the other end! Whew! What a snow storm!! The lab tech in the other vehicle was a bit shaken. He was sitting in his car at the top of the hill when I left the vet's. It looked like he needed a moment. He didn't hit the big tree on his side either, so all is good. It looks like all is in place for the art show tomorrow. My image consultant (if I had one) would be groaning in horror: no new outfit, no new haircut. I'm going to the barn before the show, so I'll probably smell like horses! I guess I'd better wash up before you, the art aficionados, arrive.

With deep and everlasting gratitude.

November 9, 2012

So today's creativity was entirely centreed around the art show in Marda Loop. I am exhausted and have not much left but a need for sleep. However, I did want to share this photo, which was taken from the front of my house (through the screen window). Here are Mama moose and mooselet, happily munching on the grass they uncovered. I love living in the country.

November 10, 2012

Thank you for Everything! With deep and everlasting gratitude.

November 11, 2012

My sense of humour seems to have left me, perhaps its run off screaming in a panic of stressful events. The odd timing of the stressors leaves me wondering about the exercises in the marketing course I'm enrolled in. Barely out of my mouth were the words "something blows your ducks out of the water," and, BAM! I have turned into Shhair Trigger, Mistress of the Dark Side. The moment by moment pain of wondering whether Neo would live or not, the uncovering of layers of perceived internal obstacles, the added commitment to the vision that drives W.I.S.H. Studio, the physical pain of old injuries, the driving in horrible road conditions, and the excitement and timelines surrounding the assembly of the yurt has been stressful. All this added to the constant concern for my mother's wellbeing and struggles in relationships with family and friends means I'm a little tired. So I'm eating healthy foods, drinking lots of fluids, and trying to stay on top of things with out verbally flaying anyone. I've had some success in this area, but need to bandage a couple of wounded egos. Sigh. As a wonderful lady once told me, I am like a little blade of grass: I may be battered down by wind or storm, but when it passes I will stand tall again and enjoy the sun's warming rays.

November 12, 2012

We've had a fine day of yurt-building! It is so exciting to see everything coming together. I can hardly wait to hold the first workshop in this amazing space!! My creativity today centred around the use of power tools and hammers so I'm going to submit a meditative mandala, something abstract, just going on feel alone.

November 13, 2012

I had another fine day of yurt building and visiting a healing Neo. What a wonderful experience to do hands on construction of the studio, to visit my horse who is now being reintroduced to the outdoors (carefully blanketed of course), and to work on catching up on the marketing course. Here we are with 37 days to the End of the Age, and everything seems to be beautiful! The trees around the yurt site received a bit of a hair cut today. I'm sure they appreciate all the dead branches at the bottom being trimmed back. It gives more energy for the rest of the tree in the spring. It's just amazing and delightful. I'm going to do another mandala, just to keep the creative juices flowing, and then I am off to sleep. Another day with NEO and the yurt tomorrow!

November 14, 2012

There are 36 days to the End of the Age, and the yurt is about two thirds done. Neo will be well enough to go home tomorrow. (We will check in with the vet in the morning). I'm reading tons of material on the marketing program, and it's amazing how much good, solid information can be packed into such a concise format! I feel that every sentence I read is important, no filler. It's kind of like good quality horse feed. I think another mandala is in order today as we have been working on the studio-in-the-round all day. I'll just carry the circle through to the creative art work for this project as well! Consistency is key, especially in anything requiring any discipline. You know, like this project is requiring from me. Then on to sleep, so I can wake up to another amazing day filled with adventure, excitement, and joy.

November 15, 2012

Talk about an incredible experience! The yurt is complete enough and just in time for tomorrow's workshop. Amid much grumbling and a little swearing, we were able to put the final piece of the puzzle together, with love of course, at 7:30 PM, and it looks great! Whew! Of course there are still odds and ends to pull into place: small things, like heat and lights, and maybe stairs. Oh, it's early morning tomorrow! Also, my horse, Neo, is well enough to go home tomorrow. I missed the call from the vet while I was out at the yurt site. Sigh. It's one more night for my boy in a nice warm barn, then out into the cold with him, fully and carefully blanketed of course. I even dreamed about horse blankets last night, horse body stockings, actually. There were visions of other horses pulling the stretchy material away from his body and then letting it go … snap! … back against his side. The woolen stocking was bright red and winter white, and it looked like a Nordic legging! I'm learning tons about personal obstacles to success. This one lesson in the marketing program seems to be lingering overly long in my field of vision. It's time to move on, I believe. I have visions of yurt decor, landscaping, pathways, labyrinths and parking spaces, natural cedar walkways through medicine wheels with stone markers at the direction points and sage planted along the stones. I see riding paths on the property and sitting places... I am excited!

November 16, 2012

Wow! It was a great day, and an exhausting day. It was the first day of the first workshop in the yurt. Woohoo! I just returned home from bringing Neo home to a nice, private paddock at Eagle Feather Riding, complete with his very own hay pile and a warm winter weight blanket. Many thanks to Adrian and Doug for helping out with the trailer and all! It's my treat for a dinner out tomorrow evening. We have left the yurt heater on for overnight, so perhaps tomorrow it will be somewhat warmer? We have yet to finalize the type of heat suitable for the size of the space. The sheer volume of air due to the height of the ceiling is intimidating! Yet will we work it out and find the right balance of sustainability and comfort. Many thanks to the beautiful students in this weekend's class! You are awesome to pull this together. With deep and everlasting gratitude.

November 17, 2012

What a day! Thirty-three days to go…. With deep and everlasting gratitude.

November 18, 2012

There are a couple of things left to do for the Studio-in-the-Round, including a more permanent heating solution and some windows. The prospect of moving all the studio supplies into the space is very motivating! I'm looking forward to hosting the art and inspiration classes and retreats in this wonderful new space. The ideas are flowing in all manner of directions, so grabbing the goals and setting them into a workable timeline is key. The last couple of days of "cats" ties into a commission piece I'm working on, so for the next while, a bit of time will be spent pulling this together for a preview on Wednesday.

November 19, 2012

Life is all about rhythm, ebb and flow, the rhythm of expansion and contraction. Sometimes we give of ourselves, sending our ripples out into the world, and sometimes we are on the receiving end. The idea is to let go of the guilt associated with not always doing the giving. It's okay to take a rest when you are exhausted or your reserves of strength need to be replenished. In fact, it is not just "okay", it is imperative to your health and wellbeing. If you are not at your best, clearest state of mind, your view of reality becomes clouded with all that "stuff" circling around in your brain. You see the world through the filter of your own mud.

One of the most amazing ways to clear the muddiness is the rhythm of a drum bath, experienced while viewing the heavens through the oculus of a yurt. The heartbeat of the drum sends out waves of relaxation, producing a theta rhythm state in the brainwaves and allowing for a centering of the body, mind and spirit, while calming the busy-thoughts. It's a wonderful, refreshing encounter with your own inner healer. I hope you have the opportunity to experience this sometime in your life. It is as though everything falls away and you are cleansed and clear. I was so impressed by the feel of this during the recent Sound of Peace drum making workshop, here at W.I.S.H. Studio, that I have created a program specifically to provide the opportunity for others to feel this amazingly beautiful centering of body, mind and spirit! This is for you: "Rhythms of Relaxation!" With deep and everlasting gratitude.

November 20, 2012

Thirty days to the End of the Age, and I am suddenly feeling the urge to stock up on grocery items for the winter. It seems like Nature agrees, for I received visits from three squirrels this morning, in the space of an hour and a half. These are the first squirrels I've seen since the snow fell, and the little ones were spaced out all along my driving route, with the last being mere yards from my door as I returned home. It feels like winter is about to descend on us, and the time for the final gathering of nuts, berries and seeds has begun in earnest. With this in mind, I have contacted a dealer of wood stoves to begin the process of heating the yurt. This is an expensive alternative with an 80% burn efficiency rate. However, due to the soapstone content of the stove itself, only one small fire a day will heat the place for 24 hours at the least. The propane boat heater is much more cost effective but may not be as efficient when it comes to the large volume of air the high ceiling of the yurt affords. Hmmmm, what to do?

I was still contemplating heating options as I drove out to volunteer my horsemanship coaching skills, when out of the fog, a huge, Great Grey Owl formed and then dispersed as the fog thickened around its elegant shape, magically suspended in silent flight. An audible sound of awe escaped me as I stared at the curl in the fog now hiding him from view. It's a good day for predators as well, my practical inner voice piped up. When I arrived at the stable some thirty minutes later, I discovered my Neo was despondent. He was eating his feed and hay, but he was definitely not himself. Leaving him to his hay, I turned my attention to the volunteering portion of the day, which consists of a challenging ride on an opinionated horse (as my boy is convalescing). My focus and skills were tested, but a strong sense of determination is brought to the surface as well. Taho, the gifts of many teachers, is teaching me and learning from me. Interesting. Returning to the stable, I found Neo has spiked a fever again. A quick call to the vet brought a visit and more medication. With blood samples in hand, she assured me we are good to leave him blanketed outside, and that she would get back to me with the test results shortly. Later, when I arrived home, Mama Moose and Mooselet (now as big as Mama) exploded out of the trees beside the house and took off to the north, right in front of my car. I was a bit startled. The owl and the moose once again book-end my experience with my horse's illness. Sigh. Next lesson: dealing with fear. With deep peace and love.

November 21, 2012

On Connecting with Nature, A conversation with a horse: Settling in to eat hay in the shed, with a warm-ish bowl of senior feed, hay cubes and medication at our feet, the conversation began something like this:

NEO, tossing head and moving away from bowl: "I smell that you know"

MYSELF, on bended knee at his feet in the frozen hay, breaking and mixing: "Hmmm, okay, let's make these hay cubes smaller and stir it together."

NEO, curiously nuzzling and then tasting the offending mash around my busy hands, his body close beside me: "That's much better, thank you."

As I watch him daintily nibble the feed, I start picking his feet (which he offers politely) and brushing his hoar frosted mane. I have a sudden memory flash of brushing Taho's mane yesterday and getting a questioning feel from Neo.

MYSELF, looking him in the eye sincerely: "Yes, he is a good horse, and I love him. But this riding him is just until you are feeling well enough to carry me again. You feel better today, don't you?"

NEO, eyes softened: "Yes."

MYSELF, tentatively: "Do you think you will get better?"

NEO, wisely with a sideways look at me: "I don't know. It's a long winter."

I pause in my brushing, and sit on the edge of a nearby wheelbarrow, looking at him.

NEO, nuzzling my hand: "You will have to let me go when it is time."

MYSELF, picking up the now empty bowl and the lead rope: "Let's go for a walk."

Off across the ice rink we call a parking lot and over to the feed barn to store the empty bowl we go, carefully picking our footing and easily reaching our destination. I was probably more in danger of a fall than my surefooted boy, but I worried about him anyway. The next stop was my car, with the dreaded syringe full of another medication. Not a needle, luckily for both of us, just a quick squirt down his throat. Right?

NEO, head high looking down his nose at me: "I can't believe you did that to me. I really hate that."

MYSELF, gently rubbing his throat and holding his muzzle up: "You are such a good boy. Please swallow it."

Carefully releasing his jaw, I lower my hand. His head follows.

NEO, out of squinted eyes: "Yes, I swallowed it. Ok?"

MYSELF, smiling up at him: "Ok. Now let's walk."

Cutting back across the ice, we reach the highest point on the property, and then we stand facing south, looking down the fence line.

MYSELF, pointing at the brown horse looking up at us: "There's Chester, come to say hello to you."

No response. I stand still and look out, just feeling and being with him. Suddenly I have the strangest sensation. It's as though he is large, bigger than his physical body, and he's looking out over all Creation, with great dignity, peace and understanding. It seems that Neo is looking out through a veil, seeing far-off things I can't yet perceive.

Unnerved, I shuffle my feet, look at him and break the moment.

"You will have to let me go when it is time," he'd said. And I wonder what he sees more clearly than I.

November 22, 2012

I'm finding inspiration. The haunting sound of a didgeridoo surges in waves against the outer edges of my being, coaxing my mind to smooth out, just as the surges of water against a lakeshore beach ease away the sandcastles and moats in my childhood memories. I am transported back to summers at my grandmother's house, sitting on the rocks with my feet buried in the sand. I hear the sound of the loons, their lonely cry echoing across the water as the sun tilts west toward the horizon. There is water lapping softly and a boat bumps against the dock, wood on wood. I smell the water plants. Having been uprooted by the waves, they now lay discarded on the beach, the many snake-like spirals and s-curves extending down the shoreline in their dark, shiny splendour. My cheeks feel the prickly sting of the chill breeze coming off this northern lake, and I feel loved. The old bark of the towering tree feels rough against my back as I lean into its embrace. Supported from behind, I gaze up at the canopy of leaves, around at the surrounding trunks and brush, and I know I am home. My sense of place tells me so. There is an instant recognition of rightness and acceptance. With sudden clarity, I realize this feeling has been transported to this time and place, here and now, just northwest of Cochrane. Instead of chilly lakeshore breezes, hoarfrost sparkles against a sky so crystal blue it causes my lids to close in order to diffuse its brilliance. Owls, moose, and deer replace the call of the loon with their own special magic, sparking my sense of belonging and thankfulness. My senses, at least many of the 53, confirm this shift. I am indeed home, no matter where I am. I have discovered a sense of harmony within and connection without.

November 23, 2012

It's the occasional ghost in the machine. Let's try posting this today. Part of the nature of this day involved the growth of the studio-in-the-round. I have been spending time planning, designing, contemplating the feel of the place and what will enhance it for others: a rock-faced chimney wall behind the heat stove; swags of rich cloth falling from the skylight down the wall to the floor; a vestibule with a coat closet and bench; spa slippers; a buffalo skin rug/Hudson Bay blanket; stone lined cedar bark pathways; medicine wheel direction markers for the outside circle of the yurt; in-floor heat under area rugs.... All of these are on the list, plus so much more. How to create and hold a space filled with the peacefulness and power of the surrounding landscape? I can do this. I hope you've marked the day of the Open House in your calendar. It's an opportunity to touch and be touched by Nature.

November 24, 2012

This is the evolution of a working title. ...It has launched me onto a path much more intriguing than??? *The Final Art-down: 355 Days to Creative Style*, Or perhaps, Creative Integrity? Thinking, thinking. As this project has moved along, day by day, I have confronted my own personal creative obstacles, my personal gremlins, and events from my past that have formed my belief structures. I have discovered a great deal about how to keep the creativity flowing, how to foster inspiration and a healthy connection to the natural world. Much of the meditative or contemplative work has been instrumental in easing the emotional upheaval of this year, from the death of my dad and my engagement to be married at the beginning of this year, to the current construction of the studio and the complications with Neo's health, the whole time frame has been a study of extremes. It's very reminiscent of my life in general: wounds and joys, difficulties and successes … a lifetime of extremes. How do you recover or move through parental rejection and mental illness, racially inspired wounding, sibling suicide attempts, teen pregnancy, adoption of self, adopting out a baby, abandonment, sexual assault, a loved one's alcohol addiction, bankruptcy, three miscarriages, verbal and emotional abuse, threatened physical violence, stalking, divorce, financial insecurity, job insecurity, near death experience, physical illness, car accidents, personal injury, post traumatic stress? I've drawn from Art, meditation, connections to Creation and all beings in Nature, as my healing paths. I teach these and other methodologies because I have personally tested them; they work. I have not only survived; I have thrived. From the ashes, rises the phoenix, and so can you. I have grown through the challenges of my life. I've found that I can accept the label of victim or I can shrug out of it, knowing things happen but that I will heal, I will move on, I will feel it and let it go, I will forgive others and myself. I will seize the joys, the abundance, the love and peace as they arise, and I will treasure every single moment of it.

November 25, 2012

Nightmares, and little sleep make Sherri a touchy girl. That and working through stuff in an effort to release it. The baby moose in this picture was just outside my bedroom window when I woke from a particularly nasty nightmare. He and his mama have been hanging around the green grass poking through the snow on our lawn. Mama seems to know we mean her no harm and that we are grateful for the opportunity to watch her and her beautiful baby. Baby, however, is starting to move like the bull moose he will soon become. The power and strength are evident in his every step. I know in a few months he will most likely move off on his own, creating a territory for himself. I wish him bon voyage. With only a few days of this years hunting season left, they are both quite skittish of anything pointed at them, but they did graciously allow a few moments for me and my camera.

November 26, 2012

I'm aligning with Moose, or rather Moose is aligning with me. As I have continued to work through the extremes of emotional events this year, the moose has become a particularly surprising addition to my days. Or perhaps not so much, as they found me in the city as well, and on the riding trail, and during the searches for an acreage. Okay, so Moose has been placing itself in my sight-lines for awhile now. It's just becoming more prominent, persistent, up front and personal at present. Moose is really getting into my space. Moose is such an unusual creature; .it lives on the borders of water and land and is able to move gracefully between both. It's symbolic of movement across boundaries. I believe the presence of Baby is significant, too, as I observe his growth alongside Mama, and his budding horns and independence. How does this fit with my current situations? What are they trying to teach me? I see a journey on this topic might provide me with some necessary insight. I'm sending out the questions, let's see what materializes. With deep peace, love, and gratitude.

November 27, 2012

Personal space issues! Wow, I've discovered an interesting facet: one that I knew but had forgotten. When things or people intrude suddenly on my personal space, I freeze and seethe. It is then difficult to let it go. Have you ever remembered something about yourself that you'd rather not? Perhaps a certain way you respond in situations, or maybe a perceived flaw that irritates you when you think about it? I'm working on letting go of the seething, and moving on with just being in the present moment. If, in my mind, I continue to go over and over the different ways I could have handled the situation, the energy I spend on this, the focus I place there, pulls me away from where I currently am. And I am left, fragmented and un-whole. If I choose, I can stay there, in that never ending cycle of regret, frustration and unhappiness. Or, I can choose to be free of this imprisonment in the past. I can choose to acknowledge it. "Grrrrrrr." I can choose to act from a place of inner peace, "no biting", or "retaliation." I can choose to let it go, "forgiving you and me." I can choose to feel the release and sense of calm that it brings. I can choose freedom from the past and peace with the simple determination of my own thoughts. If I can feel the sense of rightness and wholeness when I choose this way of being, it is a small event in a single life. Imagine if you did it, if family and friends did, too. What if, neighbours, countries, and each being chose to simply determine their own path based on creating a personal sense of wholeness and peace-filled calmness. What would the world look like then? Today's artwork is an expression of this process. I am creating, rather than breaking. With deep peace, love, and gratitude.

November 28, 2012

The journey is almost done. Twenty-three days left to this Mayan calendar and its End of Age. As I wonder what this means for us, I feel the strain of this year and the years before it. There is much to let go, much to forgive. I wonder if this period of release is tied in to this End of Age, or whether it is just a particular place on my life's journey I have reached. Tomorrow I will schedule the medical tests that have been waiting for my attention. Tomorrow. For now, I am at the gateway, standing at the edge of potential, possibility and promise.

November 29, 2012

Three hundred and thirty-three pieces of creativity, 333 days of persistent and careful searches for creative inspiration and pulling on the depths of my inner strength to continue with this project, no matter what!

There has been a change in me through this process, a deep development of confidence and an inner knowing that even when I am exhausted and empty, I can be refilled. I can start again in this moment, and the next, and the next, if I must. Being fully present in each moment, I've found, allows me to access the wellsprings of creativity easily and with flow. Now, I'm not for a moment suggesting this is easy or flowing all the time! It's just that when I am able to tune in to the moment, when I can focus, be aware, then things just flow. It's like a tap that has been turned on, and I just happen to flow along for the ride, allowing the words, ideas, images to become. Other times, it is just plain hard work, doing the work, when I don't want to, when I don't feel the tingle of creative juices flowing, when I hate the very idea of creating anything. But these are the times that have made it for me. These are the times that suddenly bring about a new idea, a wonderful program, a fantastic project, and I quickly write it down so I won't forget it. The newbie then sits in my consciousness, growing and forming on its own, like yeast in bread dough. When I go back and take a look, I may have to knead it down to size and come back later. However, it is still there, busily working its magic on its own until I am ready to form it into something I find delightful. So, here's to wonderful ideas, and the pains of birthing them.

November 30, 2012

It's the last day of November 2012! What to do when this project is over? I have an idea, but shhhh, it's a secret. There has been so much going on the last month. I've found the marketing program and a writing overview class incredibly helpful; what a wealth of information I am sorting through! The art show (thank you, Barbara & Karol Fodor) was great fun, and I met some very interesting and talented people. My studio-in-the-round, the yurt, arrived and is under construction, many thanks to Doug, Jerry, Andrew, and Alex. I couldn't have built it on my own, you are amazing! Neo, my wonderful equine friend, is recovering from his pneumonia and will soon rejoin the herd in the pasture. Tamara and Marie, and all those at Burwash Equine Services, I send you great love and thanks! (And thank you, thank you, thank you, Creator, for gifting me with his continued presence!) As you can tell, my mind is all over the place. There is so much to be grateful for, so much to appreciate, so much to love about this world I'm in. And to my new husband, who is celebrating his birthday tomorrow and will always be a kid at heart, in the famous words of Sharon, Lois and Bram of The Elephant Show:

"I love you in the morning, and in the afternoon. I love you in the evening, underneath the moon..." With great peace, great thanks, and great love.

December 1, 2012

Neo's temperature has spiked up with a fever again, as we tried, for the second time, to scale back the dosage of his medications. I am devastated. He has been doing so wonderfully the last few days. To see the fever this morning and have it continuing is heartbreaking. Thank you to Doug for stopping back in on your way home, taking the time to give him extra meds and rechecking his temperature. Thank you to the staff at Burwash for their advice. We're keeping our fingers crossed for a good morning temperature tomorrow. With prayers for Neo.

December 2, 2012

Another day in the life of an artist and horse parent. Although I've been recovering from a chest cold, I was determined to ensure the welfare of my Neo so out into the cold I went, twice. I was bundled up to be sure, but still it was cold. I was most disappointed when I discovered he had eaten too much hay and wasn't interested in any of the feed (with meds) I had to offer him this morning. With a child, you can talk them into taking their medicine, with a horse, not so much. I was frustrated and afraid for him. When I went back the second time, he did finish the bowl, so at the very least he did get the right amount of medicine in him within a 12 hour period. We will see tomorrow if it has any effect.

Tomorrow, the delivery day for "Amanda". I've included a picture of her here, even though the project itself was longer than a single day. I hope you've enjoyed watching the creation process unfold. The photo session, the choice of shot and composition, and now, finally, the finished product. As I sat at my easel and watched her come to life from the flat surface of the paper, I couldn't help but greet her with a happy, "Hello, Amanda!" This is one of the joys of creating, watching the piece develop and change, until finally it takes on its own voice. "C'est fini!" I hope she loves it! With prayers for Neo.

December 3, 2012

The adventure continues, and I am tired. When I spoke with the vet today, the "e" word came up in her conversation, so I contacted an osteopath, looked up an herbalist, and am ready to learn how to do injections in order to work on getting this under control. My prayers are that something works. My best companion, my soul mate and friend, to let you go is difficult. I need to try everything, to ensure that I have done all I can. Yet will I maintain the balance. Your dignity and joy in life is so much more important to me than just hanging on to you. You bring such a light into my life, and I honour that. With prayers for Neo.

December 4, 2012

Today was Dad's birthday. He's been gone almost a year now, so I pasted a message to his still active Facebook page wall, (No one has the password to go in and delete it.), wishing him a happy day. It was a strange, uncomfortable feeling. As a horse parent, I have to add that Neo's temperature has responded to the shot he received today, and it is back to normal. He and I are waiting to hear back from the vet about the results of his blood and lymph node tests to see if more antibiotics are required. We are working on different ways to deliver the oral steroids. Apparently, I have the only horse in the world who does not like applesauce. I thought I'd try it tonight to see if he likes it before I mix in the medicine, and it's a good thing I did. He even turned his nose up at his favourite cookie dipped in applesauce.

Oh, Neo! I will need to check in with the vet in the morning to see if there are any changes to be made to his medicines. I am learning about giving the shots, and it's difficult since I've never even held a syringe with a needle in it before. But I know Neo appreciates my efforts, and he does seem to want the shots rather than the food additive. We will see what he does with a trembling and creeped-out me, rather than the calm, cool, and collected vet, coming at him with the needle. He may change his preference. It's been a day full of strange, uncomfortable feelings. I think the artwork reflects my insides at the moment. With prayers for Neo.

December 5, 2012

Apparently, yesterday's empty stall was just waiting to be filled. Neo is all cozy and tucked in to a warm, hay-filled stall over at the vet clinic. ... We had a success for both of us: I gave him his needles, and he let me do it. There was only one bleeding wound—and it was mine. I stabbed myself getting the cap off the syringe, and then I bled all over everything: the syringe, the horse, the gloves, the tissue, the ground, ... You get the picture. I bled for him, and he didn't even flinch. That's the story of my life ... ha! I saw something today that fits with how I really feel about that: "Let the past make you better, not bitter." I love it!! Anyway, there's good news elsewhere on the home front. The new wall colour has arrived and has been installed on the studio-in-the-round! I'm lovin' it. The first part of the heating solution also arrived today, and it will be installed this weekend, along with rock wall and all that jazz. Stairs are also in the works. We're reusing some of the leftover materials from the platform construction. Yes! I can hardly wait for the Open House celebration! With prayers for Neo and his speedy recovery.

December 6, 2012

Weird... I was reviewing the dates on the blog, and I realized Thursday, December 6th didn't upload or appear at all. In fact, it is not there anywhere! I'm not sure what happened, so a quick update will have to take its place. Most of the day was spent with Neo at the Burwash clinic. In the morning, we were outside soaking in the sun (-9° Celsius). We could feel the heat coming off the hay as the absorbed sunlight radiated back, and it did act as a bit of a windbreak. As we watched a flock of Canada geese fly overhead in their v-formation, I could hear the squeak of their wings. Later in the evening, we wandered around the yard for a bit, but it was just too cold so we spent a bit of time in the corridor inside. It saddened me to see how thin he is getting and to notice that he was a bit unsteady. His breathing is laboured; the antibiotics don't appear to have kicked in yet. With prayers for Neo and his speedy recovery.

December 7, 2012

Miracles? I woke this morning feeling the Neo had died during the night. He hadn't, but the information from the vet was not good. Given that information, I decided to let Neo go, and made arrangements to have him visited by his herd mates to comfort and be with him when he passes. Then with more info from the vet at 10:30 last night, I decided to keep trying to save him. Rollercoasters aren't this brutal. I am going to sleep. Neo is having his lungs drained in the morning, and I will be at the clinic all day. With prayers for Neo and his speedy recovery.

December 8, 2012

Well, my boy is eating and drinking, and seems in good spirits. He's a fighter, and by all standards should look a lot more ill than he does. I'm going to honour that. The vets did a wonderful job, the osteopath was fantastic (for both of us), and now it is up to Neo. I dreamed of bringing him home with me here, building a stall for him in the heated garage, and walking him every day. While eating hay in the sun this morning, he pointed out how he liked to be around other horses, and how he loved the sound of the children. Back to Eagle Feather Riding he will go, as I honour that as well. With the exhaustion, creativity is an interesting thing and can take on many forms. Today I sang a song of strength and protection for my horse. I played drum-like rhythms on my leg, and the pony in the next paddock banged his feed bin at the appropriate moments, twice scaring Neo out of his skin. I laughed. The many v-formations of geese added their song to mine, and the sun blessed us with its warming light. See you in the morning, Neo. Good night all! With prayers for Neo and his speedy recovery.

December 9, 2012

I didn't wake up until noon! Now *this* is a once in a year occurrence! I sincerely needed the rest; my spirit, mind, and body have been thoroughly wrung out and hung up to dry in a hurricane. But again, I have to say this is a wonderful world, despite the bumps and bruises, etc., that I have encountered on my life's journey. I spent time with Neo. (I'm reading him a book called *The Dream Giver*. It's very good stuff.) This morning there was no feed left in his bin; he'd eaten it all. He was soaked in sweat from the warmth of the stable, though, so I dried him off as much as I could, blanketed him and took him out into the sunshine. He ate hay and drank, ate hay and ate snow lumps, walked and ate more hay. He had bright and shiny eyes, he was curious about the world, and was steady on his feet and able to walk well. (There was no wobbling like there was on Friday night.) I was a little tentative when I went to feel the lymph nodes under his jaw, not certain what I would find. It was less swollen, and the whole jaw area seemed thinner. His barrel was less round and more sleek, and he was breathing easier and fuller. It is still early yet, and given the previous relapse I am unsure whether to celebrate yet, but the signs do look promising today. We may just owe Auntie Tamara and the wonderful people at Burwash a great big hug and thank you; with another for Kevin and Sigird at BluEquine. In fact, we felt so good that we did a bit of Christmas gift getting on the way home, small tokens of affection, and a small tree to decorate later. I'm keeping my fingers crossed I just went for a cup of water, and there in my kitchen were…excavator parts, draining into my sink! Some days, I just don't know what to expect next. Today's creativity is an exploration of what lies hidden on the back of a drum. Drenched in shadow and partially obscured is the image of a running fox. I offer many thanks to Fox for being there. It was Nature's gift. With prayers for Neo and his speedy recovery.

December 10, 2012

How do I express what I am feeling today? The words all seem so trite and confining, so I'm sticking to details rather than emotion; details are much easier to convey with language. Beyond a shadow of a doubt, the results of the pathologist's tests of the fluid from Neo's lungs show cancer as the root cause of all his various difficulties for the last month. It is manageable for a couple days, which has allowed me to move him back to his herd and people friends at EFR to spend his remaining hours peacefully among those who love him.

I received a note from the ranch about an hour ago that all was well in his nighttime world. He is resting, snuggled up with his friend Radar in the shelter, while Zeus, a rugged old draft horse of indeterminate age, and an anonymous dark horse (too dark to see who it is) stand at the fence behind them. Tomorrow I will let Neo out with the whole herd for a few hours. I'll walk with him to keep him safe from some of the more energetic youngsters, but still allow him to pick his path. We will see where it takes us. Tomorrow I will book my own tests, ones that have been waiting for quite some time for completion. We will see where they take me. With prayers for Neo as he follows this new path.

December 11, 2012

You know a lot of what I teach in my workshops and classes is about connection and being "in relationship to", and I've always had to take hard looks at myself to see if I am walking my talk. It seems so strange to hear myself approaching the world in this way, so strange. Though I have to admit it is the most honest approach to life: be "there", be "big", be who you are and allow the ripples from your actions to bring change, hopefully for the highest good of all beings. As I've struggled with this day, I have come to realize the best part of me is the part that lives honestly in the moment. Here's what I learned today:

1. The gift of your presence to another being is more than just enough; it is valued beyond all.
2. Love has a flow to it that works under its own power; just step into love's stream and let it carry you.
3. Relationship is more than just the surface stuff: the joy, laughter, sadness, etc. It's a connection and alignment on a cellular level, a moving together as one.

A wise young lady pointed out that we are always surrounded by those we love. They help teach us how to fly when it is time for us to learn. With prayers for Neo as he follows this new path.

December 12, 2012

Yesterday I walked in my horse's footsteps. Among other things, we spent hours standing in the sun in the wind shelter, listening to the sound of the traffic, watching the cows across the road and the clouds reforming with the wind. To him, the shelter smells like friends, family, safety and home. As I propped my back against the pillar, I realized I could feel the tension leaving my shoulders and my neck. There is peace there, in that space. Birds scuttled across the metal roof, and other horses talked back and forth on the other side of the wall. The high rafters have a cathedral like feel, and embraced us both in the protection of their beams. We stood close and I felt the prickle of the hair on his nose as he nuzzled my hand, our secret code for cookie. I emptied my pockets on command, and I listened to the sound of his chewing. The wind picked up and I was chilled. But blanketed as he was, he didn't seem to mind, even with his struggles with pneumonia. He was soaking up the world, and the world was giving him everything it could. As we walked back up the pasture, another horse joined us, and the two had a conversation about leadership and relationship. They cuddled together in the shelter for awhile, and I left them to some horse time. Later, I returned and I followed him. He seemed intent on showing me something and we walked with purpose. The shelter up top was reviewed and found wanting, so he stood at the gate, waiting for me to open it, which I did. We marched right past his favourite hay pile, and on out into the dark, across the parking lot to the trees behind the house. We stopped as he made motions to lie down; he stopped the motion, and looked at me. This spot I know is where another horse friend chose to die, I nodded at Neo. Yes, I know. With that he marched off through the woods and down into the front pasture by the hay bale where a recent send-off for another horse friend was held. He looked at me, and ate hay. Yes, I know. He is leaving, and he wants to make sure I know. I touched his mane, and told him I know he hurts. I told him I can help him so it won't hurt when he dies and so he won't be afraid. Tomorrow, I said. And tomorrow became today. Neo walked with purpose, leading me to the spot behind the house, so we brought hay. He looked around and firmly strode off for the hay bale in the front pasture. I followed. He ate hay and listened to the people and the horses. You could feel the love surrounding him from all sides as people and horses stood together around the hay pile. There was a circle of love drawn around him, literally and figuratively. When it got to be too much, we walked with our favourite horse friend and then came back. Our friend went first, and we stopped. The intensity was a lot, so I told Neo we would move them, and we did, to give us space. It was time, so I held him as I let him go. Softly sending out love to travel with Neo as he journeys on ahead of me. I promise you I will bring cookies for when we meet again on the other side. PS: I am surrounded by wise young ladies. In the words of Tanya, when the sun sets, it rises on another horizon. Be at peace, Neo.

December 13, 2012

And so begins life without Neo. I decided to den up and lick my wounds today in a rather fox like fashion. Alone, I am able to release the emotions as they arise. There is no need to put on a happy facade or be the strong one; just feel and release, feel and release. My body hurts, my guts ache, and I look soft and washed out in the mirror. Who is this person? Where do I go from here? I have a braided clipping of his mane, it carries his scent. I know because I held it to my face as I cried. Now some may say, "Good lord girl, it's only a horse." But I have found that being "in relationship to" is not confined to human interactions. We can mourn the loss of an animal companion, a tree, a place or wherever we put our focus. Our love leaves us open to loss. This morning, I woke angry. Did they lie to me about the seriousness of his illness? Could they have fixed it if we paid more? Then I let it go. There is no treatment for horses with cancer; I know this. And it is so rare; I know this, too. All I can do is feel the pain and try my best to let it all go, holding onto none of it, taking no blame and blaming no one. My work years ago in the funeral service industry familiarized me with the "grief process". My studies in expressive art therapies, shamanism, and organic eco-psychology supplied me with tools to ease my way. The work I did with the United Church in Sunday school, Social Justice and Basics of Faith programs, gave me a sense of trust in the Divine that transcends religious tradition. My life's experiences have given me a unique perspective; I am well-equipped, so to speak. Tomorrow it will be time to start expressing this with paint. Maybe I will go to the stable and take my daughter's horse for a walk (or maybe not yet). For now, line and pen are more controlled and less explosive than the fluidity of watercolour on yupo paper, although the picture is in my mind. There is no colour yet, no joyous creation— only release. Just let it go, all of it.

With great love.

December 14, 2012

This journal is the most amazing thing. It came along at just the right time to give me a written reference of my life with Neo. I am stunned when I think about the timing and what a gift it is. Last night I went back and read all the passages since Neo became ill, and I was astounded to find such beauty in the darkness. This might be the first time I have re-read any of the entries. It brought the feel of him close to me. Today I called in with the inscription for his plaque. "His registered name is Fires King, but he goes by Neo", I said. I've offered to send a bit of his mane to the young lady who had him before me. Perhaps there are one or two others who might like a little bit? I don't know how generous I am prepared to be with it, this is all there is besides my memories and I am hanging on for dear life. And still, life carries on. I went to pay bills, choose supplies for the studio, pick up groceries, and make dinner. At times, it even felt normal. I thought about horses, looked at pictures of horses, thought about going out to see horses and be with horses, but I didn't go. Maybe tomorrow.....

December 15, 2012

The repetitive motion of grooming a horse is so soothing. I can close my eyes and feel every day of the last five years flowing through the muscle memory and I am at peace. I'm not sure going to pick up Neo's tack was a good idea today, but the experience while I was there was nice. I brushed and cleaned up Taho, patted Promise, and cried a bit while Wizzard wrapped his head around me. It is a community of horses and of people, what a wonderful gift for each of us. It was difficult to go today, I won't pretend otherwise. Yet I am glad I did, except for the bucket of brushes that are now in the car and require cleaning. While I was there, I decided how I would find my next companion. I will take Neo's halter, and just like the glass slipper, I will try it on every horse I meet in order to find my prince. It's a tall order to fill my little Neo's shoes. When I arrived home from my trip to horse-heaven-on-earth to be where Neo liked to be, there on my doorstep were three beautiful "chickens". I sat and watched them for awhile. They were completely calm and aware of me, but unthreatened. It was beautiful just watching them eat pine needles and scratch for gravel, their measured and precise steps taking them exactly where they needed to go. It was as though a thoughtful planning process went into each step, allowing them to guarantee the outcome of every movement. It's so at odds with the feeding frenzy motions they made while grazing! A teaching from the "chickens": Plan every step it takes to get there, then jump on every opportunity presented once you arrive.

December 16, 2012

Today was another day of hiding out. The mere thought of teaching a lesson without my Neo was unsettling, never mind trying to teach a child who also loved him. Thank you to Kirsten for taking my class today. I will be back in the New Year. My energy would not have been on the task at hand, to say the very least, so instead, I focused on doing studio work, pulling together the elements to bring warmth to the space, literally. The first heating unit arrived, and now the decor items have also been chosen, so it's on to assembly and ambience! Christmas shopping is waiting to be done, with little enthusiasm this year. I'm finding grief is creeping in to all my endeavours. Watching someone drag a Christmas tree brought tears to my eyes as I remembered having the opportunity to drag a Christmas tree behind Neo and opting out because I didn't want to frighten him. We could drag bouncing milk jugs on a rope, though, with great success. I'm missing him. Tomorrow I am going to go for a ride. I will see how I do.

Here we are, on the verge of a momentous event, the changing of the Mayan Age. There are barely five days left, and I can't help but wonder about the significance of this. Apparently many predictions worldwide converge on this time, but I have a suspicion that what is going to happen is not what is expected. Something wonderful this way comes. I feel love all around me; it's so incredibly beautiful. We've had tons of meteor showers the last while. The sky was so beautiful when I woke at 3:00 AM a couple nights ago. The night was crisp and bright, and the stars were so close, it was like I could reach out and touch one with my extended fingers. It's time for sleep, otherwise I will be sobbing all over the place tomorrow, and then the riding would be difficult.

December 17, 2012

Crying seemed to be the theme of the day. This is a ton more difficult than I thought it was going to be. For some reason, I am an open floodgate releasing everything and all. It is as though Neo grabbed hold of places inside my soul that needed clearing out and took them all with him when he left. All that is left for me to do is cry and wash it away, and feel it like the sting of a bandaid that is ripped off too quickly. Here I am, realizing that I, who is used to riding daily, has now been off rhythm since the end of October, and it shows. I'm losing muscle tone and connection. We will see how this goes over the holidays. I feel emptied out and out of sorts. It was nice to see everyone ride today. I volunteer with the intermediate ladies' class tomorrow. We will see whether I can make it through without dissolving into tears. I've moved Neo's mane next to the screen here, alongside a beautiful dream catcher of the same colour. Tomorrow I'm sending off a piece of the hair to the young lady who cared for him before me. I think I'll include a picture of him, the one with his mane braided. Lesson from the "chickens": It's okay to let friends get your back when you feel like sticking your head in the grass. It's only a few hours and three more full days until 4:11AM on December 21st, 2012. I'm heading off to sleep now!

December 18, 2012

Well, I managed to not cry in front of the ladies' class. I'll take my successes where I get them, thank you. It was difficult, though, when one of the students was encouraged to try another horse, leaving Taho available for me to ride. I felt exposed and uncomfortable. However, that being said, it was a wonderful ride with him. Taho has such a different mindset from my Neo. So totally different in fact, that it is freeing in a way, allowing me to focus entirely on this new being. I did a fair amount of comparison thinking, however. Yet it is funny-odd how I was reminded of both an old horse friend and Neo, through Taho's actions today. Using my body as a rubbing post for his head brought Cisco firmly to mind. Then at the end of the ride, Taho did the cookie request! It was as though the wisdom, experience and knowledge of those who are gone has somehow been absorbed and accessed by Taho. They are guiding him, somehow. All the animal beings in my world have impressed me with their kindness and heartfelt concern at the moment, which they are expressing as deeply as the human beings. Dog friends run up to greet me, whining in delight. Horse friends seek me out in the field to touch my arms or hand or to breathe on my hair. Some just stand with me, offering their service and space. It is so amazingly touching and I am surprised by the depth of the feeling aroused. I truly am surrounded by love. And here we all are, surrounded by love. Do we see it? Can we access it? Have we truly tried to step into that stream of emotion and just let it carry us? I don't know about you, but I am definitely giving it a try! We are building a rock fireplace surround for the studio heater, and I'd have to say the process of creating the space has been my creative endeavour for the day. It was fun choosing, matching and designing! A practical usage for artistic creation, you've gotta love that, too.

December 19, 2012

This morning I woke with a migraine headache and piercing, pulling muscle aches from deep in the long bones of the body. It has almost passed now, yet I still feel its shadow like a layer of darkness at the edge of my mind. I dreamed last night, and it was restless and unrestful. There is not a flicker of an image that I remember of it, either. As the day went on, the more time I spent looking online at various horses, the worse the headache became. If I left the computer, the headache started to abate. When I came back to the screen, the migraine also came back in full, screaming force. I decided to leave the computer alone for a while and just let the day unfold. There was no artwork, no creativity, just searing pain and stomach upset so I napped. Tomorrow I am off to see the wizard. No, I'm just kidding. I'm going to visit my mother. It's her birthday tomorrow, and I felt this prompting to just go take her out for lunch. Three hours there, three hours back and lunch in the middle, all on winter roads and all to follow the whisper of a feeling. But the feeling is strong, and the whisper, well, that points out that it is needed. So, off I go. I definitely won't be in Kansas anymore, and by the end of the day, there will be no place like home. It's a whirlwind trip. I will go to the ranch on Friday to pet a horse.

December 20, 2012

Here we are! The last day of the Final Art-Down!! And I filled it with a trip to visit my mother. It was a proposed whirlwind trip: in and out, and back by dinner. So, of course, every road we chose was blocked or delayed. Five hours from my door to hers, and a late lunch followed by singing, cherry cheesecake and piano music. What a wonderful visit. In fact, I'd say it had to be the best visit we have had together in a great many years. Everyone seemed pleased, even her notoriously grouchy cat that looked me deep in the eyes, decided I was good, and proceeded to encourage me to scratch his head. I'm glad I went. The drive back in the dark, on the wintery but clear roads was three and a half hours, which was not so bad. A mere 8.5 hours of driving time today! What's a little wall-to-wall traffic compared to a lovely birthday visit with family? I am glad to be home. Rupert is glad we are home, but is annoyed with us. (He actually went to sleep in the bedroom without us). It was a stressful day for my beautiful boy. This is probably the longest he has ever been at home alone as both the kids were away at work throughout the day, and apparently we'd better not do it again. He is accustomed to being at my feet while I work, so I'm certain he thought we'd abandoned him, that we were lost. Lots of love is in order to ease his worry. You know, I had thought to do this fancy worded blog for today. Yet, I find I would rather quietly say good night. What a beautiful experience this has been. Your support, encouragement and love have blessed me through the year. I couldn't have done it without you. Thank you! And sleep well.

- Sherri

PS: If you noticed a shortage of illustrations, please know … video just doesn't translate well to book form. ;-)

EPILOGUE:

After the end of the age, and the beginning of the new, the artist joins the world in celebration. Appreciating and soaking in the warmth of the late morning sun, surrounded by the busy survival activities of myriad insects, this inspired being breathes in the world and remarks on the life of the dragonfly.

These creatures of AIR, made fertile by the late summer's sun, laid eggs in summers past. There in the pond, nourished by WATER, this small life is sustained until, driven by an irresistible internal need, it climbs toward the FIRE of the sun, and change begins. Held safe in a cocoon of its own making, the whisper of a dream forms, ready to take flight. At the precise moment when all is in readiness, the cocoon opens. The dreams become reality, and they fly!

Flying at many different altitudes and trajectories, this vast flurry of bold aerial precision and delicate display is supported by Air. With their purpose defined and focused, they complete their task and the world around them benefits. The ripples of their Being clears the air, a gift for those who walk upon EARTH. Good-bye, mosquitoes.

Allegory: The artist comprehends.

Be true to your potential. Allow your dreams and vision to grow and emerge into the light. At any altitude, from the heartfelt sharing of drawing with a child, to the famed display in world galleries, and every layer in between, your Being sends ripples out into the world, touching others in ways you cannot yet see nor comprehend. Hold to your creative integrity, your artistic truth, and give it Voice. Your Being and its expression are your greatest gift to those who walk upon Earth.

Nourish the seeds of your creativity and share them with the world. The stories they tell may be just what someone else needs at that particular moment in their life. Let your artistic voice be heard. Make a difference just by being you.

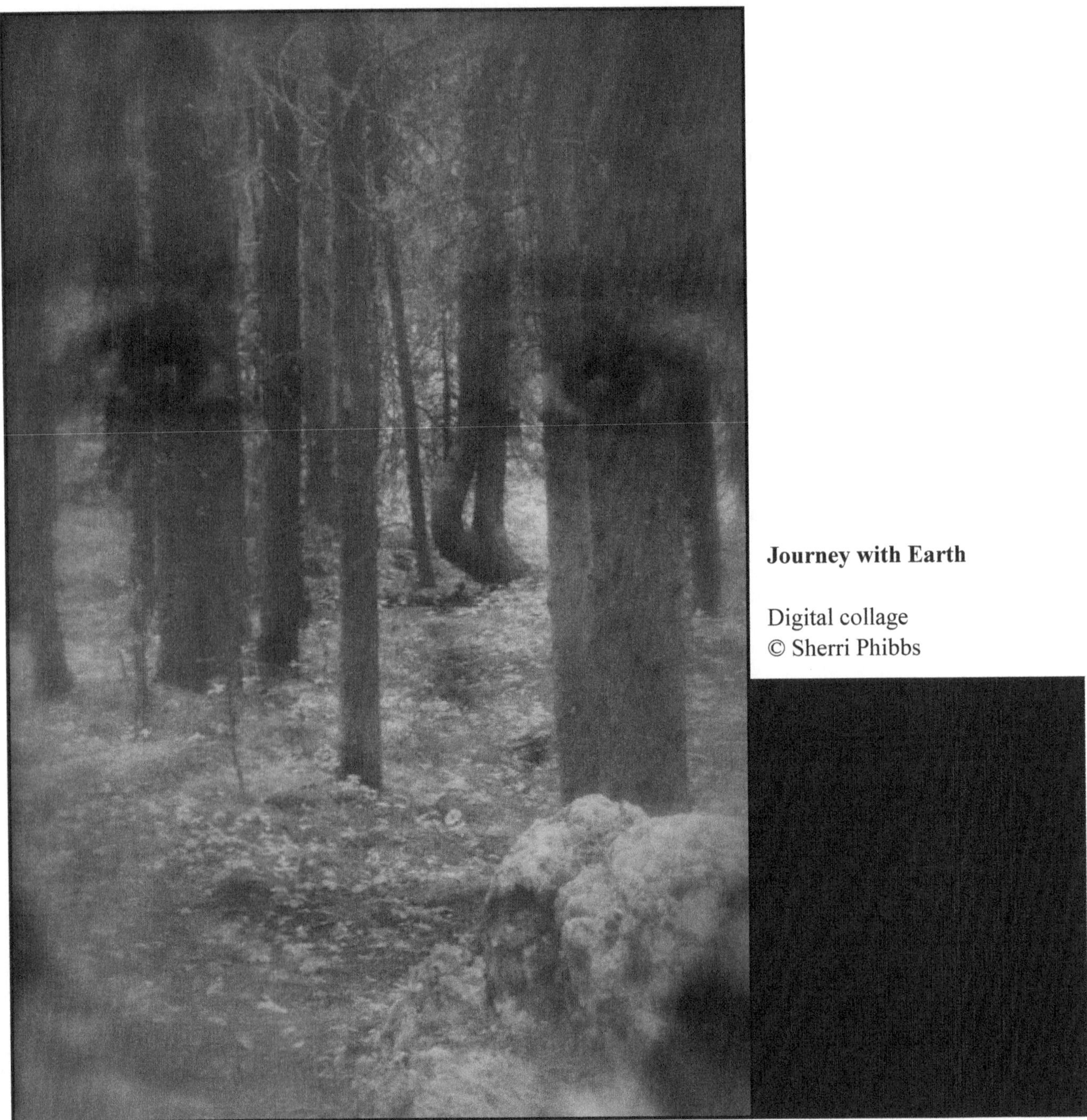

Journey with Earth

Digital collage

Strengthen Your Artistic Voice with Mini-Retreats

Platinum Intensive: Seek Your Inner Artist	3 hours
Media Exploration	2 hours
Drum Art	6 hours

That Drum Thing:

Sound of Peace Project

2 day teaching circle exploring the art of making a traditional hand-drum

All classes include nature connection exercises

www.wishstudio.ca

PSST…

That author's bio at the front sounds so stuffy! I am also a mother who cares deeply for her children and the natural world. A vibrant, strong woman who is recently remarried to a wonderful man and lives in the country with her yellow lab, Rupert, and two horses, Echo and the soon to be renamed Hotspots.

Ok, that sounds way too idyllic, where's the dark stuff? Lets see, I have a parent who has suffered from severe mental illness since she was sixteen, the year I was born, a father who abandoned me as a baby. Adopted by my step-father; my name changed so I would have the choice to hide my genetic makeup; and later divorced by him, when he and my mother's relationship came crashing down the year I graduated high school. That same year, I became a pregnancy statistic, literally starved from home; I was ostracized. Confronted by parental intolerance, I made the single most difficult decision of my life, alone, adoption. Later married and having suffered through multiple miscarriages, I became a statistic again, a divorced single mother with two small children and the need to resort to legal action to collect child support. Follow this up with car accidents, physical injuries, and post-traumatic stress…and there is more, but I think you get the picture. I am a survivor …and a determined thriver!

I have had a dream of working from my own studio for more than twenty years and last year it became a solid reality in the form of an earth-friendly yurt in the countryside.

I am looking forward to adding Eco-art Therapy certification to my repertoire, and excited to find the moment while continuing my study of ecopsychology when I own the knowledge. As a valued member of our beautiful natural world, I belong. As a valued member of our beautiful world, so too, do you!

CPSIA information can be obtained at www.ICGtesting.com
Printed in the USA
LVOW02s1916171213

365763LV00001B/1/P